D1741543

# DEEP INTEGRATION

## HOW TRANSATLANTIC MARKETS ARE LEADING GLOBALIZATION

EDITED BY

**DANIEL S. HAMILTON** AND **JOSEPH P. QUINLAN**

PUBLISHED JOINTLY BY

CENTER FOR TRANSATLANTIC RELATIONS
JOHNS HOPKINS UNIVERSITY
PAUL H. NITZE SCHOOL OF ADVANCED INTERNATIONAL STUDIES

AND

CENTRE FOR EUROPEAN POLICY STUDIES (CEPS)

*Funding for this project was made possible by a generous grant from the DaimlerChrysler Corporation Fund.*

Hamilton, Daniel S. and Quinlan, Joseph P. (eds), *Deep Integration: How Transatlantic Markets are Leading Globalization,* Washington, DC and Brussels: Center for Transatlantic Relations and Centre for European Policy Studies, 2005

ISBN 9-9766434-1-3

Center for Transatlantic Relations
American Consortium on EU Studies
EU Center Washington, DC
The Paul H. Nitze School of
      Advanced International Studies
The Johns Hopkins University
1717 Massachusetts Ave., NW. Suit 525
Washington, DC 20036
Tel: 202-663-5880
Fax: 202-663-5879
Email: transatlantic@jhu.edu
Website: http://transatlantic.sais-jhu.edu

Centre for European Policy Studies
Place du Congrès 1
1000 Brussels
Tel: 32 2 229 39 11
Fax: 32 2 219 41 51
Email: info@ceps.be
Website: http://www.ceps.be

# Table of Contents

## Section III. Politics and Markets

## Section IV. Conclusion

# Preface

Globalization is widening the scope and scale of interactions between continents to embrace more parts of the globe than ever before. Most punditry and analysis have focused on this 'widening' process, particularly its impact on developing countries. But globalization is also deepening the intensity of such interactions, and this deepening is most intense across the Atlantic.

This volume examines the phenomenon we call 'deep integration' – the extensive ties that bind the US and European economies. We attempt to offer a clearer picture of the 'deep integration' forces shaping the transatlantic economy today; to show how these interdependencies have accelerated, not loosened, since the end of the Cold War; how they prevailed despite the transatlantic political disputes of the past few years; how specific sectors of the transatlantic economy are deeply integrated; how domestic policy decisions have important transatlantic consequences; and how decision-makers on each side of the Atlantic can understand the challenges and seize the opportunities accompanying this phenomenon.

While there has been no effort to force consensus among the authors in this volume, a basic theme does connect the various contributions: transatlantic markets are in many respects the cutting edge of globalization. Key sectors of the transatlantic economy are integrating as never before, driven primarily by investment flows and foreign affiliate sales, which are 'deep' forms of integration, as opposed to trade, which is a 'shallow' form of integration. Europeans and Americans have become so intertwined that we are literally in each other's business. These linkages underpin a $3 trillion economy that provides up to 14 million 'insourced' jobs on both sides of the Atlantic. Deep integration, however, can also generate frictions when two different systems rub up against each other.

Many 'top-down' policy proposals for new transatlantic economic initiatives have been issued by business groups and think tanks, but there is little 'bottom-up' analysis of specific cases that can provide a foundation of evidence for the phenomenon of deep integration. The case studies in this volume are intended to be illustrative rather than comprehensive. Some examine specific sectors in which transatlantic cooperation to remove barriers or align standards has had positive results, and sectors in which cooperation has been less successful. Others investigate the interaction between domestic policy decisions and deep transatlantic integration. Wherever possible we have sought to quantify the economic benefits of success or the economic costs of failure, and to offer lessons to be drawn and areas to explore.

We conclude that while transatlantic markets are some of the freest in the world, they are not fully free; there is both considerable opportunity to liberalize further, and considerable need to cope with challenges that arise from open transatlantic markets.

The volume expands and deepens the analysis offered in two previous studies by the Johns Hopkins Center for Transatlantic Relations: *Partners in Prosperity: The Changing Geography of the Transatlantic Economy* (2004), by Daniel S. Hamilton and Joseph P. Quinlan, and *Drifting Apart or Growing Together: The Continuing Primacy of the Transatlantic Economy*, by Joseph P. Quinlan (2003). This study is a joint effort by the Center for Transatlantic Relations, based in Washington, DC, and the Centre for European Policy Studies (CEPS), based in Brussels.

On behalf of our two institutions, we would like to thank the DaimlerChrysler Corporation Fund for its encouragement and support of this project. Special thanks go to Michael Duignan for critical research support, and to Anne Harrington, Els Van Den Broeck and Isabelle Tenaerts for working with us to produce this volume. Each author writes in his or her personal capacity; the views expressed are those of the authors and not their institutions.

Daniel S. Hamilton
Joseph P. Quinlan

# Executive Summary

- One of the defining features of the global economic landscape over the past decade has been the increasing integration and cohesion of the transatlantic economy. Globalization is happening faster and reaching deeper between Europe and America than between any other two continents.

- The European and American economies have not drifted apart since the end of the Cold War; they have become even more intertwined and interdependent.

- Despite the perennial hype about the significance of NAFTA, the 'rise of Asia' or 'big emerging markets', the United States and Europe remain by far each other's most important commercial partners.

- The economic relationship between the United States and Europe is by a wide margin the deepest and broadest between any two continents in history – and those ties are accelerating.

- The first five years of the 21$^{st}$ century – a time of transatlantic political tension and sluggish economic growth – marked one of the most intense periods of transatlantic integration ever.

- The transatlantic economy generates roughly $3 trillion in total commercial sales a year and employs up to 14 million workers in mutually 'insourced' jobs on both sides of the Atlantic who enjoy high wages, high labor and environmental standards, and open, largely nondiscriminatory access to each other's markets.

## Investment First, Trade Second

- Transatlantic trade squabbles steal the headlines but account for only 1-2% of transatlantic commerce. In fact, trade itself accounts for less than 20% of transatlantic commerce.

- Trade flows are a misleading benchmark of transatlantic economic interaction. Foreign investment, not trade, drives transatlantic commerce, and contrary to common wisdom, most US and European investments flow to each other, rather than to lower-wage developing nations.

- When one adds investment and trade together to get a more complete picture, one sees that US economic engagement remains overwhelmingly focused on Europe. The transatlantic economy is where the markets are, where the jobs are and where the profits are.

- In 2004, total transatlantic trade in goods rose to a record $482 billion, up 22% from 2003.

- Despite the strength of the euro against the US dollar, US imports from the European Union jumped to a record $283 billion, helping to drive America's trade deficit with the European Union to an all-time high – $110 billion.

- In 2004, the US posted record imports from Germany ($77.2 billion), Italy ($28 billion), France ($31.8 billion), Italy ($28.1 billion) and a host of other European nations. Surging imports from Europe led to record US trade deficits with a number of European nations in 2004, including Germany ($46 billion).

- Despite Washington's war-related frustrations with Europe, corporate America ploughed nearly $100 billion into the European Union in 2003 and another $92 billion in 2004.

- US investment flows to the United Kingdom ($23 billion) in 2004 accounted for roughly 25% of total US investments in the European Union as a whole.

- US foreign investment to the rest of Europe approached $70 billion in 2004, or near-record highs.

- Despite the diplomatic ill-will between Washington and Paris; US investment flows to France soared to a record $6.8 billion in 2004, some 45% larger than US investments to China in the same year.

- US investment flows to Italy in 2004 ($4.2 billion) were four times as large as US flows to India ($1 billion).

- Europe remains the number one geographical location for US overseas investment. During the first half of this decade, Europe has accounted for nearly 56% of total US foreign direct investment.

- Despite European squabbles with the Bush Administration, European firms invested nearly $53 billion in the United States in 2004, up from just $6.6 billion the year before.

- French investment surged to nearly $9 billion in 2004, up from $5.1 billion in 2003. German firms invested some $6.8 billion in the United States in 2004, up sharply from investment flows of just $407 million in 2003.

- Corporate Europe has accounted for 75% of total foreign direct investment inflows into the US in the past five years. The UK accounted for 19.8% of total global investment flows into the United

States, followed by France (13.1%), the Netherlands (10.8%) and Germany (9.2%).

- Europeans invested over $100 billion in US securities in 2003-04.

- US net purchases of European equities in 2004 reached nearly $52 billion, an annual record.

## *That's where the profits are ...*

- US affiliates earned a record $100.8 billion in Europe in 2004. Earnings jumped 23% over record earnings of $82 billion in 2003.

- US affiliates booked record profits in 17 European markets in 2004.

- US earnings from Europe have nearly doubled in the past five years.

- Despite the strength of the euro, European affiliate earnings in the US surged to a record $65.7 billion in 2004, a 38.5% jump from 2003. Affiliates from nine different European nations reported record US profits in 2004.

- Earnings of European affiliates in the US have increased more than four times since the US recession in 2001.

- US affiliate income in China continues to soar, but US affiliates earned almost three times as much in tiny Ireland and more than five times as much in such countries as the Netherlands or the UK as they did in China.

- Europe is the most profitable region in the world for corporate America. In 2004, US affiliates posted record profits in 12 European countries. US companies continue to rely on Europe for half their total annual foreign profits.

- Over the past five years US companies have registered their most robust earnings growth in Poland, the Czech Republic and Switzerland, ahead of China or India. US affiliate profits in Switzerland alone were twice those earned in all of South America, 4 times that of earnings in China and 23 times that of earnings in India.

- The United Kingdom ranks as the most important single national market in the world for corporate America when it comes to global earnings, accounting for 11% of total affiliate income in the first half of this decade. Not far behind was the Netherlands, with a 10.3% share of global foreign affiliate earnings.

## That's where the jobs are ...

- Most foreigners working for US companies abroad are employed in Europe and most foreigners working for European companies abroad are employed in the United States.

- The manufacturing workforce of US affiliates in Germany alone totaled 385,000 in 2002, more than 80% larger than the number of manufactured workers employed in China by US affiliates.

- European firms employed over two-thirds of the 5.4 million US workers on the payrolls of majority-owned foreign affiliates in 2002.

## That's where the research is ...

- 61% of US corporate research and development conducted outside the US is conducted in Europe. R&D expenditures by US foreign affiliates are greatest in the UK, Germany, France and Switzerland, in that order.

- European R&D expenditures in the US are substantial and dwarf expenditures by Japan or other nations.

## That's where the markets are ...

- Europe accounted for half of the record $3 trillion in global US foreign affiliate sales in 2002, well in excess of US exports of $975 billion.

- Europe accounted for half of total global sales, more than double comparable figures for the Asia/Pacific region.

- US affiliate sales in Europe were more than double affiliate sales in the entire Asia/Pacific region.

- US affiliate sales in the UK alone exceeded aggregate sales in Latin America.

- While US foreign affiliate sales in China have skyrocketed, they have done so from a very low base, and still remain very far below comparable sales in Europe. Sales of $48 billion in China in 2002, for example, were lower than sales to Spain ($57 billion) and well below those in Germany ($242 billion) or France ($140 billion).

- Affiliate sales, not trade, represent the primary means by which European firms deliver goods and services to US consumers. In 2002, European affiliate sales in the US ($1.2 trillion) were roughly three times larger than European exports to the US.

- German affiliate sales in the US were roughly 3.3 times larger than German exports to the US British affiliate sales in the US were almost two and a half times larger than British exports to the US

- The total output of US foreign affiliates in Europe and of European affiliates in the US is greater than the total gross domestic output of most nations.

- Europe accounts for 56% of the total global output of US affiliates.

- US affiliates in Ireland accounted for 19.4% of Ireland's total GDP in 2002, a jump of 3.4% from 2001. US affiliates accounted for 6.7% of the UK's aggregate output and 5.5% of Belgium's total output in 2002.

- European affiliates account for 64% of the total output of all foreign affiliates operating in the United States.

- 60% of corporate America's foreign assets are located in Europe.

- US assets in Germany are greater than total US assets in all of South America.

- America's corporate assets in the United Kingdom exceed total US assets in the entire Asia/Pacific region.

- European firms account for 75% of total foreign assets in the United States.

- There is far more European investment in Texas alone as all US investment in Japan and China put together. In fact, European investment in many different US states, ranging from Georgia to Indiana to California, is greater, in any given year, than total US investment in Japan and China put together.

## Some barriers remain ...

- Despite the fact that transatlantic markets are among the most open in the world and are deeply integrated through dense flows of investment, affiliate sales and related-party trade, various barriers persist that prevent the emergence of a free transatlantic marketplace.

- Transatlantic tariff barriers are generally low, averaging between 3-4% of the €500 billion in annual transatlantic trade. EU tariff levels are uneven, however, and both EU and US tariffs are higher on some sensitive products.

- Because transatlantic tariffs are generally quite low and European and US industries are so deeply intertwined with each other, 'behind the border' non-tariff barriers are more important impediments to a free transatlantic marketplace.

### But a free transatlantic market could bring great benefits …

- The OECD estimates that further transatlantic liberalization could lead to permanent gains in GDP per capita on both sides of the Atlantic of 3 to 3½%, and cause additional benefits to other commercial partners.

## Sectoral Opportunities and Challenges

### Services

- Service activities are the sleeping giant of the transatlantic economy – an economic force that, if awoken and unbound, would further deepen the commercial stakes between the United States and Europe and enhance the global competitiveness of both parties.

- The service economies of the United States and Europe have never been as intertwined as they are today – in such activities as financial services, telecommunications, utilities, insurance, advertising, computer services and other related functions.

- Foreign affiliate sales of services on both sides of the Atlantic have exploded over the past decade. In fact, affiliate sales of services have not only become a viable second channel of delivery, they have become the overwhelming mode of delivery in a rather short period of time. Nothing better illustrates the ever-deepening integration of the transatlantic service economy.

- Following in the footsteps of manufacturers, US and European service companies now deliver their services more through foreign affiliate sales than through trade. In the 1970s and 1980s, firms delivered services primarily via trade. In the 1990s, foreign affiliate sales became the chief mode of delivery.

- Sales of services by US foreign affiliates in Europe soared from $85 billion in 1994 to roughly $212 billion in 2002 – a 150% increase, well ahead of the roughly 65% rise in US service exports to Europe over the same period.

- US foreign affiliate sales of services in Europe – after being roughly equal to US service exports to Europe in 1992 – were nearly double the value of US service exports in 2002.

- Europe is the most important market in the world for US foreign affiliate sales of services, just as it is the most important market for US foreign affiliate sales of goods. In 2002, Europe accounted for 53% of total US affiliate sales ($401 billion), with Asia (with 23% share) and Latin America (13%), a distant second and third, respectively.

- US foreign affiliate service sales of $98.5 billion in the UK alone in 2002 were greater than foreign affiliate service sales in all of Asia ($97 billion) and Latin America ($52 billion).

- Sales of services by US affiliates of European firms have also soared over the past decade. As Europe's investment position in services has expanded in the US, so have foreign affiliate sales of services in the US. The latter totaled $269 billion in 2002 versus $86 billion in 1994, a jump of 213%, well ahead of the 85% rise in US service imports from Europe over the same period.

- The full potential of the transatlantic service economy, however, remains hampered by internal barriers in the US and particularly in Europe. US barriers include maritime, legal, engineering, architectural and accounting services. EU15 barriers appear highest for domestic and foreign firms in accounting, maritime and legal services, and higher for foreign firms relative to domestic firms in distribution, maritime and architectural services.

- The key issue, however, remains the continued existence of service barriers within the EU itself. Copenhagen Economics estimates that liberalization of inner-EU services could result in a total welfare gain of 0.6% of EU GDP, or €37 billion, create up to 600,000 jobs and boost foreign investment by up to 34%.

- Such an initiative would be the single most important stimulus to the transatlantic services economy; lack of services reform represents a significant 'opportunity cost' to the US, the EU and the transatlantic economy.

## Civil Aviation

- The EU and US have the largest and among the most deregulated domestic aviation markets in the world, but still limit transatlantic competition and investment. As a result, the aviation industry lags in adapting to globalization even as it drives other sectors to globalize.

- A single, open transatlantic market for air transport services could increase annual passenger traffic by between 4.1 million and 11.0 million passengers on transatlantic routes, and between 13.6 million and 35.7 million on intra-EU routes, for a total increase of 17.7-46.7 million passengers per year – an increase of 9-24% in total transatlantic travel, and 5-14% in intra-EU travel.

- Consumer welfare could increase by about €5.2 billion annually, with transatlantic traffic accounting for just over half of that increase. The lion's share (up to €3.8 billion annually) would come from gains to consumers that would not involve any reduction in airline profits.

- The increased airline revenue would lead to additional economic output in 'directly related' industries ranging from €3.6-8.1 billion a year. This excludes the potential impact on industries such as tourism and leisure and excludes the 10 new EU members, and is therefore a conservative estimate.

## Commercial Aerospace

- Transatlantic trade in commercial aerospace is a healthy two-way street, with both sides importing and exporting $10-15 billion worth of equipment annually.

- At the end of 2004, Airbus had built 18.2% of the active US passenger fleet, and Boeing had built 58.7% of the active EU passenger fleet.

- The world's jetliners are all powered by Rolls-Royce, General Electric, or Pratt & Whitney turbofans.

- More US than EU airlines chose EU engines for their two main wide-body jets over the past decade, which means that US engine companies enjoy a higher market share on these aircraft in the EU than they do in their domestic market.

- Despite the open nature of transatlantic aerospace trade, a joint transatlantic jetliner industry does not now exist. Sadly, there is an increasing division between Boeing and Airbus, and between their national political backers in the US and the EU.

- The transatlantic market is so open because of a very useful WTO component, the Agreement on Trade in Civil Aircraft (ATCA). It also provides an ongoing test for politicians. Will they be able to resist the short-term rewards of intervening in commercial jetliner trade, or will they keep faith in a long-term institution that has served both sides admirably?

## Automotive Sector

- Transatlantic automotive commerce – whether in the form of visible trade or capital transfers and invisibles such as R&D – is a major underpinning of the North American and European economies.

- In Western Europe the automotive sector accounts for 10% of manufacturing output, employs 2.5 million people directly and accounts for about 3% of GDP. The situation is similar in North America, where the auto sector is the largest manufacturing industry; no other activity is linked to so much of US manufacturing or directly generates so much retail business or employment. The industry employs almost 3 million people directly, with the usual knock-on effects that some studies put as high as another 5 million people.

- Transatlantic trade in automotive products remains significant, with a more than 4-to-1 imbalance in favor of Europe. From 2000 to 2005, trade from Europe to North America grew by 45.7% compared with 10.4% from Asia to North America, and compared with -0.3% from Latin America to North America. North American exports to Europe grew by 44.1% over the period.

- The North American and West European car and light truck markets are broadly equivalent, at around 15 million each, although the type of product, imports share of the market, structure of the industry and size of the leading firms are different. Whereas European companies service the North American market largely through trade, North American companies service the European market primarily through direct investment.

- US-owned companies have around 20% of the West European market whereas Europeans have less than 6% of the North American car and light truck markets. Europe sells 1.1 million vehicles in North America annually; North Americans sell over 3 million cars and light commercial trucks in Europe. US firms account for 12% of the West European heavy truck market; West European firms have 60% of the North American heavy truck market.

- The openness of the transatlantic commerce in automotive products provides a benchmark for other sectors. Transatlantic commerce in automotive products is largely free of market-distorting arrangements and market failure. Compared with many sectors, the auto industry is an example of best practice where market-opening is concerned. In the transatlantic auto sector, there is nowhere for the inefficient to hide.

- There is very little tension in the transatlantic automotive sector. The tension tends to be with third parties, notably Japan.

- Although the transatlantic automotive market is largely open, harmonization of regulations across the Atlantic could reduce unit costs by between 5% and 7% and allow the same products – be they components, accessories or sub-assemblies like engines – to be used in both markets. Given the scale of the automotive sector, harmonization of regulations could increase transatlantic commerce significantly.

## Biopharmaceuticals

- The impact of the health care sector on the transatlantic economy is substantial and expected to grow in the coming decades due to aging populations, consumer demand for innovative medical care and post-genomic advances toward personalized medicine.

- Since the biopharmaceutical sector has globalized through the entire value chain, from research to marketing, transatlantic integration in this sector is best tracked through investment rather than trade.

- The key cross-regional investment driver is clearly the need to recover R&D costs on a worldwide basis. Major attractions of the US for European companies include its dominance in biotechnology innovation, the sheer size of the market and its relatively 'free market' pricing system – all of which are reinforced by the relocation of major research operations from Europe to the US.

- Similarly, despite slower growth and some internal market barriers, the European market remains indispensable for US companies because of rising consumer demand due to aging populations and expectations of high-tech medicines, maturing of bioscience clusters in the UK, Germany and Scandinavia, centralization of the drug approval process, and rationalization of supply chains.

- Each side faces various barriers to fuller integration, however. Bioscience is emerging as the innovation driver across many sectors ranging from health care to energy, food and bio-defense, and is deeply rooted in transatlantic interconnections, and yet public policies lag behind the private sector in spurring transatlantic integration.

- Public policies on both sides of the Atlantic need to be more proactive and harmonized, in areas ranging from research funding to pricing and reimbursement, in order to provide appropriate support for this vibrant sector.

## Financial Markets

- Europe's capital markets accounted for 31% of the global financial stock in 2003, up from 28% in 1999. This compares to 37% for the US, whose share declined from 40% in 1999.

- The exponential growth of transatlantic portfolio investment over the past decade, together with EU financial reforms, has led to a regular financial markets regulatory dialogue with the US that could be considered a model for other areas of deeper transatlantic economic cooperation.

- Significant reductions in the cost of the capital and regulatory burdens, for example, may be expected from the April 2005 US-EU agreement on the equivalence of accounting standards, which will effectively allow companies to use one single accounting standard in the EU and US.

- It would be difficult to measure the benefits of a fully integrated transatlantic financial market, however, particularly since such a market does not yet exist within the EU itself. One analysis suggests that full transatlantic integration of the securities markets could lead to a 9% reduction of the cost of capital for listed companies, 60% reduction in transaction costs and an almost 50% increase in trading volume. A fully integrated capital market could be expected to eliminate a variety of additional duplicate costs.

- Closer transatlantic regulatory dialogue can be positive, but a high degree of international cooperation between regulators could also replicate the dangers of excessive or opaque regulatory intervention at the national level.

## *Telecommunications*

- Over the past two decades, the information and communication technologies sector has become the most important engine of economic growth, productivity and welfare for developed and developing countries. The ICT industry is estimated to have reached €2.044 trillion in 2005, of which the US and the EU account for 29.3% and 32.1%, respectively.

- Europe accounts for 30.7% and the US for 21.6% of the €1.126 trillion global telecommunications sector. Nine of the world's top 10 telecommunications firms are based either in the US or in the EU.

- The transatlantic telecommunications sector is a success story of soaring productivity, plummeting prices, rapid innovation and increasingly open transatlantic competition with beneficial results on both continents. There are few remaining restrictions on foreign ownership and wide participation by foreign communications operations.

- Transatlantic telephone calls today cost only 15 cents per minute, and there is more than 700,000 hours of daily calling across the Atlantic. Transatlantic capacity has increased from scores of channels to hundreds of thousands of channels, and traffic volume has expanded more than 20 times since 1980 level.

- This sector is also an example of cutting-edge issues of globalization that are affecting the US and EU first but which neither side has adequately addressed, such as management of common resources, e.g. spectrum (perhaps leading to an international marketplace for spectrum rights), and emerging issues of interoperability and intellectual property rights.

- The 1998 EU-US Mutual Recognition Agreement on communications equipment spurred various efforts to advance further transatlantic telecoms integration between the respective telecoms markets. Such a market is still hindered, however, by diverging regulatory frameworks, incompatible standards and non-tariff barriers.

- The EU and US are converging in moving towards wireless access and mobile technologies, even though telecoms industries still differ in many respects. 3G platforms are reducing (but not eliminating) incompatible standards on the two sides of the Atlantic. The future shape of the telecoms industry depends on the convergence between fixed and mobile technologies and on the increasing convergence between telecoms, multimedia and broadcast industries.

- If the US is to realize its goal of universal broadband coverage by 2007, and if the EU is to realize its Lisbon goal of becoming a dynamic and competitive knowledge-based economy, each will need to work to create a more homogeneous and pro-competitive regulatory environment on the two sides of the Atlantic. Barriers exist, however, notably US federal and state regulatory obstacles to inward FDI and incomplete market liberalization in the EU.

- The European Commission estimated that the liberalization of telecommunications and electricity markets would lead to a GDP increase of 0.4-0.6% and an employment boost of 0.6%

- The Commission also calculated that increasing total EU R&D expenditure from 1.9% to 3% of GDP by 2010 would lead to a GDP level increase of 1.7% by 2010 (0.25% per year), increases of Total Factor Productivity (0.8%), employment (1.4%) and real income (3%) by 2010 and further GDP level increases of 4.2%, 7.5% and 12.1% in 2015, 2020 and 2030, respectively.

- In the US, a recent study calculated that "each year of delay will cost the US economy about $12 billion of investment spending and about $33 billion of GDP and will deter the creation of more than 212,000 jobs".

## Domestic Policies and Deep Transatlantic Integration

### *Deficits/Imbalances in the Transatlantic Economy*

- Even though the US has a large and growing trade deficit with the EU, which still remains one of the largest of its bilateral deficits, this has generated little political heat for two reasons. First, the EU and the US produce similar goods (not the case for China trade), avoiding issues of cheap labor and 'social dumping'; and second, accumulated investments across the Atlantic are so large that more than one-half of all transatlantic trade is intra-firm trade, which means that even large shifts in exchange rates do not generate protectionist pressures.

- The US current account deficit is also unlikely to generate transatlantic tensions, since it has largely resulted because emerging markets have massively increased their savings. This has one simple implication for transatlantic relations: the main mechanism to rein in the US current account deficit is not the bilateral exchange rate dollar/euro, but an increase in global interest rates, which would compress US excess demand for savings from the rest of the world. It is thus possible that all will remain quiet on the transatlantic front.

### *Transatlantic Dimension to the Lisbon Agenda*

- There is a 'missing link' to the EU's Lisbon Agenda to become a top, competitive, knowledge-based economy – harnessing transatlantic cooperation to leverage growth and innovation, rather than portraying the issue as 'Europe vs. America'.

- While the EU and US should advance liberalization together in key sectors included in the Doha round of multilateral trade negotiations, there are clear opportunities to complementary transatlantic market-opening initiatives in such areas as agriculture, services, financial markets, telecommunications, non-tariff barriers and the movement of people, anti-dumping provisions, trade disputes and innovation policies.

### *Transatlantic Corporate Governance Reform*

- High-profile corporate fallouts of recent years have underscored the interconnection and interdependency of the transatlantic economies and the need for regulators and legislators to work cooperatively to improve transatlantic auditing and governance policies.

- The transatlantic dimension of corporate governance is a unique experiment in corporate law reform. The development of 'transatlantic practice' in corporate governance is underway – an uneven but palpable process leading to the adoption of some common standards and a certain degree of convergence in legal techniques to solve similar problems.

- Impediments remain on both sides of the Atlantic, however, and regulatory diversity may actually facilitate the establishment of a truly transatlantic marketplace.

## Climate Change/Transatlantic Emissions Markets

- The climate change challenge can only addressed as long as all emitters participate, including all industrialized countries and at least the major emitters from developing countries.

- Although the US has not ratified the Kyoto Protocol, US companies are already affected by the implications of the Kyoto Protocol and the EU emission trading scheme (ETS). Not only are their European affiliates directly subject to emission limits, they are indirectly affected by changes in energy prices. Most importantly, perhaps, companies will gain experience with carbon management.

- Once it is up and properly running, the €45 billion EU carbon market should turn over at least four or five times more than the underlying physical stock of allowances. If Russia, Ukraine, Canada or Japan would join, let alone the US, the sums become gigantic. A global greenhouse gas emissions market would easily be worth $100 billion.

- The deep integration of the transatlantic business community means that US and European businesses have much to gain by a transatlantic greenhouse gas emissions market, and much to lose by failure to achieve such a market.

- Huge differences in carbon constraints on both sides of the Atlantic would make further transatlantic market integration almost impossible. On the other hand, a breakthrough in one of the most controversial transatlantic disputes could be a major boost to a more integrated transatlantic market.

## REACH – Chemicals Regulation

- The European Commission's REACH proposal to overhaul the entire EU chemicals regulation and replace it with a single system with very different rules and incentives will apply to the whole value chain of chemicals and their derivatives, including applications to millions of intermediate and final goods. Practically no industry escapes the reach of REACH.

- US business has every interest in following REACH carefully. The chemical industry is of course directly affected. Potentially, the stakes could be high. In addition to $60 billion in chemicals trade and $4 billion in US FDI to Europe in the chemicals industry (the first layer of the value chain), it is estimated that well over $400 billion of 'downstream products' made by US firms with chemicals sold to the EU could be affected.

## Conclusion

- The transatlantic economy is the freest in the world. But it is not free. A concerted effort to create a truly free transatlantic market could generate significant benefits in growth, jobs and consumer welfare on both sides of the Atlantic.

- The transatlantic economy is the laboratory of globalization. It is precisely because the United States and Europe have been at the forefront of a more integrated global economy that the possibilities – and potential limits – of globalization are likely to be defined first and foremost by the transatlantic relationship. Yet neither the framework for our relationship nor the ways our governments are currently organized adequately capture these new realities.

# SECTION I

# DEEP INTEGRATION AND THE TRANSATLANTIC ECONOMY

# 1.  The Transatlantic Economy Today: Neither Mars nor Venus – Mercury!

## *Daniel S. Hamilton and Joseph P. Quinlan*

It is fashionable these days to proclaim the transatlantic partnership passé. Such loose talk, however, ignores two bottom-line economic facts. First, despite the perennial hype about 'big emerging markets', the economic relationship between the United States and Europe is by a wide margin the deepest and broadest between any two continents in history. Second, these ties that bind have become stronger, not weaker, since the end of the Cold War, tightened even further during George W. Bush's first term, and have remained robust despite troubling growth prospects for some key European economies.

Robert Kagan's quip that Americans are from Mars and Europeans are from Venus has been reinforced by transatlantic disputes over Iraq since 2003. However, a related tale of recent years is that both Mars and Venus should take greater heed of Mercury, the god of commerce.

For the transatlantic partnership, the last few years have been characterized by political bust and economic boom. Even as diplomatic relations between the US and Europe reached new lows, and as each side of the Atlantic has encountered recessionary pressures, the economic ties that bind the two parties have only grown stronger. Indeed, in the past few years, transatlantic business has never been better.

By our estimates, transatlantic commerce totaled roughly $3 trillion in 2004. That figure includes total two-way trade between the United States and Europe, plus total foreign affiliate sales, adjusted for potential double counting of affiliate sales and exports/imports.

Transatlantic trade, foreign direct investment, portfolio flows and affiliate profits have all rebounded robustly from the US cyclical economic downturn of 2001-02, and continue strong even as some key European economies struggle with low growth now. In 2004, for instance, total transatlantic trade in goods rose to a record $482 billion, up 22% from the prior year. Notwithstanding the strength of the euro against the US dollar, US imports from the European Union jumped to a record $283 billion, helping to drive America's trade deficit with the European Union to an all-time high of $110 billion.

In 2004, the US posted record imports from Germany ($77.2 billion), Italy ($28 billion), France ($31.8 billion), Italy ($28.1 billion) and a host of other European nations. Surging imports from Europe led to record US trade deficits with a number of European nations in 2004, including Germany ($46 billion).

Strong trade flows have been complemented by robust levels of foreign direct investment. Despite Washington's war-related frustrations with Europe, corporate America ploughed nearly $100 billion into the European Union in 2003 and another $92 billion in 2004. As is customary, US investment flows to the United Kingdom ($23 billion) in 2004 accounted for roughly 25% of total US investments in the European Union as a whole.

Even after adjusting for massive flows to the UK, however, US foreign investment to the rest of Europe approached $70 billion in 2004, or near-record highs. Interestingly, despite the diplomatic ill will between Washington and Paris, US investment flows to France soared to a record $6.8 billion in 2004, some 45% larger than US investments to China in the same year. US investment flows to Italy in 2004 ($4.2 billion) were four times as large as US flows to India ($1 billion). Greece, Russia and the Czech Republic all received record annual inflows of US foreign direct investment in 2004.

Europe remains the number one geographic location for US overseas investment. In 2004, the region accounted for 41% of the global total. That is a rather low percentage given that during the first half of this decade, Europe accounted for nearly 56% of total US foreign direct investment. However, the figures for 2004 were skewed by a large one-off US investment in Australia, which lowered the global total destined for Europe.

*Table 1. 2004: Another Record-Setting Year for the Transatlantic Economy*

The following all-time highs were recorded in 2004:

**Transatlantic Investment**

| | |
|---|---|
| European net purchases of US government agency bonds | $84.4 billion |
| French net purchases of US corporate bonds | $7.4 billion |
| German net purchases of US corporate bonds | $11.7 billion |
| US net purchases of European equities | $51.7 billion |
| | |
| US foreign direct investment flows to Czech Republic | $300 million |
| US foreign direct investment flows to France | $6.8 billion |
| US foreign direct investment flows to Greece | $274 million |
| US foreign direct investment flows to Russia | $430 million |

*Sources*: Bureau of Economic Analysis, US Department of Commerce; US Department of the Treasury.

*Table 2. Transatlantic Profits (affiliate income)*

| | |
|---|---|
| US profits in Europe | $100.8 billion |
| US profits in Belgium | $2.8 billion |
| US profits in Czech Republic | $437 million |
| US profits in Finland: | $507 million |
| US profits in France: | $6.3 billion |
| US profits in Germany | $7.0 billion |
| US profits in Greece | $270 million |
| US profits in Hungary | $546 million |
| US profits in Ireland | $10.2 billion |
| US profits in Italy | $2.9 billion |
| US profits in Luxemburg | $7.2 billion |
| US profits in Netherlands | $18.2 billion |
| US profits in Norway | $2.3 billion |
| US profits in Poland | $635 million |
| US profits in Portugal | $483 million |
| US profits in Spain | $4.3 billion |
| US profits in Switzerland | $12.2 billion |
| US profits in United Kingdom | $19.7 billion |
| European profits in the US | $65.7 billion |
| Belgium profits in the US | $637 million |
| Denmark profits in the US | $368 million |
| Finland profits in the US | $390 million |
| France profits in the US | $8.5 billion |
| Germany profits in the US | $8.5 billion |
| Ireland profits in the US | $1.2 billion |
| Italy profits in the US | $520 million |
| Netherlands profits in the US | $13.2 billion |
| Norway profits in the US | $242 million |
| Spain profits in the US | $287 million |
| United Kingdom profits in the US | $19.5 billion |

*Source*: Bureau of Economic Analysis, US Department of Commerce.

*Table 3. Transatlantic Trade*

| | |
|---|---:|
| Total transatlantic trade in goods | $482 billion |
| US trade deficit with European Union | $110 billion |
| US current account deficit with the European Union | $134.3 billion |
| US imports from the European Union | $282.6 billion |
| US exports to Germany | $31.4 billion |
| US imports from Germany | $77.2 billion |
| US trade deficit with Germany | $45.9 billion |
| US imports from Austria | $5.8 billion |
| US trade deficit with Austria | $3.8 billion |
| US exports to Belgium | $16.9 billion |
| US imports from Belgium | $12.4 billion |
| US exports to Czech Republic | $822 million |
| US imports from Czech Republic | $1.8 billion |
| US trade deficit with Czech Republic | $939 million |
| US exports to Denmark | $2.1 billion |
| US imports from Denmark | $3.9 billion |
| US imports from Finland | $3.9 billion |
| US exports to France | $21.2 billion |
| US imports from France | $31.8 billion |
| US exports to Hungary | $1.1 billion |
| US Imports from Ireland | $27.4 billion |
| US trade deficit with Ireland | 19.3 billion |
| US imports from Italy | $28.1 billion |
| US trade deficit with Italy | $17.4 billion |
| US exports to Netherlands | $24.3 billion |
| US imports from Netherlands | $12.6 billion |
| US imports from Norway | $6.5 billion |
| US trade deficit with Norway | $4.9 billion |
| US imports from Poland | $1.8 billion |
| US trade deficit with Poland | $901 million |
| US imports from Portugal | $2.2 billion |
| US trade deficit with Portugal | $1.2 billion |
| US exports to Slovenia | $192 million |
| US imports from Slovenia | $512 million |
| US exports to Spain | $6.6 billion |
| US imports from Spain | $7.5 billion |
| US trade deficit with Spain | $835 million |
| US imports from Sweden | $12.7 billion |
| US trade deficit with Sweden | $9.4 billion |
| US imports from Switzerland | $11.6 billion |
| US trade deficit with Switzerland | $2.4 billion |
| US imports from United Kingdom | $46.4 billion |
| US trade deficit with United Kingdom | $10.4 billion |

*Source*: US Census Bureau.

The fact that many in Europe were staunchly opposed to the policies of the Bush Administration did not prevent European firms from investing nearly $53 billion in the United States in 2004, up from just $6.6 billion the year before. French investment surged to nearly $9 billion in 2004, up from $5.1 billion the year before. German firms invested some $6.8 billion in the United States in 2004, up sharply from investment flows of just $407 million the year before. Corporate Europe remains a key source of foreign capital for the United States, accounting for 75% of total foreign direct investment inflows into the US over the 2000-04 timeframe. During this period, the United Kingdom accounted for 19.8% of total global investment flows into the United States, followed by France (13.1% of the total), the Netherlands (10.8%) and Germany (9.2%).

*Figure 1. Corporate America's Bias toward Europe (US foreign direct investment outflows to Europe as a % of total)*

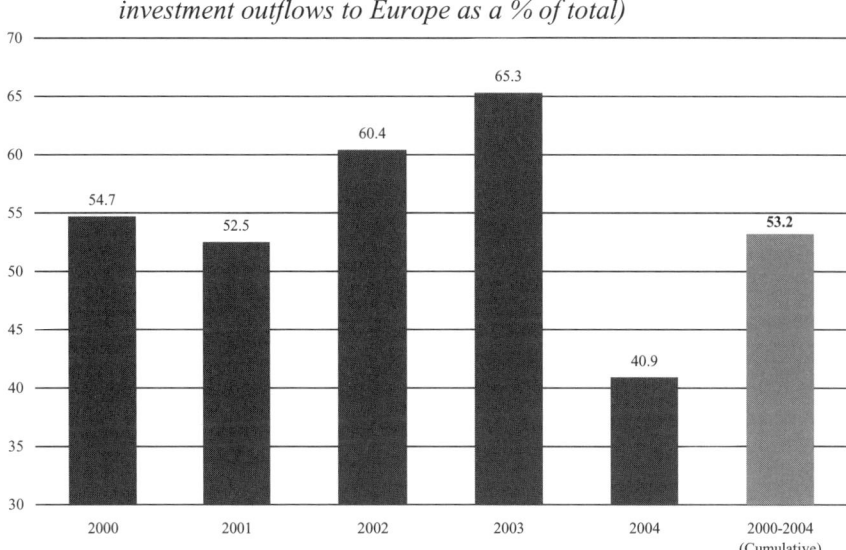

*Source*: Bureau of Economic Analysis, US Department of Commerce.

European investors have also remained important foreign investors in US dollar-denominated securities over the past few years. European net purchases of US government agency bonds totaled a record $84.4 billion in 2004. In the US corporate bond market, net purchases of US corporate bonds by French investors totaled $7.4 billion in 2004 – an all-time high. German net purchases of US corporate bonds in 2004 also hit a record $11.7 billion. In total, eurozone investors (which excludes the United Kingdom) in 2004 were net purchasers of $55 billion in US securities. This capital infusion helped the debt-stretched United States cover its massive savings shortfall.

Over the two years 2003 and 2004, European investors sank over $100 billion in US securities (US Treasury notes, government agency bonds, corporate bonds and US stocks).

*Figure 2. Euroland Net Purchases of US Securities 1988-2004*

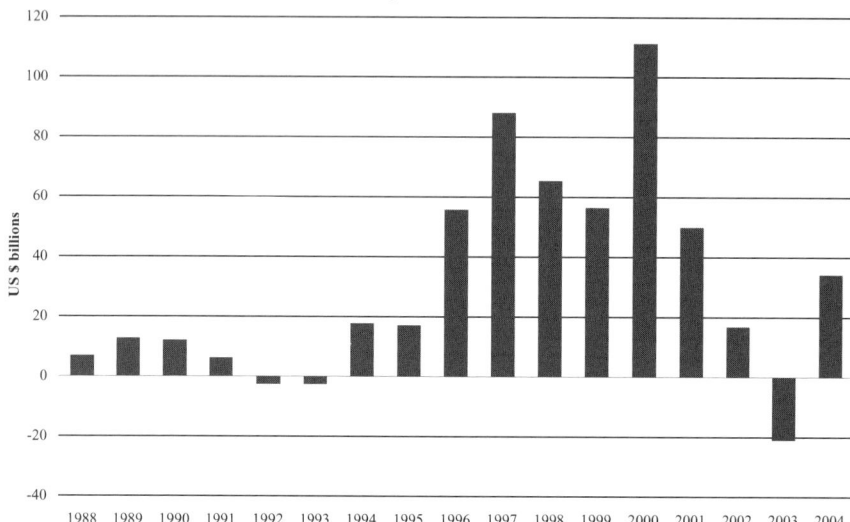

Excludes purchases from the United Kingdom.
*Source*: US Treasury Department.

Portfolio flows from the US to Europe were also robust in 2004, with US net purchases of European equities reaching nearly $52 billion, an annual record.

The past few years have also been record years for transatlantic profits as measured by foreign affiliate income. Despite all the talk of transatlantic boycotts and of a consumer backlash on both sides of the ocean, business has never been better for US and European multinationals.

*Figure 3. A Banner Year for Transatlantic Profits (1994-2004)\**

* Income of affiliates.

*Source*: Bureau of Economic Analysis.

Over the past two years, US foreign affiliates in Europe have booked record profits, courtesy of the steep decline of the US dollar against the euro. The weaker the dollar, the more inflated the dollar-based earnings of US foreign affiliates have become. The result: US affiliates earned a record $100.8 billion in Europe in 2004, with strong gains across the board. Earnings jumped 23% over record earnings of $82 billion the year before, when US affiliate earnings in 12 European markets reached record highs. In 2004, US affiliates booked record profits in 17 European markets, with record earnings reported not only in such traditional markets as Germany, France and Italy, but also in the markets of new EU members Poland, Hungary and the Czech Republic. This broadly-based profits surge from Europe helped boost total US pretax corporate profits to record levels in 2004. Between 2001 and 2004, US affiliate income (earnings) from Europe nearly doubled.

2004 was also a record profit year for European affiliates operating in the United States. Notwithstanding the strength of the euro – a significant drag on European earnings – European affiliate earnings surged to a record $65.7 billion in 2004, a 38.5% jump from 2003. Affiliates from the following nations reported record US profits in 2004: France, Germany, Belgium, Finland, Ireland, the Netherlands, Norway, Spain and the United Kingdom. Earnings of European affiliates in the US have increased more than four-fold since the US recession in 2001. The earnings recovery has been driven by robust US demand, which has offset both the negative effect of the appreciation of the euro and the British pound, and weak European growth during the past few years. Much of the sharp rise in corporate profits in Europe in 2003 and 2004 was due to strong US demand.

While US affiliate income in China continues to soar (rising to a record $3.5 billion in 2004), US affiliates earned almost three times as much in tiny Ireland ($10.2 billion) and more than five times as much in such countries as the Netherlands ($18.2 billion) or the UK ($19.7 billion). In 2004 US affiliates posted record profits in France, Germany, Ireland, the Netherlands, Norway, Poland, Spain, Switzerland, Belgium, Finland, the Czech Republic and Greece. US companies continue to rely on Europe for half their total annual foreign profits.

Europe also remains the most attractive overseas destination for US foreign direct investment. Despite all the talk about US firms decamping for China and India, more than 53% of total US capital outflows of $760 billion this decade – $405 billion – has been sunk in Europe. Over the past decade US firms have ploughed ten times as much capital into the Netherlands as into China, and twice as much into the Netherlands as into Mexico. There is far more European investment in Texas alone than US investment in Japan and China put together. In fact, European investment in many different US states, ranging from Georgia to Indiana to California, is greater, in any given year, than total US investment in Japan and China put together.

In sum, Europe and the United States remain each other's most important foreign commercial markets, a fact lost on opinion leaders on both sides of the Atlantic over the past few years. No other commercial artery in the world is as integrated and fused together by foreign investment. Some 12-14 million workers on both sides of the Atlantic depend on the transatlantic economy for employment. Hundreds of European firms are intertwined in the US economy, just as hundreds of US firms are embedded in the European Union. Workers, employers and shareholders in various countries benefit tremendously from this relationship.

# 2. The Transatlantic Economy Today: Seven Ties that Bind

## *Daniel S. Hamilton and Joseph P. Quinlan*

It has long been our contention that one of the most dangerous deficits affecting the transatlantic partnership is not one of trade, values or military capabilities but rather a deficit in understanding among opinion leaders of the vital stakes Americans and Europeans have developed in the success of each other's respective economies.

Much has been written in recent years about transatlantic divisions and the widening gulf that separates the United States and Europe. There has been comparatively little analysis or recognition of the economic glue that continues to bind the two parties together. Policy-makers, politicians and pundits on both sides of the Atlantic fail to appreciate a critical fact: the transatlantic economy is tightly bound together by foreign investment, a deep form of cross-border integration – as opposed to trade, which is a rather shallow, underdeveloped form of integration.

This is reflected in the massive capital investment of the United States in Europe and Europe's outsized investment commitment in the United States. Exports and imports have become the most common measurement of cross-border economic activity between nations, but trade alone is a misleading benchmark of international commerce. Foreign direct investment and the activities of foreign affiliates are the backbone of transatlantic commercial activity.

## The Ties that Bind – Quantifying the Transatlantic Economy

The primacy of foreign direct investment in driving transatlantic commerce reflects the underlying commercial infrastructure that links the United States with Europe. This infrastructure has been under construction for over a century, but remains largely invisible to policy-makers on both sides of the Atlantic. Over the past few years we have suggested that seven key indices offer a clearer picture of the 'deep integration' forces shaping the transatlantic economy today. This chapter updates those indices with the latest available figures. The bottom-line story they tell: transatlantic commercial ties have never been stronger and never as important. Moreover, these transatlantic ties tightened considerably during George W. Bush's first term in office. They continue to be strong despite sluggish growth in some key European markets.

*Figure 1. The Transatlantic World vs. the World Economy*

**Share of World Total**

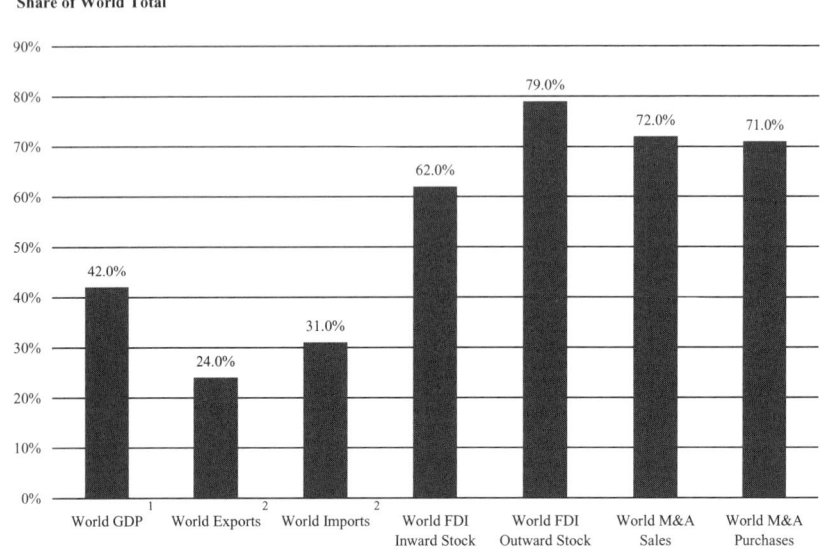

¹ Based on PPP estimates.
² Excluding intra-EU trade.
*Sources*: UN, IMF, official government sources, figures for 2003.

## 1. Gross Product of Foreign Affiliates

The total output of US foreign affiliates in Europe ($342 billion in 2002) and of European affiliates in the United States ($290 billion) is greater than the total gross domestic output of most nations. On a global basis, the aggregate output of US affiliates topped $600 billion in 2002, with Europe accounting for 56% of the total.

The presence of US affiliates in some European nations is particularly noteworthy. The gross output of US affiliates in Ireland, for instance, represented 19.4% of Ireland's total GDP in 2002, a jump of 3.4% from 2001. US affiliates accounted for 6.7% of the UK's aggregate output in the same year and 5.5% of Belgium's total output.

In the United States, European affiliates are major economic producers in their own right. British firms are particularly important – their US output totaled nearly $90 billion in 2002. Output from German affiliates operating in the US totaled $57 billion, while output from French affiliates was nearly $41 billion in 2002. Overall, foreign affiliates contributed more than $453 billion to US aggregate production in 2002; output from European affiliates totaled $291 billion, or 64% of the total attributable to foreign affiliates.

*Figure 2. America's Major Commercial Arteries*

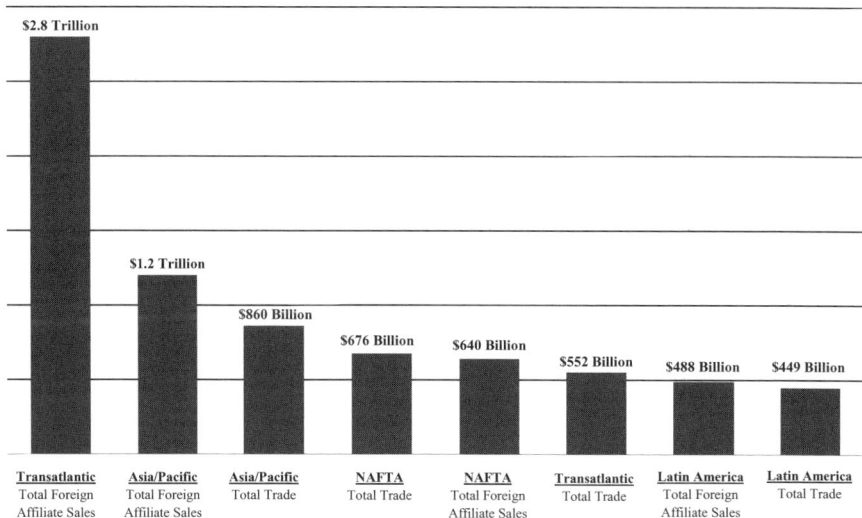

*Note*: Foreign Affiliate Sales: Data for 2002; Total Trade: Data in goods & services, 2002.
*Source*: US Department of Commerce.

## 2. Overseas Assets of Foreign Affiliates

America's global commercial presence is unsurpassed, with total foreign assets of corporate America tallying roughly $6.9 trillion in 2002. The bulk of these assets – roughly 60% – were located in Europe, with the largest share in the United Kingdom, followed by the Netherlands and Germany. US assets in Germany alone ($351 billion) were greater than total US assets in all of South America. America's corporate assets in the United Kingdom ($1.6 trillion) exceeded total US assets in the entire Asia/Pacific region.

*Table 1. Global Engagement: US Foreign Affiliate Sales vs. Trade*

|  | $ billions, 2002 |
|---|---|
| Global Affiliate Sales of US | 2973.2 |
| Total US Exports | 975.9 |
| Total Affiliate Sales in US | 2043.5 |
| US Imports | 1397.7 |
| US Affiliate Sales in Europe | 1479.5 |
| US Exports to Europe (G&S) | 273.9 |
| European Affiliate Sales in US | 1246.6 |
| US Imports from Europe (G&S) | 363.6 |

*Figure 3. Sales of US Affiliates in Europe vs. US Exports to Europe*

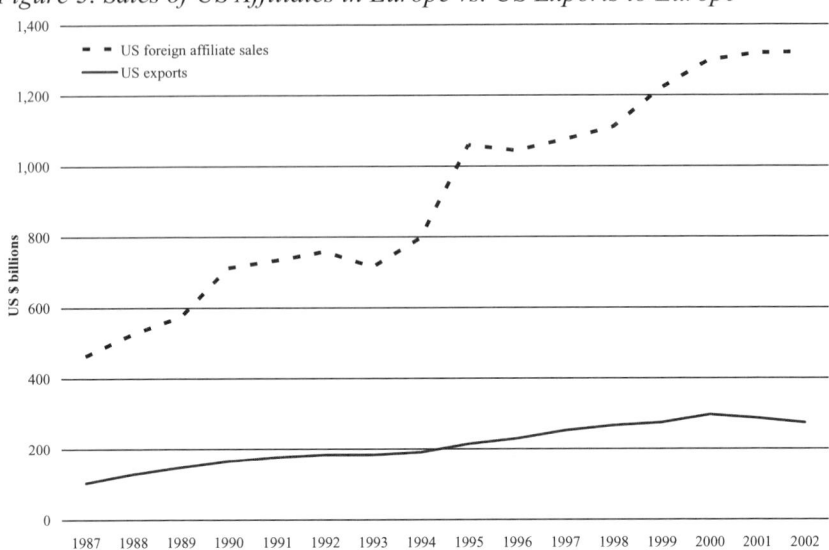

*Source*: Bureau of Economic Analysis, US Department of Commerce.

*Figure 4. Sales of European Affiliates in the United States vs. US Imports from Europe*

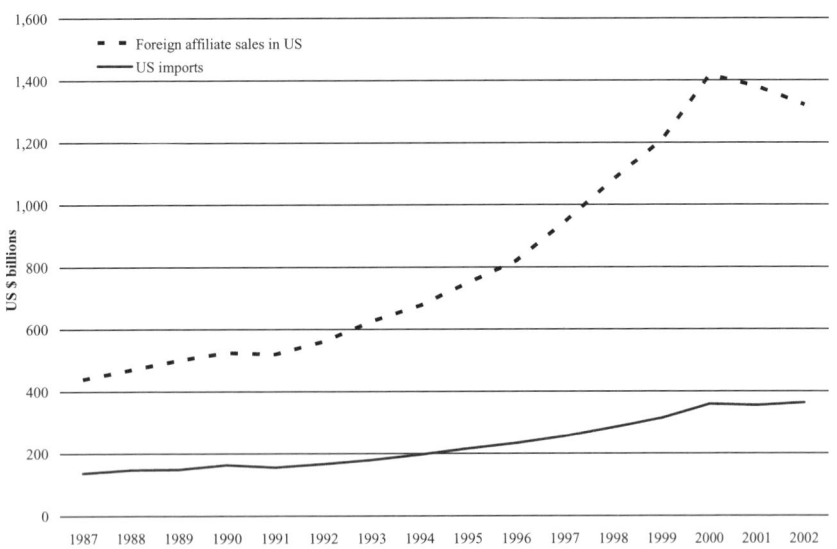

*Source*: Bureau of Economic Analysis, US Department of Commerce.

What about foreign-owned assets held in the US? European firms held some $3.4 trillion in US assets in 2002, roughly 75% of total foreign assets in the United States. The stock of Europe's investment in the US is distributed widely across industrial sectors and geographic regions. Indeed, European companies were the top foreign investors in 44 states, and ranked second in the remaining six states in 2002. Switzerland and the United Kingdom ranked as the largest holders of US assets in 2002, with Swiss affiliates in possession of $878 billion worth of US assets and British firms holding $820 billion in assets.

## 3. Affiliate Employment

The continuing debate about 'outsourcing' is generating more heat than light, often leading pundits and the public to the easy – but erroneous – conclusion that the bulk of corporate America's overseas workforce toils in low-wage nations like Mexico and China. The real story is rather different. Most foreigners working for US companies abroad are employed in the industrialized nations, notably Europe.

US firms employed 4.1 million workers in Europe in 2002. The European workforce of US majority-owned foreign affiliates was almost evenly split between manufacturing and service workers. The number of manufacturing workers in Europe has leveled off in recent years, although US firms still employed roughly 1.9 million manufactured workers in 2002. The manufacturing workforce of US affiliates in Germany alone totaled 385,000 in 2002, more than 80% larger than the number of manufactured workers employed in China by US affiliates. The transportation equipment sector continued to be the largest source of manufacturing employment in Europe; wholesale employment was among the largest sources of service-related employment, and includes employment in such areas as logistics, trade, insurance and other service-enhancing activities.

The same is true for European companies. Despite stories on the continent about home-grown European companies decamping for cheap labor markets in eastern Europe or Asia, most foreigners working for European companies outside the EU are American. European majority-owned foreign affiliates directly employed roughly 3.8 million American workers in 2002. The top five employers in the US were firms from the United Kingdom (995,000), Germany (676,000), the Netherlands (547,000), France (468,000) and Switzerland (430,000). European firms employed over two-thirds of the 5.4 million US workers on the payrolls of majority-owned foreign affiliates in 2002.

*Table 2. Top Five European Employers of US Workers\**

| | | |
|---|---|---|
| 1. | United Kingdom | 995,000 |
| 2. | Germany | 676,000 |
| 3. | The Netherlands | 547,000 |
| 4. | France | 468,000 |
| 5. | Switzerland | 430,000 |

\* Directly employed by majority-owned European affiliates, 2002.

*Source*: Bureau of Economic Analysis, US Department of Commerce.

In short, the transatlantic workforce directly employed by US and European foreign affiliates is roughly 8 million people. That is nearly double the number of total workers employed by US firms in NAFTA partners Canada and Mexico.

On a global basis, US companies directly employed 9.7 million workers in 2002, with roughly 42% in Europe.

As we have stressed in our last annual surveys, these figures understate the employment effects of mutual investment flows, since these numbers are limited to direct employment, and do not account for indirect employment effects of non-equity arrangements such as strategic alliances, joint ventures and other deals. Moreover, affiliate employment figures do not include jobs supported by transatlantic trade. Trade-related employment is substantial in many US states and many European regions.

In total, and adding in indirect employment, we estimate that the transatlantic work force numbers some 12-14 million workers. Europe is by far the most important source of 'insourced' jobs in America, and the US is by far the most important source of 'insourced' jobs in Europe.

## 4. Research and Development (R&D) of Foreign Affiliates

While most firms still tend to center their R&D expenditures in their home country, foreign affiliate R&D has become more prominent over the past decade as firms seek to share development costs, spread risks and tap into the intellectual talent of other nations. Alliances, cross-licensing of intellectual property, mergers and acquisitions and other forms of cooperation have become more prevalent characteristics of the transatlantic economy in the past decade. The advent and speed of the internet on both sides of the Atlantic has powered greater transatlantic R&D.

Research and development among US foreign affiliates topped $21 billion in 2002. The bulk of such activity was carried out in the developed nations, where the largest pool of skilled labor resides. In 2001, the last year of country information, Europe accounted for 61% of total US foreign affiliate R&D, with the United Kingdom, Germany, France and Switzerland representing markets where R&D expenditures by US affiliates were the greatest.

No comparable country figures for Europe's R&D investment in the United States are available, although on an aggregate basis, expenditures on R&D preformed by majority-owned US affiliates totaled $27.5 billion in 2002. A significant share emanated from world-class leaders from Europe, given their interest in America's highly skilled labor force and the research intensity of many European sectors, including chemicals, telecommunications and automobiles.

## 5. Intra-Firm Trade of Foreign Affiliates

While cross-border trade is a secondary means of delivering goods and services across the Atlantic when compared to foreign investment, the modes of delivery – affiliate sales and trade – should not be viewed independently of each other. They are more complements than substitutes, since foreign investment and affiliate sales increasingly drive trade flows. Indeed, a substantial share of transatlantic trade is considered intra-firm trade or related-party trade, which is cross-border trade that stays within the ambit of the company – for instance when BMW of Germany sends parts to BMW of South Carolina, when LaFarge or Michelin sends intermediate components to their plants in the Greater Cincinnati area, or when 3M sends component parts for its office products or communications sectors from St. Paul to its affiliates in Germany or the UK. The tight linkages between European parent companies and their US affiliates is reflected in the fact that roughly 58% of US imports from the European Union consisted of related-party trade in 2004. The percentage was even higher in the case of Ireland (89.3%) and Germany (62.1%). Meanwhile, roughly 30% of US exports to Europe in 2003 represented-related party trade.

Against this backdrop, it is hardly surprising that the three-year slide of the US dollar against the euro has done little to correct America's trade deficit with Europe. Following such a large shift in prices or exchange rates, Economics 101 would have predicted a rebalancing of bilateral trade. Economic theory would have expected US export growth to outstrip US import growth, leading to an improvement in the overall trade balance. In fact, the opposite occurred: America's trade deficit (in goods and services) with the European Union actually widened by 17% in 2004, with the deficit jumping to a record $104.4 billion.

In the end, what is missing from the debate over trade and missing from conventional analysis is the fact that an unusually large percentage of US imports from Europe is considered related-party trade, or trade between a parent and an affiliate. Parent-affiliate trade is less responsive to shifts in prices or exchange rates and more attuned to domestic demand. Accordingly, while a strong euro, in theory at least, would be associated with a decline in European competitiveness in the US, the fact that many European multinationals produce, market and distribute goods on both sides of the ocean gives firms a high degree of immunity to a dramatic shift in exchange rates.

*Table 3. Related-Party Trade 2004*

|  | US Imports: 'Related-Party Trade' as % of Total | US Exports: 'Related-Party Trade' as % of Total |
|---|---|---|
| European Union | 57.9 | 30.4 |
| France | 48.9 | 31.8 |
| Germany | 62.1 | 32.2 |
| Netherlands | 53.3 | 35.9 |
| United Kingdom | 58.5 | 27.7 |
| Other European Union | 47.0 | 27.5 |

*Source*: US Census Bureau.

## 6. Foreign Affiliate Sales

US foreign affiliate sales hit a record $3 trillion in 2002, the last year of available data, well in excess of US exports of $975 billion in the same year. Europe accounted for half of total global sales. Sales of US affiliates in Europe totaled $1.5 trillion, more than double the comparable figures for the Asia/Pacific region. Affiliate sales in the United Kingdom ($389 billion) exceeded aggregate sales in Latin America. While US foreign affiliate sales in China skyrocketed in the 1990s on account of surging US foreign direct investment, they did so from a very low base, and still remain very far below comparable sales in Europe. Sales of US affiliates in China in 2002 totaled just $48 billion, lower than sales to Spain ($57 billion) and well below those in Germany ($242 billion) or France ($140 billion).

*Figure 5. US Foreign Direct Investment in China vs. Europe (1994-2004)*

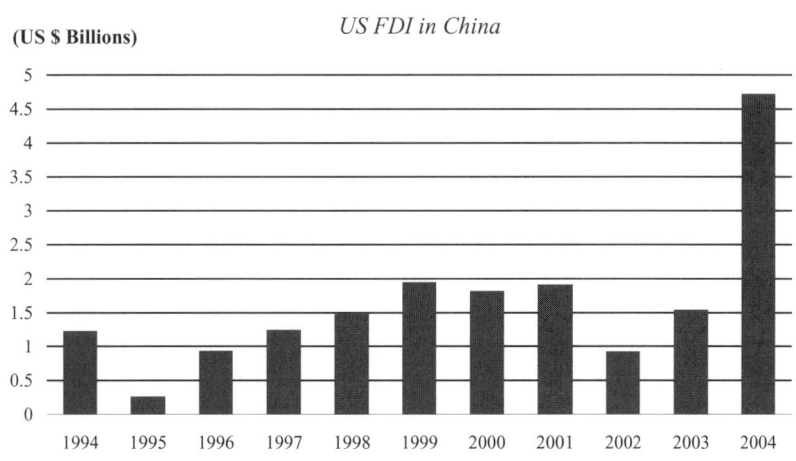

**(US $ Billions)**

■ China ■ Europe

**(US $ Billions)** *US FDI in China*

*Source*: Bureau of Economic Analysis, US Department of Commerce.

Affiliate sales are also the primary means by which European firms deliver goods and services to US consumers. In 2002, for instance, majority-owned European affiliate sales in the US ($1.2 trillion) were more than three times larger than US imports from Europe. In the case of Germany, the gap between foreign affiliate sales and imports was even wider, with German affiliate sales ($290 billion) roughly 3.3 times larger than US imports from Germany ($87 billion). British affiliate sales in the US of $315 billion were almost two and a half times larger than US imports from the UK in 2002.

## 7. Foreign Affiliate Profits

When it comes to the bottom line – the earnings of US multinationals – Europe remains by a relatively wide margin the most profitable region in the world for corporate America. In 2004, Europe accounted for 47% of total US foreign affiliate income, a proxy for global earnings. Corporate America's earnings in Europe were double those in the Asia-Pacific region and triple those with NAFTA partners Mexico and Canada. US foreign affiliate income from Europe was a record $100.8 billion in 2004, up sharply from the record levels of 2003 ($82 billion). Behind the surge in profits is the steep slide of the dollar against the euro, pound and Swiss franc, which helped inflated dollar-based earnings of US affiliates in Europe. Over the first half of this decade Europe has accounted for 53% of total US affiliate income.

Lavish media coverage tipping China or India as the hot growth markets of this decade obscures the fact that over the past five years, US companies have registered robust earnings growth in other places, like Poland, where cumulative affiliate earnings jumped 1,011% in the first half of this decade versus the second half of the 1990s. Over the same period, cumulative affiliate earnings soared by 940% in the Czech Republic, greater than the rise in earnings in either India (758% increase) and or China (286% increase). While these growth rates in earnings are remarkable, all proceed from a relatively low base – US corporate earnings in Poland and India were each roughly $1.85 billion over the 2000-04 period. What is perhaps most striking is the fact that Switzerland ranked third worldwide as a source of earnings growth for U.S companies over the past five years, and from a more sizable base. In 2000 Switzerland accounted for only 1.6% of US foreign affiliate earnings; by 2004 Switzerland accounted for 6.4% of earnings ($43.77 billion) – twice that of Corporate America's total earnings in South America, 4 times that of earnings in China and 23 times that of earnings in India.

The United Kingdom, however, ranks as the most important market in the world for corporate America when it comes to global earnings. On average, the UK represented nearly 11% of total affiliate income in the first half of this decade. Not far behind was the Netherlands, with a 10.3% share of global foreign affiliate earnings.

US profits continued in other European markets as well. Over the past five years US companies have earned three times as much in tiny Ireland than in China, for example.

*Table 4. Top Five Foreign Earners in the United States, 2004 ($ billions)*

| 1. | United Kingdom | 19.532 |
|---|---|---|
| 2. | The Netherlands | 13.207 |
| 3. | Japan | 12.080 |
| 4. | France | 8.515 |
| 5. | Germany | 8.494 |

Similarly, the United States is the most important market in the world in terms of earnings for many European multinationals. Profits of European foreign affiliates in the United States totaled $65.7 billion in 2004, with the earnings driven by strong U.S demand, which offset the adverse price effect from the strength of the euro and the British pound. The sectors most exposed to the US market include telecoms, automobiles, media, technology, capital goods, utilities and pharmaceuticals.

*Figure 6. The US Earnings Boost from Europe (US foreign affiliate income from Europe)*

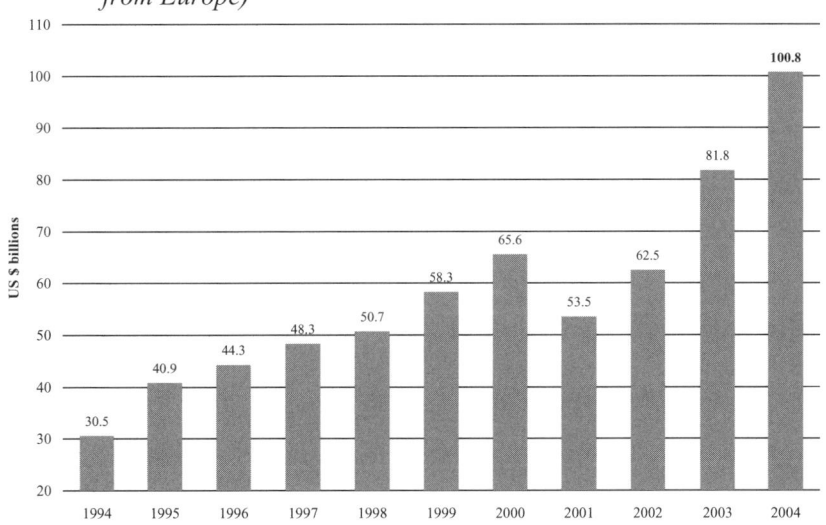

*Source*: Bureau of Economic Analysis, US Department of Commerce.

*Figure 7. US Foreign Affiliate Income Earned Abroad
(as a percentage of the global total, 2004)*

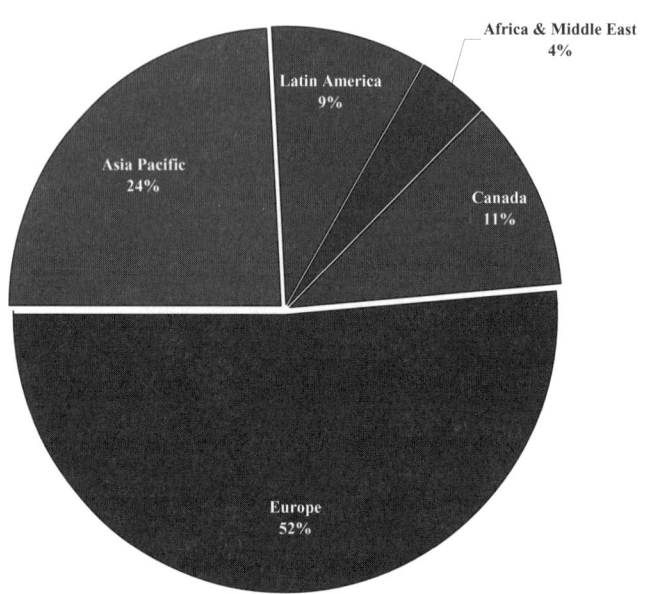

*Source*: Bureau of Economic Analysis, US Department of Commerce.

In short, these seven indices convey a more complete and complex picture of international economic flows than simple tallies of exports and imports. Foreign direct investment, not trade, is the backbone of the transatlantic economy, with many other indicators of market growth derived from the level and depth of these investment linkages.

Table 5. Total EU Exports to the US vs. EU Exports to the World

| | 2000 | | | 2001 | | | 2002 | | | 2003 | | | 2004 | | |
|---|---|---|---|---|---|---|---|---|---|---|---|---|---|---|---|
| | Total US ($ Bil.) | Share of Extra-EU Total | Share of World Total | Total US ($ Bil.) | Share of Extra-EU Total | Share of World Total | Total US ($ Bil.) | Share of Extra-EU Total | Share of World Total | Total US ($ Bil.) | Share of Extra-EU Total | Share of World Total | Total US ($ Bil.) | Share of Extra-EU Total | Share of World Total |
| Austr. | 3.4 | 19.0% | 5.0% | 3.6 | 19.5% | 5.1% | 3.9 | 18.7% | 4.9% | 4.8 | 18.5% | 4.9% | 6.9 | 21.1% | 6.0% |
| Belg. | 10.9 | 25.6% | 5.9% | 10.6 | 25.7% | 5.6% | 16.8 | 31.5% | 7.9% | 16.9 | 29.2% | 6.7% | 20.0 | 28.6% | 6.5% |
| Denm. | 3.0 | 20.2% | 5.9% | 3.5 | 21.8% | 6.9% | 3.6 | 20.3% | 6.4% | 4.1 | 19.9% | 6.2% | 3.6 | 16.7% | 5.4% |
| Finl. | 3.4 | 19.8% | 7.4% | 4.2 | 24.3% | 9.8% | 4.0 | 22.7% | 9.0% | 4.3 | 20.4% | 8.2% | 3.9 | 15.2% | 6.4% |
| Fran. | 28.1 | 24.2% | 8.7% | 27.7 | 23.6% | 8.6% | 26.0 | 22.0% | 7.8% | 26.3 | 19.6% | 6.7% | 29.9 | 19.0% | 6.7% |
| Germ. | 56.4 | 28.7% | 10.3% | 60.3 | 28.6% | 10.6% | 62.9 | 27.7% | 10.3% | 69.0 | 25.9% | 9.3% | 78.5 | 24.3% | 8.8% |
| Greece | 0.6 | 11.1% | 5.4% | 0.5 | 11.6% | 5.6% | 0.5 | 9.9% | 5.2% | 0.9 | 14.3% | 6.3% | 0.8 | 11.8% | 5.3% |
| Irel. | 12.9 | 43.8% | 17.0% | 14.0 | 43.3% | 16.8% | 14.6 | 46.8% | 16.7% | 19.1 | 54.5% | 20.5% | 21.2 | 53.2% | 20.2% |
| Italy | 24.5 | 25.8% | 10.4% | 23.5 | 23.9% | 9.7% | 24.5 | 23.6% | 9.8% | 24.9 | 21.0% | 8.3% | 27.5 | 19.5% | 8.0% |
| Lux. | 0.3 | 30.6% | 4.1% | 0.3 | 18.8% | 2.8% | 0.3 | 20.9% | 2.7% | 0.3 | 16.0% | 1.9% | 0.3 | 16.7% | 1.8% |
| Neth. | 10.0 | 23.1% | 4.4% | 9.7 | 22.3% | 4.2% | 11.1 | 22.8% | 4.6% | 13.2 | 22.4% | 4.5% | 14.7 | 20.4% | 4.2% |
| Norw. | 4.6 | 36.1% | 8.0% | 4.6 | 37.6% | 8.0% | 5.2 | 37.2% | 8.6% | 5.9 | 38.5% | 8.7% | 6.9 | 38.7% | 8.4% |
| Port. | 1.4 | 31.2% | 6.0% | 1.4 | 30.2% | 5.7% | 1.5 | 30.5% | 5.8% | 1.8 | 29.6% | 5.7% | 2.2 | 30.3% | 6.0% |
| Spain | 5.5 | 17.7% | 5.0% | 5.1 | 16.6% | 4.6% | 5.4 | 16.8% | 4.6% | 6.4 | 16.2% | 4.1% | 7.0 | 14.6% | 3.9% |
| Swed. | 8.9 | 25.1% | 10.2% | 8.6 | 26.0% | 11.1% | 9.4 | 27.0% | 11.4% | 11.7 | 27.5% | 11.5% | 11.9 | 26.2% | 10.7% |
| Switz. | 10.6 | 33.9% | 13.1% | 9.6 | 31.2% | 11.6% | 10.5 | 31.3% | 12.0% | 11.4 | 30.0% | 11.3% | 10.9 | 23.0% | 9.1% |
| UK | 44.8 | 38.6% | 15.8% | 42.8 | 36.8% | 15.9% | 42.9 | 37.0% | 15.5% | 48.2 | 36.0% | 15.7% | 50.8 | 33.4% | 15.0% |
| Europe Total | 229.2 | | | 229.9 | | | 243.1 | | | 268.9 | | | 297.0 | | |

Source: IMF Department of Trade Statistics.

Table 6. Total EU Imports from the US vs. EU Imports from the World

| | 2000 | | | 2001 | | | 2002 | | | 2003 | | | 2004 | | |
|---|---|---|---|---|---|---|---|---|---|---|---|---|---|---|---|
| | Total US ($ Bil.) | Share of Extra-EU Total | Share of World Total | Total US ($ Bil.) | Share of Extra-EU Total | Share of World Total | Total US ($ Bil.) | Share of Extra-EU Total | Share of World Total | Total US ($ Bil.) | Share of Extra-EU Total | Share of World Total | Total US ($ Bil.) | Share of Extra-EU Total | Share of World Total |
| Austr. | 2.9 | 20.0% | 4.1% | 2.9 | 19.0% | 3.8% | 2.7 | 17.3% | 3.5% | 2.2 | 11.6% | 2.2% | 2.3 | 10.6% | 2.0% |
| Belg. | 13.3 | 25.7% | 7.6% | 12.4 | 24.6% | 7.0% | 12.6 | 23.6% | 6.4% | 13.3 | 22.2% | 5.9% | 15.7 | 20.8% | 5.5% |
| Denm. | 1.9 | 15.3% | 4.3% | 2.0 | 17.0% | 4.4% | 1.9 | 16.2% | 3.9% | 1.8 | 12.8% | 3.3% | 2.3 | 13.5% | 3.5% |
| Finl. | 1.6 | 13.5% | 4.8% | 1.4 | 10.3% | 4.2% | 1.2 | 9.1% | 3.7% | 1.6 | 11.6% | 3.7% | 1.7 | 10.0% | 3.3% |
| Fran. | 24.6 | 22.0% | 7.4% | 24.2 | 22.3% | 7.4% | 22.3 | 21.2% | 6.8% | 21.0 | 17.4% | 5.3% | 23.7 | 16.2% | 5.1% |
| Germ. | 42.8 | 21.2% | 8.6% | 40.7 | 21.2% | 8.3% | 37.8 | 19.8% | 7.7% | 43.6 | 18.9% | 7.3% | 46.4 | 16.9% | 6.5% |
| Greece | 0.9 | 8.2% | 3.2% | 1.0 | 8.0% | 3.5% | 1.5 | 10.4% | 4.7% | 2.3 | 11.6% | 5.1% | 2.3 | 10.5% | 4.4% |
| Irel. | 8.2 | 37.7% | 16.2% | 7.6 | 39.0% | 15.0% | 7.9 | 42.9% | 15.3% | 8.4 | 40.1% | 15.7% | 8.2 | 36.9% | 13.6% |
| Italy | 12.5 | 13.0% | 5.3% | 11.5 | 12.3% | 4.9% | 11.8 | 12.3% | 4.9% | 11.6 | 10.1% | 3.9% | 12.1 | 8.7% | 3.5% |
| Lux. | 0.4 | 21.4% | 3.4% | 0.6 | 25.5% | 4.9% | 0.5 | 19.6% | 3.9% | 0.4 | 9.2% | 2.1% | 0.6 | 12.9% | 3.0% |
| Neth. | 21.9 | 21.6% | 10.2% | 20.7 | 20.6% | 9.9% | 19.8 | 19.5% | 9.1% | 21.1 | 17.5% | 8.0% | 24.7 | 16.6% | 7.8% |
| Norw. | 2.2 | 22.3% | 6.9% | 2.2 | 23.0% | 6.9% | 2.1 | 21.9% | 6.1% | 2.1 | 17.7% | 5.1% | 2.4 | 16.7% | 4.9% |
| Port. | 1.2 | 12.5% | 3.1% | 1.4 | 15.5% | 3.7% | 0.8 | 10.2% | 2.2% | 0.9 | 9.0% | 1.9% | 1.2 | 9.9% | 2.2% |
| Spain | 6.6 | 13.4% | 4.6% | 6.0 | 12.4% | 4.2% | 5.7 | 11.0% | 3.7% | 6.3 | 9.7% | 3.0% | 7.4 | 9.0% | 2.9% |
| Swed. | 4.9 | 22.5% | 6.7% | 3.5 | 18.9% | 5.4% | 3.2 | 17.2% | 4.8% | 3.3 | 14.4% | 3.9% | 3.6 | 15.0% | 3.5% |
| Switz. | 6.5 | 32.7% | 7.8% | 5.7 | 30.3% | 6.7% | 5.5 | 32.9% | 6.6% | 5.3 | 29.9% | 5.5% | 10.0 | 33.2% | 7.6% |
| UK | 45.0 | 27.7% | 13.4% | 45.1 | 27.5% | 14.0% | 39.9 | 24.9% | 11.9% | 39.2 | 22.3% | 10.2% | 41.9 | 19.3% | 9.2% |
| Europe Total | 197.4 | | | 188.6 | | | 177.3 | | | 184.3 | | | 206.4 | | |

Source: IMF Department of Trade Statistics.

*Table 7. The Ties that Bind – Top Ten FDI Destinations and Investors*

**US FDI by Country, Top Ten Destinations, 2003**
(% share in historic cost basis)

| Rank | Country | % Share |
|------|---------|---------|
| 1 | United Kingdom | 15.2% |
| 2 | Canada | 10.8% |
| 3 | Netherlands | 10.0% |
| 4 | Belgium/Luxembourg | 5.1% |
| 5 | Switzerland | 4.8% |
| 6 | Germany | 4.5% |
| 7 | Japan | 4.1% |
| 8 | Mexico | 3.4% |
| 9 | Singapore | 3.2% |
| 10 | Ireland | 3.1% |
| | **Total** | **64.2%** |

**FDI Positions in US, Top Ten Investors, 2003**
(% share in historic cost basis)

| Rank | Country | % Share |
|------|---------|---------|
| 1 | United Kingdom | 16.7% |
| 2 | Japan | 11.6% |
| 3 | Germany | 10.8% |
| 4 | Netherlands | 10.6% |
| 5 | France | 10.4% |
| 6 | Belgium/Luxembourg | 8.4% |
| 7 | Switzerland | 8.2% |
| 8 | Canada | 7.6% |
| 9 | Ireland | 1.9% |
| 10 | Australia | 1.8% |
| | **Total** | **88.0%** |

*Source*: Bureau of Economic Analysis, US Department of Commerce.

*Table 8. America's FDI Roots in Europe*

| $ billions | US FDI to Europe | % of US total |
|---|---|---|
| European Total | 963.1 | 53.8% |
| Mining | 20.8 | 21.1% |
| Utilities | 8.5 | 31.6% |
| Manufacturing | 177.9 | 47.1% |
| Food Products | 11.3 | 48.8% |
| Chemicals | 51.9 | 57.5% |
| Primary Metals | 10.5 | 45.7% |
| Machinery | 11.3 | 52.8% |
| Other Manufacturing | 46.6 | 41.4% |
| Wholesale | 89.5 | 63.7% |
| Information | 30.3 | 63.8% |
| Banking | 38.1 | 60.0% |
| Finance (ex. banks) | 116.4 | 38.8% |
| Services | 21.1 | 51.4% |
| Other | 460.5 | 66.4% |

*Note*: Historical-cost basis, 2003.

*Source*: Bureau of Economic Analysis, US Department of Commerce.

*Table 9. Europe's FDI Roots in the U.S.*

| $ billions | European FDI to US | % of US total |
|---|---|---|
| Total from Europe | 1000.5 | 72.6% |
| Manufacturing | 376.6 | 79.2% |
| Food Products | 15.8 | 82.7% |
| Chemicals | 111.0 | 90.2% |
| Primary Metals | 14.3 | 73.7% |
| Machinery | 30.6 | 80.1% |
| Other Manufacturing | 105.5 | 69.4% |
| Wholesale | 106.7 | 58.6% |
| Retail | 18.8 | 74.7% |
| Banking | 61.6 | 69.8% |
| Information | 97.9 | 88.6% |
| Finance & Insurance (ex. banks) | 132.4 | 71.3% |
| Real Estate | 20.8 | 44.2% |
| Services | 24.8 | 87.6% |
| Other | 162.3 | 71.5% |

*Note*: Historical-cost basis, 2003.

*Source*: Bureau of Economic Analysis, US Department of Commerce.

*Figure 8. US and Europe Represent the Majority Stake in the Global Equity Market (regional values expressed as a share of the world total)*

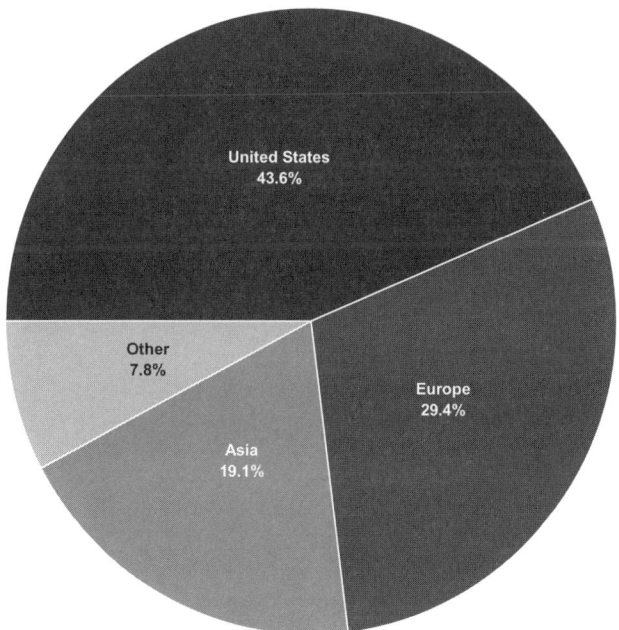

*Note*: Data as of May 31, 2005.

*Source*: FactSet.

# 3. The Transatlantic Economy Today: Remaining Barriers and Benefits from Further Liberalization

## *Daniel S. Hamilton and Joseph P. Quinlan*

Despite the fact that transatlantic markets are among the most open in the world and are deeply integrated through dense flows of investment, affiliate sales and related-party trade, various barriers persist that prevent the emergence of a free transatlantic marketplace. These include traditional tariff barriers, as well non-tariff barriers and regulations that restrict foreign ownership of domestic resources, assign monopoly status to government enterprises, pose significant regulatory hurdles for prospective foreign investors or discriminate between domestic and foreign bidders.[1]

## Transatlantic Tariff Barriers

Transatlantic tariff barriers are generally low, averaging between 3-4% of the €500 billion in annual transatlantic trade. Tariff levels in the European Union, however, are more widely dispersed than those in the US, and tariffs in both the EU and the US are higher on specific products in sensitive sectors, such as textiles, wearing apparel and leather products, or as a result of preferential trade agreements.[2]

The highest barriers to trade between Europe and the US are in agriculture, with particularly high rates of protection for rice, sugar and dairy products. CEPR has estimated the average MFN tariff on agricultural goods to be 17.3% in the EU and 10.6% in the United States. Transatlantic agricultural

---

[1] For an assessment of these barriers for certain industries, see the contributions to the 2004-2005 US-EU Stakeholder Dialogue (available at http://www.ustr.gov/World_Regions/Europe_Mediterranean/Transatlantic_Dialogue/Section_Index.html); see also OECD, *The Benefits of Liberalising Product Markets and Reducing Barriers to International Trade and Investment: The Case of The United States and the European Union,* Economics Department Working Paper 432, Paris, June 2005, pp. 7-10.

[2] Transatlantic Business Dialogue, "Report to the 2005 US-EU Summit: A Framework for Deepening Transatlantic Trade and Investment," April 2005 (http://128.121.145.19/tabd/media/TABD2005SummitReportFINAL051.pdf); and OECD, ibid.

liberalization would result in substantial benefits for developing countries in particular.[3]

*Figure 1. Applied Tariff Levels in the EU, the US and the OECD (2003)*

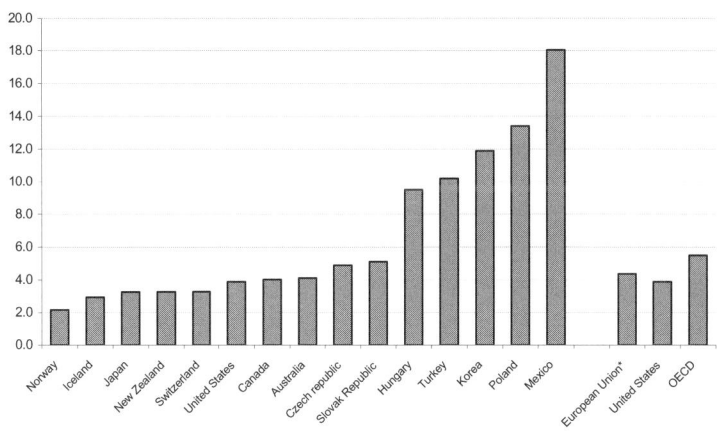

* EU 15
*Source:* OECD

In manufactures, average transatlantic tariffs are low. CEPR estimated the average MFN tariff on manufactures to be 4.2% for the EU and 5% for the US. The high volume of transatlantic trade in manufactures, however, means that further reductions in these barriers would still yield significant benefits.[4]

## Non-Tariff Barriers/Contingent Protection

Because transatlantic tariffs are generally quite low and European and US industries are so deeply intertwined with each other, non-tariff barriers are more important impediments to a free transatlantic marketplace. Remaining non-tariff barriers consist largely of domestic regulations, including safety norms, different health, environmental or engineering standards, rules of origin or labeling requirements. Such measures are due in part to different societal preferences and priorities, but also to a significant degree to a lack of coordination or adequate information exchange between regulators and legislators on each side of the Atlantic, who are subject to different legal mandates or engage in different oversight procedures.

---

[3] OECD, op. cit., p. 19; Hylke Vandenbussche, Ian Wooton and Anthony J. Venables, *Enhancing Cooperation between the EU and the Americas: An Economic Assessment,* CEPR, London, 2002, p. 66.

[4] Vandenbussche et al., ibid.

*Table 1. Ad-valorem Equivalent Measures of Applied Border Protection in the United States and the European Union, 2001*

|  | United States | | European Union | |
|  | On total imports | On imports from EU15 | On total imports | On imports from US |
|---|---|---|---|---|
| Paddy rice | 3.6 | 4.5 | 36.7 | 73.6 |
| Wheat | 0.2 | 2.5 | 0.2 | 1.3 |
| Cereal grains | 0.0 | 0.0 | 4.2 | 7.8 |
| Vegetables, fruit, nuts | 0.6 | 2.7 | 7.0 | 4.4 |
| Oil seeds | 2.9 | 6.5 | 0.0 | 0.0 |
| Sugar cane, sugar beet | 0.2 | 0.2 | 5.6 | 0.0 |
| Other primary agriculture | 1.7 | 1.9 | 1.1 | 8.9 |
| Bovine cattle, sheep, goats, horses | 0.0 | 0.0 | 3.5 | 0.7 |
| Natural resources | 0.0 | 0.0 | 0.0 | 0.0 |
| Bovine cattle, sheep and goat meat products | 2.8 | 1.4 | 13.5 | 19.8 |
| Meat products | 0.6 | 1.1 | 3.1 | 24.4 |
| Vegetable oils and fats | 1.0 | 1.2 | 4.0 | 5.2 |
| Diary products | 18.2 | 20.0 | 3.0 | 32.0 |
| Processed rice | 4.4 | 6.5 | 51.5 | 93.8 |
| Sugar | 25.4 | 23.4 | 62.9 | 23.2 |
| Other food products | 2.5 | 5.3 | 3.0 | 15.3 |
| Beverages and tobacco products | 1.4 | 1.5 | 1.4 | 8.3 |
| Textiles | 7.9 | 8.5 | 1.8 | 6.4 |
| Wearing apparel | 9.9 | 10.1 | 3.2 | 10.1 |
| Leather products | 12.2 | 7.4 | 2.8 | 4.5 |
| Other manufacturing | 1.0 | 1.6 | 0.5 | 1.7 |
| Agriculture average[*] | 1.1 | 2.8 | 2.8 | 13.1 |
| Manufacturing average[*] | 1.9 | 1.9 | 0.7 | 2.1 |

[*] Denotes trade-weighted average.

*Source*: OECD, GTAP (version 6.05).

Other forms of contingent protection include antidumping measures, countervailing duties and safeguard clauses. In 2002, CEPR estimated that contingent protection accounted for about 30% of the total cost of protection. While the OECD has cautioned that accurate quantification of both border and behind the border non-tariff measures is still not completely reliable today, CEPR estimated the welfare cost to the US alone of the active antidumping cases in one year to be $4 billion.[5]

A particularly challenging yet potentially significant area for liberalization is government procurement, which represents nearly 15% of the world's GDP. Many governments on both shores of the Atlantic maintain restrictions in this area; more transparent and competitive procurement practices could open up potentially enormous market opportunities and deliver a broader choice of better quality goods and services to governments and citizens.

## Sectoral Barriers

These barriers to transatlantic integration tend to be concentrated in certain sectors of the economy. In general, barriers in manufacturing tend to be low, while barriers in services and agriculture tend to be relatively high. Since agriculture comprises a relatively small and services a relatively high percentage of overall transatlantic economic output and employment, gains from liberalization in services relative to agriculture would be quite high. Two OECD charts paint a clearer picture of these barriers. Figure 2 outlines anti-competitive regulation in selected service sectors, while Figure 3 presents more narrowly focused FDI controls across manufacturing and a range of service sectors.

*Figure 2. Product Market Regulations in Service Sectors in the EU, the US and OECD (OECD Indicator, 2003)*

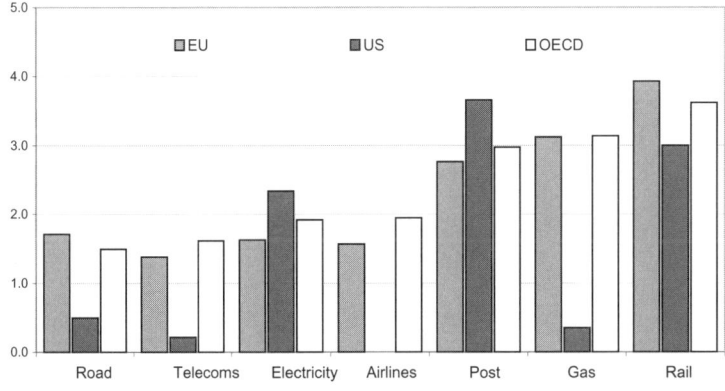

---

[5] OECD, op. cit.; Vandenbussche et al., op. cit.

*Figure 3. Sectoral Barriers to FDI in the EU, the US and OECD (2001)*

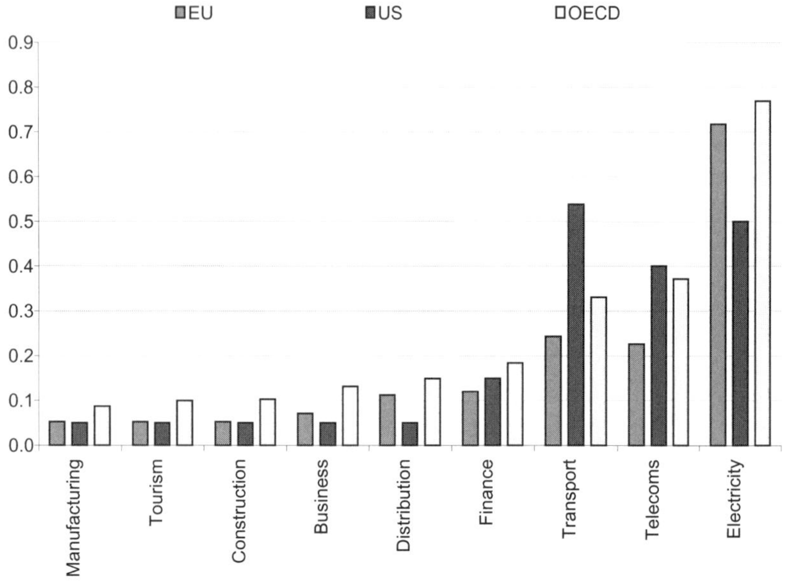

*Note*: The indicator ranges from 0 (least restrictive) to 1 (most restrictive).

*Source*: Stephen S. Golub, *Measures of Restrictiveness on Inward FDI in OECD Countries*, OECD Economic Studies No. 36, OECD, Paris, 2003.

These charts underscore that competition-restraining regulations tend to be more extensive in the EU than in the US for six of the seven sectors, the exception being postal services.[6] FDI controls on manufacturing are low in both the US and the EU. In Europe, the OECD reports that sectoral barriers to FDI appear highest in transport services, telecommunications and particularly electricity. In the US FDI restrictions on transport services and telecommunications are higher than in the average EU country. While electricity restrictions are also high, they are lower than the levels of most European countries.[7] In chapter 4, we examine the extent of the transatlantic services market – the 'sleeping giant' of the transatlantic economy – and

---

[6] Vandenbussche, et al., op. cit., p. 43. Another study by Patrick A. Messerlin compared the regulatory environment in the EU and North America in seven different sectors. He concluded that on a scale of 0 to 6, from least to most restrictive, the US rated 1.7, Mexico 2.7, Canada 2.8 and the EU 3.3. See P.A. Messerlin, *Measuring the Costs of Protection in Europe: European Commercial Policy in the 2000s,* September 2001, Institute for International Economics, Washington, DC.

[7] OECD, op. cit., p. 19.

estimate the benefits that could result from further services liberalization within the EU Single Market as well as across the Atlantic.

## Potential Benefits of Further Transatlantic Liberalization

In June 2005, an OECD report estimated that a package of structural reforms in the EU and the US that included reduction of competition-restraining regulations, tariff barriers and FDI restrictions could lead to permanent gains in GDP per capita on both sides of the Atlantic of up to 3 to 3 1/2%, and cause additional benefits to other OECD countries of up to 1 1/2% of GDP per capita. Over the course of an average 40-year working life of an individual, the OECD estimates that the cumulated addition to earnings would equal between one-half and more than a full year's worth of earnings. Moreover, the implied reforms are relatively narrow and exclude labor market, financial market, agricultural or tax reforms, any of which could also strengthen transatlantic economic integration and performance. Thus the OECD study is conservative in its conclusions; gains from transatlantic liberalization could be significantly higher.[8]

The OECD study suggested that such output gains would require ambitious reforms in key sectors. Competition-restraining regulations in most EU15 countries would have to be reduced considerably in domestic air, rail and road transportation, electricity and gas, and telecommunications. The United States would have to focus reforms on electricity and rail transportation. The greatest reduction of restrictions on foreign direct investment in the United States would need to come in transportation services, while in the European Union it would need to be most extensive in electricity generation. Reductions in tariff levels in the European Union would have to be concentrated on agricultural products; in the United States, tariff reductions would imply relatively more adjustment to rates of protection on textiles, apparel and other manufactured goods.[9]

A separate study by CEPR in 2002 came to similar conclusions, underscoring that the mutual benefits of further transatlantic economic cooperation could be very large. CEPR estimated that dismantling remaining tariff and non-tariff barriers between the US and the EU could result in welfare gains for the EU ranging from 0.7%-2% of GDP. These gains reflect the annual income gain to the EU from transatlantic liberalization, accruing in perpetuity. In value terms, the lower range estimates correspond to an increase of between €39-€51 billion, with prices to EU consumers going down by 2.5% and an increase of 1 million EU jobs. The upper range

---

[8] OECD, op. cit., pp. 5-7.

[9] OECD, op. cit.

corresponded to the gains of the Single Market estimated by the Cecchini report. For the US, the lower range estimate of static welfare gains – reflecting only the dismantling of tariffs on goods trade – was 0.2% of US GDP (1990), the equivalent of some $15 billion, corresponding to an increase of 300,000 new US jobs. The upper range totaled 1% of US GDP.[10]

*Table 2. Impact of Reforms on EU and US Export Levels, OECD Panel Data Studies*

*% changes*

| Country | Reduction in bilateral tariffs | Easing FDI restrictions | Reduction in domestic regulation | Total impact of reforms |
|---|---|---|---|---|
| Austria | 0.6 | 1.5 | 29.0 | 31.0 |
| Belgium | 1.0 | 2.2 | 24.9 | 28.1 |
| Denmark | 0.8 | 3.1 | 21.3 | 25.3 |
| Finland | 1.4 | 2.1 | 24.7 | 28.2 |
| France | 1.2 | 2.3 | 28.5 | 32.0 |
| Germany | 1.6 | 2.4 | 25.4 | 29.3 |
| Greece | 0.6 | 6.5 | 35.0 | 42.1 |
| Ireland | 2.7 | 2.1 | 21.0 | 25.7 |
| Italy | 1.8 | 2.6 | 26.3 | 30.6 |
| The Netherlands | 0.7 | 2.1 | 27.0 | 29.7 |
| Portugal | 0.8 | 2.7 | 25.9 | 29.4 |
| Spain | 0.8 | 2.7 | 26.4 | 29.8 |
| Sweden | 1.5 | 2.1 | 21.0 | 24.7 |
| United Kingdom | 2.1 | 2.8 | 23.7 | 28.6 |
| **United States** | **3.5** | **1.0** | **17.5** | **22.0** |
| **EU15 (excluding intra-EU trade)** | **4.7** | **2.9** | **23.0** | **30.7** |
| **EU15** | **1.4** | **2.4** | **25.6** | **29.4** |

*Source: OECD.*

In short, given the size and the deep inter-linkages between the US and European economies, the removal of remaining tariff and non-tariff barriers, coupled with enhanced economic and regulatory cooperation between the US and the EU, could be the catalyst for a significant boost in economic growth, employment, investment and innovation across the transatlantic marketplace, and could further enhance the attractiveness of the transatlantic economy in a globalizing world. Lower barriers within the transatlantic economy, new economic dynamism, closer regulatory cooperation and greater transparency would also enhance market access and simplify the complex maze of regulations faced by third parties. Such efforts would also enable the US and

---

[10] Vandenbussche et al., op. cit.

the EU to act as pathfinders for regulatory policy cooperation and market opening beyond the transatlantic economy, acting as a motor for multilateral market-opening measures.

*Table 3. Impact of Reforms on GDP per Capita Levels, OECD Panel Data Studies (% increase in GDP per capita levels)*

| Country | Reduction in bilateral tariffs | Easing FDI restrictions | Reduction in domestic regulation | Total impact of reforms |
|---|---|---|---|---|
| Austria | 0.1 | 0.3 | 3.0 | 3.4 |
| Belgium | 0.1 | 0.1 | 0.8 | 1.0 |
| Denmark | 0.2 | 0.3 | 2.2 | 2.8 |
| Finland | 0.2 | 0.3 | 2.7 | 2.9 |
| France | 0.2 | 0.4 | 3.4 | 4.0 |
| Germany | 0.3 | 0.3 | 3.0 | 3.6 |
| Greece | 0.2 | 0.5 | 2.7 | 3.3 |
| Ireland | 0.1 | 0.0 | 0.6 | 0.7 |
| Italy | 0.2 | 0.3 | 2.8 | 3.3 |
| The Netherlands | 0.1 | 0.2 | 1.7 | 2.0 |
| Portugal | 0.1 | 0.4 | 2.7 | 3.3 |
| Spain | 0.1 | 0.4 | 2.7 | 3.2 |
| Sweden | 0.2 | 0.3 | 2.1 | 2.5 |
| United Kingdom | 0.4 | 0.2 | 2.4 | 3.0 |
| **United States** | **0.9** | **0.4** | **1.7** | **3.1** |
| **EU15** | **0.3** | **0.3** | **2.8** | **3.5** |

*Source:* OECD.

It is worth noting that efforts to forge a truly free transatlantic market must be accompanied by parallel efforts to complete the EU's Single Market, since internal EU commercial barriers are also barriers to truly open transatlantic commerce. Other parallel efforts include the Doha round of multilateral trade negotiations and global efforts to liberalize services.

The following chapters investigate more closely the dynamics of transatlantic market integration. Our authors describe the barriers to and drivers of integration in the key markets of services, finance, commercial aerospace, civil aviation, biopharmaceuticals, telecommunications and automotive manufacturing. We then examine how domestic political decisions and regulatory mechanisms on each side of the Atlantic interact with deep transatlantic market integration in four illustrative cases: the potential transatlantic impact of the EU's REACH Directive on chemicals; US-EU differences over climate change and the potential for transatlantic emissions trading markets; issues of corporate governance, particularly the transatlantic impact of the US Sarbanes-Oxley Act; and the transatlantic dimensions of the EU's Lisbon Agenda regarding innovation and competitiveness.

These cases are not intended to be exhaustive. There are other important sectors of the transatlantic economy. Other policy areas also deserve attention. A number of new US regulations governing trade and security following the attacks of September 11, 2001, for example, were advanced with little or no consultation with EU governments or companies, with significant consequences for transatlantic commerce. Similarly, various competition policy decisions by the European Commission have taken US officials and companies by surprise. A comprehensive examination of the full range of US-EU interaction is beyond the scope of this volume. These case studies are intended to underscore the quasi-domestic nature of some aspects of transatlantic relations today, and to illustrate the types of issues that arise when domestic decision-making interacts with deep transatlantic integration. We end with some conclusions for policy.

# DEEP INTEGRATION AND THE TRANSATLANTIC ECONOMY: SECTORAL ANALYSES

# 4. The Sleeping Giant: Services in the Transatlantic Economy

## Daniel S. Hamilton and Joseph P. Quinlan

Service activities are the sleeping giant of the transatlantic economy – an economic force that, if awakened and unbound, would further deepen the commercial stakes between the United States and Europe and enhance the global competitiveness of both parties. At present, however, the full potential of the transatlantic service economy remains hampered by internal barriers, regulations and obstacles in the United States and, in particular, in Europe.

As a recent report from the OECD[1] has noted, restrictions at the sectoral level are largely centered in service activities, with sectoral barriers in the European Union and the United States highest in such sectors as transport services, telecommunications, and electricity. Restrictive regulations in these and other sectors have hampered economic growth and reduced the economic efficiencies of the transatlantic economy over the past few decades. Regulatory reform, on the other hand, would help promote growth, create employment and increase the value of cross-border trade and investment.

### The Globalization of Services

Service activities are rapidly being reshaped on a global basis. Functions that were once considered non-tradable (e.g. data processing, education and medical services) are now being traded regularly. Activities long classified as domestic endeavors (advertising, legal services and consulting) today easily take place across borders. Industries that were once the domain of the overregulated public sector (telecommunications, insurance and electric utilities) have been privatized and, in many cases, opened to foreign competition. Consequently, service activities have spread globally, notably across the Atlantic.

The global role of services has been recast in large measure because of the accelerating pace of technological change. In Europe and many other parts of the world, technological advances have appreciably lowered the cost of communications, making it more feasible and efficient to retrieve, process and disseminate multiple forms of information. Just as container ships made the physical export of goods possible in the past, fiber-optic cables have made it possible to export more data, information and other knowledge-based

---

[1] OECD, *The Benefits of Liberalising Product Markets and Reducing Barriers to International Trade and Investment: The Case of the United States and the European Union,* Economics Department Working Paper 432, Paris, June 2005.

services that used to be considered non-tradable. In short, communications technology increasingly allows firms to split and disperse parts of service functions to foreign affiliates or to non-equity joint partners.

As communications costs have fallen, the information infrastructure has expanded and the Internet has proliferated, knowledge-based services of both the United States and Europe have become more linked, promoting more trade and foreign investment in services. Industry deregulation, a more liberal investment environment and falling communications costs all converged in the 1990s to drive a transatlantic investment boom in services. Other variables supporting transatlantic service investment include the rising share of services in economic activity on both sides of the Atlantic; the growing service intensity of the production of goods; and greater competitive pressures in service markets that have pushed firms to seek markets abroad and strengthen their competitiveness.

Against this backdrop, more than three-quarters of global mergers and acquisitions (M&As) in the services sector took place among developed nations during 1987-2003, with the bulk of the transactions occurring either within Europe or across the Atlantic. According to UN figures, services accounted for 36 of the top 100 cross-border M&A deals in 1987-1995 and for 64 of the top cross-border M&A deals in 1996-2003.

Today, the service economies of the United States and Europe have never been as intertwined as they are today, notably in such activities as financial services, telecommunications, utilities, insurance, advertising, computer services and other related functions.

## Enhanced Economic Integration through Services

Following in the footsteps of manufacturers, US and European service companies now deliver their services more through foreign affiliate sales than through trade. In the 1970s and 1980s, firms delivered services primarily via trade. In the 1990s foreign affiliate sales became the chief mode of delivery.

Sales of services by US foreign affiliates in Europe soared from $85 billion in 1994 to roughly $212 billion in 2002, the last year of available data. That marks a 150% increase, well ahead of the roughly 65% rise in US service exports to Europe over the same period. After being roughly equal to US service exports to Europe in 1992, foreign affiliate sales of services in Europe were nearly double the value of US service exports in 2002, with US service exports to Europe totaling $117.5 billion.

Europe is the most important market in the world for US foreign affiliate sales of services, just as it is the most important market for US foreign affiliate sales of goods. Indeed, of total affiliate service sales of $401 billion in 2002, Europe accounted for 53% of the total, with Asia (with 23% share) and Latin America (13%), a distant second and third, respectively.

*Figure 1.US-Europe service linkages*

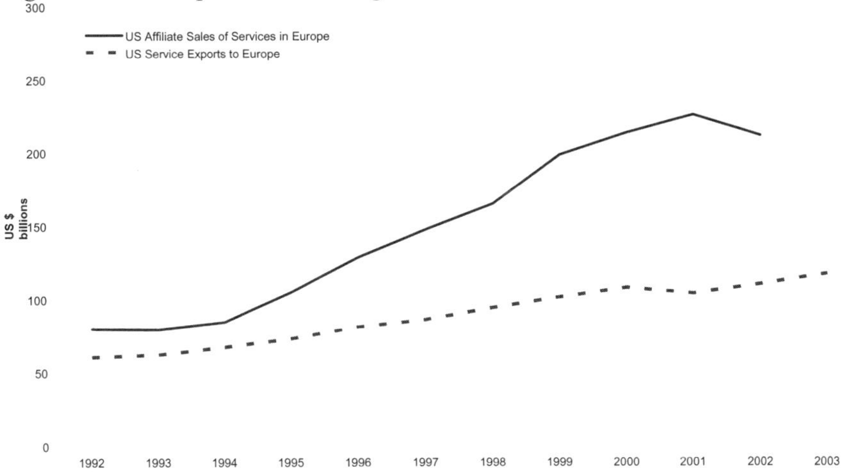

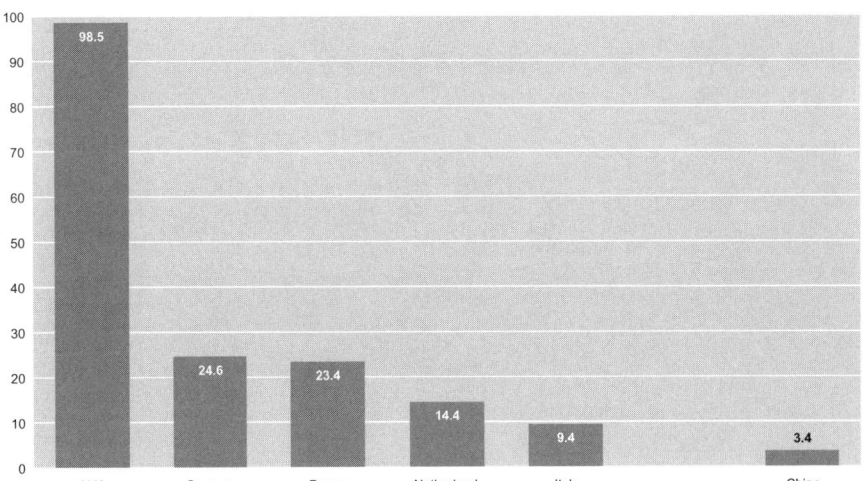

*Source*: Bureau of Economic Analysis, US Department of Commerce.

*Figure 2. Service Sales of US Foreign Affiliates Abroad – Europe vs. China*

*Source*: Bureau of Economic Analysis, US Department of Commerce.

By country, the UK, whose various service sectors are most aligned with those of the US, accounted for the largest share of US affiliate sales not only in Europe but also the world. In fact, foreign affiliate service sales of $98.5 billion in the UK in 2002 were greater than foreign affiliate service sales in all of Asia ($97 billion) and Latin America ($52 billion). In Europe, Germany ($24.6 billion), France ($23.5 billion) and the Netherlands ($14.4 billion) trailed the UK.

*Figure 3. Sales of Services to Europe by US Affiliates, by Country, 2002*

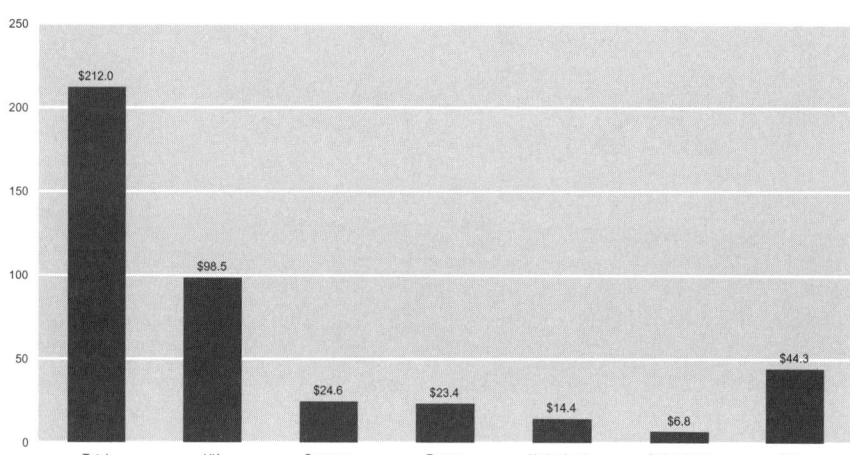

*Source*: Bureau of Economic Analysis, US Department of Commerce.

By industry, sales of services to Europe by US affiliates are quite diverse, with information ($41.9 billion) and financial and insurance ($41 billion) leading the way.

*Figure 4. Sales of Services to Europe by US Affiliates, by Industry, 2002*

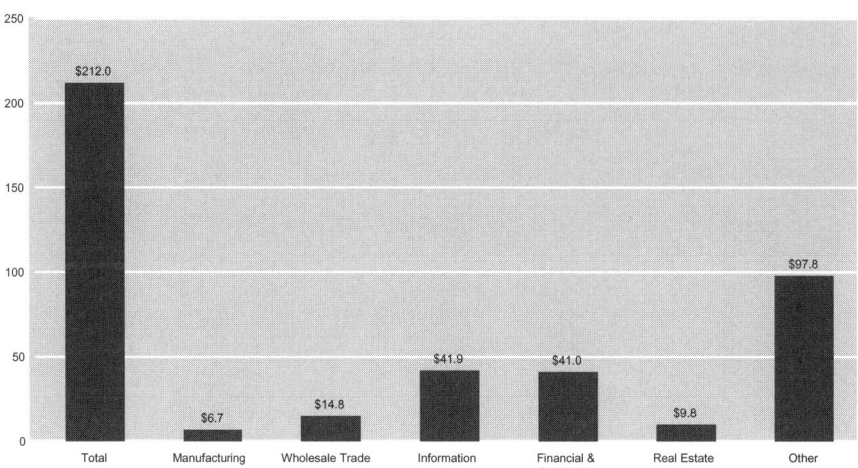

*Source*: Bureau of Economic Analysis, US Department of Commerce.

Sales of services by US affiliates of European firms have also soared over the past decade. As Europe's investment position in services has expanded in the US, so have foreign affiliate sales of services in the US. The latter totaled $269 billion in 2002 versus $86 billion in 1994, a jump of 213%. US service imports from Europe expanded over the same period, by roughly 85%, well below the rate of growth of affiliate sales of services.

*Figure 5. Europe – US Service Linkages*

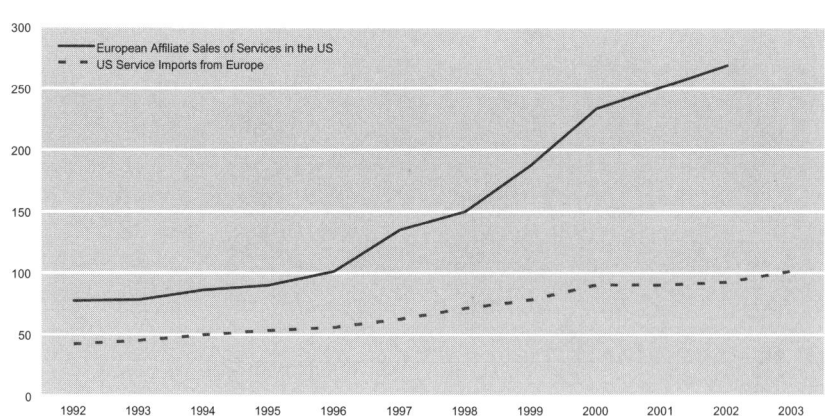

*Source*: Bureau of Economic Analysis, US Department of Commerce.

Leading the way were British service firms, whose US affiliate sales in services totaled $67 billion in 2003, or 25% of total European affiliate sales. German, French and Dutch affiliates in the US posted substantial sales of services as well, totaling $44 billion, $42 billion and $33 billion, respectively, in 2002.

*Figure 6. Sales of Services to US by European Affiliates, by Country*

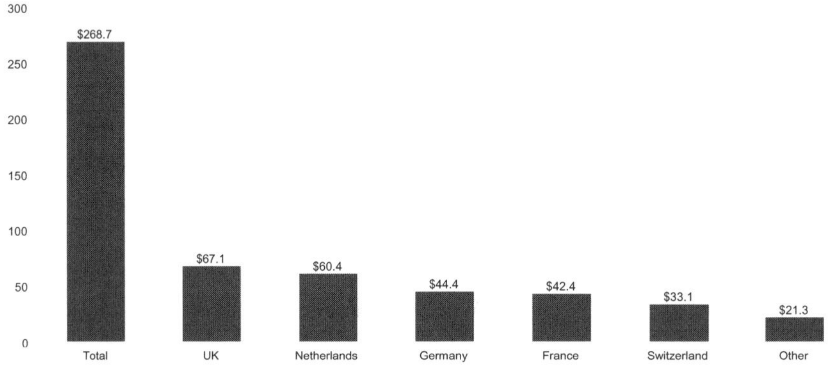

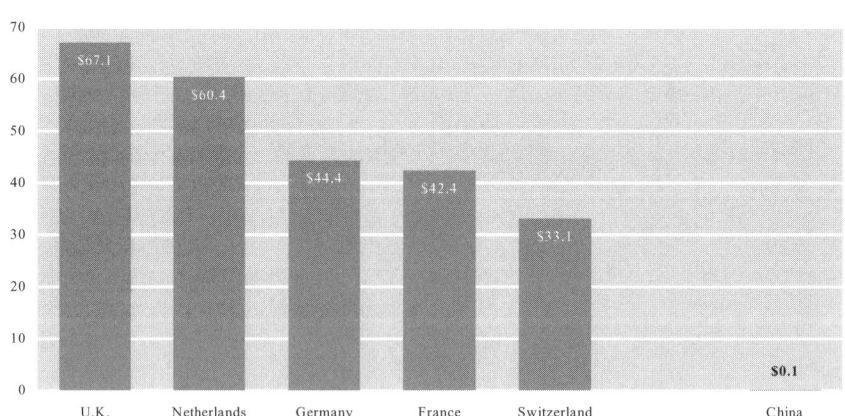

*Source:* Bureau of Economic Analysis, US Department of Commerce.

*Figure 7. Sales of Services to US by Foreign Affiliates, Europe vs. China, 2002*

*Source:* Bureau of Economic Analysis, US Department of Commerce.

Financial and insurances services accounted for one-third ($89.6 billion) of total services sales in the US by European affiliates, followed by manufacturing services ($34.4 billion), information services ($31 billion), professional and technical services ($25.6 billion) and a variety of other service sectors.

*Figure 8. Sales of Services to US by European Affiliates, by Industry 2002*

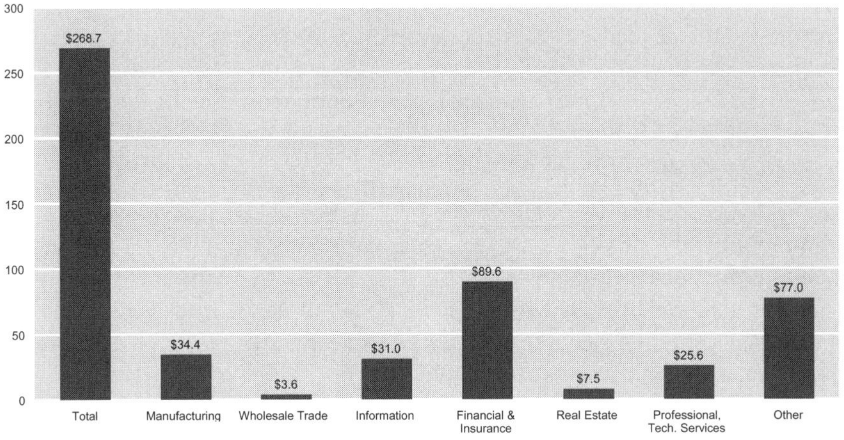

*Source*: Bureau of Economic Analysis, US Department of Commerce.

In short, foreign affiliate sales of services on both sides of the Atlantic have exploded over the past decade. In fact, affiliate sales of services have not only become a viable second channel of delivery for US and European multinationals, they have become the overwhelming mode of delivery in a rather short period of time. Moreover, countries where services accounted for close to 60% of overall employment – such as the US, UK, the Netherlands and Norway – had the best record of job creation within the OECD.[2]

## The Services Directive: Impact on the Transatlantic Economy

Despite the major significance of the transatlantic services economy, barriers remain on both sides of the Atlantic. US barriers are most prominent in maritime, legal, engineering, architectural and accounting services. In the EU15 as a whole, barriers appear highest for domestic and foreign firms in accounting, maritime and legal services, and higher for foreign firms relative

---

[2] Tobias Buck, "OECD stresses services market reform benefits", *Financial Times*, April 27, 2005.

to domestic firms in distribution, maritime and architectural services.[3] The key issue, however, remains the continued existence of service barriers within the EU itself. Liberalization of inner-EU services would be the single most important stimulus to the transatlantic services economy.

The EU has been committed to a common market for services and goods since its inception in 1957. The EU Single Market was supposed to materialize on January 1, 1993, providing freedom of movement in goods, capital, people and services. Seven years later, EU leaders agreed to announce by the end of 2000 "a strategy for the removal of barriers to services." Five years later, however, goods continue to move across the Union largely without difficulty, while services remained hampered by 25 different sets of national rules and regulations – even though services account for almost 70% of GDP and jobs in the EU.[4]

Through an initiative called the Services Directive, the European Commission seeks to break down service barriers all at once, rather than by tackling liberalization sector by sector. The Services Directive covers a wide range of services provided to businesses and consumers in all 25 member states. The Directive seeks to provide "a legal framework that will eliminate the obstacles to the freedom of establishment for service providers and the free movement of services between the Member States."[5]

---

[3] See C. Findley and T. Warren (eds), *Impediments to Trade in Services: Measurement and Policy Implications,* London: Routledge, 2000; K. Kalirajan, "Restrictions on Trade in Distributive Services", Productivity Commission Staff Research Paper, Canberra: AusInfo, August 2000; D. Nguyen-Hongh, "Restrictions on Trade in Professional Services", Productivity Commission Staff Research Paper, Canberra: AusInfo, August 2000; Copenhagen Economics, *Economic Assessment of the Barriers to the Internal Market for Services. Final Report,* Copenhagen, January 2005.

[4] See Tobias Buck, "A recipe for jobs or a race to the bottom? The EU debates a single market in services", *Financial Times*, March 15, 2005; AmCham EU submission to the US-EU Stakeholder's Dialogue, December 6, 2004; Daniel Gros, "Europe needs the single market in services", *Financial Times*, April 7, 2005; and Copenhagen Economics, ibid.

[5] European Commission, "Directive of the European Parliament and of the Council on Services in the Internal Market", Proposal, COM(2004) 2 final/3, March 5, 2004.

While some controversial elements[6] of the current Services Directive have caused some member states to question its implementation, analysts estimate that it could be the single most important initiative to improve the continent's competitiveness and employment. Copenhagen Economics, a think tank consultancy in Denmark, estimates that the Services Directive would yield significant economic gains. European consumers, businesses, governments and foreign investors would benefit from enhanced productivity, higher employment, increased wages and lower prices. A comprehensive study by Copenhagen Economics concluded that implementing the Services Directive could result in a total welfare gain of 0.6% of EU GDP, or €37 billion, create up to 600,000 jobs and boost foreign investment by up to 34%.[7] A second study by Dutch economists, published in 2004, came to similar conclusions. Given the dense interconnections in the transatlantic service economy, implementation of the Services Directive would be very likely to boost US direct investment in the EU considerably.

Implementing the Services Directive would be akin to waking the sleeping giant of the transatlantic economy – services. Ultimately, it could produce a number of benefits and gains for the both the United States and Europe, including the following:

- *Boost transatlantic foreign direct investment flows.* Like the Single Market program, which sparked a rise in more service-related foreign investment, notably in transportation and telecommunications, the elimination or reduction of barriers to service activities in Europe would attract more foreign direct investment from leading service firms in the United States. Under such a scenario, Europe would most likely remain the top destination of US foreign direct investment, continuing the trend of the past half-century. Service deregulation would also promote more intra-European foreign investment, leading to consolidation and greater efficiencies in various service activities.

- *Lower prices while raising productivity and growth.* Service reform and deregulation would trigger greater cross-border competition in services, which would ultimately lead to lower prices, benefiting both consumers and businesses. Productivity levels would rise as costs declined and as firms leveraged more competitively priced services. Since services are a critical component of many manufacturing industries, greater service deregulation in Europe would yield a competitive boost to Europe's

---

[6] This includes the so-called 'country of origin' principle, which would grant companies the right to provide services in all member states as long as they follow the laws of their home state, which has caused some critics to warn of 'social dumping'.

[7] Copenhagen Economics, op. cit.

manufacturing sector. Finally, falling prices, combined with rising productivity, would help boost real economic growth in the EU and a rise in European corporate earnings. In monetary terms, Copenhagen Economics estimates that total value added in the services sector would increase by approximately €33 billion.[8] Without competitive business services, meeting the EU's Lisbon Agenda objective of forging a world-class knowledge economy in the next few years will be quite difficult.

- *Improve wages and create jobs.* The service sector of the EU already accounts for nearly 70% of total employment; a new regulatory framework that removes tariffs and non-tariffs to services would drive the percentage even higher. Copenhagen Economics estimates that implementation of the Services Directive would boost real wages in the EU by 0.4% and create 600,000 jobs.[9] Net employment gains would be most noticeable in the new enlargement economies, where service employment (as a percentage of total employment) lags the EU average. In 2003, for instance, only 55.8% of the Czech Republic's work force was employed in services, well below the OECD average of 68.6% in 2003. In Slovakia, the service sector employed only 55.9% of the total work force, while service employment in Poland and Portugal, as a percentage of the total, was 53% and 54.7%, respectively. In terms of service employment catching up to the EU average under a more liberal service framework, Germany and Greece would also benefit, considering that service employment accounts for just 65.6% of total employment in the former and just 61.1% in the latter economy.

- *Stimulate greater cross-border trade in services.* A more deregulatory environment for services would promote greater cross-border transactions in services, helping to boost not only intra-EU trade in services but also cross-border transatlantic trade in services. Cross-border transatlantic trade in services is already quite robust, with total transatlantic trade in services (US service exports to Europe + US service imports from Europe) amounting to $219 billion in 2003. That is more than double the level of a decade ago.

US service exports to Europe totaled $117.4 billion in 2003, with Europe accounting for 40% of the global total. Of the top ten markets in the world for US service exports, five are transatlantic partners, with United Kingdom ranked first in the world. Germany ranked fourth, followed by France (6th), Switzerland (8th), and the Netherlands (9th). Of US service imports, roughly 45% were accounted for by Europe in 2003. Service imports from Europe topped $100 billion for the first time in 2003, with

---

[8] Ibid.

[9] Ibid., pp. 31-32.

service imports from the United Kinggom the largest in the world ($30 billion).

## The Way Forward

Removing barriers to trade and investment in services is one of the key challenges before transatlantic policy-makers. While services presently account for the largest share of gross domestic product in virtually all of the nations that comprise the transatlantic economy, the role of services could be even larger and growth-enhancing if the political will was present to push ahead with more service deregulation and reform.

The lack of service reform represents a significant opportunity cost to the United States, the European Union and the transatlantic economy. The lack of reform could very well undermine the growth, attraction and efficiency of the transatlantic economy – the rest of the world is not standing still.

# 5. Beyond Open Skies: The Economic Impact of a US-EU Open Aviation Area

*Dorothy Robyn, James Reitzes and Boaz Moselle*

Although aviation is an enabler of globalization, paradoxically, the airline industry itself remains subject to highly restrictive national controls on cross-border competition and investment. Government-to-government bilateral agreements often limit the routes that international air carriers can fly, the number of flights they can schedule and the fares they can charge. All but a few countries prohibit foreign competition in their internal markets, by banning both the operation of foreign air carriers between domestic points ('cabotage') and cross-border ownership of national airlines. Government signatories to bilateral agreements even restrict cross-border investment in *foreign* carriers through a so-called 'nationality clause' that requires carriers to be 'substantially owned and effectively controlled' by citizens of the country where they are based.

The European Union and the United States have the largest and among the most deregulated domestic aviation markets in the world. However, despite the success of airline deregulation in their domestic markets, Europe and the United States still limit transatlantic competition and investment. To be sure, bilateral 'Open Skies' agreements between the United States and individual EU member states have eliminated most controls on the quality, quantity and price of aviation services, but such agreements still stop short of full liberalization, and major markets are not covered.

As a result of this system, the aviation industry lags in adapting to globalization even as it drives other sectors to globalize. As an editorial in the Financial Times put it, "In an era of supposedly borderless markets and global competition, the world airline industry remains stuck in a time warp."[1] This regulatory time warp imposes significant costs on consumers and air carriers alike. And while archaic regulation is not the principal cause of the financial crisis currently confronting major carriers in the United States, Europe and elsewhere, it impedes their long-term recovery.

The European Commission has endorsed the elimination of *all* commercial restrictions on EU-US aviation competition and investment. The Commission's goal is to create a single open market encompassing the provision of air transport services not only between, but also within Europe

---

[1] "Lowering the Flag", *Financial Times,* June 8, 2000.

and the United States. We refer to this as an 'Open Aviation Area' because it would amount to a free trade area in air transport.

To inform the debate, the Commission asked The Brattle Group in 2002 to analyze the economic effects of complete EU-US aviation liberalization.[2] This chapter discusses the analysis and findings of that study. First, to set the stage, we review the history of transatlantic aviation liberalization and describe the remaining restrictions and their effects. Second, we describe our analysis of the impact that elimination of these restrictions could be expected to have on competition, economic efficiency and consumer welfare. In particular, we estimated the benefits from three sources: i) airline cost savings from increased competition and consolidation, ii) reductions in air fares as a result of improved pricing coordination on transatlantic interline routes and iii) output expansion from replacement of restrictive bilateral agreements. Third, we analyze the merits of concerns raised about the potential impact of US-EU liberalization in three key areas – national security, airline labor and aviation safety. Finally, we summarize recent developments, including last year's failed US-EU negotiations.

Two caveats are in order. First, our quantitative analysis was limited to the 15 countries that were EU members in 2002, and thus did not include the 10 new EU members that acceded in 2004. The expansion of our analysis to include these 10 countries would increase the economic benefits of a US-EU Open Aviation Area; thus, the numbers reported here are conservative. Second, the numbers reported here were calculated at a time when the currency conversion between the dollar and the euro was almost exactly one to one. Since that time, the dollar has depreciated, and thus the sums reported in euros may be overstated.

To summarize, our quantitative analysis suggests that, over the long term, a US-EU Open Aviation Area would:

- increase transatlantic travel by up to 11 million passengers a year – a 24% increase;

- boost intra-EU travel by up to an additional 35.7 million passengers a year – a 14% increase;

- increase economic output in directly related industries by up to $8.1 billion a year; and

---

[2] See Boaz Moselle et al., "The Economic Impact of an EU-US Open Aviation Area", The Brattle Group, December 2002.

- create about $5.2 billion a year in consumer benefits through lower fares and increased travel, with more than half of those benefits going to transatlantic passengers.

To be conservative, we did not try to quantify benefits in the US domestic market. Although we think US domestic passengers will benefit from an Open Aviation Area, the US market is already highly competitive because entry is fully open to domestic carriers, if not to foreign carriers.

Our qualitative analysis finds that claims regarding the potential for international liberalization to harm national security, labor and airline safety do not stand up to scrutiny. Among our conclusions:

- A US-EU Open Aviation Area would not harm national security. If a European entity bought or established a US carrier for business and other reasons, it would operate it as a US subsidiary, and that legal arrangement would preserve Department of Defense leverage. As evidence, foreign-owned, US-incorporated ocean shipping companies have top secret clearance and transport a great deal of US military cargo.

- Nor would US airline labor suffer significant harm. Direct labor substitution would be very limited because of legal and institutional factors that give US pilots considerable bargaining leverage. Although there is greater potential for indirect labor substitution, even that would likely be limited because the US-EU wage gap is so small.

- Creation of an Open Aviation Area poses challenges for US and European regulators, but these challenges are manageable and do not threaten airline safety.

## The US-EU Market: Economic Restrictions and Their Effects

### *Transatlantic Liberalization*

Although major impediments to competition remain, air transport between Europe and the United States has been significantly liberalized in the last 25 years. Inspired in part by the success of US domestic airline deregulation, the United States negotiated liberal 'open market' agreements in the late 1970s and 1980s with various European governments, beginning with the Netherlands. Belgium, Germany and Luxembourg followed.[3] In exchange for

---

[3] See Rigas Doganis, *The Airline Business in the 21st Century,* London: Routledge, 2001, pp. 23-30. 'Open market' is Doganis' term for these agreements.

access to more (but not all) US cities, European governments agreed to let US carriers fly from any point in the United States to specified points in their country. In addition, the agreements eliminated all restrictions on the frequency of flights and the seat capacity on those flights, provided greater opportunities for innovative and competitive pricing, removed restrictions on charter operations and allowed for the designation of multiple airlines. The latter provision was of interest largely to the United States because most other countries had only one international carrier (their so-called 'flag carriers').

Predictably, international traffic increased and fares dropped following liberalization. Between 1987 and 1993, the number of passengers traveling on US airlines between the United States and foreign destinations increased by 47%, while domestic traffic increased by only 6%.[4] (Liberalization had a similar impact within the European Union, where member states had negotiated open-market-style agreements on a bilateral basis.[5])

By the early 1990s, as a result of structural changes in the airline industry, the limits of open market agreements were becoming more apparent. US airline deregulation and the industry consolidation that followed had produced several carriers with large national networks and a strong commercial orientation. These carriers saw greater opportunities for expansion in international markets than within the more mature US domestic market. And in Europe, where international traffic already constituted a substantial part of flag carriers' revenue, the trend toward privatization and away from state aid was putting increased pressure on carriers to become self-sufficient.[6]

In response to these factors, the United States and individual European governments in the 1990s negotiated bilateral 'Open Skies' agreements that went beyond the earlier open market agreements – in effect, deregulating international travel between the United States and the other country. A typical Open Skies agreement allows carriers from either signatory country to fly to any point in the other country with no restrictions on fares or frequency of service. In addition, carriers receive unlimited fifth freedom (also known as 'intermediate' and 'beyond') rights – i.e. the right to carry traffic between the other country and a third country. Finally, carriers from

---

[4] US General Accounting Office, *International Aviation: Airline Alliances Produce Benefits, but Effect on Competition is Uncertain*, GAO/RCED-95-99, April 1995, p. 2.

[5] Doganis, op. cit., p. 27.

[6] Ibid., pp. 30-32.

the two countries can engage in code-share and other commercial arrangements.

## Remaining Restrictions

### *Output-Restricting Agreements*

Ten of the 25 EU member states have not signed Open Skies agreements with the United States, and they account for about half of all EU-US traffic.[7] We refer to the US bilateral agreements with these 10 countries as 'output restricting', because they limit to some degree the volume of traffic to and from the United States. The most restrictive agreement is Bermuda 2, which governs US-UK aviation, the largest single transatlantic aviation market. For passenger services, the 1977 Bermuda 2 agreement:

- restricts access to Heathrow, London's preferred airport, to two airlines each from the United States (currently, American and United) and the United Kingdom (currently, British Airways and Virgin Atlantic);

- limits the number of US cities eligible for non-stop service to and from Heathrow and Gatwick Airports; and

- effectively caps entry in most markets at one US and one UK airline.

In addition, the British government has used Bermuda 2 to limit the number of flights US airlines can offer and to disallow pro-competitive pricing initiatives. All-cargo services between the United States and the United Kingdom operate under a more liberal regime, with no limits on entry, capacity, pricing or which cities can be served in either country. However, fifth freedom operations are restricted to three US airlines and only nine countries.[8]

Bermuda 2 imposes huge costs on UK and US business travelers. Bermuda 2 also imposes major costs on US cargo carriers and the UK shippers they serve. Federal Express, which has its major European hub in Paris, operates daily service from the United States to Stansted Airport outside of London,

---

[7] The 10 member states are: Cyprus, Estonia, Greece, Hungary, Ireland, Latvia, Lithuania, Slovenia, Spain and the United Kingdom.

[8] Under Bermuda 2, US cargo carriers have 'beyond' rights only to Belgium, Germany, India, Iran, Jordan, Lebanon, the Netherlands, Syria and Turkey. Thus, they cannot travel from the United Kingdom to many commercially important markets, including France, Italy and Spain in Europe, as well as China, Hong Kong and Japan in Asia.

where it delivers UK-bound express cargo and collects UK cargo outbound for the European continent. Because it does not have fifth freedom rights from the United Kingdom to France, Federal Express must transport the UK outbound cargo to Paris by truck or train, or hire an EU carrier to fly it to Paris. At the same time, Federal Express planes must fly empty from Stansted to Paris.

As another example, under the US-Ireland air services agreement, a US carrier serving Ireland must operate as many flights to Shannon as it does to Dublin (the so-called '50/50 rule'). Irish carriers, in turn, are limited in the number of US gateways they can serve. These restrictions limit air services between the United States and Ireland to the detriment of consumers and air carriers in both countries.

## 'Open Skies' Agreements

Although Open Skies agreements eliminate all restrictions on output, they retain a number of restrictive features of traditional air services agreements, either by omission or by explicit provision. With respect to transatlantic competition, perhaps the most restrictive feature is the *nationality clause*, which provides that only airlines that are 'substantially owned and effectively controlled' by nationals of the signatory state can operate direct service between that state and the United States. For example, a German-owned airline may operate direct service from Frankfurt to Chicago, but it may not operate direct service from Paris to Chicago. A senior US transportation official recently described the differential impact this provision has on Europe versus the United States:

> Consider, first, two different trans-Atlantic aviation route maps as they appear today...The first map shows – with lines connecting every conceivable transatlantic city pair – all of the opportunities currently available to every US airline wishing to fly to Europe...There are some famously anachronistic restrictions at London's Heathrow Airport and some other less important exceptions, but it's still pretty difficult to see the outlines of the continents under the dense tangle of available routes on this first map – the opportunities available to US carriers.
>
> The second map looks very different. It shows the transatlantic city pairs currently available to EU carriers. Instead of the dense tangle of routes we saw on the first map, this map shows a separate spray of routes coming out of each EU country to the United States. The airlines of each of our many EU Open Skies partners are certainly allowed to fly to and from any city in the US, but all those flights must funnel in and out of their individual home countries. At the present time, in other words, no EU carrier has the ability under the current

bilateral agreements to do what every US carrier can do: connect any point in the US to any point in Europe.[9]

The nationality clause is a traditional air services provision that serves the same function as rules of origin in preferential trade agreements – namely, to prevent third countries from obtaining negotiated privileges through the back door. However, by denying European airlines the right to serve US destinations from anywhere in the European Union, this provision thwarts internal European liberalization and integration.

To elaborate, EU flag carriers must base their operations in their home countries, because transatlantic traffic constitutes a substantial part of the revenue of most European carriers. Moreover, it would be difficult for one European flag carrier to challenge a competitor in another EU country, because it could not fly directly to the United States from that country.

The nationality clause is also a barrier to EU consolidation. Restructuring via mergers and acquisitions is one of the key drivers of change in most industries, and the European Commission has indicated a desire to see Europe's airlines consolidate. However, if one of the merging airlines were from a non-Open Skies EU country (and several of the more likely merger candidates are), it is likely that the United States would effectively block the transaction.[10]

In sum, the current regulatory regime leads to an 'artificial' proliferation of hubs or mini-hubs in Europe to serve the transatlantic market. At the same time, transatlantic routes are effectively insulated from entry by more efficient competitors from different EU member states. Thus, the current system impedes the evolution of an efficient network design in Europe.

---

[9] "International Aviation Priorities", remarks by Jeffrey N. Shane, Under Secretary for Policy at the US Department of Transportation, at Phoenix Sky Harbor International Airport's Aviation Symposium, April 27, 2005.

[10] For example, British Airways explored the acquisition of KLM in 2000. Because the United States had an Open Skies agreement with the Netherlands but not with the UK, US officials made clear that such an acquisition would not give British Airways additional access to the United States through the 'back door' of the Netherlands. More significantly, they cautioned that the merger would cost KLM its longstanding Open Skies rights to the United States. A senior Clinton Administration official announced at the time that "if KLM comes under effective control of British Airways while Bermuda 2 still governs US-UK air services, KLM will immediately lose the benefits of the US-Netherlands Open Skies Agreement". Remarks to the International Aviation Club by Dorothy Robyn, Special Assistant to the President for Economic Policy, National Economic Council, July 18, 2000.

Although airline alliances provide a way around some of these restrictions, they have their own serious limitations.

A second major restriction that persists even under an Open Skies agreement is the statutory limit on *foreign ownership and control of domestic airlines.* Under US law, at least 75% of the voting stock of a US airline must be owned by US citizens, and US citizens must also control the airline. EU law has similar restrictions, although the cap on foreign ownership is higher – 49%. In addition, some EU member states have their own prohibitions on airline takeovers by non-EU investors.

The restrictions on foreign ownership and control also preclude a *right of establishment.* Such a right allows an airline or other investor from one country to establish an airline in another country and to operate it under the laws and regulations of the other country. Thus, although UK entrepreneur Richard Branson would like start up a low-cost airline in the United States and operate it as a US company, he would not be able to control it.

Open Skies agreements effectively preserve a number of other restrictions as well, although their impact on competition is less significant:

- *Stand-alone cabotage.* An airline from one Open Skies country cannot carry domestic traffic solely between two points within the territory of the other Open Skies country. For example, Lufthansa cannot carry US domestic passengers solely between two airports inside the United States. Likewise, a US airline cannot carry German domestic passengers between two airports in Germany.

- *Consecutive ('fill-up') cabotage.* An airline from one Open Skies country cannot carry domestic traffic between two points within the territory of the other, even in the course of providing international service. For example, on a flight from Paris to Mexico City via New York and Chicago, Air France can drop off Paris-originating passengers, and pick up Mexico-bound passengers, in both New York and Chicago; but it cannot carry US domestic passengers solely between New York and Chicago.

- *Wet leasing.*[11] US carriers can 'lease-out' US aircraft and crew to foreign carriers, but they are prohibited from 'leasing-in' foreign aircraft and crew. EU carriers do not face such an absolute prohibition, although leasing-in of third-country aircraft is limited to temporary needs and exceptional circumstances.

---

[11] 'Wet leasing' involves the lease of aircraft and crew, in contrast to 'dry leasing', which involves the lease of aircraft without crew.

- *'Fly America' requirements.* Most US government commercial air transport, domestic as well as international, must take place on US airlines. This includes the transport of US government personnel and cargo, as well as most items handled by the US Postal Service. However, on international flights, foreign code-share partners of US-flag carriers can transport US government personnel, cargo and mail under the US carrier's code on routes covered by their code-sharing agreement.

## US-EU Open Aviation Area

To remove these market distortions, the European Commission has endorsed the elimination of *all* commercial restrictions on US-EU competition and investment. The resulting US-EU Open Aviation Area would amount to a free trade zone in air transport encompassing not just transatlantic operations but operations within the European Union and the United States as well.

There is support for an Open Aviation Area on both sides of the Atlantic, including among many (although not all) flag carriers seeking greater commercial flexibility. While economists and aviation policy experts generally favor the proposal because it embraces market principles, specific groups, including airline labor unions and some US Department of Defense officials, express serious concerns about key provisions. Moreover, US carriers have been reluctant to battle with their pilots on this issue in the current climate. Largely based on the position of these groups, the US government, despite having blazed the trail on aviation liberalization for more than two decades, has not endorsed significant elements of a US-EU Open Aviation Area.

## Economic Impact of an Open Aviation Area

To quantify the benefits of an Open Aviation Area, we focused on three efficiency effects: cost savings, price reductions and output expansion. Using a variety of quantitative methods, we estimated the impact of each effect on prices, passenger traffic volume and consumer welfare.

### Economic Benefits of More Efficient Firms Replacing Less Efficient Firms

In a liberalized market, more efficient airlines would replace less efficient ones, or less efficient airlines would adopt the practices of more efficient ones, leading to significant cost savings and an increase in industry efficiency. This substitution would occur through two mechanisms: industry restructuring (e.g. mergers, acquisitions, joint ventures), and increased competition (e.g. a carrier from one EU country could establish a transatlantic hub in another EU country).

This same process of expansion and consolidation would allow air carriers to exploit size-related economies, leading to further efficiency gains. For example, a merger or 'deep' alliance might allow two carriers to spread certain fixed costs over more passengers (scale economy). The carriers might achieve added savings by reconfiguring their combined network to connect more flights to certain hub airports (scope economy). They might also achieve higher utilization – e.g. by combining traffic to raise load factors (density economy).

We used route-level cost data for US and EU carriers to estimate the potential for cost savings under an Open Aviation Area. Our primary source was a database of airline costs and revenues provided by the European Commission's Directorate General for Energy and Transport and originally commissioned from British Aerospace (BAe). The database estimates airline costs on a route-by-route basis, using essentially the same cost categories used by the International Air Transport Association (IATA). To preserve carrier anonymity and commercial confidentiality, it groups airlines into 'low', 'medium' and 'high' cost categories and presents average costs for each category rather than cost figures for individual airlines.

First, we used these data, together with qualitative industry input, to identify five cost categories for which the variation in costs across airlines was the largest and the potential for network efficiencies the greatest. The categories were: flight deck crew; cabin attendants; passenger service; ticketing, sales and promotion; and general and administrative.

Second, we determined a 'best practice benchmark' for these five cost categories. Specifically, we used 'medium-cost' airlines rather than 'no frills' airlines as our benchmark for industry best practice. It would be unreasonable to claim that traditional airlines could reduce their passenger service costs to those of Ryanair or easyJet, because traditional airlines provide a higher level of in-flight service.

Third, for each cost category, we calculated the savings that would result if high-cost airlines cost were to reduce their costs to the benchmark level. These calculations were done on a route-by-route basis within four geographic regions: the transatlantic, northern Europe, southern Europe and north-south European routes. We limited our comparison to carriers that already served an individual region. That is, we excluded US carriers from our analysis of intra-EU routes, and our analysis of the three intra-EU regions ignored EU carriers that did not already serve that particular region.

*Table 1. Estimated Impact of Cost Reductions*

| | Flight type | | |
|---|---|---|---|
| | Intra-EU | Transatlantic | All flights |
| Current costs (€ million/year) | 39,531 | 28,578 | 68,110 |
| Potential savings (€ million/year) | 2,268 | 621 | 2,888 |
| Percent of current costs | 5.7% | 2.2% | 4.2% |

*Note:* These figures were calculated as of December 2, 2002, when €1 = $0.9927. Consequently, these figures may be overstated due to currency changes since that time.

Table 1 shows our results. We estimate that the potential cost savings to the airline industry from greater 'productive efficiency' are about €2.9 billion annually, or 4.2% of total costs. Nearly 80% of the savings would come from intra-EU, as opposed to transatlantic, operations. We further estimate the impact if these savings were passed through to consumers in price reductions. In addition to the direct benefit of €2.9 billion a year, these savings would produce an annual increase in consumer welfare of as much as €370 million due to the increase in passenger traffic that lower prices would generate.

### Economic Benefits of Pricing Synergies owing to Transatlantic Integration

By facilitating deeper forms of integration between US and EU carriers, liberalization would allow improved price coordination on transatlantic interline routes (i.e. routes that require passengers to fly on two or more airlines to reach their destination). Without coordination, each carrier will set the fare for its leg of the flight without considering how it will affect demand for the other legs. If the same carriers are allowed to coordinate, each will have an incentive to set *lower* fares so as to increase combined profits. This process, which seems counterintuitive to many non-economists, is known as 'elimination of double marginalization'.

We assessed the impact of improved price coordination by interlining carriers in an Open Aviation Area. In particular, we relied on previous studies that examined the fare difference on transatlantic interline routes when the route is covered by an airline alliance, as opposed to no alliance. Economists Jan Brueckner and W. Tom Whalen analyzed fares on US international routes to assess whether alliances result in lower fares on interline routes as a result of improved price coordination.[12] The authors found that alliance partners charge interline fares that are between 18% and 28% below the prices charged by non-allied airlines on the same route. They concluded that when allied airlines are allowed to share revenues or profits and engage in coordinated fare-setting, consumers benefit from lower interline prices. Moreover, they found that alliances increased consumer welfare overall, even though they may reduce competition, and thus raise prices somewhat on gateway-to-gateway routes.

To produce indicative estimates of these benefits, we made three calculations. First, we calculated fares and volumes for traffic on all transatlantic interline routes not currently subject to price coordination. (We excluded routes covered by the four output-restricting bilateral agreements, because we considered those separately.) To determine fares, we used average passenger revenues for all transatlantic routes as derived from the revenue, volume and load factor information in the BAe database. With respect to traffic volume, we used an industry estimate that around 10% of total transatlantic traffic involves interlining carriers that do not engage in price coordination. We applied this figure to total US-EU transatlantic traffic volumes derived from the US Department of Transportation T-100 data.

Second, we estimated the size of the fare reductions that improved price coordination among transatlantic carriers would produce. We relied on the Brueckner and Whalen results showing that existing alliances have produced fare reductions on interline routes ranging from 18% to 28%.

Third, we calculated the increased traffic volume that would result from these price reductions. We used two estimates of the price-responsiveness (elasticity) of demand – a lower bound estimate of 1.0 and an upper bound estimate of 2.5.

Using these steps, we estimate the gains to consumers that would result if there were comparable fare reductions on transatlantic routes not currently subject to price coordination. Table 2 summarizes our findings, showing an estimated annual benefit to consumers of between €629 million and €1.347 billion, depending on passengers' responsiveness to changes in price (the elasticity of demand).

---

[12]   See Jan K. Brueckner and W. Tom Whalen, "The Price Effects of International Airline Alliances", *Journal of Law & Economics* 43, No. 2, October 2000, pp. 503-545. The majority of the alliances examined in Brueckner and Whalen's analysis were subject to antitrust immunity. International airline alliances may have other, less desirable effects as well. These potential anti-competitive effects of alliances are the subject of ongoing research by Brueckner and by The Brattle Group.

*Table 2. Annual Impact of Increased Interline Price Coordination*

|  | Lower bound scenario | Upper bound scenario |
|---|---|---|
| Increased passenger volume ('000s/year) | 975 | 5,654 |
| Increase in consumer surplus (€ million/year) |  |  |
| From price decreases for existing customers | 571 | 888 |
| From increased traffic | 59 | 458 |
| Total | 629 | 1,347 |

*Note*: The lower bound scenario assumes an 18% price reduction and a price elasticity of demand of 1.0, while the upper bound scenario assumes a 28% price reduction and a price elasticity of demand of 2.5.

### Economic Benefits of Eliminating Output Restrictions

At least three mechanisms would lead to expanded output (passenger traffic) in a liberalized market. First, cost savings from the first two efficiency effects described above would be passed through to consumers (at least in the long run) in the form of lower prices, leading to increased passenger demand for travel. Second, price reductions resulting from improved price coordination on transatlantic interline routes would increase demand. Third, US bilateral agreements with Greece, Ireland, Spain and the United Kingdom all restrict output to varying degrees; an Open Aviation Area would eliminate these restrictions. (Recall that our analysis did not include the ten newly acceded EU members, six of which have output restricting agreements with the United States.)

We estimated the impact on airline industry output of liberalizing those four 'output-restricting' bilateral agreements. Our methodology involved estimating the impact of prior, 'partial' transatlantic liberalization – namely the Open Skies agreements of the 1990s. Specifically, we estimated the impact of these Open Skies agreements by using statistical techniques to analyze historical data on passenger traffic as well as market cost and demand variables. By controlling for these economic variables, we isolated the contribution of Open Skies agreements to changes in the volume of transatlantic passengers over time. We used this result as a lower-bound estimate of the output expansion that would accompany the replacement of the four output-restricting bilateral agreements in an Open Aviation Area.

Our analysis found that, controlling for other factors, the 1990s Open Skies agreements led to a 10% increase in the number of transatlantic passengers. To estimate the impact of liberalizing the four remaining output-restricting bilateral agreements, we simply extrapolated from that result, as shown in Table 3. By this measure, an Open Aviation Area would lead to an additional 2.2 million passengers traveling annually between the United States and Greece, Ireland, Spain and the United Kingdom. As Table 4 shows, the corresponding impact on consumer welfare would range from €0.6 billion to €1.5 billion a year.

*Table 3. Estimated Volume Increases from Lifting of Output Restrictions for Non-Open Skies Countries*

| Country | Actual volume in 2000 ('000s) [1] | Predicted % increase from open skies agreement [2] | Predicted volume in 2000 ('000s) [3] = (1+[2]) x [1] | Change in volume in 2000 ('000s) [4] = [3] – [1] |
|---|---|---|---|---|
| Greece | 342 | 10% | 377 | 35 |
| Ireland | 1,587 | 10% | 1,748 | 161 |
| Spain | 1,825 | 10% | 2,011 | 185 |
| UK | 17,810 | 10% | 19,617 | 1,807 |
| Total | 21,564 | 10% | 23,753 | 2,188 |

*Source*: DOT International T-100 Data.

*Table 4. Predicted Increase in Consumer Surplus due to Lifting of Output Restrictions (€ million/year)*

| Country | Lower bound scenario | | | Upper bound scenario | | |
|---|---|---|---|---|---|---|
| | Gain due to price decreases for existing customers | Gain due to increased traffic | Total gains | Gain due to price decreases for existing customers | Gain due to increased traffic | Total gains |
| Greece | 18 | 1 | 19 | 8 | 0 | 8 |
| Ireland | 95 | 5 | 99 | 39 | 2 | 41 |
| Spain | 106 | 5 | 112 | 44 | 2 | 46 |
| UK | 1,181 | 58 | 1,239 | 486 | 24 | 510 |
| Total | 1,401 | 69 | 1,469 | 577 | 29 | 605 |

*Notes*: Calculated for routes where volume and bi-directional fares are both available.

Utilities January 2001 fares.

The lower bound scenario assumes an elasticity of 1.0, while the upper bound scenario assumes an elasticity of 2.5.

These labels are used to be consistent with the rest of the analysis, even though the assumptions behind the two scenarios result in greater gains in the lower bound scenario than in the upper bound scenario.

*Source*: DOT International T-100 Data and BAe Database.

## Total Economic Impact

Combining the results from Tables 1 through 3, we developed indicative estimates of the total economic impact of an Open Aviation Area on two key measures: passenger traffic volume and consumer welfare.

As Table 5 shows, we estimate that passenger traffic would increase annually by between 4.1 million and 11.0 million passengers on transatlantic routes, and between 13.6 million and 35.7 million on intra-EU routes, for a total increase of 17.7 million to 46.7 million passengers per year. *These are significant increases. They represent an increase of 9-24% in total transatlantic travel, and 5-14% in intra-EU travel.*

*Table 5. Total Estimated Increase in Passenger Volume ('000s/year)*

| Effect | Area | Lower bound scenario | Upper bound scenario |
|---|---|---|---|
| Cost savings | Transatlantic | 968 | 3,169 |
| Price synergies | Transatlantic | 975 | 5,654 |
| No output-restricting bilaterals | Transatlantic | 2,188 | 2,188 |
| *Subtotal* | | *4,131* | *11,011* |
| Cost savings | Intra-EU | 13,527 | 35,720 |
| Total | | 17,658 | 46,731 |

As Table 6 shows, we estimate that an Open Aviation Area would increase consumer surplus by a large amount – from €5.1 billion to €5.2 billion annually.[13] Transatlantic traffic accounts for €2.7 billion to €2.8 billion, or just over half of that increase. The lion's share (€3.1 billion to €3.8 billion annually) comes from gains to consumers that do not involve any reduction in airline profits.

We also quantified the impact of an Open Aviation Area on industries that supply direct inputs to aviation, such as aircraft and computer equipment. As Table 7 shows, we estimated that the increased airline revenue would lead to additional economic output in 'directly-related' industries ranging from €3.6 billion to €8.1 billion a year. Note that this figure excludes any of the

---

[13] For Table 5 through Table 7, the lower bound scenario represents an assumed elasticity of 1.0, while the upper bound scenario represents an assumed elasticity of 2.5. For the price synergies results, the lower bound scenario also assumes an 18% price decrease, while the upper bound scenario assumes a 28% price decrease.

potential impact on industries such as tourism and leisure that would be among the most significant beneficiaries of aviation liberalization.

*Table 6. Total Estimated Increase in Consumer Surplus (€ million/year)*

| Effect | Area | Lower bound scenario | | | Upper bound scenario | | |
|---|---|---|---|---|---|---|---|
| | | Gain due to price decreases for existing customers | Gain due to increased traffic | Total gains | Gain due to price decreases for existing customers | Gain due to increased traffic | Total gains |
| Cost savings | Transatlantic | 621 | 41 | 662 | 621 | 158 | 778 |
| Pricing synergies | Transatlantic | 571 | 59 | 629 | 888 | 458 | 1,347 |
| No output-restricting bilaterals | Transatlantic | 1,401 | 69 | 1,469 | 577 | 29 | 605 |
| Subtotal | | 2,592 | 168 | 2,760 | 2,085 | 645 | 2,730 |
| Cost savings | Intra-EU | 2,268 | 83 | 2,351 | 2,268 | 216 | 2,483 |
| Total | | 4,860 | 251 | 5,111 | 4,353 | 860 | 5,213 |

*Table 7. Revenue Impact on Directly-Related Industries (€ million/year)*

| Effect | Lower bound scenario | | | Upper bound scenario | | |
|---|---|---|---|---|---|---|
| | Revenue | Direct economic impacts | Direct-plus indirect economic impacts | Revenue | Direct economic impacts | Direct-plus indirect economic impacts |
| Pricing synergies | 571 | 571 | 1,053 | 2,908 | 2,908 | 5,365 |
| No output-restricting bilaterals | 1,401 | 1,401 | 2,584 | 1,484 | 1,484 | 2,738 |
| Total | 1,971 | 1,971 | 3,637 | 4,392 | 4,392 | 8,103 |

## Potential Impact of Liberalization in Three Key Policy Areas

Opponents of international aviation liberalization argue that it will have an adverse impact in at least three areas – national security, airline labor and aviation safety. Below, we analyze the merits of these claims in the context of a US-EU Open Aviation Area.

## Would an open aviation area jeopardize US national security?

Some in the US Department of Defense (DOD) are concerned that international aviation liberalization could threaten the Civil Reserve Air Fleet (CRAF), a critical component of America's military readiness. Under the CRAF program, US commercial air carriers pledge to provide military airlift in a defense emergency in exchange for exclusive access to US government peacetime business. DOD officials fear that allowing foreign investors to acquire US air carriers would jeopardize the military's dependable access to this emergency capability. DOD concerns rest on three assumptions:

- US air carriers are more dependable than foreign air carriers.

- If a foreign entity bought a US air carrier, it would operate as a foreign carrier.

- If the US government changed its *statutory policy* to allow foreign ownership of US carriers, it would open itself up to problematic *transactions*.

The first assumption is generally valid. US carriers *are* more dependable because the US government has legal leverage over them (it could revoke the operating certificate of a non-compliant CRAF carrier, seize the aircraft and call up the carrier's reservist-pilots to fly them, etc.). The US government's leverage with foreign carriers is far more limited.

However, the second assumption is flawed. Legal requirements and business strategy almost certainly would compel the European buyer of a US carrier to operate it as a US subsidiary, giving the US government the identical leverage. The alternative – operating as a European carrier in US domestic commerce – would amount to stand-alone cabotage. Cabotage operations on that scale would be highly impractical from a commercial standpoint. In addition, most US aviation law experts believe that, even if the statutory restriction on stand-alone cabotage were eliminated under an Open Aviation Area, a foreign carrier operating in US domestic commerce would be subject to all of the laws and regulations that apply to other US-based companies.[14] In sum, because the European buyer of a US carrier would (by choice or mandate) exercise its right of establishment, DOD's dependable access to the aircraft would be preserved.

---

[14] Presumably, the same logic would apply to a US carrier operating in European domestic commerce. The legal argument would not necessarily extend to the transport of domestic traffic as part of international service (i.e. consecutive or 'fill-up' cabotage).

Only one scenario would put CRAF aircraft at risk – if a US carrier (whether US- or foreign-owned) re-flagged its international operations to Europe, presumably to substitute lower-wage EU pilots. But this scenario is unlikely, and there are ways to preclude it.

As evidence that this approach (i.e. US incorporation under a right of establishment) protects national security, DOD already allows participation by foreign-owned commercial vessels in its Voluntary Intermodal Sealift Agreement (VISA) program – the maritime equivalent of CRAF – and the closely linked Maritime Security Program (MSP). Much of VISA and MSP capacity comes from ships that meet US 'citizenship' requirements and fly the US flag despite being foreign-owned. For example, the Danish-owned, Norfolk-based Maersk Line, Limited has top-secret clearance and transports half of all DOD's peacetime maritime cargo.

The third assumption also is flawed. Even if it were to allow foreign ownership of US carriers, the US government still could block or restrict individual transactions, using the Exon-Florio amendment to the Defense Production Act. Under Exon-Florio, an interagency executive-branch Committee on Foreign Investment in the United States (CFIUS) reviews foreign mergers solely to determine if they would harm US national security. Since 1988, CFIUS has imposed conditions on a number of transactions to protect US national security.

A second DOD concern is that elimination of market access restrictions (Fly America requirements and the ban on cabotage) would make the CRAF program more costly. Because CRAF is financed indirectly, by giving participating carriers exclusive access to the market for US government air transport services, it requires no direct funding. Economists have long criticized cabotage and Fly America restrictions: by excluding foreign carriers from the US government market, they impose direct and indirect costs on users. On balance, the US government would *save* money if it paid US carriers directly to participate in CRAF and opened the government market to all qualified carriers. As noted above, however, stand-alone cabotage is impractical for legal and business reasons. Moreover, elimination of Fly America requirements may be politically impractical in the near term, because it would require the US Congress to appropriate money for a program that is currently 'free' in budgetary terms. If Fly America restrictions were maintained, it would diminish somewhat the benefits of an Open Aviation Area, but European carriers could get around that restriction by exercising their right of establishment.

We conclude that a US-EU Open Aviation Area would not jeopardize the CRAF program or US national security more broadly.

## How would an open aviation area affect workers and wages?

Economic theory tells us that by liberalizing trade and investment in aviation, an Open Aviation Area could facilitate the substitution of less expensive foreign workers for more expensive domestic workers ('labor substitution'), either directly or indirectly. In fact, a major impediment to US-EU liberalization is the concern by labor groups that US pilots and flight attendants would be replaced by lower-wage EU flight crew on transatlantic flights. US pilots point to two scenarios that are of particular concern. The first is a US-EU merger: for example, if Delta were to buy Aer Lingus and substitute Irish pilots on transatlantic flights. Under the second scenario, a US carrier would re-flag some or all of its transatlantic operations to, say, Portugal – what labor groups refer to as flying a 'flag of convenience' – so as to substitute lower-wage EU flight crew.

Based on a comparison of US-EU wage differences and an analysis of legal and institutional barriers to labor mobility, we draw three conclusions. First, *the potential for direct labor substitution appears to be very limited*. Under US immigration law, US carriers cannot avoid using US flight crew for their domestic operations, which account for nearly 75% of their total revenue. This gives US pilots significant bargaining leverage with which to prevent US carriers from engaging in direct labor substitution. US pilots have already negotiated protection against the comparable risk associated with international alliances and other international operations, and that process will only accelerate as the prospects for liberalization improve. Moreover, pilots are organizing themselves in parallel with the cross-border airline alliances, and these international pilot alliances will thwart airline efforts to introduce competition in aviation labor markets.

In addition, the lack of significant US-EU wage disparity would limit the appeal of direct labor substitution for US carriers under an Open Aviation Area. Pilots and flight attendants at major airlines in the EU15 member states earn only about 15% less than their US counterparts. There is, however, a far wider wage gap between US flight crew and their counterparts in the 10 member states that acceded in 2004. Still, these countries have relatively few qualified pilots, and it is expensive to train new ones. Moreover, because new member state pilots are scarce and well-informed, their wages will converge with those of other pilots in a competitive market.

Second, *the potential for indirect labor substitution is greater*, by comparison – particularly over the long run. Under this scenario, relatively lower-wage transatlantic carriers such as Virgin Atlantic would take market share from high-wage US and EU carriers. *But, even here, any adverse impact on US labor would be limited* because US and EU wage levels, which are not that far apart to begin with, will converge in a competitive market.

Third, *the pejorative discussion of 'flags of convenience' in the context of US-EU aviation liberalization is fundamentally misleading.* The checkered history of open-registry vessels in the maritime industry, which opponents of liberalization often cite, has limited relevance for an Open Aviation Area. US carriers are unlikely to re-flag for the reasons cited above, and high-wage EU carriers are equally unlikely to re-flag for a different reason: they can hire workers from lower-wage EU countries even without re-flagging. Finally, even if re-flagging were to occur under an Open Aviation Area, it would not pose a threat to airline safety or labor conditions, given the high standards in place in Europe and the United States.

Although our analysis suggests that airline workers would not be harmed seriously by liberalization, it nevertheless may be desirable to cushion them against possible losses under an Open Aviation Area. Policy-makers should avoid policies that distort competition (e.g. mechanisms to preclude re-flagging). Far preferable are policies that directly compensate dislocated workers, although policy-makers would have to make a credible commitment to honor such policies.

## Would an open aviation area harm airline safety?

Western Europe and the United States have aviation safety records that are (in the words of safety expert Arnold Barnett) "astoundingly close to perfect". In part, these records reflect the strength of government regulatory systems that subject aviation to a higher level of safety scrutiny than that received by any other industry. US and European safety systems are part of a longstanding international regulatory regime that has proven highly effective in those parts of the world where it is fully implemented. Most important:

- The International Civil Aviation Organization (ICAO) develops and disseminates detailed international standards covering every aspect of aviation.

- Member countries, through their national or regional civil aviation authority (CAA), apply and enforce ICAO standards. Specifically, CAAs are responsible for the safe operation of air carriers that bear their nation's flag.

More recently, the United States and ICAO have begun formal programs to assess whether third-country CAAs comply with ICAO standards. Regulators in the United States and elsewhere use the results of these assessments to limit or deny access to their national airspace by carriers from non-compliant countries.

Although a US-EU Open Aviation Area would not alter the strong regulatory structure in place in Western Europe and the United States, proposals for international liberalization, generally, have raised concerns from labor groups and questions from aviation regulators at the US Federal Aviation Administration (FAA).

Labor groups warn that increased international competition could force carriers to cut spending related to safety. US airline deregulation prompted similar concerns in the late 1970s and 1980s. However, extensive research found no evidence that deregulation had any adverse impact on safety, and the US accident rate improved during deregulation roughly in line with long-term trends. A second concern is that practices fostered by globalization (e.g., international code-sharing) make it easier for carriers to avoid national regulatory oversight. While these practices do make safety regulation more complex, an Open Aviation Area would pose no new or added risk.

Most FAA officials view international liberalization as an issue that should be decided on the basis of economic policy, not safety, considerations. However, they urge that liberalization be carried out in a way that preserves or enhances safety. One issue is how to handle operations by EU carriers inside of the United States under an Open Aviation Area – primarily, fill-up cabotage or wet leasing that is cross-border in nature. Under international rules, those operations would be the regulatory responsibility of European authorities; but FAA officials worry that Congress would impose direct FAA oversight, subjecting the operator to two regulatory standards. As an alternative to having no oversight or direct oversight, the FAA might certify such operations using its Bilateral Aviation Safety Agreement, a mechanism currently used to facilitate reciprocal certification of aircraft and aeronautical products. A second FAA issue concerns international flights to and from the United States under an Open Aviation Area. The key is to preserve aviation authorities' ability to know precisely who has operational control of, and regulatory control over individual flights.

In sum, although an Open Aviation Area would challenge regulators, it would not harm aviation safety, given the generally high level of regulatory oversight in Europe and the United States. Globalization of aviation is unavoidable. Aviation authorities in the United States and Europe are devoting ever more time and resources to dealing with the international dimensions of regulatory oversight. US-EU aviation liberalization would focus and accelerate this important effort. In the end, that could be one of the most valuable contributions of an Open Aviation Area.

## Recent Developments

Although creation of a US-EU Open Area remains a seemingly distant goal, a great deal has happened since our study was published in early 2003. The precipitating event was a November 2002 ruling by the European Court of

Justice (ECJ). In a group of cases brought by the European Commission against selected member states, the ECJ ruled that the nationality clause was a violation of the Treaty of Rome, and told the member states in question to remove the clause from their bilateral agreements. In June 2003, after months of internal debate, member states granted the European Commission its long-sought mandate to negotiate international air services agreements on their behalf, albeit with certain restrictions. That same month, at the US-EU Summit, President Bush and his EU counterparts announced the start of comprehensive air services negotiations.

A year later, following six formal rounds of talks, the European Commission and the US government reached a major agreement that stopped short of an Open Aviation Area but that nevertheless went beyond traditional Open Skies. The agreement eliminated most of the remaining restrictions on US-EU aviation competition, with the notable exception of the prohibition on foreign ownership and control, which also precludes a right of establishment.[15] Most important, the agreement replaced the problematic nationality clause with an 'EU carrier clause'. In addition to resolving member states' internal legal problem, that clause was intended to facilitate consolidation of the fragmented EU airline industry. The agreement also replaced all of the existing bilateral agreements with a single EU-wide Open Skies agreement, thus extending the Open Skies model to the 10 EU member states that do not have such an arrangement with the United States. In addition, the agreement opened up Heathrow Airport to all US carriers, although it did not provide any takeoff or landing slots.

Despite the European Commission's strong support for the agreement, it was rejected in June 2004 by the EU Transport Ministers, whose approval was required. Not surprisingly, the UK was the most vocal objector, but several member states with Open Skies agreements also opposed the agreement. The naysayers maintained that granting the US its major wish – greater access to Heathrow – would leave them little leverage to induce for the United States to return to the table later and negotiate access to its domestic market. However, in a speech delivered a month later, John Byerly, a senior official at the State Department who led the US delegation, left little doubt that the

---

[15] Shortly before it reached an agreement with the Commission, the Bush Administration proposed legislation to raise the cap on foreign ownership from 25% to 49% of voting stock, but that proposed change, which met with only limited support in Congress, would have had little practical effect without a simultaneous change in the prohibition on foreign control. The agreement also left the prohibition on cabotage in place, although that restriction, in contrast to the limitation on foreign ownership and control, has little commercial effect.

real impediment was continued protectionism on the part of British Airways, Lufthansa and several other European carriers:

> Publicly, the Association of European Airlines had long called for a Commission mandate and for EU-wide negotiations with the United States. Privately, however, individual European carriers – many of which enjoy protected positions on international routes to third countries negotiated by their national governments – expressed concern that the Commission might pursue a more independent course, one that could work to their commercial disadvantage. Why, they implied, should member states give the Commission an early win that could only bolster its quest to negotiate market-opening agreements with other countries?[16]

The European Commission was also stung by the no vote. (According to Byerly, the Commission's Minister for Energy and Transport, Madame Loyola de Palacio, complained publicly about some European carriers' desire to maintain 'closed market shares' that make 'victims' of consumers.) However, the Commission remains intent on getting an agreement. In an effort to put pressure on the member states, the Commission recently ordered 11 European countries to renounce their bilateral agreements with the United States, in keeping with the ECJ's 2002 decision.

The Bush Administration is sympathetic to the Commission's agenda: in a recent speech, a senior DOT official all but endorsed elimination of restrictions on foreign ownership of US airlines.[17] However, the Administration does not yet appear ready to expend the political capital necessary to secure congressional support for that long-overdue change in the law. Thus, as much as the United States would like to conclude the 2004 agreement, it is reluctant to restart talks without some guarantee of success.

Despite the seeming stalemate, support for a US-EU Open Aviation Area is growing, slowly but surely. The issue has been studied and debated extensively in the last several years on both continents, and supporters and

---

[16] "US-EU Aviation Relations – Charting the Course for Success", remarks to the International Aviation Club by John R. Byerly, Deputy Assistant Secretary for Transportation Affairs, US Department of State, July 13, 2004.

[17] Remarks of Jeffrey N. Shane, op. cit. Shane said that "the one industry in which capital is not allowed to flow freely across national boundaries, ironically, is the very industry that has facilitated the globalization of all the others – commercial aviation. It does not seem radical in 2005 to suggest that it is time to reconsider the justification for a law that restricts US airlines' access to the global capital marketplace."

opponents are gradually finding common ground.[18] If a European 'white knight' were to express interest in a financially troubled US carrier, it is likely that Congress – presumably with support from US airline labor – would amend the foreign ownership law in short order to make the rescue possible. Absent this scenario, which does not seem likely, complete liberalization may still be several years away. But it is increasingly seen as inevitable.

---

[18] As one illustration, an American Bar Association (ABA) working group recently reached unanimous agreement to recommend elimination of statutory restrictions on foreign ownership and control of US airlines subject to three (admittedly controversial) conditions that are designed to deal with national security and labor concerns. Four years earlier, a similar ABA working group was unable to reach any consensus because of disagreements over the implications of a change in the law for national security and labor. "Working Group Position Statement on Relaxing Airline Foreign Ownership Restrictions", *The Air & Space Lawyer*, Winter 2005.

# 6. Commercial Aerospace and the Transatlantic Economy

## *Richard Aboulafia*

### A Very Useful Agreement

Transatlantic trade in commercial jetliners and their associated components is a major success story. This industry has achieved a very high level of supply-chain internationalization, and jetliners from the US and the EU are increasingly sold to airlines on both sides of the Atlantic. Despite the recent dispute over EU launch aid for Airbus aircraft and contracts for US military and technology development for Boeing, the US and the EU have achieved an impressive level of jetliner industrial integration.

A rough metric of this trade is shown in Figure 1. Much of the trade is in the form of defense equipment, where the US enjoys a strong advantage, so Europe actually has a better position in commercial aerospace. In the figure the EU is represented by only its top five EU aerospace players – France, Germany, Italy, the Netherlands and the UK – although these constitute over 80% of the EU's aerospace output and market. The important point, however, is that aerospace trade is clearly a healthy two-way street, with both sides importing and exporting $10-15 billion worth of equipment annually.

*Figure 1. US-EU Aerospace Trade ($ billion)*

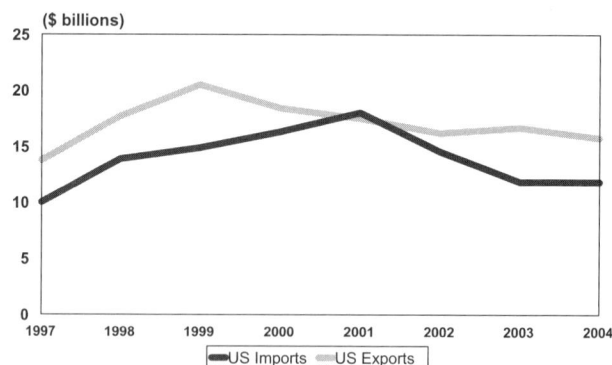

* Top five EU aerospace trade partners – France, Germany, Italy, the Netherlands and the UK (data derived from the AIA/ITA)

*Source*: Teal Group Corporation.

This success is largely the result of a very useful WTO component, the Agreement on Trade in Civil Aircraft (ATCA).[1] At the very least, a maturing global attitude towards this industry is reflected in the ATCA. Even where the ATCA did not remove trade barriers, it did codify their removal and extend the precedent to new signatory nations.

The ATCA was created as a component of the General Agreement on Tariffs and Trade, negotiated during the Tokyo Round of multilateral trade negotiations. From the standpoint of transatlantic jetliner trade, the treaty's most important effects include the elimination of:[2]

- tariffs on imported aircraft, engines and parts;

- quantitative import restrictions, such as quotas;

- government influence over aircraft purchase decisions through incentives or 'unreasonable' pressure on aircraft purchasers; and

- elimination of mandatory subcontracts associated with aircraft sales.

It also inludes the avoidance of using technical measures, such as standards, to restrict civil aircraft trade unfairly. Art. 4.1 of the ATCA summarizes the objective: "Purchasers of civil aircraft should be free to select suppliers on the basis of commercial and technological factors". The implication is that no other factors, such as local content, technology transfer or government mandate, should play a role in airline purchase decisions. Art. 4 also precludes mandatory purchases of local equipment (also known as offsets) in exchange for jetliner sales. In other words, a signatory nation cannot mandate that the selling company purchase its national products in exchange for a jetliner sale to that signatory nation's airlines.[3]

Transatlantic commercial aerospace trade takes three primary forms. The first is purchases of aircraft. The second is purchasing equipment for use in jetliners. Finally, there are joint ventures and alliances among US and EU manufacturers, to co-produce and co-design new equipment. Each of these categories offers strong examples of successful transatlantic trade and merits

---

[1] The Agreement on Trade in Civil Aircraft, Annex 4a of the World Trade Organisation Agreement of 1994, WTO, Geneva (retrieved from http://www.wto.org/english/docs_e/legal_e/air-79_e.pdf).

[2] A good summary of the ATCA provisions can be found in a recent jetliner study by the US Department of Commerce, International Trade Administration, *The US Jet Transport Industry: Competition, Regulation, and Global Market Factors affecting US Producers*, Washington, D.C., March 2005, (retrieved from http://www.ita.doc.gov/td/aerospace/jet_transport_study.htm).

[3] Agreement on Trade in Civil Aircraft, op. cit.

individual discussion. This paper also considers the risks to and benefits of US-EU commercial aerospace trade.

## Aircraft Purchasing

Because of the ATCA, US- and EU-based airlines are free to purchase commercial aircraft from Boeing or Airbus (or from Brazil's Embraer or Canada's Bombardier). Increasingly, they are exercising this option.

Airbus's first big break in the US market occurred with the sale of A300s to Eastern Airlines in 1978. Since then, the European plane-maker has gone from strength to strength. Pan Am was the second customer. In the 1990s, America West, United and USAirways all became customers. JetBlue built the second most successful low-cost carrier (after Southwest Airlines) in the US using an all-Airbus fleet.

Meanwhile, Boeing managed to keep a very strong presence in Europe. While its market share inevitably fell as Airbus matured (in terms of product line and sales force), it has continued to sell jets successfully to a free and open market. Most notably, France and Germany, which at another time might have been termed Airbus 'home market' countries, have continued to take large numbers of Boeing jetliners. Consistently praising its Boeing 777 fleet, Air France continues to order additional 777s instead of the competing Airbus A340. Most recently, in May 2005 Air France has joined the firms in the launch order book for the 777-200 cargo version.

The low-cost carrier (LCC) market illustrates this trade equality. Just as the US LCC market is split between Airbus and Boeing carriers, EU LCCs are evenly split too. Of the two dominant LCC players, Ryanair has an all-Boeing fleet, while EasyJet mostly has Airbus aircraft. Owing to the politicized nature of the LCC business (they depend on de-regulation, low-cost airport access and the general goodwill of politicians) the LCCs make an interesting test case for market openness.

Figure 2 clearly indicates the increase in Airbus's US market position. In 1999, a mere 403 planes belonging to US carriers (active fleets of passenger planes, excluding cargo) were built by Airbus – just 10.8% of the fleet. By the end of 2004, this figure had increased to 676 aircraft – 18.2% of the fleet. In addition, backlogged (unfilled) Airbus orders for US carriers were approximately equal, implying continued strong growth in Airbus's fleet share.

*Figure 2. US Airline Large Jet Fleets (all planes above 100 seats)*

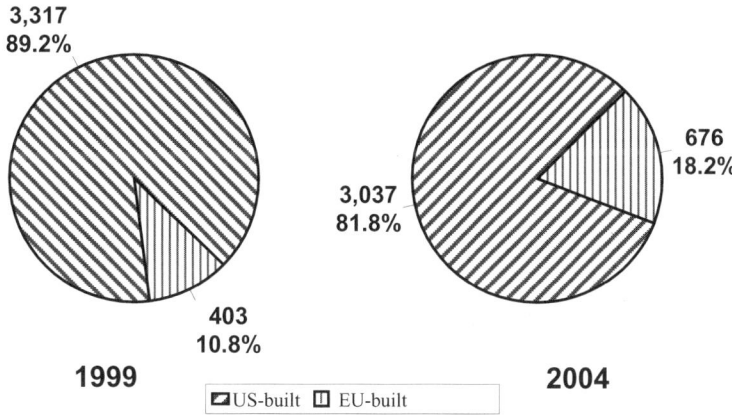

**1999**  **2004**

US-built  EU-built

*Source:* Teal Group Corporation.

Meanwhile, EU carrier Boeing and legacy McDonnell Douglas jetliner fleets have continued to diminish, both in relative and absolute terms. Figure 3 shows how the position of US manufacturers in the EU has shrunk from 1,246 aircraft (or 69.8% of the fleet) in 1999 to 1,157 aircraft (or 58.7% of the fleet) in 2004.

In short, the numbers indicate that there are no serious barriers to selling jetliners across the Atlantic. The market standing enjoyed by Airbus and Boeing in both US and EU markets is gradually equalizing. Although some commentators still discuss the desirability of jetliner transplant factories to facilitate civil market access, the reality is that this step is not necessary at all.

Ironically, owing to this trade liberalization, Airbus has extensively benefited from the US government aid provided after the attacks on September 11, 2001. Among the 10 carriers who received the most aid, four have taken mostly Airbus aircraft over the last four years.

The proposed US Airways/America West airline merger, which was announced in May 2005 highlights a related phenomenon. Airbus is an active member of the financing team behind the new entity, providing support in exchange for an order for Airbus's new A350 wide-body aircraft (and to support two key markets for Airbus's A320 narrow-body family).

Because of the trade liberalization engendered by the ATCA, Airbus and Boeing directly employ relatively few people outside of their home countries. Boeing has a small administrative presence in Europe, while Airbus employs approximately 500 persons in the US, primarily in training, engineering, and customer service roles. Airbus claims to support 120,000 US jobs[4] although, most of this employment in the US as well as that associated with Boeing's economic activity in the EU revolve around contract work for systems and structures. Nevertheless, these indirect jobs are also a transatlantic trade success story. Figures 4 through 7 present both a retroactive and forward look at trade in Airbus and Boeing aircraft.

*Figure 3. Large Jet Fleets among EU Airlines (all planes above 100 seats)*

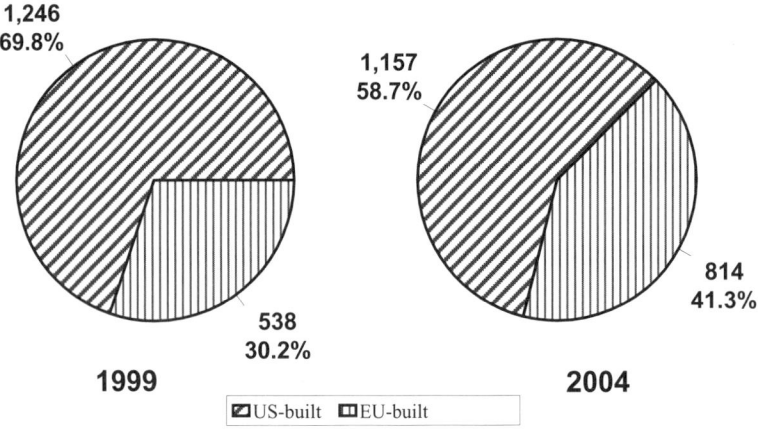

*Source:* Teal Group Corporation.

---

[4] See http://www.airbus.com.

*Figure 4. History and Forecast for Commercial Jetliners*

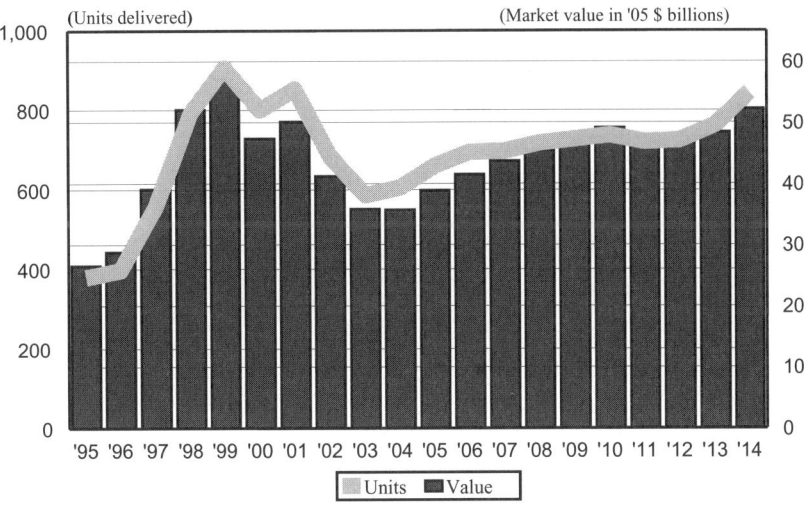

*Source*: Teal Group Corporation.

*Figure 5. Historical Jetliner Orders and Deliveries (all Airbus and Boeing aircraft)*

The end of an extended boom cycle

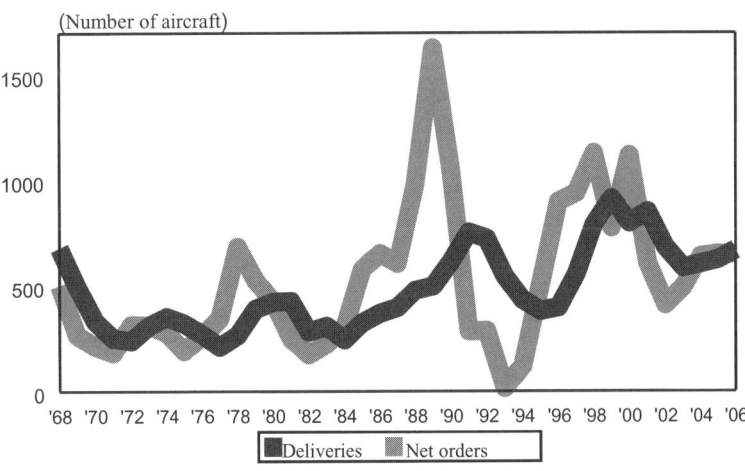

*Source*: Teal Group Corporation.

*Figure 6. Comparative Backlog Values – Airbus Growth since Boeing-MDC Merger, 787 Stops the Trend*

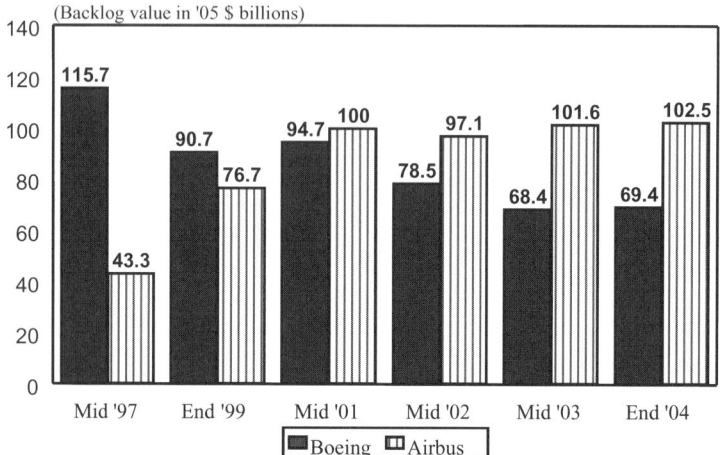

*Source*: Teal Group Corporation.

*Figure 7. Outlook for Jetliner Market Share – 787 Holds the Line (assumes current A350 launch)*

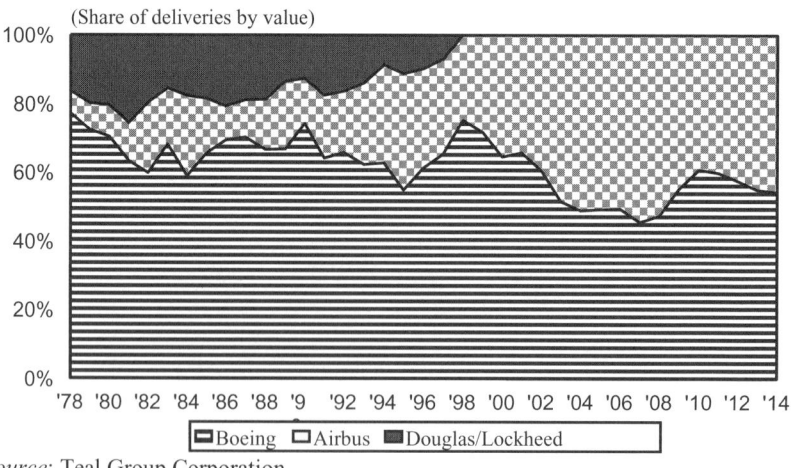

*Source*: Teal Group Corporation.

## Aircraft Contract Sourcing

Subcontracting is broadly divided into two categories. One covers discrete aircraft systems, which are nearly always contracted out. The second category is airframe work, subcontracted out at the prime contractor's discretion.

Discrete systems, the first category, include engines, avionics (airborne electronics), landing gear, interiors and other systems (such as the environmental control system or the auxiliary power unit). These subcomponents comprise 60-65% of the value chain of a commercial jetliner. The second category entails discretionary contracts primarily for the airframe. Airframe work typically comprises 35-40% of the value chain of a commercial jetliner.

### Aircraft Systems

The bulk of transatlantic jetliner contract work covers individual systems. This trend is owing both to the importance of these systems within the jetliner value chain, and to the strong market dominance enjoyed by the US and EU contractors with these systems. Almost all of the prime contractors for these systems are domiciled in the US, the UK and France. Several prime and some secondary contractors are domiciled in Germany, Italy, Japan and the Netherlands.

Engines are the single highest-value systems. The world's jetliners are all powered by Rolls-Royce, General Electric or Pratt & Whitney turbofans; they are manufactured by these contractors alone, in concert with one another or with other major subcontractors.

Almost all twin-aisle (wide-body) and about half of the single-aisle (narrow-body) jetliners offer a choice of engines, to be determined by the airline. In fact, until 1988 all Airbuses were delivered with US engines – either General Electric or Pratt & Whitney.

As with jetliners, there is strong evidence of robust transatlantic trade in engines. An analysis of two wide-body twinjets that have seen fierce engine manufacturer competition in the last 10 years – Airbus's A330 and Boeing's 777 – produces interesting numbers, as may be seen in Figure 8. For example, more US airlines than EU airlines have chosen EU engines (from Rolls-Royce) for these aircraft. Yet, the two US engine companies enjoy a higher market share on these two aircraft in the EU than they do in their domestic market.

*Figure 8. US-EU Engine Orders for the Airbus 330 and the Boeing 777*

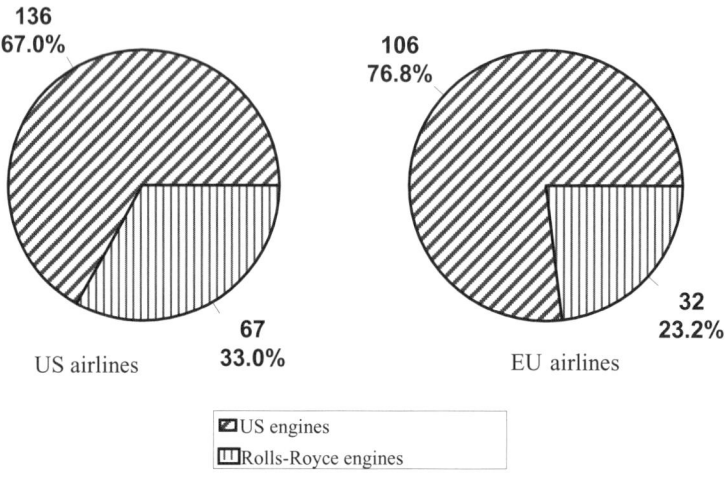

*Source:* Teal Group Corporation.

The myriad other aircraft systems are much tougher to quantify and seldom involve a customer choice within a single airframe. As Table 1 indicates, however, a look at systems contracts placed for the most recent Airbus and Boeing jetliners – the A380 and 787 – reveals very strong evidence of transatlantic trade. As a result of its acquisition of legacy businesses, BAE Systems, which owns 20% of Airbus, has substantial systems roles on most Boeing aircraft, including the 747.

Most systems contractors endeavor to obtain a diverse portfolio for their engines, landing gear, etc. Over-reliance on the prime contractors of either of the two jetliners is considered a bad strategy. In any event, contractors seek to leverage their systems development work over as broad a range of platforms as possible.

Therefore, when Airbus claims economic benefits for the US related to the contract work it places in companies located there or when Boeing makes similar claims for the EU, they are overlooking the fact that these benefits usually accrue to either side. For example, whether an airline buys a Boeing 737 or an Airbus A320 with a CFM56 engine, General Electric receives exactly the same economic benefits. In short, the estimated indirect jobs are fungible and mostly independent of trade.

*Table 1. Systems Contracts Placed for Airbus and Boeing Jetliners*

| US systems on the Airbus A380 | |
| --- | --- |
| Company | Systems |
| Goodrich | Multifunction probes, evacuation slide systems, ice detector, elevator actuators, lower level cargo mechanical system, cabin attendant/cockpit occupant seats |
| Hamilton Sundstrand (United Technologies) | Air generation system, ram air turbine |
| Honeywell | Electrical distribution-secondary, aircraft environment surveillance system, flight management system |
| Parker | Fuel measurement and management system |
| Rockwell Collins | Communications and navigation equipment, avionics ether switch |
| TRW | Cargo loading system, elevator actuators, control systems |
| EU systems on the Boeing 787 | |
| Company | Systems |
| Dassault Systemes | Product development software |
| Labinal (SNECMA) | Electrical wiring system |
| Messier-Bugatti (SNECMA) | Electrical brake system |
| Messier-Dowty (SNECMA) | Main and nose landing gear |
| Smiths Aerospace | Common core avionics system, actuation systems, power drive units |
| Techspace Aero | Has a 3% share in GenX engine (General Electric's 787 engine) |
| Thales | Integrated standby flight display |
| Volvo Flygmotor | Has a 6% share in GenX engine |

*Source:* Author's data.

## Airframe Contracts

Transatlantic contracting for airframe work is less active than for component (systems) contracting, for two main reasons. First, Airbus retains a relatively high percentage of airframe work in-house. Second, Asian aerostructure contractors enjoy higher levels of government support than US or EU contractors and are better able to participate as risk-sharing (cash-providing) partners.

There are notable exceptions to these limitations, however. The biggest EU transatlantic aero structures contractor is Finmeccanica's Alenia unit. The Italian company is taking an estimated 13% share in Boeing's 787 airframe. It also has major roles in the 717 and 767 programs.

France's Latecoere has achieved notable success as a specialty aero structures provider for both Boeing and Airbus. It recently won the contract to build passenger doors for Boeing's 787. Meanwhile, owing to the evolution of European industrial restructuring, Airbus parent EADS provides ailerons for Boeing's 777. For similar reasons, BAE Systems Aerostructures provides wing-fixed leading edges for the 777.

This success in transatlantic equipment trade is largely related to the ATCA. The agreement makes the mandatory transfer of commercial work illegal. Governments are barred from "attaching inducements of any kind to the sale or purchase of civil aircraft".[5] This stipulation frees jetliner contractors to make aircraft component decisions based on technology, quality and value.

## Joint Programs

Despite the open nature of transatlantic aerospace trade, a joint transatlantic jetliner industry does not now exist. Sadly, there is an increasing division between Boeing and Airbus and between their national political supporters in the US and the EU. Yet historically there have been notable transatlantic joint ventures and the engine industry provides a good model for the future.

Regarding aircraft, there is an interesting history behind the internationalization of passenger aircraft programs. Most notably, Fokker of the Netherlands granted a license to Fairchild for production of its F27 44-seat turboprop transport. Fairchild built over 200 F27s at its Maryland factory. Fairchild also signed an agreement with Saab covering production of its 33-seat Saab 340, but later reduced its role to major subcontractor.

More recently, before McDonnell Douglas merged with Boeing and exited the jetliner business, it considered a joint jetliner venture with Airbus. Specifically, the two companies discussed mating the fuselage of McDonnell Douglas's MD-11 with the larger wing of Airbus's A330. The resulting product, the AM 300, would have seated up to 400 persons and competed with Boeing's four engine 747 with the economics of a three-engine jetliner.

Further, in the mid 1990s, Boeing initiated discussions with Airbus member companies (but not Airbus itself) covering joint development of a new large transport (with 500 seats or above) and a supersonic jet transport (with about 250 seats). These discussions produced nothing substantive.

---

[5] Agreement on Trade in Civil Aircraft, op. cit.

Aside from the political and product divergence between Airbus and Boeing, the idea of jetliner joint ventures has not happened for another reason: it is not necessary for market access. Thanks to the ATCA, both sides can sell freely in the other company's territory, removing a key driver behind the creation of joint programs. Yet there are other drivers, including resource pooling, risk spreading and technology sharing.

Today, the engine industry offers two examples of transatlantic, co-prime business relationships. The two primary engines for single-aisle jetliners are built by such arrangements, including:

- **CFM International.** This is a joint venture between General Electric and France's SNECMA. The CFM56 engine powers all Boeing 737s and just over half of the Airbus A318/319/320/321 fleet. It uses core technology from General Electric's F101 engine, developed for the US Air Force B-1 bomber and SNECMA technology developed for France's Mirage fighters.

- **International Aero Engines (IAE).** This is a multinational program comprising Rolls-Royce (32.5%), Pratt & Whitney (32.5%), Japan Aero Engine Corporation (23%) and Germany's Motoren und Turbinen Union (12%). The V2500 engine powers just under half of the Airbus A319/320/321 fleet, as well as McDonnell Douglas's legacy MD-90 fleet.

These two engines represent a strong future trend, in terms of teaming arrangements and cross-border industrial alliances. To compete in new markets with new technology development, companies are increasingly looking to spread risk and share costs. The CFM56 program began because General Electric wanted to challenge the Pratt & Whitney JT8D, which enjoyed a dominant market position. The V2500 resulted because Pratt & Whitney needed a JT8D replacement and lacked the resources to go head-to-head with General Electric and SNECMA.

Again, this approach has not been adapted by airliner primes, although Boeing's 787 makes extensive use of Japanese industry participation (35% of the airframe). Further, if jetliner technology moves on to a new level of technological sophistication with supersonic aircraft, for example, the logical approach would be through a multinational consortium along CFM/IAE lines.

## Benefits

The benefits of transatlantic jetliner trade are impossible to quantify. Yet they are very real and broadly fall into five categories:

1. **Price reduction related to competitive jetliner offers**. Since the US and EU markets can only sustain one manufacturer, jetliner autarky would allow monopoly pricing. This would mean higher list prices, and no discounts (today, a 30% discount from the list price is more or less standard). Ultimately, it would cost the consumer more to fly as these higher capital costs would be passed from the manufacturer to the airline to the flying public.

2. **Qualitative improvements owing to competition**. Jetliner autarky would remove the impetus for technology development, new product launches and current product improvement. Boeing would have taken considerably longer to launch its 767 wide-body twinjet if it were not for Airbus's innovative A300, the world's first wide-body twinjet.

3. **Technology sharing through joint venture** (as described above).

4. **A 'best technology' approach to component selection**. The extension of free trade down to the component and subcomponent level ensures low prices, technical innovation and high quality at all levels of the component chain.

5. **Multiple market exposure**. Worldwide air transport markets do not rise and fall in tandem. For prime and subcontract manufacturers, it is much better to be exposed to as many markets as possible, allowing access to at least one healthy market when one or more of the others are in recession. This point is as equally true for new equipment sales as it is for aftermarket exposure (sales of spare parts, service work, etc.).

## Threats

The biggest threat to this international market is political pressure aimed at promoting selection of a particular manufacturer's aircraft. There have been no notable accusations by the EU of US political pressure seeking to induce US carriers to purchase Boeing jets. The US has hinted at EU pressure on European carriers to purchase Airbus planes, but has filed no particular complaints as far as core EU countries are concerned.

New problems could arise as the EU grows. The new EU states are more susceptible to political pressure, because of the importance of EU markets for their goods and their desire to be accepted as full EU members.

The EU has been accused by the US of taking advantage of this dynamic, most notably in the Czech Republic. According to the US Department of Commerce, in 2002 the European Commission admonished the Czech

Republic for eliminating a tariff differential that favored Airbus, thereby pressuring the Czech Republic to order Airbus aircraft.[6]

A related threat concerns the attachment of inducements to aircraft sales to the new EU states. Most of the older EU members have economies and societies that are basically too sophisticated to care about local work in exchange for jetliner purchases. For the most part, airlines are in private hands or will be soon. Deregulation in the EU has also given airlines independence from their home markets and they now serve many regions. Therefore, the individual governments have no real ability to demand these commercial offsets.

Again, however, EU enlargement could change this healthy situation. In 1992, Romania's airline Tarom ordered five 737s, followed by four more in 1999. In return, Boeing gave the country production tools and contracts for aircraft components. Greg Dole, Boeing's Director of International Trade Policy, remarked: "This [ATCA] was a very new agreement. I don't think the salespeople really were being asked or should have known this was illegal. Our contracts staff probably should have engaged [in] this more fully."[7]

Another danger concerns the political pressure routinely placed on foreign carriers (non-US or EU), even in ATCA signatory nations, to purchase Airbus or Boeing equipment. The US has been accused of using its strategic might to gain advantage over purchase decisions, primarily in such allied countries as Saudi Arabia, Taiwan and Japan.

The Taiwanese and Japanese cases provide two recent examples. In Taiwan, 16 senators and at least four representatives sent a letter asking that China Airlines re-consider an Airbus order and go with Boeing instead (China Airlines did indeed order some Boeing aircraft as a result).[8]

Airbus and the European Union have also accused the United States of using similar tactics in Japan, which has remained a loyal Boeing client for both military and commercial aerospace equipment. After the most recent purchase by All Nippon of Boeing 737s, a European Commission spokesperson suggested that their "reasons weren't entirely commercial".[9]

---

[6] US Department of Commerce, International Trade Administration, op. cit., p. 83.

[7] Quoted in the *Seattle Times*, June 1, 2004.

[8] See "US Lawmakers Push Taiwan to Cancel Airbus Deal, Hire Boeing", *Wall Street Journal*, September 12, 2002, p. A13.

[9] See "Commentary: Airbus's wings clipped in Japan deal", *Bloomberg News*, May 15, 2003.

Most recently, in May 2005 Airbus accused the US of exercising political pressure to secure an Air India order for Boeing 777s and 787s over competing Airbus planes. One claim was that India purchased the planes to offset US government criticism of a growing US-India trade gap.[10]

This alleged political pressure to buy a particular plane is matched by an unfortunate trend towards offering commercial incentives to purchase aircraft, which are clearly illegal under the ATCA. In 2004, Airbus implied that a prospective Indian Airlines order for its jets would result in $630 million worth of subcontract and other work given to Indian industry – a clear violation of the ATCA agreement.[11]

In effect, there is the risk of 'blowback' from all of these political maneuverings: if they become an accepted practice in jetliner sales outside the US and EU, they could become a standard part of doing business everywhere, even in the US and EU home markets.

At the very least, politicians in the US and EU might use resentment over lost sales owing to political interference in export markets to generate protectionist sentiment at home. Despite the current trade dispute over jetliner subsidies, at the time of writing neither side is currently using the WTO to stop government intervention in sales campaigns.[12]

Another issue overlooked in current trade disputes has to do with technology development funds for subcontract suppliers. While this is less immediately threatening than support for jetliner prime contractors, it effectively undermines the principal of free trade in subcontracts.

Both the US and EU have given extensive support to their national subcontractors, especially for engine manufacturers. Since 1988, the UK government has provided £949 million for the development of Rolls Royce's civil jet product line, of which only £314 million has been repaid.[13]

The effort to promote national engine champions is particularly pernicious, because it results in aircraft that are more heavily European or Amercian (by value). For example, in the late 1990s, both Airbus and Boeing launched new, long-range 300/400-seat derivative aircraft families with a single

---

[10] See "Lex: Protectionism", *Financial Times*, May 10, 2005 (retrieved from http://news.ft.com/cms/s/d059856a-c185-11d9-943f-00000e2511c8.html).

[11] See "Airbus to Place Orders in India if it Wins Bid, Standard Says", *Bloomberg News*, March 2, 2004.

[12] US Department of Commerce, International Trade Administration, op. cit., p. 142.

[13] US Trade Representative, *2005 National Trade Estimate Report on Foreign Trade Barriers*, Washington, D.C., March 30, 2005, pp. 213-215.

engine choice. Boeing's 777-200LR/300ER family offered only General Electric engines, while the competing Airbus A340-500/600 family offered only Rolls-Royce engines. These actions made the aircraft more 'vertical' in their national composition, one being heavily American and the other heavily European. Thankfully, since then, both sides have retreated from this trend, launching new aircraft with full, international engine alternatives.

For the most part, the support given by governments to systems contractors ultimately benefits both sides; improved subsystems technology and lower costs helps both Airbus and Boeing aircraft. Yet with the A380, there is an unfortunate precedent being set. France's 2005 government budget provides 330 million in A380 development money, not just for Airbus, but also for French equipment manufacturers developing subsystems for the A380.[14] In essence, the French government is skewing the balance of trade in jetliner subsystems away from US competitors and towards French ones.

The absence of meaningful foreign direct investment (FDI) in the aerospace sector compounds these risks to trade. EADS, the Airbus parent with an 80% share, is largely owned by major European stakeholders, including Daimler Chrysler, Lagardere, and the Governments of France and Spain. These large institutions own about 70% of EADS and the remainder largely comprises French and German financial institutions, while a few percent are employee-owned. Boeing, by contrast, is more widely floated, with no shareholder owning more than about 10% of the company, and most owning less than 1%, but most of these are based in the US.

In short, there is very little manufacturer-ownership money crossing borders in the jetliner industry. FDI increases and balances support for continued open borders and again, its absence in this sector should be a source of concern.

Last, there is the threat of creeping protectionism. While this industry has seen no suggestions of 'voluntary' quotas or other market protection measures, politicians are increasingly aware of jetliner imports and their relevance to trade. This is largely related to the politically heated battle over subsidies. Most notably, in May 2003, US Representative John Mica said he wanted airlines to provide plastic cards in seat pouches that inform passengers where their aircraft was made.[15] This is roughly analogous to the textile industry period when foreign labeling came into vogue.

---

[14] Ibid.

[15] See "Lawmaker wants airlines to say where planes were made", *Bloomberg News,* May 16, 2003.

The current US WTO trade complaint, firmly launched in May 2005, and the likely resulting EU counter-complaint will exacerbate all of these threats. Politicians in both the US and EU will probably use the dispute to further protectionist aims.

Equally dangerous is the prospect of a trade war resulting from any forceful WTO ruling. WTO enforcement provisions can be blunt instruments. A ruling might give one side the right to retaliate with barriers or other trade-distorting measures; any retaliation could set off a series of actions that unravel the tremendous progress made towards globalizing the commercial aerospace industry.

## Lessons

The ATCA provides a most compelling lesson for transatlantic trade from the commercial aerospace industry. While not a flawless treaty (there is disagreement about the wording in several clauses) it does apply a useful principle: private enterprise should be free to make business decisions without political interference. This principle has nearly universal applicability to many traded goods and services.

The application and enforcement of the ATCA is of course an ongoing issue, providing new lessons for transatlantic trade as the jetliner market evolves. It also provides an ongoing test for politicians: Will they be able to resist the short-term rewards of intervening in commercial jetliner trade or will they keep faith in a long-term institution that has served both sides admirably?

# 7. The Transatlantic Outlook for the Biopharmaceutical Sector

## Françoise Simon

The impact of the health care sector on the transatlantic economy is substantial and expected to grow in the coming decades due to several trends: aging populations, consumer demand for innovative medical care, and post-genomic advances toward personalized medicine leading to a portfolio shift toward effective but expensive biologics and targeted small molecules.

Within this sector, biotechnology and pharmaceuticals have effectively merged due to several factors: top biotechnology firms such as Amgen have matured and emerged as mid-cap biopharmaceuticals. Through acquisitions and internal research, pharma companies such as Johnson & Johnson, Lilly and Roche have become major biotechnology players. Innovation also depends on global alliance and equity networks linking small biotech firms and Big Biotech or Big Pharma.

Through the value chain from R&D to manufacturing and marketing, the industry has globalized. Multinationals have manufacturing sites on both sides of the Atlantic to rationalize their supply chains and to facilitate price negotiations with national agencies. For US and European biotechs, sales and marketing are often carried out through local partners, due to their limited resources outside of their home markets.

For these reasons, the appropriate measure of economic integration in this sector is investment rather than trade.

This chapter will first review health care expenditures, sector performance and economic impact in the US and Europe. It will then analyze integration drivers and barriers at the policy level, from Medicare reform and the focus on drug safety in the US to national reimbursement policies and parallel trade in Europe. Analysis will then shift to the industry and in particular to innovation networks and consolidation across the Atlantic.

## International Health Care Spending

US health care spending per capita continues to exceed that of other OECD countries by huge margins and with disappointing outcomes. Expenditures reached $1.7 trillion in 2003 (15.3% of gross domestic product), i.e. $5,670 per person. Prescription drugs accounted for $179 million, or 11% of health spending. Their 2003 growth of 10.7% marked a fourth consecutive year of decline – due to increased generic penetration and co-payments shifting costs to consumers.[1]

Despite this slowing growth, US expenditures tower over those of major European countries. An OECD comparative study listed British spending per capita at less than 41% that of the US. Even Germany reached only 57% of the American spending level, on a purchasing power parity basis (Table 1). The gap is projected to increase; the Center for Medicare and Medicaid Services (CMS) forecasts that the US will spend $3.4 trillion on health by 2013, or 18.4% of GDP.

*Table 1. Health Spending in OECD Countries*

| Country | Total spending/capita PPP | Average annual growth 1991-2001 (%) | Health spending as % of GDP |
|---------|---------------------------|-------------------------------------|-----------------------------|
| US | $4,887 | 3.1 | 13.9 |
| Germany | $2,808 | 2.4 | 10.7 |
| France | $2,561 | 2.4 | 9.5 |
| Italy | $2,212 | 1.5 | 8.4 |
| UK | $1,992 | 4.1 | 7.6 |
| Spain | $1,600 | 3.2 | 7.5 |
| Japan | $2,131 | 3.9 | 8 |

*Source:* Organization for Economic Cooperation & Development, 2002 (data for 2001); growth rates calculated from national currencies (not purchasing power parities).

This high US spending level does not translate into better outcomes on most measures of human development. For instance, Europe performs better than the US on life expectancy and neonatal mortality. In 2000, Europe averaged 75.6 years for men and 81.7 for women, versus, respectively, 74.1 years and 79.5 years in the US.[2]

This may be attributed partly to factors such as the lack of US universal insurance, managed care restrictions on preventive health care and inefficiencies in reimbursement systems.

---

[1] Cynthia Smith et al., "Health Spending Growth Slows in 2003", *Health Affairs,* 24, 1, Jan/Feb 2005, pp. 185-186.

[2] *European Competitiveness Report 2004*, European Commission staff working document, SEC (2004) 1397, pp. 129-130.

## Sector Performance

Higher expenditures and drug prices turned the US into a global growth engine over past decades, but the sector is now at an inflection point throughout major markets.

Biopharmaceutical sales reached $550 billion worldwide in 2004 (including $518 billion in major markets audited by IMS Health), but growth slowed markedly, at 7% versus 10% compound annual rate of the preceding five years. There was also a greater convergence between the US and major European markets, with 8% growth in the US and 6% in the European Union.[3] Nevertheless, the US still accounts for 46% of the world market (versus less than 30% for EU25), and thus remains a major investment magnet for European companies (see Table 2).

*Table 2. Pharmaceutical Sales by Region*

| | 2004 Global sales | | % Growth (constant $) | |
|---|---|---|---|---|
| World Audited Market | $ Billion | % Global sales | 2004 | CAGR 99-03 |
| North America | 248 | 47.8 | 7.8 | 13.7 |
| European Union | 144 | 27.8 | 5.7 | 8.8 |
| Rest of Europe | 9 | 1.8 | 12.4 | 10.9 |
| Japan | 58 | 11.1 | 1.5 | 3.3 |
| Asia/Africa/Australia | 40 | 7.7 | 13.0 | 10.3 |
| Latin America | 19 | 3.8 | 12.4 | 1.5 |
| Total IMS Audited | $518 | 100.0% | 7.1% | 10.0% |

*Note:* Excludes unaudited markets and Estonia, Lithuania, Belarus, Bulgaria, Dominican Republic, Russia and Ukraine

*Source:* IMS Health MIDAS, MAT December 2004.

While global growth will continue to be driven by aging populations (not only in the OECD but also in emerging markets such as China), a flow of

---

[3] *Intelligence.360: Global Pharmaceutical Perspectives*, IMS Health, 2004, pp. 8-10.

innovative therapies and consumer demand for high-tech care, there are some moderating factors: a universal focus on cost containment, more cautious regulators and the increased role of US federal and state agencies in drug purchasing. For those reasons, the global market is projected to grow at only 6-9% through 2008.

Growth in the North American market is likely to remain in the single digits through 2008. In addition to cost containment, negative pressure on growth will come from major patent expirations. From 2006 to 2008, products that generated revenues of about $70 billion in 2004 will lose patents. These include Merck's Zocor (simvastatin), with over $5 billion in sales, and Pfizer's Norvasc (amlodipine), which recorded $4.5 billion in sales. In contrast to Big Pharma's slowdown, two bright growth areas are the biotechnology and generics subsectors – the former driven by innovation and the latter by cost containment.

In 2004, biotech drugs generated over $44 billion in worldwide sales, with overall growth of 20%. Biologics accounted for 27% of research pipelines.

Among mid-size biotechs, Gilead Sciences was profitable in 2004, reaching over $1 billion in revenues and growing by nearly 43%, thanks to its HIV/hepatitis product line. Even a mature biotech such as Amgen grew by 26% and reached nearly $11 billion in global sales.

Both US and European pharma companies show an increasing reliance on biotech products. Roche led the industry, as biologics generated over 45% of its 2004 sales and nearly 70% of its net present value. Next came Johnson & Johnson and Lilly, with approximately 25% of their sales from biologics.[4]

The generic side grew equally fast. Canada's Apotex reached over $1 billion in global sales, with growth of 42% in 2004, and in the US, Par and Ivax grew by more than 30%.[5] In Europe, Novartis expanded its Sandoz division into the largest generic company with the $7 billion acquisition of Germany's Hexal and its US subsidiary, Eon Labs. This brought Sandoz's 2004 combined proforma sales to $5 billion, with a portfolio of more than 600 active ingredients.[6] Novartis also took the lead in biosimilar medicines with the 2004 approval in Australia of its generic human growth hormone, Omnitrope.

While Europe shares negative trends with the US, such as cost containment, major national markets differ sharply in their strategies and growth rates (see Table 3).

---

[4] Lehman Brothers, *Generic Biologics*, April 12, 2005, pp. 3-5.

[5] *Global Strategic Management Review*, IMS Health, May 10, 2005, p. 16.

[6] "Largest Generic Company Created", *Med Ad News*, May 2005, p. 20.

*Table 3. Key Market Trends in US and European Pharmaceutical Industries*

| | Sales ($ billion, 2004) | Growth 2003-04 (%) | Key Trends |
|---|---|---|---|
| Germany | 29.4 | 1.6 | New reference prices for patented drugs<br>Manufacturer discounts of 16% on prescription drugs |
| France | 28.5 | 7.2 | New reference prices for large classes (statins)<br>Delisting of drugs with low medical benefit |
| UK | 20.0 | 8.1 | 7% price cut (Pharmaceutical Price Regulation scheme)<br>Focus on cost effectiveness by National Institute of Clinical Excellence (NICE) |
| Italy | 18.9 | 4.7 | 6.8% price cut by Italian National Medicines Agency<br>60% clawback of manufacturer overspending |
| Spain | 13.9 | 8.5 | Price cuts of 4%, reduction in wholesaler & pharmacist margins |
| US | 236.0 | 7.7 | Cost containment (Medicare reform, generic growth)<br>Focus on safety/consumer promotion |

*Source: Intelligence.360/Global Pharmaceutical Perspectives*, IMS Health, 2004.

The German market remains the largest at $29 billion in 2004 sales but with an anemic growth of 1.6%, due to an expansion of reference pricing to patented drugs. For instance, in the statin class of cholesterol reducers, Germany plans to reduce reimbursement for Pfizer's Lipitor (atorvastatin) to the level of generic simvastatin.

France closely follows Germany at $28.5 billion in sales, but grew by over 7% in 2004. This gap may moderate with the expansion of reference prices to large classes such as statins, a delisting of drugs with low medical benefit and an effort to curb over-prescribing.

The United Kingdom grew by over 8% to $20 billion in sales, but this was partly due to the strong growth of generics (25%), boosted by the patent expiry of major drugs such as pravastatin. A price reduction policy continues with 7% cuts under the Pharmaceutical Price Regulation Scheme (PPRS) in 2005.[7] The UK also leads Europe in its focus on pharmacoeconomic data to demonstrate the cost effectiveness of new drugs, as recommended by the National Institute of Clinical Excellence.

## Economic Impact of the Biopharmaceutical Sector

According to a study by the Milken Institute, biopharmaceuticals employed 406,700 people in 2003 in the US (including over 198,000 in biotechnology). It was among the most productive sectors with real output per worker of $157,300. The industry was directly responsible for nearly $64 billion in real output and a total of almost $173 billion when the economic impact across other sectors was incorporated. The sector nearly doubled in size over the past two decades and accounted for over 8% of all industrial R&D, despite representing only 0.3% of total non-farm employment.

The Milken Institute econometric model projects that employment in the biopharma sector will grow to nearly 540,000 people in the next decade. If multiplier dynamics are fully applied, the sector will have a total impact of 3.6 million jobs by 2014. Multipliers include the *indirect impact* (jobs, wages or output generated by all supplier industries) and the *induced impact* (higher employment and wages in supplier industries leading to more purchases of goods and services, which in turn generate more income to spend in the local economy).

With these multipliers factored in, the US biopharmaceutical sector accounted for 2.7 million jobs, or over 2% of non-farm employment in 2003. For every job in the sector, an additional 5.7 jobs were created elsewhere. By contrast, the retail and textile sectors generated, respectively, only 0.9 and 2.9 jobs.

On a regional level, the industry is highly clustered on the two coasts, with California directly accounting for nearly 70,000 jobs and key northeast states (Massachusetts, New Jersey, New York and Pennsylvania) directly generating nearly 140,000 jobs.[8]

A European Commission report on competitiveness[9] showed labor input (either measured by numbers employed or total hours worked) growing faster in the US than in the EU15. For both the US and the European Union,

---

[7] *Intelligence.360*, IMS, pp. 16-19.

[8] R. De Vol et al., *Biopharmaceutical Industry Contributions to State and US Economies,* Milken Institute, Santa Monica, CA, October 2004 (http://www.milkeninstitute.org/pdf/biopharma_report.pdf), pp. 1-2, 5-6.

[9] *European Competitiveness Report 2004*, op. cit., pp. 138-143.

growth in hours worked has been higher in the health sector than in the overall economy, but the latter Europe shows significant variance: Germany and the Netherlands have larger increases in labor input than France or the UK. Related factors are varying shortages of health professionals (nurses in particular) and labor skill levels.

Capital input, specifically equipment capital, also shows higher growth rates in the US than in most EU countries. This gap can be partly attributed to a greater US focus on information technology, and also to a reduction in EU hospital investment, as technology has reduced hospitalizations and length of stay, and led to a decrease in hospital beds across Europe.

The same discrepancy is found in the biopharmaceutical sector. Another study conducted in 2000 for the European Commission found Europe less competitive than the US in this respect, largely as a consequence of the industry's performance in Germany and Italy, by contrast with relatively better results in the UK, Ireland, Sweden and Denmark.[10] Germany continued to under perform vis-à-vis other markets, registering the lowest European growth in 2004, due to aggressive cost-containment policies ranging from expanded reference pricing to manufacturer discounts.

## Integration Drivers and Barriers

Since the biopharmaceutical sector has globalized through the entire value chain, from research to marketing, transatlantic integration can be tracked through investment rather than trade.

The key cross-regional investment driver is clearly the need to recover R&D costs on a worldwide basis. Estimates of drug costs from molecule to market, taking into account high attrition rates, vary from $802 million (Tufts Center for Study of Drug Development) to over $1 billion (Lehman Brothers).[11]

A major draw for European companies is also the sheer size of the US market (46% of world sales by value) and its relatively 'free market' pricing system – although restrictions are being rapidly applied by private and public payers.

First and foremost, the major appeal of the US market for European firms is its dominance in biotechnology innovation. This has caused a much-

---

[10] A. Gambardella, L. Orsenigo and F. Pammoli, "Global Competitiveness in Pharmaceuticals. A European Perspective", Report for the Directorate General Enterprise of the European Commission, 2000.

[11] Tufts Center for the Study of Drug Development, Tufts University, presentation by Kenneth Kaitin (http://csdd.tufts.edu) and Lehman Brothers, op. cit.

lamented 'brain drain' for several decades, and is now reinforced by the relocation of major research operations from Europe to the US. For instance, Novartis moved much of its research to Cambridge, Massachusetts in order to be at the core of the Boston area biotech cluster.

In coming years, however, the US market will be constrained on several levels, ranging from sharper regulator scrutiny to the increased role of public agencies in drug purchasing, as well as the high growth of generics, favored by legislators as well as public and private payers.

Despite the slower growth of the European market, it remains indispensable for US companies to be implanted there because of several factors: rising consumer demand due to aging populations and expectations of high-tech medicines, maturing of bioscience clusters in the UK, Germany and Scandinavia, and centralization of the drug approval process.

In addition, manufacturing in Europe has several benefits, including the rationalization of supply chains. For instance, Wyeth built in Ireland a major biomanufacturing plant to expand its capacity in this area. Local production also facilitates job creation. On the other hand, Europe still suffers from substantial barriers to integration, from national reimbursement policies that often delay drug launches to parallel trade within the Union and extensive cost containment policies (see Table 4).

*Table 4. Integration Barriers and Drivers*

|  | Drivers | Barriers |
|---|---|---|
| United States | Need to recover R&D costs in global markets<br><br>Investment attractiveness of US market<br><br>Bioscience innovation clusters<br><br>EU biopharma need for US partners | Focus on safety/regulator scrutiny<br><br>Increased influence of federal and state agencies on price<br><br>High growth of generics in US/ patent disputes lost by originator firms<br><br>Legal restrictions on stem cell research/other bioethics issues |
| Europe | Consumer demand for new medications, population aging<br><br>Centralization of drug approval process<br><br>Emerging bioscience clusters<br><br>Benefits of EU manufacturing sites (supply chain rationali- zation, price setting | National reimbursement policies<br><br>Parallel trade within EU<br><br>Cost containment (expanded reference pricing, pro-generic policies)<br><br>Pharmacoeconomic requirements |

## US Regulation: From Medicare to Bioethics

The 2003 Medicare Prescription Drug and Modernization Act (MMA) was initially announced at a $400 billion price tag from 2006 to 2016, but this cost has since been sharply revised upward and many of its provisions remain controversial. The provision of outpatient drug benefits for the 40 million Medicare beneficiaries will increase the federal government's share of the national drug bill to more than 49% by 2014. This will increase price pressure from a number of factors: greater transparency through public dissemination of prices by the CMS, preferred drug lists favoring generics and tiered formularies.[12]

Although drug trans-shipment from Canada to the US has been prominent in press headlines, it has not had a major impact on the market thus far. Importation by states and individuals remains low, and will be further constrained by Canada's limited capacity and planned Canadian policies to block exports to the US by online pharmacies.

The US Department of Health and Human Services (HHS) Task Force on Drug Importation issued a final report in December 2004 that opposed any broad opening of US borders for prescription drugs, and ruled out individual importing due to an expected $3 billion cost to regulate product inflow. The report advised Congress to legalize importation only for certain high-volume, high-cost drugs, since any system to track products and to sample imports by the Food and Drug Administration (FDA) would likely require hundreds of millions of dollars to set up and maintain.[13]

Far more worrying for US and European companies is the intensified focus on drug safety, following the 2004 recall by Merck of its arthritis drug Vioxx (rofecoxib) and added warnings for other drugs in the COX-2 inhibitor class, such as Pfizer's Celebrex (celecoxib), due to cardiovascular side effects revealed by large clinical trials. This had direct consequences for European manufacturers: Novartis temporarily withdrew its application to market its anti-arthritic Prexige in the European Union and postponed its application in the US.

Following several high-profile recalls, such as that of Bayer's statin Baycol, this event represents a turning point in the way regulators, health professionals and patients view safety issues in major markets.

---

[12] CMS Report, 2005 (http://www.healthaffairs.org), cited by Jill Wechsler, "Creeping Single-Payerism?", *Pharmaceutical Executive*, March 2005, pp. 43-44.

[13] Jill Wechsler, "No Surprises", *Pharmaceutical Executive*, February 2005, p. 42.

The US Congress and consumer groups have called for stricter approval standards, greater independence for the FDA from the pharmaceutical industry and tighter controls on direct-to-consumer advertising (DTC); the latter is seen as responsible for artificially inflating demand for the COX-2 class, which might have been restricted to a more targeted patient population, instead of the more than 20 million people who have used these therapies.

The Medicare bill authorized the HHS Agency for Healthcare Research and Quality (AHRQ) to support more studies on the comparative effectiveness of medical interventions, including prescription drugs for the top 10 conditions affecting the elderly, from heart disease to arthritis, depression, cancer and asthma. The 2005 budget includes $15 million for this initiative.

Probable policy changes in the post-Vioxx era include:

- A 'conditional approval' system requiring regular assessment of safety and efficacy data to allow continued marketing of a drug.

- Expanded post-approval studies to be required by the FDA.

- Intensified pharmacological vigilance; adverse event reporting would move from voluntary to mandatory; the Medicare drug benefit could provide essential prescribing and utilization data.

- Curb on DTC advertising, especially for products that raise safety concerns; the FDA's Division of Drug Marketing Advertising and Communications (DDMAC) issued 12 warning letters in 2004 (versus 4 to 5 in previous years) to marketers about exaggerated benefits, minimized risks and unsupported claims in drug advertising. DDMAC plans a year-long consumer survey to assess understanding of risks and benefits; previous studies showed that consumers seldom read clinical summaries in ads and usually do not understand the ones they read.[14]

If these steps are partly or wholly implemented, they will have direct financial consequences for both US and European manufacturers: Late-stage clinical studies already account for most of the $800 million to $1 billion R&D costs; post-approval studies would greatly increase that cost. In addition, added regulator scrutiny will lead to approval delays. The demand for greater global transparency of clinical trials will also strengthen the case for a single global regulatory dossier.

---

[14] Jill Wechsler, "Side Effects", *Pharmaceutical Executive,* February 2005, pp. 40-41, and "FDA on DTC: Get Serious", *Pharmaceutical Executive*, March 2005, p. 22.

In addition to these marketing constraints, the US market is losing attractiveness for local R&D by European companies, due to its restrictions on stem cell research and other bioethical concerns. In 2001, federally-funded embryonic stem cell research was limited to cell lines already in existence. Although 78 were then identified, only 19 are actually available for study. To counter a 'brain-drain' threat and related loss of competitiveness, California approved in late 2004 state funding of $3 billion for stem cell research, and other states such as New Jersey followed suit. Universities including Harvard, Stanford and the Massachusetts Institute of Technology have also allocated private funds in this area.[15] Given the magnitude of the National Institutes of Health (NIH) budget (over $28 billion), these steps may not be sufficient to prevent some exodus of stem cell research to less restrictive countries such as Singapore.

Last but not least, a policy area that will severely affect both US and European manufacturers relates to biosimilar products, or generic biologics. American and European authorities have converged in their postponement of market authorization. The European Medicines Agency (EMA) guidelines on biosimilars are still a work in progress, and the FDA's draft scientific guidance is expected in 2006. Generic biologics are currently sold in countries such as India, and the door to OECD markets was opened in 2004 with Australia's approval of the Novartis human growth hormone, Omnitrope.

Biosimilar approval would have a massive impact on Big Biotech and several Big Pharma firms, since most first-generation biologics are already off-patent, including epoetin alfa (Amgen's Epogen and Johnson & Johnson's Procrit) and most interferons.

The industry's stance is that bioequivalence between two biologics cannot be proven, citing cases such as that of Johnson & Johnson's Eprex (epoetin alfa). A difference in one manufacturing step between the US and Europe led to adverse reactions and to the withdrawal of one formulation from the EU. In this context, it is unlikely that the FDA will apply a single regulation to all follow-on biologics. A roadmap including clinical trial hurdles may be issued for a subset of less complex, lower-risk biologics such as insulin and human growth hormone. These were approved under the Food Drug and Cosmetics Act (FDCA), which contains a statute 505(b)(2) allowing the use of clinical data to establish comparability to the innovator product. By contrast, most biologics are approved under the Public Health Service Act (PHSA), which does not include this provision.

---

[15] Nicole Gray, "Unleashing the Promise", *Pharmaceutical Executive,* April 2005, pp. 90-91.

As biogenerics emerge in future years, they are unlikely to disrupt industry economics to the extent that small molecule generics have done. Due to the high cost of biomanufacturing, biosimilar discounts may range from 30-50% of the originator price – whereas standard generics can reach an 80% discount range.[16]

## EU Regulation: From Pricing to Parallel Trade

The strongest barrier to transatlantic integration remains the fragmented national reimbursement systems in the European Union. To address record healthcare budget deficits, European governments are implementing aggressive cost containment measures, which are projected to limit compound annual growth in the top five markets to 4-7% in the coming years.

In addition, country-by-country reimbursement negotiations significantly slow product launches. Europe is therefore less attractive than the US both on price levels and speed to market.

Cost-containment measures are converging across top markets, from manufacturer discounts and price cuts (Germany, UK, Italy) to reference pricing and delisting of low-benefit prescription medicines or OTC drugs (Germany, France). There is no relief from the new EU members: although they show higher growth rates, they are enthusiastically adopting the same cost-containment strategies. Poland adopted the German reference price scheme and volume restrictions similar to those in France, and Hungary uses the French and Spanish methods of price negotiations and international price referencing.

Wide price differentials remain across Europe. The spread around the average European price ranged from -20% to +20% in the top five markets, and was much higher in the rest of Europe. There is also little price consistency between the US and Europe. Among 2003 launches, the average European price was 29% lower than the American level for Abbott's rheumatoid arthritis drug Humira, and reached new depths for lifestyle and follower drugs: 55% to 65% less for Bayer's Levitra and Lilly's Cialis (erectile dysfunction) and 79% less for Crestor (follower statin by AstraZeneca).

On the bright side, first-in-class products and biologics are generally able to command narrower global price ranges. For example, Lilly's Forteo (recombinant parathyroid hormone for the treatment of osteoporosis) was

---

[16] Lehman Brothers, op. cit., pp. 6-11.

launched at an average European price only 3% lower than its American level.

In addition to price pressures, reimbursement negotiations delay market access in Europe. On average, new products reach only about 20% of EU15 markets six months post-launch. Here again, breakthrough products tend to diffuse faster: Lilly's Forteo reached more than 40% of the EU-15 after six months on the European market. This gap may narrow, however, as formulary listings and co-pay tier restrictions increasingly slow down diffusion in the US market.[17]

Parallel trade accounting for about 5% of the European market, at a cost of over €1 billion to originators, represents another investment barrier. Authorized by the EU principle of free movement of goods and services, and mandated by the German government as a cost containment measure, parallel trade has slowed down recently, partly because of pharma companies' efforts to manage their supply chains more effectively. This was supported by a court ruling that GlaxoSmithKline did not break European law by limiting sales to Greek wholesalers suspected of parallel trade. Further pressure will come from patent expirations in large drug classes, leading to generics across Europe.

A study carried out by the London School of Economics in six product categories (ACE I and II blockers, anti-psychotics, proton pump inhibitors, statins and selective serotonin reuptake inhibitors) from 1997 to 2002 found only modest savings from parallel trade for health insurers, at less than €50 million (or €100 million with manufacturer discounts). Due to cost-sharing structures in the UK, Germany, the Netherlands and Sweden, financial benefits to patients amounted to zero, and were marginal in Denmark and Norway.[18]

## Innovation: From National Policies to Global Networks

Despite cross-regional investment barriers, biopharmaceutical companies are sourcing innovation globally and have active transatlantic collaborations. At the public policy level, Europe lags behind the United States, and this threatens the maturation of innovation clusters in the region.

The industry faces an innovation problem globally. FDA drug approvals declined in 1999-2002, and only slightly rose in the last two years, despite

---

[17] *Pricing and Reimbursement Review*, IMS Health, 2003, pp. 7, 11, 18-21.

[18] Pavos Kanavos, "Pharmaceutical Parallel Trade in the European Union: Impact on Stakeholders", *Progressions/Global Pharmaceutical Report,* Ernst & Young, 2004, pp. 21-22.

the fact that the industry spent almost $50 billion on R&D in 2004 (see Figure 1).

*Figure 1. New Drug Approvals*

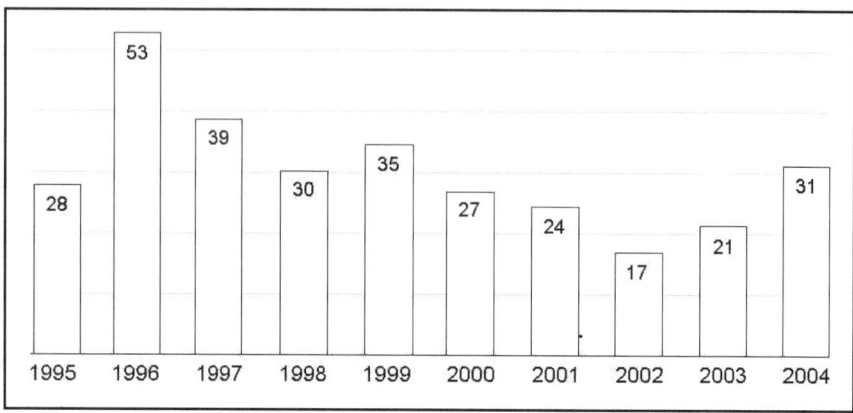

*Source*: US Food and Drug Administration, 2004.

Contributing factors include the higher risk and complexity of post-genomic science, dealing with over 5,000 biological targets rather than the 500 addressed by traditional small molecules. The question 'is bigger better?' may also apply to biology research. With an annual research budget of $7 billion, Pfizer may have reached the limit of manageable innovation, and GlaxoSmithKline addressed this problem by splitting its own research into 6 semi-independent units. Big Biotech, like Big Pharma, increasingly depends on outside innovation. Amgen bought Immunex in 2001 for $16 billion to access high-potential products such as its rheumatoid arthritis drug Enbrel (etanercept), and it acquired Tularik in 2004 for $1.3 billion partly for its small-molecule research. These acquisitions are complemented by hundreds of alliances.

Leading players are therefore highly dependent on innovation from clusters of small biotechs, universities and major health centers. In the commercialization of biotechnology, Europe can claim 30% of global sales, but half comes from Roche's shareholding in Genentech. Blockbuster drugs of European origin accounted for 42% of the total by 2004, but the world share of revenues for European companies declined from 30% in 1994 to 24% ten years later.[19]

---

[19] *Intelligence.360*, op. cit., p. 79.

This is partly related to the huge transatlantic imbalance in research support. In the US, NIH has a 2004 budget of nearly $28 billion. Through a joint program with the Small Business Administration, it encourages R&D for small firms with Small Business Innovation Research grants. This budget was increased by 10% in 2003-04.

Across industry sectors, there is a significant gap between the US and Europe in both public and private financing. Some help may come from national initiatives such as the 2003 French incentives for Young Innovative Enterprises, exempting them for up to eight years from most taxes and, social contributions. The UK also announced a ten-year 'Strategy for Science.'

At the European level, a new goal to increase Europe's R&D investment to 3% of GDP was set in Barcelona in 2002, but governments have since been keener to contain costs than to reverse the damage caused by long-term disinvestments. While European businesses increased R&D spending by over 50% in 1995-2001, their US counterparts raised it by 130%. Accession of the new member states will increase the EU's scientific stock, but their commercialization experience and venture capital are both minimal.[20]

An EU-wide harmonization of capital market rules would be a crucial step to a true single capital and stock market in Europe. The post-2000 retrenchment of risk capital and the arrival of many new companies with the same financing need (due to the success of programs such as Germany's Bio Regio in the 1990s) have combined to threaten start-ups in key markets.

In 2003 the European Investment Bank committed half a billion euros for the European Investment Fund to invest in high technology, and the European Commission's 6th Framework Program for Research allocated over €810 million to the life sciences and food sectors; about 10% of the budget will go to small and medium-sized enterprises (SMEs). In the US, public funding is strongly reinforced by private finance. After lean years in 2001-03, US biotech fundraising rebounded in 2004 with nearly $20 billion in financing and another $11 billion from partnering. Both levels dwarfed European biotech funding.[21]

Among pillars of innovation, Europe ranks well on labor skills, scientific education and academic medical centers, but it still lags on capital markets, venture capital and reimbursement policies (see Table 5).

---

[20] *Refocus: The European Perspective*, Ernst & Young, 2004, pp. 14, 22, 48-52.

[21] *Life Sciences and Biotechnology – A Strategy for Europe*, Second progress report for the European Commission; SEC (2004) 438, pp. 8-12.

*Table 5. Pillars of Innovation*

| Reimburse-ment /access | Intellectual property | Regulatory environment | Gov't funding for R&D | Business context | Human resources |
|---|---|---|---|---|---|
| Market prices<br><br>Technology assessment<br><br>Parallel imports | Length of market exclusivity<br><br>Strength of patent enforcement<br><br>Global IP standards | Registration and filing fees<br><br>Transparency<br><br>Global/ regional harmonization | Technology transfer<br><br>Gov't grants<br><br>Number of academic medical centers | R&D tax credits<br><br>Corporate taxes<br><br>Capital markets | Highly skilled workers<br><br>Risk-taking culture<br><br>Incentives for higher education |

*Source:* Ernst & Young, *Progressions*, Global Pharmaceutical Report, 2004.

## Industry Consolidation: From M&As to Alliances

Despite discrepancies in public policy, the industry's need for global innovation and marketing has led to significant cross-border integration. Of the top ten Big Pharma companies by global sales, half are European, and some US firms grew by merging with European companies (Pfizer and Pharmacia). Intra-European consolidation is also growing; while the Sanofi/Aventis $66 billion merger was the result of overt government intervention, Novartis (Ciba-Geigy and Sandoz) and Astra-Zeneca merged because of market forces such as the need for global scale (see Table 6).

*Table 6. Top 10 Corporations by Global Pharma Sales*

|  | 2004 Global sales | | % Growth (constant $) | |
|---|---|---|---|---|
|  | $ billion | Global sales % | 2004 | CAGR 99-03 |
| Pfizer | 50.9 | 9.8 | 4.9 | 12.3 |
| GlaxoSmithKline | 32.7 | 6.3 | 1.9 | 9.4 |
| Sanofi-Aventis | 27.1 | 5.2 | 9.1 | 12.7 |
| Johnson & Johnson | 24.6 | 4.7 | 8.0 | 16.7 |
| Merck & Co. | 23.9 | 4.6 | 3.5 | 12.4 |
| Novartis | 22.7 | 4.4 | 7.5 | 11.3 |
| AstraZeneca | 21.6 | 4.2 | 9.3 | 8.1 |
| Roche | 17.7 | 3.4 | 10.7 | 8.1 |
| Bristol-Myers Squibb | 15.5 | 3.0 | -3.2 | 4.6 |
| Wyeth | 14.2 | 2.7 | 9.8 | 11.9 |
| Total Top 10 Corporations | $ 250.9 | 48.4% | 5.8% | 10.9% |

*Source:* IMS Health, MAT, December 2004.

Big Biotech is dominated by US companies, but Europe's Serono, Shire and Elan are in the top tier. A new trend is the transformation of mid-size European pharma companies into biotechs, as was shown by UCB's acquisition of Celltech for $2.7 billion.

Consolidation will continue for both pharma companies and biotechs. As Big Pharma's largest company, Pfizer still holds less than 10% of the world market, and both large and mid-size pharma companies will continue to merge to maintain growth rates, access products or gain critical mass.

The sheer number of biotechs dictates further consolidation. There are nearly 1,500 companies in the US, of which only about 300 are publicly held, and a handful have profits from marketed products. Europe counts over 1,800 companies, of which only about 100 are public. Germany alone has nearly 350 firms, of which fewer than 15 are public – and most have financing needs that are not met by local venture capital.[22]

While there is little cross-national partnering in Europe, global collaborations sharply increased in 2004, to over 500 alliances (Figure 2).

*Figure 2. New Biotech-Pharma Collaborations*

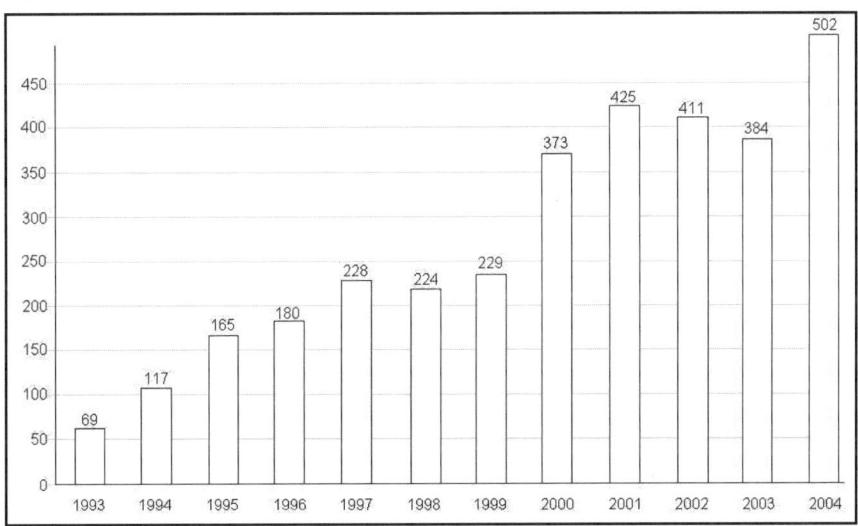

*Source:* BioWorld Financial Watch, American Health Consultants, BioCentury.

---

[22] Burrill and Company, presentation of the Burrill 2005 Biotech Report, San Francisco, May 9, 2005.

A significant trend is the rise of biotech/biotech partnerships in a field that was historically dominated by the Big Pharma/biotech satellites model.

This is partly due to Big Biotech's increasing need to insource innovation, and to the perception by small biotechs that they may have a better cultural fit with other biotechs than with Big Pharma.

Due to the global nature of biopharmaceutical innovation, these networking strategies will continue to grow both between and within regions.

## Conclusion

As bioscience emerges as the innovation driver across many sectors ranging from health care to energy, food and biodefense, the industry's public policies and private investment patterns will be a bellwether for high technology in general.

A general conclusion from this analysis is that public policies lag behind the private sector in spurring transatlantic integration. Biopharmaceutical companies have globalized their value chain from research to marketing, have formed global innovation networks and are taking their products to market through ever-increasing partnerships.

Public policies on both sides of the Atlantic need to be more proactive and harmonized, in areas ranging from research funding to pricing and reimbursement, in order to provide appropriate support for this vibrant sector.

# 8. The Transatlantic Automotive Sector

## Garel Rhys

North America and Western Europe were the original centers of automotive production and remained dominant until the Japanese industry emerged as an international force in the 1960s, but particularly in the 1970s. As a result, links between these two world regions were established early in the development of the automotive sector.

## Background

Even before 1920, the size of the US market was such that there were opportunities to make vehicles in high volumes and to reap economies of scale that were out of the reach of the fragmented national European industries. As a result, US car prices were on average 50% lower than those in Europe before 1920. Thus, there was a considerable flow of vehicles from North America to Europe with very few going in the reverse direction. In addition, there were the beginnings of considerable investment in vehicle-making plants by the likes of Ford (in the UK in 1911) and others, but this really took off in the inter-war period. These investments were aimed at circumventing the massive increase in tariff barriers (see Table 1) erected by European countries to protect their auto industries from US competition and to serve what was a growing local market.

*Table 1. Import Duties on Passenger Cars (%)*

|      | US        | France  | Germany | Italy   | UK      |
|------|-----------|---------|---------|---------|---------|
| 1913 | 45        | 9-14    | 3       | 4-6     | 0       |
| 1924 | 25-50     | 45-180  | 13      | 6-11    | 33.3    |
| 1937 | 10        | 47-74   | 40      | 101-111 | 33.3    |
| 1950 | 10        | 35      | 35      | 35      | 33.3    |
| 1960 | 8.5       | 35      | 35      | 35      | 33.3    |
| 1973 | 3         | 0/10.9  | 0/10.9  | 0/10.9  | 0/10.9  |
| 1983 | 2.8       | 0/10.5  | 0/10.5  | 0/10.5  | 0/10.5  |
| 2004 | 0/2.5/10  | 0/10    | 0/10    | 0/10    | 0/10    |

*Sources*: Alan Altshuter et al., *The Future of the Automobile*, Society of Motor Manufacturers and Traders (SMMT).

The flow of trade in vehicles output from the pre-1920 period was limited until the years following World War II, and then it was mainly from Europe to North America. The relatively open and prosperous North American market was a huge attraction to companies and governments in Europe wishing to earn foreign exchange to finance essential imports. Tariff protection in Europe remained enormous, compared with the US, from 1945-1970. It took the various GATT rounds ('Dillon', but particularly 'Kennedy') to reduce European tariffs significantly, but even today they are much higher than US tariffs on passenger cars (see Table 1).

In addition to tariff protection, diverging car designs in the US and Europe in the 1930s meant that demand for US cars in post-war Europe was limited. In effect, they were too large for the European roads of the time (which is also largely true today), and placed high demands on the restricted supply of petrol, which was rationed until the early mid-1950s. As a result, at no time during the late 1940s and early 1950s did US car exports worldwide reach the levels of the 1920s, despite excess demand during this period. This was not the case for trucks, since countries were more inclined to buy essential capital items such as trucks needed for reconstruction and development.

## Current Position

The pattern of automotive trade between Europe and North America over the last 25 years is shown in Table 2.

*Table 2. Pattern of Trade ($ billions)*

|                                | 1981 | 1999 | 2000 | 2003 |
|--------------------------------|------|------|------|------|
| North America to Europe        | 1.9  | 7.4  | 6.8  | 9.8  |
| Europe to North America        | 6.3  | 28.2 | 28.0 | 40.8 |
| Asia to North America          | 13.7 | 49.2 | 54.7 | 60.4 |
| North America to Asia          | 0.2  | 4.6  | 5.4  | 5.4  |
| North America to Latin America | -    | 11.8 | 15.9 | 13.3 |
| Latin America to North America | -    | 25.3 | 30.8 | 30.7 |

*Sources*: GATT and WTO.

The striking phenomenon is that trade *from* North America to other world regions is not a major trade flow compared with flows into North America or intra-North American trade, which was $94.8 billion in 2003. North America – particularly the US – remains what it has been throughout the post-war years: an open and liberalized market ready to absorb large numbers of imported cars notwithstanding the voluntary export arrangements imposed by the Japanese on themselves at the behest of North American auto industries and government. The balance of payments position in automotive products of the US and the European Union further illustrates this fact (see Table 3). In

2003, the US imported $112 thousand million more than it exported in automotive products compared with $46 billion in 1990. The European Union exported to the world $58 billion more in automotive products than it imported in 2003, compared with $22 billion in 1990. Of course, the Japanese balance of payments situation these figures dwarfs (see Table 3).

*Table 3. Balance of Payments in Automotive Products ($ millions)*

|  | 1990 | | 2003 | |
|---|---|---|---|---|
|  | Exports | Imports | Exports | Imports |
| US | 32,547 | 79,320 | 69,245 | 181,283 |
| European Union (outside the EU) | 45,751 | 23,329 | 124,973 | 66,523 |
| Japan | 66,230 | 7,315 | 102,734 | 11,130 |

*Source*: WTO.

## Significance of the Transatlantic Automotive Sector

Trade in automotive products between Western Europe and North America remains significant with a more than 4-to-1 imbalance in favor of Europe (Table 2). Also, from 2000 to 2005, trade from Europe to North America grew by 45.7% compared with 10.4% from Asia to North America, and compared with -0.3% from Latin America to North America. Given that North American exports to Europe grew by 44.1% over the same period, the trade imbalance did not worsen much in percentage terms, although it did in absolute numbers. The growth of European exports to North America compared with those from Latin America, where many US firms operate and export to North America, is a good performance.

In 2003, Western Europe exported $380 billion of which $270.6 billion was intra-European trade while North America exported $126 billion, of which $94.8 billion was intra-North American trade. So while Europe sold almost $110 billion of automotive products to the world, North America sold $31.5 billion. North America is not a significant exporter in world terms. Therefore, the imbalance in trade with Western Europe is not in any way unusual. In fact this is offset by the effects of major US investments in vehicle-making in Western Europe, which is more than an adequate substitute for the lack of vehicle exports. Cars made in Europe by US firms are a significant part of the overall equation.

The North American car and light truck market is broadly equivalent to the West European car market, at around 15 million each. However, US-owned companies have around 20% of the West European market, whereas Europeans have less than 6% of the North American car and light truck markets. So while Europe sells 1.1 million vehicles in North America, mainly imports, North Americans sell over 3 million cars and light commercial trucks in Europe. At the same time, US firms account for only 12% of the West European heavy truck market via Paccar's control of DAF and Foden, but West European firms DaimlerChrysler and Volvo have 60% of the North American heavy truck market. Both markets are similar, varying around a typical figure of 300,000 units a year. However, the American share of European car production more than offsets the European dominance of the Class 8 heavy truck market via the control of Freightliner by DaimlerChrysler and White, Mack and GM heavy trucks by Volvo Trucks.

This trade position plus the nature of direct investment by North American and West European companies in each other's markets has produced a state of affairs where there is very little tension internally in the transatlantic automotive sector. The tension tends to be with third parties, notably Japan.

In 2003, the share of North American automotive products in the region's trade in merchandise was 12.7% of exports and 15.8% of imports, and for Western Europe the figures were 12.1% and 11.0%, respectively. In terms of the share of automotive products in trade in manufacturers by North America, they account for 16.8% of exports and 20.2% of imports, and in Western Europe the respective figures are 15% and 14.6%. In short, not only are automotive products important, but they are also important to a similar degree in both regions.

The total production of passenger cars in Western Europe, including in the new EU member states, was 15.9 million in 2003 and 16 million in 2004. In North America, the figures were 15.9 million and 15.8 million, respectively. The latter includes light trucks (LTs), which in the main are included in 'car' figures in Europe. In Western Europe the automotive sector accounts for 10% of manufacturing output, employs 2.5 million people directly and accounts for about 3% of GDP. In addition, through its research & development (R&D) and investment in production and information systems, the industry is central to technological developments in the EU. It also contributes greatly to Western European trade with a trade surplus to offset deficits in many other sectors.

The situation is similar in North America, where the auto sector is the largest manufacturing industry; no other activity is linked to so much of US manufacturing or directly generates so much retail business or employment. The industry employs almost 3 million people directly, with the usual knock-on effects that some studies put as high as another 5 million people. The dynamic effects are the same as in Europe, and although the industry has a balance of payments deficit, over 80% of sales are from domestic output, constituting a major import saving.

The automotive sector as a whole is robust in both Western Europe and North America. Despite problems and challenges facing individual firms, car and light truck production together with the supply chain is at or about record levels, with little likelihood of a major structural decline any time soon.

European car production has been revitalized by firms fully conversant with what needs to be done to achieve maximum efficiency on the supply side and attractive products on the demand side. More specifically, Europe is the primary source of specialist car production while its main comparative advantage is in the manufacture of heavy trucks and buses. The volume car industry is vibrant and has been reinforced by Japan's inward investment.

In North America the inward investment by the Japanese and others has created a new industry capable of making over 2.5 million units a year, more than most national motor industries. This is offsetting the problems faced by the more traditional US-owned makers. The real strength of the North American automotive industry is no longer in car making – less than half of the US market is in the hands of GM, Ford and DaimlerChrysler – but in light trucks, which is largely in US hands because of considerable tariff protection (see Table 4). Japanese firms are investing in truck production in North America, however, so increased competition will occur. US manufacturers face serious challenges because: a) they have seen much of their car market disappear, b) they now depend on light truck production for financial underpinning, but this sector is under attack by Japanese firms on the one hand and environmentalists on the other and c) their position in the European market has weakened in the last decade.

*Table 4. US Market Share (%) (cars and LTs)*

|  | 2002 | 2003 |
| --- | --- | --- |
| GM | 28.3 | 28.6 |
| Ford | 20.9 | 21.5 |
| DaimlerChrysler | 14.1 | 14.4 |
| Toyota | 11.2 | 10.4 |
| Honda | 8.1 | 7.4 |
| Nissan | 4.8 | 4.4 |
| Hyundai | 3.8 | 3.6 |
| Mitsubishi | 1.9 | 1.8 |
| VW Group | 1.8 | 2.0 |
| BMW | 1.4 | 1.4 |
| Mazda | 1.6 | 1.5 |
| Subaru | 1.1 | 1.1 |
| Suzuki | 0.4 | 0.4 |
| Isuzu | 0.2 | 0.3 |

*Source*: SMMT.

Transatlantic commerce plays a major role in maintaining the growth of the West European motor industry, especially in the executive and luxury car sector. Western Europe exports around 1 million cars a year to North America out of a total production of 15 million, and a North American market of 8.5 million cars. The export of light trucks to North America is tiny, but will grow as Land Rover (Ford) sales develop. This is by far Europe's largest export market. Trade in the opposite direction is small, with 7,000 cars and 41,000 trucks being exported to Europe in 2003. As already indicated, however, North America's presence in the West European market is via the local subsidiaries of US firms, rather than through trade (see Table 5). These are GM's Opel, Vauxhall and Saab brands and Ford's own brand plus the Premier Automotive Group of Jaguar, Volvo, Land Rover and Aston Martin. In 2004 these had 21.5% of the West European markets (see Table 5, although only Volvo of PAG is listed). These subsidiaries are amongst the largest in US firms' portfolio, and are responsible for many of the cars designed and developed to sell in the world market outside North America. In short, transatlantic commerce, whether in visible trade and capital transfers or invisibles such as R&D, is a major underpinning of the two regions' automotive sectors.

*Table 5. The West European Market Share (%)*

|  | 1990 | 1995 | 2001 | 2003 | 2004 |
|---|---|---|---|---|---|
| VW | 15.5 | 16.8 | 18.9 | 18.2 | 17.7 |
| GM* | 12.1 | 13.1 | 10.8 | 10.6 | 10.6 |
| PSA | 13.2 | 12.0 | 14.4 | 14.8 | 14.4 |
| Ford (Blue Oval) | 11.7 | 11.9 | 8.8 | 8.6 | 8.9 |
| Volvo | 2.0 | 1.8 | 1.5 | 1.5 | 1.7 |
| Renault | 9.9 | 10.3 | 10.6 | 10.6 | 10.4 |
| Fiat Group | 14.6 | 11.1 | 9.6 | 7.4 | 7.7 |
| Rover | 2.8 | 3.1 | 1.1 | 1.0 | 0.9 |
| BMW Group | 2.8 | 3.3 | 3.5 | 4.4 | 3.6 |
| DaimlerChrysler | 2.8 | 3.4 | 6.4 | 6.5 | 6.1 |
| Toyota | 2.7 | 2.5 | 3.7 | 4.7 | 5.1 |
| Nissan | 2.9 | 3.1 | 2.5 | 2.8 | 2.5 |
| Honda | 1.2 | 1.4 | 1.0 | 1.4 | 1.5 |
| Japanese (total) | 12.0 | 10.1 | 10.4 | 12.7 | 13.1 |
| Korean |  | 1.5 | 2.8 | 2.5 | 2.9 |

* From 2003, Daewoo's share (0.9%) was also included in the GM figure. In 2004, it was 0.8%.

*Source*: SMMT.

## An 'Open' Relationship

Transatlantic commerce in the automotive sector is open to a very large degree. European car imports face a 2.5% import duty while North American exports encounter a 10% tariff in Western Europe. The imbalance in trade is not due to this tariff discrepancy but to the type of vehicle made in the US In the main they are too large in body and engine size for European conditions. Furthermore, US firms have shown little, if occasional, enthusiasm for selling US products in Europe, preferring to use their local subsidiaries geared to meeting European conditions. They conduct their transatlantic business primarily through investment rather than trade. Apart from some concerns over technical, safety and emissions issues, there are no great concerns about the openness of transatlantic trade in this sector. There are no quotas or voluntary export restraints and modest import duties.

Because trade in automotive products is so open, the question of the opportunity costs of continued barriers and lack of further economic integration in this sector does not really arise. If US customers want smaller, more fuel-efficient vehicles, then they can buy them from abroad or from transplant operations. North American car prices are among the lowest in the world, which is testimony to the competitiveness of the market. In the heavy truck sector, competition is intense, with European-controlled firms challenging the remaining US-owned companies, Navistar and Paccar. Local operating conditions and customer preference are the key to the dominance of North American-built, but not owned, firms in this sector. The area where tariff protection may be abetting the manufacture of over-large and gas-guzzling vehicles is the light truck area. However, the tariff protection is geared at Japanese products, not European ones, so transatlantic trade conditions are not an issue. As regards Europe, North American products are not entirely appropriate to European conditions, except for some light trucks and imports from US Japanese transplants. Trade is governed by corporate decision-making, not by the state of trade regulations.

## Convergence or Divergence?

The automotive sectors in Western Europe and North America are different. The type of product, imports' share of the market, structure of the industry and size of the leading firms are different in each case. The size of the mass-market car in North America, but especially the light truck, is much larger than the 'average' European product. In this regard, the North American industry is out of line with the rest of the world: even though GM and Ford are the most global of companies they find it difficult to design a 'world car' suitable for North America and elsewhere. The cars made by the transplants are nearer the world norm and to this extent the car designs are converging, but much has to be done before similar products are made on both sides of the Atlantic. In the case of heavy trucks, there is only some evidence of convergence, and in the world of light trucks divergence is continuing. It is here that the 'American Dream' of large vehicles and large engines continues to be experienced.

In 2005, for the first time, the West European new car market may see over one-half of its cars having diesel engines. In North America, the diesel light-vehicle market is very small, due to the very low price of gasoline and severe technical regulations. North America is showing greater interest in hybrids than is Western Europe, however, because diesel is not being used to attack the $CO_2$ problem. This could lead to divergence via non-tariff barriers. A convergence of engine size and future fuel sources would probably emerge if North America raised fuel taxes to international levels, but this is not likely to occur and not just for political reasons. A curious alliance is being formed between consumerists and environmentalists who see an increase in fuel prices as letting US firms off the hook by forcing consumers to buy smaller vehicles, rather than obliging manufacturers to supply expensively developed large vehicles with environmentally cleaner characteristics. If the North American market shifted its preference to smaller vehicles, then it would be easier for North American firms to make world cars. This would cut development costs and give much larger production runs and greater economies of scale. In effect, North American firms have to run two operations, one for North America and one for 'the rest of the world' European firms face no such imperative since they are not part of the market for the big volume-made vehicles. The West European large car is for the more specialist end of the market.

The North American and West European industries are different and, in some ways, this divergence may be increasing, for instance as regards future fuel sources. This as yet, however, does not create friction in transatlantic commerce in this area. The developments are not due to protectionist or special interest pressures, although there are differences in the preferences of consumers on each side of the Atlantic. On the other hand, harmonization of fuel taxes would have a major impact on the convergence of such preferences.

The market structures (Tables 4 and 5) in North America and Western Europe are very different. In North America, the two top firms have 50% of the market, whereas in Western Europe the top two firms have 28% of the market. The top five have 82% and 63%, respectively. But the North American industry is changing. The erstwhile dominance of Ford and GM is being eroded and genuine multi-firm competition is appearing as never before. In Western Europe, the 'European' market share is a myth with very different shares posted in the different national markets of Europe (e.g. Fiat has 26% of Italy, but 2% of the UK car market). However, as European integration proceeds the 'European' share will become more real, and the seemingly competitive picture in Table 5 will become a reality. Hence the two regional markets are converging in terms of form *and* behavior. This will strengthen the links between them, since their philosophy and aspirations will continue to coincide.

## Measures to Increase Trade

Although there are no real obstacles to transatlantic commerce in the auto sector, a large flow of trade only occurs in one direction. Hence, it is not the removal of regulatory obstacles that will increase integration but ways and means to make North American-made vehicles more attractive to European consumers. At present over 80% of cars made in Western Europe have engines of less than 2 liters; in the US over 80% of cars and light trucks have engines *over* 2 liters. This complementarity of product is not generating business for North American firms, however, since the types of vehicle made are inappropriate for European conditions. This does not just mean size but operating characteristics such as performance. The North American motor industry's lack of interest in directly exporting to Western Europe duplicates its trade flows with other parts of the world. In 2003, only 117,000 cars and 245,000 commercial vehicles were exported to the world. Hence, North America's export performance in vehicles is a general problem, and not one peculiar to its relations with Western Europe. Any increase will require a change in North American vehicles, a change of policy by US firms to supplement European production by imports, and greater integration of European and North American production programs by Asian producers. In short, if the North American auto industry wants to export more, it will have to become more export-orientated. The activities of some of the North American component firms show that such a philosophy can be very rewarding.

For their part, the European manufacturers must improve their act to launch an attack on the volume car markets of North America, which have been lost to the Japanese. Among the European volume market brands, only VW has any sort of business in North America. The French and Italian makers are conspicuous by their absence. Some Japanese products sold in North America are sourced in Western Europe, and the components sector has had some success supplying North American firms from Europe. Renault's links with Nissan may be the way for the French company to return but the prospects of Fiat and Peugeot in North America do not appear promising. As Table 2 shows, Western Europe has had a successful push into North America since 2000, with improved and more competitive products, but even though Asian makers are sourcing more production in North America, their export performance is 50% better than the Europeans. The appearance of some European transplant manufacturers in North America with incremental products may increase the sales volume and value.

## Do Barriers to Trade Exist?

Because commerce in transatlantic automotive products is already so liberalized, any further liberalization can only be minor. As a result, no extra significant beneficial knock-on effects would be likely. If West European or North American automotive enterprises want to sell in each other's markets, then there are no protectionist issues preventing them from doing so. Perhaps what is required are further efforts at increasing knowledge to improve transparency. However, both industries and their respective authorities are adept at commercial marketing, but no doubt continuous improvement means that something can always be done. This may be particularly so at the supply-chain level where component and systems suppliers are all too often ignorant of possibilities.

This means that any barriers to deeper transatlantic commerce are not regulatory or fiscal, but more likely to result from competitive dynamics. That is, the products of one or both industries are not attractive enough in the other market. Although Western Europe exports one million vehicles to North America, this is only 11.8% of the car market and 6.6% of the car and LT market. The former is similar to the 10% import penetration of the West European car market and the latter to the 6% import share of the Japanese car market. Japanese imports hold 19% of the North American car market, apart from transplant production. Western Europe does not make cars for the North American large car volume market and makes very few pick-ups, sports utility vehicles and minivans suitable for the US market. This is because only a limited 'home' market would exist for such vehicles. To serve the North American market, BMW and Daimler have established plants in the US, but Ford's Land Rover subsidiary will supply from the UK. Similarly, the Europeans realized the best place to make North America-type heavy trucks is in North America, through the purchase of US firms. It appears that any significant increase in transatlantic trade in automotive products, which the West European performance since 2000 has shown is possible, must be based on the overall competitiveness of the firms involved, which includes such characteristics as price, quality, delivery, reliability, service and repair.

The area where harmonization could reduce unit costs and generate trade is in technical regulations. After all, the harmonization of such was seen as a major benefit of the creation of the single market in the EU post-1992. Such a harmonization that allowed vehicle homologation in Western Europe and North America to coincide could reduce unit costs by between 5% and 7%

and allow the same products – including components, accessories and sub-assemblies such as engines – to be used in both markets. This would have great trade potential. After all, where tariff barriers are small, any non-tariff issue becomes important. Harmonization of regulations could increase trade by a significant amount.

## The Non-Transatlantic Competitive Challenge

Enough has been said to indicate that where world trade between regions is concerned, it is the Japanese who are the main force. In trade with North America, the West Europeans export around one million vehicles a year but the Japanese export over 1.6 million. The Europeans export 130,000 vehicles to Japan but import over one million from them. Also from Asia, the South Korean motor industry exports 725,000 vehicles to North America, taking 2,000 in return. The Koreans export 500,000 vehicles to Western Europe, taking 16,000 in return. If North American industry was able to integrate its North American and European operations, the quality, economies of scale and model program of such an eventuality could strengthen their position against the leading Japanese producers, remembering that Mazda, Suzuki, Isuzu and Subaru are linked to North American firms. Similarly if the West European volume producers were able to duplicate the performance of their premium brands, such as Mercedes Benz, BMW and MINI, Jaguar, Audi, Volvo and Land Rover, they would return to the North American market, perhaps mainly at the expense of Asian producers. This is much easier said than done, given the present impressive record of Toyota, Hyundai, Honda and, to a lesser extent, Nissan (the latter being controlled by Renault). If all predictions are realized, then China, and possibly India, will become major challengers by 2015.

## Automotive Trade: A Lesson in Market Opening

The openness of the transatlantic commerce in automotive products provides a benchmark for other sectors. The European industry has never threatened the existence of the North American auto industry in the way the Europeans feared US competition in the period from 1920 to 1970 (see Table 1) and illustrated by the relative tariff protection. As a result, European imports were tolerated and were often seen in the 1950s and 1960s as a safety-valve for diverting criticism of the North American producers that they did not offer small cars and had no intention of doing so at that time. Equally, the North American producers established themselves in Europe to make cars and commercial vehicles, providing jobs, using local suppliers and becoming accepted as 'European' producers. Also by manufacturing in a number of European countries, they were able to gather a wide constituency of support.

The R&D facilities, the best-practice operations and acceptable products all added to their acceptance by the European auto sector and market. So although there has developed a great imbalance in the trade flows to Europe's advantage, the activities of US plants in Europe has created an impression of balance and fairness in auto trading arrangements.

Transatlantic commerce in automotive products demonstrates that opportunities may exist but companies must be competitive to grasp them. The European manufacturers face only a 2½% import duty in the US and 6% in Canada. Under such circumstances, their ability to carve out a significant share of these markets depends upon their competitiveness. The relatively small share of the North American market held by European firms other than the specialists such as Mercedes Benz or BMW is due to a lack of competitiveness amongst the mass-market producers and the lack of competitiveness of the European operations of the North American companies in comparison with their Japanese associates such as Mazda, Isuzu, Suzuki and Subaru. In short, best-practice market opening depends upon competitiveness.

Competition in the auto sector has not been greatly distorted by 'unfair' practices such as subsidy and market sharing. This has removed a potential source of friction from transatlantic commerce in automotive products.

As said above the main threats to each other's auto industries are not each other. Rather it is Japan, and particularly Toyota, which is the 'Airbus' of the auto sector. The Japanese pose a threat to the dominance of GM and Ford in the global market for the first time ever. To this extent European exports are marginal. In the opposite direction, the development of North American-owned auto production sites in Europe with all the beneficial effects that flow for the local economies are a substitute for direct imports. In a sense these facilities are an 'offset' arrangement, compensating for European auto trade flows into North America. What is so often an artificial and costly device in aerospace has emerged through market forces in response to pre-war trade barriers. This has also occurred in the heavy truck industry where European direct investment in North American companies secures their future and is an offset for the very large hold that General Motors and Ford have on the European auto markets. The sector is characterized by openness in trade and investment flows in both directions.

Another feature of the relationship is that the bulk of trade flows are complementary rather than substitutes, as in the case of the Japanese. The main auto products sold to North America from Europe are specialist cars, which only compete with a small minority of North American car producers such as Lincoln and Cadillac. The main counter flow is mini-vans and sports utility vehicles plus components and major sub-assemblies such as engines. This also reduces the potential for friction and conflict.

Technology transfer has been liberal in the relationship between the automotive sectors in North America and Europe. The companies often cooperate and collaborate and engage in joint ventures. So while the sector is highly competitive, there is an underlying trust between the North American and West European players.

The result of all this is that transatlantic commerce in automotive products is largely free of market-distorting arrangements and market failure. Failures are mainly the result of entrepreneurial mistakes rather than institutionally-inspired distortion. Compared with many sectors, the auto industry is an example of best practice where market-opening is concerned. In the transatlantic auto sector, there is nowhere for the inefficient to hide.

# 9.  A Transatlantic Financial Market?[1]

## Karel Lannoo

Back in the early days of the European Single Market, a 'reciprocity' provision in the second banking directive caused much uproar in transatlantic relations. According to this clause, the EU could ask trading partners to grant access to their markets in a manner that was reciprocal to the one obtained for third countries in the EU. It was claimed that the European Union was becoming a 'fortress' and that the United States would never accept being forced to change its regulatory structure. Although the provision has never actually been applied, it took more than 10 years before officials started to have regular discussions on coming to more equivalence in regulatory regimes on both sides. This dialogue culminated in an agreement on April 22, 2005 between the US Securities and Exchange Commission (SEC) and the European Commission on equivalence of accounting standards.

Yet equivalent standards also have some drawbacks. First, financial markets on both sides are fundamentally different in structure, meaning that it is not easy to find issues that are of comparable importance. Moreover, EU financial markets are still largely fragmented and consolidated at the national level, meaning that the benefits of the Single Market still have not been realized within the EU. Second, the process may be seen as a way to reduce regulatory competition, which could limit the benefits of equivalence.

## A Bank-Based versus Market-Based Financial System

The EU and US financial systems continue to differ fundamentally. In comparing the size of bank, bond and equity markets in the US and the EU, it is striking to note that a highly developed banking market and a (much) less-developed bond and equity market characterize the EU, while the opposite is true for the US (see Figure 1). This asymmetry between the two systems largely results from regulatory differences, in particular the universal

---

[1] This chapter builds upon earlier work by the author. For a more extensive discussion of ongoing EU financial market regulation issues and references, see K. Lannoo and J.-P. Casey, *Financial Regulation and Supervision beyond 2005*, CEPS Task Force Report, CEPS, Brussels, February 2005. For US-EU issues, see M. Draghi and R. Pozen, *US-EU regulatory convergence: Capital market issues*, John M. Olin Discussion Paper Series No. 444, Harvard Law School, Cambridge, MA, 2003; and also E. Posner, "Market power without a single market: The new transatlantic relations in financial services", mimeo, George Washington University, Washington DC, June 2004.

banking system in Europe and the segmentation of the US financial system by the 1933 Glass-Steagall Act, which separates commercial banking from investment banking. In addition, the 1933 Securities Act laid the basis for the market-based financial system in the US as we know it today.

The segmentation of the US financial industry stimulated tough competition between intermediaries. It provided the environment in which capital market financing, specialization and innovation emerged, creating the most competitive industry worldwide. As noted by Chief Economist at the European Investment Bank Alfred Steinherr, "In no other industry has the United States been as resolutely superior as in the financial industry. (...) All significant innovations have come out of the US financial system."[2]

*Figure 1. Amounts of Bonds Outstanding, Total Domestic Stock Market Capitalization and Bank Assets, end 2003 (in billions of euros and as a percentage of GDP)*

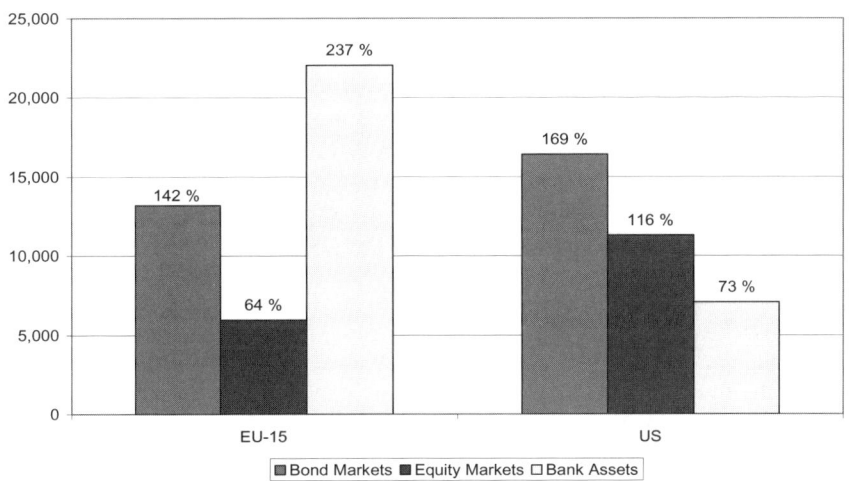

Competition between commercial banks, investment banks and brokers in the US stimulated a process of disintermediation and securitization. Caps on short-term bank deposits led to the emergence of higher-yielding money market mutual funds. Banks responded by transforming liabilities into negotiable certificates of deposits, on which interest could be paid without restrictions. In order to obtain a share of the profitable loan market, investment banks stimulated corporations to securitize their loans. As a

---

[2] A. Steinherr, *Derivatives, the Wild Beast of Finance*, New York: John Wiley & Sons Inc., 1998, p. 29.

result, the balance sheets of banks became fully disintermediated and securitized and relationship banking disappeared. The growth of a deep and liquid money and capital market had deprived relationship banking of its implicit insurance value and made valuations more important. The key principle of transparency, which underlies US financial, securities and accounting law, emerged.

In Europe, the universal banking system has remained dominant, having been taken as the model in the EU's 1992 program of financial market liberalization. There was no incentive for banks to securitize debt and capital markets remained underdeveloped. Furthermore, the regulatory framework for direct issues on capital markets left much to be desired and differed from one member state to another. For example, until recently corporate bonds were discouraged in Germany through very strict emission criteria, including the obligation to issue the bonds only in the domestic currency of the local market, with unfavorable tax treatment. Governments wished to keep close control of the local debt securities market to ease public finance.

So far, there has been no real break in the structure of the EU financial system. Bank assets to GDP have continued to grow and stood at 237% of GDP in 2003, but there has been a pronounced growth of debt securities markets in the EU, which increased from 84% of GDP in 1992 to 142% in 2003. The creation of the euro has allowed Europe's capital markets to deepen, accounting for 31% of the global financial stock in 2003, up from 28% in 1999. This compares to 37% for the US, whose share declined from 40% in 1999.[3]

The realization that the EU would not fully capture the benefits of economic and monetary union, but also that its financial system was missing out on innovative investments, led to the adoption of the Financial Services Action Plan (FSAP) in 1999 and the reform of its system of financial lawmaking and supervisory cooperation as discussed in the 2001 'Lamfalussy' report. By mid-2004, a new regulatory framework was in place for the issuance of securities on capital markets (Prospectus Directive, 2003/71/EC), market disclosure (Transparency Directive, 2004/109/EC), tackling insider trading and market manipulation (Market Abuse Directive, 2003/6/EC) and promoting fair trade and the best execution of securities transactions (Markets in Financial Instruments Directive, 2004/39/EC). The effects of these directives should allow a more market-based system to develop.

---

[3] McKinsey Global Institute, *Global Financial Stock Database*, 2005.

## EU-US Dialogue on Financial Markets Regulation

The success of the EU in reforming its financial regulatory and supervisory structure led to the start of a regular dialogue with the US, which could be considered a model for other areas of transatlantic or bilateral trade cooperation. Although the direct motive was the impact of the EU's Conglomerates Directive (2002/87/EC) on US firms, it has become a permanent feature, focusing on a broader set of financial market issues and involving the EU Commission and Lamfalussy Committees on the one side and the US Treasury, the SEC and Federal Reserve Board on the other. The aim is to improve understanding and identify potential conflicts in regulatory approaches on both sides of the Atlantic and to discuss issues of mutual interest.[4] As noted by EU Commissioner for the Internal Market and Services Charlie McGreevy in New York on 20 May 2005, "The goal must be mutual recognition of equivalence. You can also call it the home-country principle. If you agree to accept each other's system as equivalent then duplicative requirements disappear. You can then operate in the other country under the rules of your home country."[5] Hallmarks so far have been the agreements on the equivalence of rules for auditor oversight and accounting standards, but difficult issues remain on the agenda, such as the implementation of the Basel Accord and the direct access to EU exchanges by the US market.

The background to the start of the regulatory dialogue was the exponential growth of transatlantic portfolio investment in the second half of the last decade. Purchases of US equities by EU investors grew from $144 billion in 1990 to reach $2,631 billion in 2000. At the same time, US investors also stepped up their diversification into EU equities, rising from $141 billion in 1990 to reach $1,937 billion in 2000.[6] This trend was mainly driven by

---

[4] See the *Joint Report to leaders at the EU-US Summit on 25-26 June by participants in the Financial Markets Regulatory Dialogue*, for the June summit held at Dromoland Castle, Ireland (retrieved from http://europa.eu.int/comm/internal_market/finances/docs/general/eu-us-dialogue-report_en.pdf); both of the parties at the meeting agreed to "intensify" their cooperation.

[5] See "The integration of Europe's financial markets and international cooperation" by C. McCreevy, Concluding Remarks at the Euro Conference in New York on April 20, 2005. There is no full agreement on the terminology. While the EU uses the phrase 'mutual recognition', US authorities prefer 'equivalence', which may be more correct, as supervisory accountability remains at the federal level. See also the testimony of Alexander Schaub, Director-General of the European Commission DG on the Internal Market, before the US House of Representatives Committee on Financial Services, May 13, 2004.

[6] B. Steil, *Building a Transatlantic Securities Market*, International Securities Markets Association, Zurich, 2002, pp. 17-23.

institutional investors. Moreover, the emergence of a more securitized and disintermediated financial system increased the attractiveness of the EU market for US firms.[7]

Until a few years ago, the EU was not considered a credible partner for discussions on financial regulatory and supervisory matters. Progress toward the adoption of the FSAP, however, changed things. Still, US regulators were hardly interested in discussing some form of equivalence with other countries. It strictly applied the principle of territoriality and considered its financial regulatory system superior.[8] Then the corporate scandals of Enron and others altered things further. Serious flaws had been revealed in the US securities supervisory system and its accounting standards were no longer held to be superior. At the same time, because of the scandals, new laws such as the Sarbanes-Oxley Act (2002) were adopted, creating severe problems at the transatlantic level.

The issue regarding auditor oversight results from the passage of the Sarbanes-Oxley Act in the US, which created the Public Company Accounting Oversight Board (PCAOB), and required all audit firms to be registered with the PCAOB, including EU-based audit firms with US-listed clients. A declaration of intent on the equivalence of rules for auditor oversight, reached between the European Commission and the US PCAOB in March 2004,[9] would lift the requirement for EU-based audit firms. It stipulates, however, that EU member states create auditor oversight

---

[7] See the testimony of Marc Lackritz, President of the Securities Industry Association, at a Congressional hearing of the Committee on Financial Services on May 22, 2002, who stated, "Our very largest members engaging in global business receive about 20% of their net revenues from Europe. And I might add that that is about two times more than the net revenues that we receive from Asia. And we employ about 35,000 Europeans in the business."

[8] Evidence of this attitude was revealed by former Chairman of the SEC Arthur Levitt in a *Financial Times* article, *in tempore non suspectu*, concerning the International Accounting Standards (IAS). He argued that the US GAAP (Generally Accepted Accounting Principles) was "the most transparent and comprehensive disclosure regime in the world" and that the US should never recognize IAS as equivalent. See A. Levitt, "The world according to GAAP: Global capital markets cannot work without uniform, high-quality financial reporting standards", *Financial Times*, May 2, 2001.

[9] This declaration of intent was made public by European Commissioner Frits Bolkestein and US PCAOB Chairman William McDonough in Brussels on March 25, 2004.

authorities, which are not yet present in all member states, and agree on the European Union's draft 8th Company Law Directive on the statutory audit, as a precondition.[10]

The agreement on equivalence between International Financial Reporting Standards (IFRS) and US Generally Accepted Accounting Principles (GAAP), reached between the European Commission and the US SEC on April 22, 2005, probably has the most far-reaching implications. It would effectively allow companies to use one single accounting standard in the EU and US. So far, the US has always required firms to reconvert their accounts to the US GAAP when listing on US capital markets, whereas the EU requires listed firms and issuers to report in IAS or the equivalent from 2005 onwards. The agreement allows US firms to continue to issue bonds on EU capital markets in the US GAAP, whereas the SEC will eliminate the need for companies using the IFRS to reconcile to US GAAP standards possibly as soon as 2007, but no later than 2009.[11]

The transatlantic dialogue has also proliferated to the supervisory side, where the Committee of European Securities Regulators and the US SEC announced a cooperation agreement on June 4, 2004 covering increased communication about regulatory risks in each other's securities markets and the promotion of regulatory convergence in the future. This move was followed by a cooperation initiative with the US Commodities and Futures Trading Commission on October 21, 2004. The same form of extended cooperation is happening in the areas of banking and insurance, with the Committee of European Banking Supervisors and the Committee of European Insurance and Occupational Pensions Supervisors.

Other issues still on the agenda are the latest capital adequacy rules resulting from the new Basel Accord and the direct access of EU exchanges to the US market. Whereas the EU would leave all EU-licensed banks the choice of which approach to follow for the measurement of their minimum level of regulatory capital, US regulators would allow only the advanced internal ratings-based approach of the new Basel Accord to some 20 internationally active banks and apply the old Basel I framework to all the other banks. This action would seriously distort the playing field for EU banks in the US market, while US banks would have the full range of choices in the EU. The

---

[10] See the Proposal for a Directive of the European Parliament and of the Council on statutory audit of annual accounts and consolidated accounts and amending Council Directives 78/660/EEC and 83/349/EEC, COM(2004) 0177 final of March 15, 2004.

[11] See D.T. Nicolaisen, "A Securities Regulator Looks at Convergence", *Northwestern University Journal of International Law and Business*, April 2005.

justification of the US supervisors that these internationally active banks control 99% of the foreign assets in the US banking system does not take into account the significant stake EU banks have in the US banking system. In addition, it will also hamper integrated risk-management and supervisory reporting within these groups, with all the negative consequences this may entail.

A similar distortion applies with regard to trading on regulated stock markets. Whereas US-regulated stock markets are directly accessible for EU licensed brokers, the same is not the case for EU regulated markets in the US. American authorities argue that the level of investor protection in the EU stock market is not equivalent to what is in place in the US. From the EU perspective, this is seen as a protectionist measure. While all major EU stock exchanges operate a screen-based trading system, the major US stock exchange, the New York Stock Exchange (NYSE), maintains a floor-based trading structure. Having direct access to the EU-regulated market would allow US brokers to trade directly on EU stock markets, thereby not only reducing the listings of EU firms on the NYSE, but also threatening the antiquated trading structure of the world's largest exchange.[12]

## Benefits of a Transatlantic Market

Although the agreements reached in the context of the transatlantic agenda clearly have benefits, how to quantify these is not evident. Some studies have been undertaken on the specific aspects of the transatlantic financial market, but an overall figure would be almost impossible to distill. Moreover, as an integrated financial market does not yet exist at the EU level, how could the benefits of a transatlantic market be measured?

As regards the integration of securities markets, Steil has estimated that full transatlantic integration may lead to a 9% reduction of the cost of capital for listed companies. This study is based on the assumption that greater competition between the more efficient, automated trading structures on the EU side and the more competitive brokerage industry in the US would reduce transaction costs by 60%. This cost reduction would also lead to an increase in trading volume of almost 50%.[13] On top of that, a fully integrated capital market would also do away with the duplicate costs and fees companies incur through listing on multiple markets. By mid-2005, there

---

[12] J. Board et al. for example do not expect substantial benefits from introducing EU screens in the US – see *Distortion or distraction: US restrictions on EU exchange trading screens*, Corporation of London, City Research Series, No. 3, 2004.

[13] Steil, op. cit., pp. 28-30.

were 235 EU companies with listings in the US, whereas there were 140 US companies with listings on the London Stock Exchange, Deutsche Börse and Euronext.

A much more important reduction in the cost of the capital and regulatory burden would accrue from the agreement on the equivalence of accounting standards, although no studies have been carried out on the aggregate benefit of this equivalence, as far as we are aware. This exercise would certainly be a complex undertaking, as many elements need to be taken into account. First, there are the costs for European companies of converting their accounts to the US GAAP, as a condition for listing on the US capital market (the US GAAP is accepted in most EU markets), of which individual figures exist. Second, there is the advantage of having mutually accepted accounting languages, which means that analysts on both sides will trust firms' financial statements, leading to higher investment across the Atlantic (and certainly in the EU). Third, the agreement does away with the cost of the confusion and the lack of credibility caused by converting accounts to another language, often depressing the stock price. An example is Deutsche Bank's shift to the US GAAP in 2002, which led to net profit distortions in the US GAAP of minus 88% for 2001 to plus 220% in 2000 because of differences in the tax treatment of the disposal of industrial holdings.[14] Analysts therefore considered the changeover a strategic mistake.

At a more general level, stronger market integration could be an important incentive to stimulate the competitiveness of the EU financial services industry, which is lagging behind its American counterpart in performance. Return on assets in the EU banking industry stood at about 0.4% in 2003, compared with 1.4% in the United State, a performance that has stabilized at these levels for the last few years.[15] The strong productivity growth observed in the US in the second half of the 1990s can largely be attributed to a limited number of services that use information and communications technology intensively, including certain financial services. Hence, there is a need to stimulate EU financial market integration.[16] Segmented markets at the retail level in the EU, such as in mortgage lending or investment funds

---

[14] See *Financial Times*, September 10, 2002.

[15] See the *Global Financial Stability Report*, International Monetary Fund, Washington, DC, April 2005.

[16] Annex I of the European Commission's recent *Green Paper on Financial Services Policy (2005-2010)*, (COM(2005) 177, Brussels, May 3, 2005) reiterates the economic benefits of financial integration – on which studies had been published in 2002 showing the impact on the lower cost of capital and increase in GDP growth.

prevent firms from exploiting economies of scale and increasing their overall performance, which ultimately increases costs for the end-users of financial services.

Would transatlantic dialogue therefore only have beneficial effects? Not necessarily: the danger is not imaginary that it may lead to over-regulation – that the one side may hope the other will follow its standards, even if circumstances or needs may be different. Examples are the implementation of the new Basel Accord in the United States or the impact of the Sarbanes-Oxley Act on corporate governance regulation in the European Union. In these two cases, circumstances are different and do not require full equivalence, although there are clearly pressures from both sides respectively to level up the host-country model to the one presently applicable at home.

Within certain bounds, competition between regulatory regimes can be healthy – something that is also noticeable in the EU. Nevertheless, a high degree of international cooperation between regulators replicates the dangers of excessive regulatory intervention at the national level: an (unaccountable) regulatory leviathan with monopoly authority, which does not need to pay great attention to the quality of regulation, and an opaque entity subject to capture by special interest groups. Not only does this scenario have the ability to reduce welfare by excluding some economic options that free market competition would have enabled market participants to choose from, but it also removes the freedom to choose in the first place, a value from which economic actors may derive some utility. In addition, excessive regulatory cooperation at the international level outside the contours of a clearly defined legal framework effectively amounts to a lack of democratic legitimacy.

Two forces – one public, one private – can explain why excessive regulatory convergence leaves little room for innovation in securities market regulation. To begin with, a common standard or regulatory regime enjoying a monopoly need not pay much attention to upstart rivals, so there is little incentive for regulators to improve their regime or to introduce better standards when they cooperate closely at the international level. In addition, there is an inherent risk in 'benevolent planners' choosing what they believe to be the most appropriate market structure, because they may impose the wrong market structure and respond inadequately to changes in demand or to the introduction of new technologies, which may warrant a need to radically alter the market structure.[17]

---

[17] See L. Harris, *Trading and Exchanges*, Oxford: Oxford University Press, 2003.

With regard to private forces, as the incumbent standard is challenged on efficiency grounds, pioneers with low switching costs may migrate to the new standard, undermining the entrenched standard in the process. Yet, firms with high switching costs owing to scale effects will be loathe to part from the old standard. They may deliberately stifle innovation to maintain a certain market infrastructure that is advantageous to them. Such behavior can explain why outdated trading systems such as that employed by the NYSE are still in existence.[18]

---

[18] Ibid.

# 10. Transatlantic Telecommunications: Markets, Policies and Issues

## Michael Tyler and Matthew Dixon

### 1.    Introduction and Overview

Transatlantic telecommunication, reliable, inexpensive and increasingly taken for granted, enables all of the other kinds of transatlantic commerce and economic integration. Financial markets on one side of the Atlantic respond within seconds to changes on the other side. Manufacturers on one side of the Atlantic incorporate components or whole major assemblies, built on the other side, all flowing across the Atlantic under tightly coordinated 'just-in-time' logistics. Massive quantities of media content news, opinion, information and entertainment flow across the Atlantic every day. This can happen because the telecommunications industry provides immense capacity, high reliability and quality, and remarkably low prices. Transatlantic telephone calls to and from virtually all of the European Union countries now rarely cost the user more than $.20 per minute and often cost much less. Data transport has become so inexpensive and effortless that users on one side of the Atlantic accessing a website on the other side, through the Internet, are usually entirely unaware of the cost per megabyte or per minute, or even that they are accessing a resource on the other side of the Atlantic.

This chapter discusses how that state of affairs – astounding in relation to all previous eras of communication – developed. It provides a profile of transatlantic telecommunications today and outlines an agenda of remaining issues for public policy that should be addressed across the Atlantic community of countries, if this achievement is to be sustained and extended through the 21st century.

By 'transatlantic telecommunications' we mean three distinct (although inter-related) kinds of activity:

- the carriage of international telecommunications traffic – voice, data and video – between North America (the United States and Canada) and Europe;

- the extension of telecommunications operators' networks, originally set up as national networks, across the Atlantic so that US networks have been able to gain 'points of presence' (PoPs) in Europe and vice-versa; and

- participation in the domestic communications markets of North America and Europe by foreign (European and North American, respectively) telecommunications operators, either directly or by taking an ownership interest in (or acquiring outright) established local telecommunications operators.

We show how each of these areas has evolved and comment on the current issues affecting each of them.

## 2. Development of Transatlantic Telecommunications: Background to Today's Industry Structure and Issues

### 2.1 Origins

Economic interdependence and integration across the Atlantic have been enabled and stimulated by telecommunications since the 1860s, when transatlantic telegraph services first came into use. Yet massive day-to-day use of telecommunications in business and personal life can reasonably be dated to the mid-1980s, when the volume of transatlantic voice and fax calling for the first time exceeded 1 billion minutes per year (in other words, more than 45,000 hours of transatlantic conversations on an average day).

Transatlantic telecommunication has been accompanied from the start by remarkable accomplishments, drastic challenges and profound social and economic impacts. The first transatlantic telegraph cable, an enterprise instigated by Cyrus Field, vividly demonstrated all three aspects. The first cable, laid in 1858 from Valentia, Ireland, to Trinity Bay, Newfoundland, conveyed an inaugural telegram from Queen Victoria to President Buchanan of the US, expressing the hope that the cable would prove an "additional link between the nations whose friendship is founded on their common interest and reciprocal esteem". Buchanan responded "that it is a triumph more glorious, because far more useful to mankind, than was ever won by conqueror on the field of battle". He further wished that "the Atlantic telegraph, under the blessing of heaven, prove to be a bond of perpetual peace and friendship between the kindred nations, and an instrument destined by Divine Providence to diffuse religion, civilization, liberty, and law throughout the world".

The cable promptly failed a few days later, never to function again, demonstrating that technological triumphs should not be taken for granted. Perhaps subsequent experience might also prompt rueful reflections on how far superior technical means of communication really lead to better human behavior. Nevertheless, once replacement transatlantic cable systems were laid in 1865 and 1866 with better technology, the commercial benefits of transatlantic telecommunications were never again in doubt.

The evolution from the dots and dashes of words in Morse Code trickling through the telegraph cable, to today's torrent of voice, data and video, was gradual at first, but accelerated dramatically from the mid 1950s. The first transatlantic telephone service, radio-based, was started in 1927, with tiny capacity and priced in the region of $15 per minute (about $150 at today's value of money). TAT-1, the first transatlantic telephone cable, was completed in 1956, providing a grand total of 36 telephone channels. Further cables of much greater capacity followed, as did communications satellites, starting with AT&T's Telstar I, launched in 1962 and used for television broadcasts and data communications as well as voice.

## 2.2 The Era of Mass Scale

The road from these early beginnings led to today's world of $.15 per minute transatlantic telephone calls and more than 700,000 hours of daily calling across the Atlantic. Between the 1950s and the 1980s, transatlantic capacity increased from scores of channels to hundreds of thousands of channels and prices began to be reckoned in cents per minute rather than dollars. As Figure 1 shows, by the 1990s the dollar-a-minute transatlantic telephone call was fast becoming a fading memory. It is noteworthy that this happened first and fastest on the US-UK route, as revealed in Figure 1.

*Figure 1. Average US Prices for Telephone Calls to Selected European Countries*

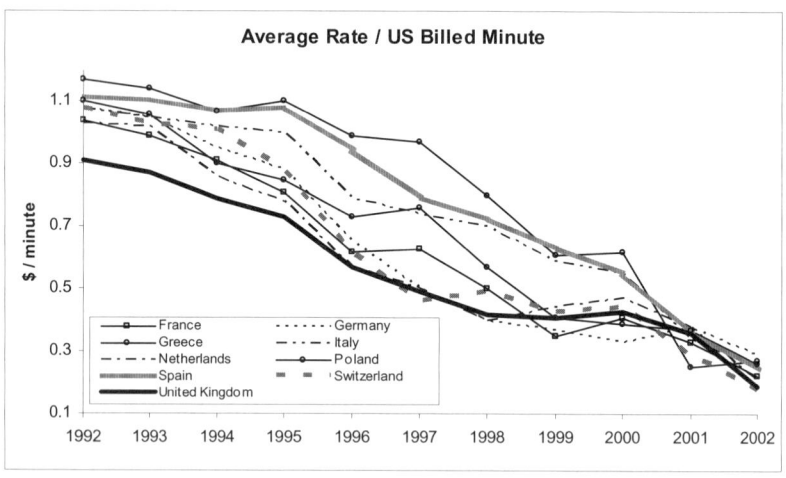

*Source:* FCC, *Trends in the International Telephony Industry,* Washington, D.C., 2004.

The UK was the first European country that had headed down essentially the same road toward a regulated multi-competitor industry structure that the US had already embarked upon in the 1970s. The UK's Telecommunications Act of 1984 (privatizing British Telecom or BT) and the licensing of competitors opened the market to competition. It did so in a broadly similar way as the US Execunet decision of 1977, the break-up of AT&T and industry restructuring from January 1984 under Judge Greene's Modification of Final Judgment (MFJ) and the series of pro-competitive decisions of the Federal Communications Commission (FCC) and the courts in the US.

Low prices, combined with high service quality and ample capacity, created mass-scale use of transatlantic telecommunications, as Figure 2 shows. No longer was a transatlantic telephone call the preserve a handful of financiers, political office holders and members of top management. In the first half of the 1980s, traffic doubled; then it doubled again by 1990. In the 1990s, the pattern was repeated, but now the scale was much larger: in 2000, the traffic volume was about 20 times the 1980 level and growth continued unabated into the 21$^{st}$ century.

*Figure 2. US-Europe Voice Traffic (both directions combined) 1980-2002*

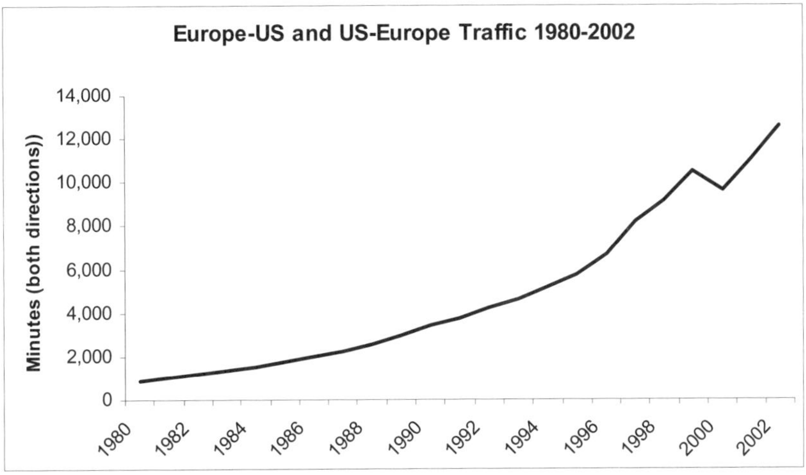

*Source:* FCC, *Trends in the International Telephony Industry,* Washington, D.C., 2004.

Some further notable features of the large-scale transatlantic telecommunications business, as it took shape in the 1990s, are apparent in Figures 3 and 4. Figure 3 shows the large (and, through most of the 1990s, widening) gap between the volume of traffic from Europe to the US and the much larger volume of traffic from the US to Europe.

This gap, partly reflecting the more competitive conditions in the US, with lower prices for calls, resulted in very large net out-payments by US operators under the settlement arrangements that formed an integral part of the traditional correspondent system, and consequently growing pressures for change in the accounting rate system. These pressures were reflected in petitions to the FCC, in FCC policy positions, in bilateral negotiations between the US government and European governments and in multilateral trade-in-services negotiations held under the auspices of the WTO agreement and its predecessor the GATT. All these factors contributed to the recent transformation of transatlantic telecommunications described in the next section.

*Figure 3. Voice Traffic, 1992-2002*

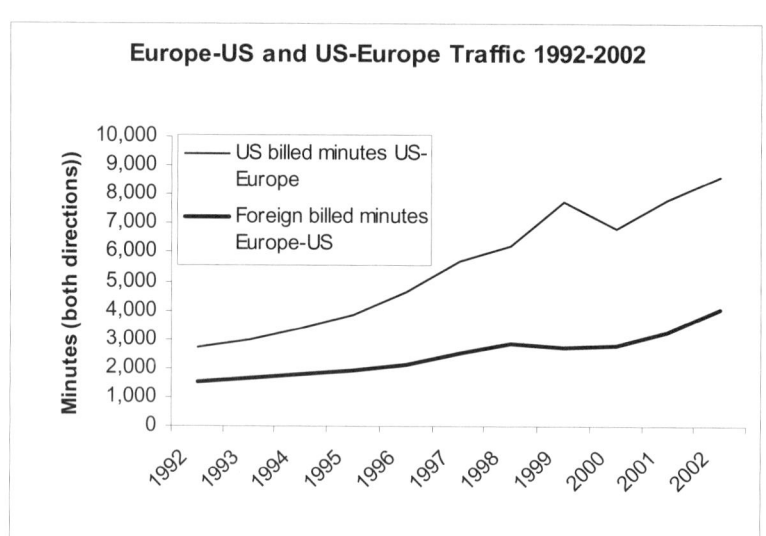

*Source:* FCC, *Trends in the International Telephony Industry,* Washington, D.C., 2004.

Finally, Figure 4 completes the picture for basic telephone service by showing the pattern of traffic growth for several different country-pairs. Perhaps the most striking feature of this pattern is the very strong growth apparent, especially since 2000, in US-UK traffic. This reflects the effects over time of the pro-competitive policy stance of the UK government, the openness of the market to competitive entry, and the consequent pressure on the incumbent operator (BT) to keep its services and prices fully competitive.

*Figure 4. Voice Traffic between the US and European Countries*

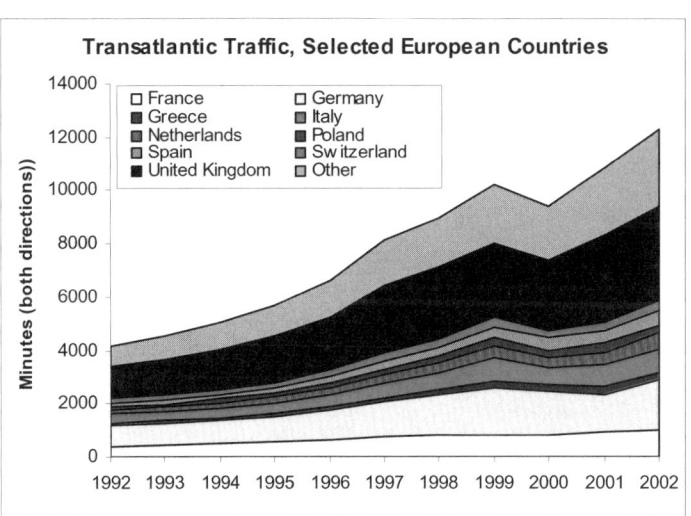

Transatlantic Traffic, Selected European Countries

*Sources:* FCC, Tyler & Company analysis.

This period not only saw the rapid expansion just described and evolutionary changes toward a more competitive industry structure (with newer players such as MCI and Sprint in the US and Mercury in the UK participating in the correspondent system), but also the emergence of radically new developments that have begun to reshape the telecommunications industry. Although reshaping always takes much longer than the breathless commentaries of business journalists might lead us to believe, reshaping has undoubtedly been in progress since the early 1990s. Notable features of the reshaping included:

- the transition of the Internet from a network used mainly by universities and a few leading-edge businesses to a familiar, indeed ubiquitous, tool of everyday life and work. In 1991, the International Telecommunication Union (ITU) (a United Nations specialized agency that plays a central role in international telecommunications) reported 4.4m Internet users worldwide; in 2001, this had risen to half a billion;

- the emergence of Internet voice telephony, using voice-over-Internet protocol (VoIP) technology to provide telephone calls over the Internet as a low-cost competitive alternative to conventional international telephone service;

- the extension of national telephone networks across the Atlantic, creating truly international networks ('trans-national networks') under a single ownership and management for the first time; and

- the emergence of a number of other new modes of operation (later described in detail), which, unlike trans-national networks, were affordable for smaller companies, thus greatly reducing the barriers to entry in the transatlantic telecommunications business. Trading-exchange operations emerged such as Arbinet (based in the US) and Band-X (based in the UK) through which smaller players as well as larger ones could buy and sell traffic and wholesale services to transmit and complete calls.

In the next section, we describe more fully the reshaping of transatlantic telecommunications that resulted from these far-reaching developments. We do so by first reviewing how the transatlantic telephone service business worked before the reshaping; then discuss the impact of the forces for change; and finally seek to give a balanced picture of the situation today, indicating the (many) elements of continuity as well as the far-reaching changes that are in progress.

## 3. Structure and Structural Change

### 3.1 The Old Structure: Traffic Exchange between National Correspondents

Transatlantic telecommunication reached the dollar-a-minute, 2-3 billion minute per year, mass-scale stage of the late 1980s, apparent at a glance in Figures 1 and 2, under essentially the same traditional, historical industry structure that had prevailed since the late 19th century. Because this structure shaped much of the transatlantic telecommunications business as it is today and large elements of it remain in place, an outline of it is essential to understanding the present, despite the far-reaching structural changes that have taken place since the 1980s. The traditional structure originally consisted largely of national 'incumbent' operators such as AT&T in the US; and BT, France Telecom, Telecom Italia and their numerous other national counterparts in Europe, exchanging traffic. BT, for example, would sell a UK-to-US call in the UK, pass it to AT&T for completion in the US and pay AT&T a fee (based on notional price called an 'accounting rate') for doing so. This structure has often been called the 'correspondent system'. As new operators were licensed such as MCI or Sprint in the US, Mercury in the UK, or Tele2 in Sweden, they too joined the correspondent system.

One useful summary of the correspondent system for the exchange of transatlantic traffic takes the form of the following three short points:

- Incumbent national operators own domestic networks and international gateways.

- The gateways in a pair of countries are linked by international transmission facilities (cable or satellite), which are owned by the national operators under a variety of arrangements (but were traditionally thought of as 'half-circuits' meeting at a notional mid-point between the two countries).

- Under 'settlement' arrangements, operators notionally pay each other for terminating each international call, according to a settlement rate, which represents an agreed share (usually 50%) of an internationally agreed wholesale price (the accounting rate). Such arrangements provide for periodic settlements between the two operators of the net balance of such charges.

The pattern varied a little from case to case. For example, the US side historically had 'record' carriers providing non-voice (text and data) services alongside AT&T's voice services. From January 1984, the newly formed regional Bell operating companies (RBOCs) carried originating international calls to AT&T, and terminated international calls passed to them by AT&T. Some European countries also had variations on this type of arrangement, with a division between the international carrier and separate domestic, regional or local operators. In the US, as MCI and Sprint grew through the 1980s and 1990s, they joined AT&T as part of the US pillar of the correspondent system. Still, the broad lines of that system were more or less universal and more or less stable over time; and, as the numbers in Figures 1 and 2 show, the system worked.

Today, the same companies are still and will continue to be, very important players and a large majority of the telephone traffic across the Atlantic is still passed from one of the incumbent national carriers in Europe (the former national monopolies) to AT&T, MCI or Sprint in the US; or vice versa. The terminology has changed, but the reality of the market structure has changed much less. The economics of the reciprocal exchange of traffic remain an important factor stabilizing the market structure. Nevertheless, fundamental changes are emerging as discussed in the next section.

## 3.2 Forces for Change

Two fundamental forces have begun to transform the structure of transatlantic telecommunications (discussed in more detail in the next section):

- the emergence of newer modes of operation that represent alternatives to the correspondent system, even in its current modernized form; and

- the changing regulatory frameworks emerging from a combination of national regulatory and legislative activity and international negotiations resulting in international treaty law.

## Newer Modes of Operation

Alongside the old-established correspondent system described above, which has been relabeled and modified, but is still very much in business (to paraphrase from Mark Twain, rumors of its death have been greatly exaggerated), newer alternative modes of operation have emerged:

- leased-line resale;

- refile, hubbing and re-origination;

- trans-national networks, in which a network initially set up with national scope is extended to include PoPs in other countries: in this case, across the Atlantic;

- international alliances; and

- Internet telephony.

We briefly discuss each of these in turn, indicating how their respective roles and impacts have varied over time.

## Leased-Line Resale

In leased-line resale, newer operators make up for the limited reach of their own network facilities by renting leased line capacity from more established carriers and using it, in conjunction with their own switching capabilities, to provide international telephone services. Calls originate on the pre-existing public, switched telephone network (PSTN), usually provided by a long-established 'incumbent' operator such as an RBOC, AT&T or BT. These are then transmitted to the destination country by a leased line or other bulk private transmission facility, before terminating through the destination PSTN. This mode of operation, often called 'international simple resale' (ISR), was historically a major factor in making cheap transatlantic calls available to European and North American consumers, by greatly reducing the barriers to entry for smaller operators.

## Refile, Hubbing and Re-origination

In a refile operation, a telecommunications operator sends international traffic to an intermediate 'hub' country (e.g. one where a more competitive, open market ensures lower charges), for 'reorigination' to the ultimate destination country. The operator in the intermediate country settles the termination charge with the incumbent in the ultimate destination, who has no indication of the actual origin of the call.

## Trans-national Networks with Foreign PoPs

The example of MCI WorldCom (notwithstanding the financial travails that the company underwent subsequently because of fraud) illustrates well how trans-national networks have emerged. In the 1990s, the US company MFS not only pioneered the concept of independent Metropolitan Area Networks (MANs) (alongside another US company, TCG) and built numerous MANs across the US, but extended this activity to the construction of MANs in many European cities as well. By acquiring MFS and connecting its various MANs on both sides of the Atlantic to international links and to MCI WorldCom's US domestic long-distance ('inter-exchange') network, MCI WorldCom became able to carry transatlantic calls all the way from a US customer to any one of numerous foreign PoPs. The PoPs connected locally into the pre-existing foreign PSTN. This by-passed the old correspondent system, and thus the payment of settlements to foreign correspondent carriers, substituting instead much smaller charges for local interconnection. In some cases, MCI WorldCom was even able to carry the call end-to-end over its own facilities, launching comprehensive facilities-based competition with the incumbent operator within the destination country. The role of the foreign incumbent's network in terminating incoming transatlantic calls was diminished, and for calls to locations connected to the destination MAN ('on-net' locations), it disappeared altogether.

## International Alliances

Telecommunications operators have attempted several times to pool or share transmission capacity and certain classes of traffic and revenue, under diverse alliance arrangements. Most examples have been in the market for worldwide telecommunications services to multinational corporations (MNCs): they have at various times included Concert (led by AT&T and BT) and Global One (led by France Telecom, Deutsche Telekom and Sprint). Yet most examples have not been successful. Both Concert and Global One disappeared in 2001.

## Internet Telephony

Internet telephony has been 'waiting in the wings' to play a major role in the transatlantic telephone service business, providing a low-price alternative, since it was first demonstrated commercially in the mid 1990s. Similarly IP telephony – using similar Internet protocol (IP) technology, but not over the public Internet – has been expected for a long period to become a major feature in the marketplace. Two factors have led this potential to become a large-scale reality in the mid-1990s:

- the emergence of technology, such as the advanced software codec provided by Skype, which assures an acceptable quality of voice signal; and

- the recent enormous expansion in broadband access, for example DSL, which provides large numbers of residential and small business customers with a sufficiently fast data connection.

Together these allow consumers and service providers to substitute data for voice telephony services. The most basic form of this substitution requires nothing more than a software client application operated by the end-user on an Internet-connected personal computer. At the other extreme are ranges of high-end IP services. Between these two poles are many hybrid solutions that effectively resell or repurpose data transmission capacity for use in all or part of a voice call.

## Evolving Roles of the New Modes of Operation

In the transatlantic marketplace, the mix between the various new modes of operation has varied rapidly over time. Leased-line resale, refile, hubbing and re-origination have played an important role in bringing about the onset of competition. They have greatly reduced the barriers to entry into the international telephone service business, but in recent years have shown a diminishing return as competitive market pressures have reduced the pricing anomalies between different types of switched calls and leased line pricing, which were 'arbitraged' by these modes of operation. Trans-national networks were expected, in the heyday of MCI WorldCom and by the efforts of Cable & Wireless of the UK, to build a truly global network. The reality has proven in the event to be much more modest: there has certainly been some interpenetration of networks across frontiers, with the establishment of foreign PoPs, but most traffic is still exchanged through an updated form of the traditional correspondent system. In our view, the greatest strategic significance of trans-national networks is a competitive safeguard: a competitive 'sword of Damocles' hanging over each correspondent operator.

## 3.3 Changing Public Policy, Legislation and Regulation

In this section, we discuss the impact of changing public policy, legislation and regulation under three headings:

- US public policy, legislation and regulation;

- European public policy, legislation and regulation, at both the EU level and the national level; and

- international agreements.

In each case, we do not purport to cover the entire immense range and complexity of national (and EU) telecommunications law and policy. Instead, we simply pick out those aspects we consider most salient for an understanding of today's transatlantic telecommunications business and the agenda of current policy issues affecting it.

### US Public Policy, Legislation and Regulation

In many respects, the US telecommunications environment is still strongly shaped by the provisions of the 1934 Communications Act, which created the FCC. The 1996 Telecommunications Act extensively revised pre-existing law, notably by clarifying and extending the FCC's authority to choose to 'forbear' from regulation when it finds that market conditions justify this. Further, the 1996 Act clarified and relaxed the conditions under which the RBOCs would be allowed to provide long-distance ('inter-exchange') and international services. Finally, it gave the US the ability to make certain international market-opening commitments, as discussed below. Out of all the complex history of US public policy, legislation and regulation for telecommunications, we have selected the following strands of this history as having particular relevance to an understanding of today's industry structure and policy environment for transatlantic telecommunications:

- the Modification of Final Judgment (MFJ) settling the Department of Justice/AT&T anti-trust case. From January 1984, this broke up the pre-existing Bell system into a new and reduced (but still very large) AT&T and the segregated RBOCs;

- a series of case-by-case FCC decisions on the extent to which non-US telecommunications operators were permitted to carry traffic into the US from abroad, or from the US to other countries (as distinct from exchanging traffic with US operators under the traditional correspondent system);

- the development by the FCC of a doctrine codifying its approach to such decisions, known as the equivalent competitive opportunities (ECO-) test, and based in essence on a doctrine of reciprocity, i.e. only allowing telecoms operators from outside the US the same opportunities extended to US-based operators;

- a period of controversy over the ECO-test doctrine, following ratification of the WTO Basic Telecommunications Agreement (discussed below) by the US Senate and focusing on two incompatible approaches involved – strict reciprocity, in the case of the ECO-test; and the principles of national treatment and most favored nation that apply to the application of market-opening commitments made by national governments under the Basic Telecommunications Agreement (like all WTO agreements);

- the resulting revocation of the ECO-test doctrine in FCC decisions of November 1997, which retained certain safeguards against anti-competitive behavior by foreign operators (mainly designed to prevent them leveraging market power in their home markets to gain an advantage in the US) and which were claimed to be non-discriminatory and therefore legitimate under the WTO Basic Telecommunications Agreement. The application of this is well illustrated by the FCC's recent consideration of Deutsche Telekom's acquisition of WorldStream. Some observers have criticized this regime as deterring competitive entry and investment by creating uncertainty as to what will and will not be permitted;

- a current controversy (addressed by an FCC policy statement in November 2004) over the FCC's use of its radio licensing powers, and whether the way it does this is equitable to foreign telecoms operators (the FCC claims it has little discretion under current US law to waive various restrictions that foreign operators are objecting to); and

- the ORBIT Act, which reflected the objections of several US commercial satellite communications players to competition from Intelsat, Inmarsat and certain other satellite operating organizations benefiting from international treaty rights. The ORBIT Act imposed far-reaching preconditions on these organizations before they would be permitted to compete fully in the US market. This delayed the full removal of barriers to entry in satellite communications for many years; but with recent changes of ownership (the affected organizations are now primarily owned by private equity investors), the ORBIT Act obstacles appear to have been largely overcome.

Overall, this complex history has moved the US regulatory environment for transatlantic telecommunications a very long way toward providing for a transatlantic 'single market' comparable to the single market that now exists throughout the EU. Nevertheless, as indicated by the last two aspects we cited, difficulties and obstacles are by no means a thing of the past.

## European Public Policy, Legislation and Regulation (EU and National)

The evolution of European telecoms markets has been shaped by the interaction of national and EU level policy, regulation and legislation. We discern four stages. In the first stage, some EU member states, notably Sweden and the UK, took a lead in moving toward a more pro-competitive policy and a multi-player industry structure (e.g. the UK's privatization of BT and the establishment of the BT-Mercury duopoly in 1984). In the second stage, beginning at the end of the 1980s, these 'leading edge' countries moved to a more radically pro-competitive approach. The UK for example abolished the duopoly and established essentially open entry into the domestic fixed-service business. Additional countries moved at the national level toward a pro-competitive policy. At the European level, the EU's 1990 Framework Directive became law throughout the EU member states. This legislation established basic principles for the licensing of operators and for harmonization of 'network access' (for example, interconnection rights for new operators) in EU member states.

The third stage involved a package of more detailed EU measures designed to extend the EU Single Market, by then long-established for trade in goods, to telecommunications services. This package, which came in to force at the beginning of 1998 made it mandatory for national regulatory authorities (NRAs), such as OFTEL in the UK (subsequently, OFCOM) to provide that national regulatory rules:

- ensure non-discriminatory licensing in each EU country of telecoms operators from other EU countries;

- permit unrestricted ownership of domestic telecoms operations in each EU country by telecoms operators from other EU countries;

- mandate unrestricted rights of interconnection to the pre-existing PSTN in each EU country for telecoms operators from other EU countries, on non-discriminatory terms and at prices bearing a reasonable relationship to costs; and

- forbid various specific forms of anticompetitive behavior by incumbent operators.

These rules were extended to benefit certain associated European countries not in the EU (notable Norway and Switzerland); they were also (as we describe more fully below) extended by means of the WTO Basic Telecommunications Agreement, to benefit telecoms operators from other WTO member countries, including the US and Canada. All of this was intended to come into force simultaneously on January 1, 1998 and despite some delays in the case of the WTO agreement, all of it was in fact in force by the end of 1998.

The fourth stage of the evolution was the new regulatory framework (NRF), introduced in 2002. This superseded the pre-existing EU legislative framework, although not the provisions of the WTO agreement. The NRF consists of several separate legislative instruments, together with guidelines for their application issued by the European Commission. It requires NRAs under the oversight of the Commission to use the following process for regulatory decisions:

- definition and analysis of markets according to principles of competition law and economics;

- assessment of significant market power (SMP) within those markets. The concept of SMP is aligned with the competition law concept of market dominance, and NRAs are permitted to regulate only where they can show that a telecoms operator has SMP and that there is consequent economic harm (or the potential for harm); and

- the design and imposition of remedies that are proportionate to the problems resulting from SMP.

The framework is based on two key principles:

- technology neutrality – regulatory measures should not discriminate between equivalent services delivered over different technological platforms, for example along the PSTN or cable-TV systems; and

- a forward-looking basis – unlike competition law (which, with the exception of consideration of proposed mergers, is applied on an *ex post* basis in response to identifiable abuses by a market player), the market definition, SMP analysis and design of remedies are all undertaken on an *ex ante* basis.

The most important practical effects of the NRF legislation, from the point of view of this chapter, have been:

- the licensing of telecoms operators, such as newer entrants that do not have SMP in European markets, has become little more than a formality, except where scarce radio spectrum (which may already have been assigned) is involved; and

- most European incumbent telecom operators have been found to have SMP in fixed line and data communications markets. As a result, they have been subject to remedies generally centering on the mandated provision of wholesale network access, including regulated interconnection and provision of wholesale network services (often including local loop unbundling), to their competitors. They have also been subject to a degree of separation of wholesale and retail activities (usually accounting separation for ensuring transparent regulated pricing of interconnection and related wholesale offerings used by competitors).

International agreements to which the EU (which nowadays acts on behalf of all member states in such matters) is a party have had the effect of extending to telecoms operators from outside the EU, on a non-discriminatory basis, the various rights of unrestricted licensing and interworking with the incumbent's networks. In the case of European countries not yet in the EU (such as Norway, Switzerland and various Eastern European countries), this was assured by the European Economic Area (EEA) Treaty and various Association Agreements. For a much wider group of countries, including the US and Canada, it was assured by the WTO Basic Telecommunication Agreement, which we discuss below.

## International Agreements

The efficient operation of transatlantic telecommunications businesses depends, to a much greater extent than is usually appreciated, on two kinds of international agreements concerning:

- technical and operational matters, such as the use of radio frequencies and the geostationary orbit, numbering, and technical standards and compatibility; and

- commercial matters, especially market access and participation across national frontiers.

The first of these, involving institutions ranging from the ITU to the Internet Engineering Task Force (IETF) is of great practical importance and we fear the potential consequences of not-so benign neglect: to maintain high quality operations in an increasingly complex and diverse environment will require more resources, not less.

The second of these has been critical in creating a competitive transatlantic marketplace: the centerpiece of a complex web of bilateral and multilateral agreements is the WTO Basic Telecommunication Agreement.

## 3.4   WTO Basic Telecommunication Agreement

Foreign operators' freedom to establish their own interconnections with incumbent networks was assured under the WTO Basic Telecommunications Agreement. The agreement was concluded in 1997 and came in to force during 1998. Technically a protocol to the General Agreement on Trade in Services (GATS), it was adopted as part of the WTO Treaty (the Marrakech Agreement) finalized in 1995 and implemented to varying timetables in the years immediately following. Under the agreement, national governments committed to 'schedules of commitments' in varying degrees to different measures to open their telecommunications markets to competition. In practice, American, Canadian and European governments made some of the most far-reaching market-opening commitments and these commitments have been transposed (not without some conflict and controversy) into national (and in Europe, EU) legislation and regulation. The commitments addressed the following areas: rights of entry for foreign competitors in domestic and international fixed markets, rights of foreign operators to establish networks and non-discriminatory interconnection at cost-based prices.

## 4.   Current Industry Structure and Market Dynamics: The Impact of Technological, Commercial, Legislative and Regulatory Forces for Change

This section discusses the state of transatlantic telecommunications today, focusing especially on the impact that can already be seen from the new modes of operation and the changing policy, legislative and regulatory environment, described above. We discuss in turn two different aspects of the telecoms business spanning the Atlantic:

- the carriage of international telecoms traffic – voice, data and video – between North America (the US and Canada) and Europe, whether under correspondent relationships or through newer modes of operation such as the extension of telecoms operators' networks, originally set up as national networks (although interconnected to other national networks) across the Atlantic, so that US networks gained PoPs in Europe and vice-versa; and

- participation in the domestic communications markets of North America and Europe by foreign (European and North American respectively) telecoms operators, either directly or by taking an ownership interest (or even by outright acquisition) of established local communications operators.

## 4.1 The Carriage of International Telecommunications Traffic

An overview of the current state of the market for international telecoms traffic – voice, data and video – across the Atlantic shows that the various 'forces for change' we reviewed in the previous section have had a substantial effect. Scholars debate endlessly about the relative importance of the various factors. For example, did the WTO Basic Telecommunication Agreement change the course of events, or did it merely record and consolidate what was happening anyway? Here we do not attempt to answer such questions or even debate whether or not they matter: there is no doubt that the cumulative effect of all these factors has led to a much more competitive environment, with a trans-national competitive marketplace across the Atlantic region of the world. Rather, we point to three notable aspects of the current state of the market, all of them manifestations of themes already identified.

First, increasing competition from new entrants has eroded incumbents' market share considerably. One of the many indications of this is provided by the European Commission's data on the market shares of the incumbent telephone companies in Europe, such as BT or France Telecom. These data, summarized in Figure 5, show that while incumbent market shares across all communications services have declined substantially as communications markets have become more liberalized, incumbents have enjoyed far lower market shares in international communications than in local ones.

*Figure 5. Average Market share of Incumbent Firms in EU-15 Countries*

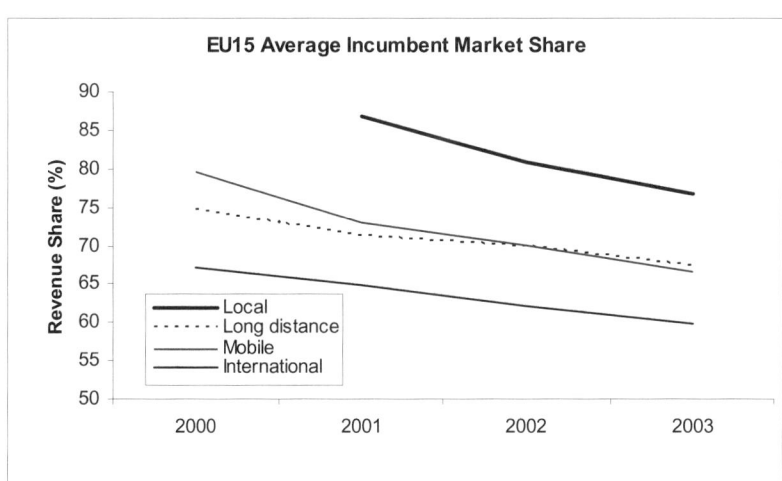

*Source:* European Commission, *Implementation of the Regulatory Framework in the Member states – 10th Report*, COM(2004) 759 final, Brussels, December 2, 2004.

Second, available capacity has continued to increase, driven by both new physical transmission capacity and by using existing capacity more efficiently. In particular, there is still a significant overhang of unlit transatlantic capacity. While the cost of lighting this capacity is by no means negligible, its availability suggests continued downward price pressure.

*Figure 6. Cable Capacity*

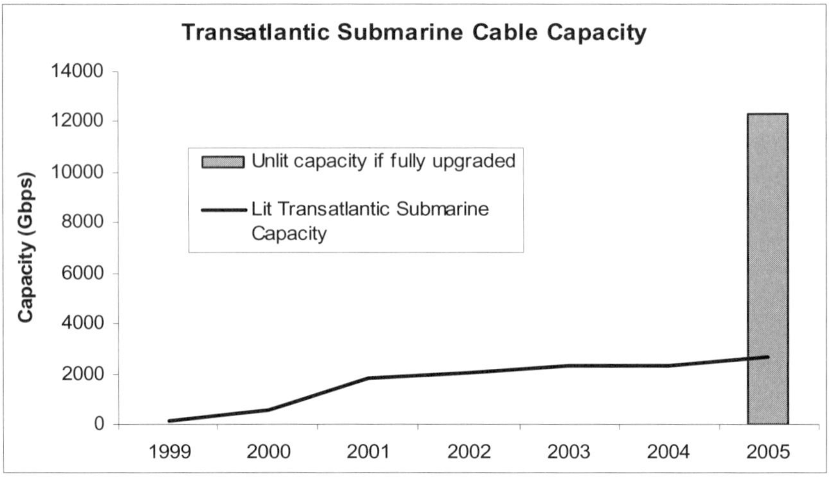

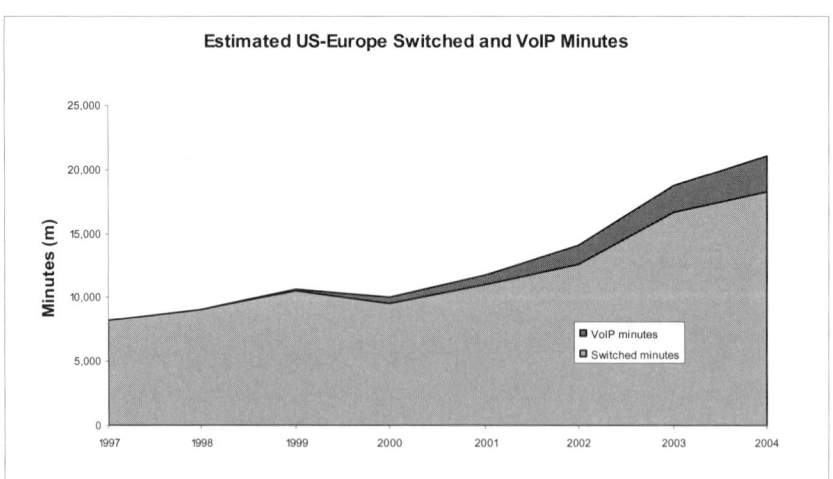

*Source:* Telegeography, 2004.

*Figure 7. Estimated of Transatlantic Switched and VoIP Minutes*

*Sources:* Telegeography, 2005; FCC; Tyler & Company Analysis.

Third, the impact of Internet telephony on the industry, although many commentators have exaggerated it so far, is now quite significant. Figure 7 shows our estimate of the number of VoIP minutes on transatlantic routes, derived from using data on worldwide circuit-switched and VoIP minutes. These figures do not include computer-to-computer VoIP where, for example, Skype claims to have 'served' 7 billion minutes since its launch in 2003. The effect is to create additional price pressure and open up major new opportunities for entrants.

## 4.2 Trans-national Market Participation and Investment

A review of the current degree of openness of European and US telecommunications markets shows few remaining restrictions on foreign ownership and wide participation by foreign communications operations. There are a very few exceptions; in some cases there are notification requirements for ownership changes. In the US the FCC retains legal authority to deny radio licenses to companies with more than 25% foreign ownership on the grounds of public-interest.

Companies on both sides of the Atlantic have participated in each other's markets, both by directly owned operations and by taking ownership stakes. This has been most pronounced, as Table 1 shows, in the faster evolving and growing markets: in mobile communications and in cable networks whose ability to offer voice and data communications services has increasingly made them major competitors to incumbents' PSTN-based services. It has also taken place in wholesale capacity markets, with the acquisition and construction of fiber-optic backbone networks. Although the Table 1 is necessarily selective, the scale of these participations demonstrates that what has arguably been the major item on the international policy agenda of the last 20 years, namely to lower barriers systematically to competitive entry, has in large part been achieved.

### New Players

Superficially, one might ask how it is that in an era of market liberalization, a list of leading players on major routes including transatlantic routes would turn up names familiar to the industry for at least 20 years (in the case of the American long distance carriers) and longer (in the case of the European incumbents). In fact, competition has been generated largely by the emergence of *new markets* based on new technologies and only to a lesser extent by competitive entry into existing markets.

Table 1. *Transatlantic Participation and Ownership of Telecommunications Services – Selected Examples*

| Type of transaction/ participation | Target/ vehicle | Business | Acquirer/ owner | Acquirer/owner business | Date | Current status |
|---|---|---|---|---|---|---|
| Transatlantic joint venture | Global One | International voice and data | France Telecom, Deutsche Telecom, Sprint | Incumbent and competitive carriers | 1996 | Concluded/dissolved: in 2000, other partners bought out by France Telecom; in 2001, acquired by Equant |
| Europe-US acquisition | MCI (Tier 1 backbone only) | Voice and data transmission | Cable & Wireless | Voice and data telephony | 1998 | C&W America filed for bankruptcy in 2003, Cable and Wireless America, Inc. filed for Chapter 11 bankruptcy; bought by Savvis Communications in 2004 |
| Transatlantic joint venture | Concert | International voice and data including VoIP | BT & AT&T | Incumbent national carriers | 1998 | Dissolved in 2001; assets returned to BT & AT&T |
| US-Europe acquisition | Kabel NRW/ish ($2.5bn) | Cable television, Internet and telephony | Callahan Associates | Financial investment group | 2000 | Kabel NRW/ish acquired after insolvency by a consortium of banks including Citigroup and Deutsche Bank in 2003 |
| US-Europe acquisition | Telewest | Cable television, Internet and telephony | Microsoft | Computer software and diverse other interests | 2000 | The stake taken was reduced from 30% after competition concerns from were expressed by the European Commission. The stake was sold in 2003 to IDT |

*Table 2. Cont'd.*

| | | | | | | |
|---|---|---|---|---|---|---|
| Europe-US acquisition | Voice-Stream ($24 bn) | Mobile telephony | Deutsche Telekom/T-Mobile | Mobile telephony | 2001 | Currently operating under the T-Mobile brand |
| US-Europe acquisition | Noos | Cable television, Internet and telephony | United-GlobalCom | International data and voice communications | 2004 | Currently operating under the Noos brand |
| US-Europe acquisition | Eutelsat | European satellite voice and data communications | Texas Pacific Group and Spectrum Equity Investors | Private equity | 2004 | TPG and Spectrum currently holding stake in Eutelsat |
| Europe-US acquisition | Cingular networks in California and Nevada | Mobile telephony | Deutsche Telekom/T-Mobile | Mobile telephony | 2005 | Currently operating services in Nevada and California |
| US-Europe acquisition | Mobilcom | Mobile telephony | Texas Pacific (incl. TPG Axon Cap.) | Private equity | 2005 | TPG currently holding stake in Mobilcom |

*Source*: Authors' data.

Most obviously, the growth and consolidation of the mobile telephony market has created a small number of very large and powerful players (such as Vodafone) and fixed-to-mobile substitution is now a significant factor in consumer demand for traditional services.

Further, the emergence of the cable industry as a competing provider of fixed-line telephony services and the convergence of voice and data communications services have created powerful new sources of competition for traditional telecommunications. Participation in these markets has proved an effective route to transnational competition.

## 5. The Outlook and the Policy Agenda

From one point of view, one might even ask why there is a policy agenda in transatlantic telecommunications. We have shown that the sector is a success story: soaring productivity, plummeting prices and rapid innovation. We have also considered how increasingly open transatlantic competition has grown and added to this favorable result. It contributes strongly to productivity gains in user industries, and since every industry is a telecommunications user (although some, like financial services and international trade, are naturally more intensive users than others), the beneficial effect is pervasive across the economy. The industry consumes little energy, hardly pollutes at all (except perhaps for some concerns, still very much subject to further research, about the possible biological effects of radio frequency energy). So what is there to make policy about?

We have picked out four key areas we foresee as being important for future policy debate, intentionally highlighting some that are relatively 'low profile' and perceived as specialized and technical or whose importance has yet to be fully recognized. These four are:

- sustaining key measures to facilitate competitive entry and physically efficient operation. These include the management of the numbering plan and addressing as well as standards for interworking/ interoperability among the growing range of networks, technologies and players;

- managing the remaining issues concerning market entry, open competition and non-discriminatory treatment of foreign telecommunications operators within the North Atlantic region. Even as a 'single transatlantic market' emerges, that is not to say that it is ever free of disputes or issues;

- management of common resources such as spectrum, the role of innovative approaches to this resource (e.g. spectrum trading), with a possible international marketplace for spectrum rights; and

- emerging controversies pitching the public interest in interoperability against intellectual property issues raised by proprietary formats (e.g. voice communication codecs integrated into online chat software applications).

Because of the pervasive importance of telecommunications as an essential infrastructure and productivity enhancer for other sectors throughout the economy, which we emphasized at the beginning of this chapter, successfully managing policy issues in these and other areas will be of major importance to the Atlantic economy as a whole.

# 11. Telecommunications Services: A Transatlantic Perspective

## *Andrea Renda*

### Introduction: The Telecommunications Anomaly

Over the past two decades, the information and communication technologies (ICT) sector has gradually become the most important engine of economic growth, productivity and welfare for developed and developing countries. The ICT industry in 2005 was valued at €2.044 trillion. The transatlantic economy accounts for 61.4% of the global ICT industry, with the United States and the EU respectively comprising 29.3% and 32.1% of the total.

Yet the two regions have experienced starkly different patterns of growth in this sector. The US showed a real productivity boost during the late 1990s, thanks to the development of its ICT sector, which appears to have driven two-thirds of US economic growth.[1] Today, even after the Internet bubble, US growth has gradually resumed, with estimates of 3.9% for 2005 and 4.5% in 2006.[2] The EU, on the other hand, not only lags consistently behind the US, it is being outperformed by Asian countries, notably South Korea, India, China and Japan. The European Commission reported that as much as 40% of the productivity growth in the EU between 1995 and 2000 stemmed from ICT, although an important productivity gap remains between the EU and the US, which can be explained largely by the EU's lower investments in ICT.[3]

Both the US and the EU have formulated ambitious goals in the ICT sector. On March 26, 2004, President George W. Bush launched the new US broadband policy, aiming at achieving universal broadband availability no later than 2007. At the March 2000 European Council meeting in Lisbon, European Union leaders declared the EU's ambition to become the most competitive and dynamic knowledge-based economy by 2010, highlighting ICT as a main driver to achieve that goal. The key role of information and communications technology in the Lisbon strategy was also confirmed in the

---

[1] See *inter alia* D. Jorgenson, "Information Technology and the U.S. Economy", *American Economic Review*, Vol. 91, No. 1, March 2001, pp. 1-32.

[2] Data derived from the European Information Technology Observatory (EITO), *2005 Annual Report*, EITO, Frankfurt.

[3] See B. Van Ark and O. Mahony, *EU Productivity and Competitiveness: An Industry Perspective – Can Europe Resume the Catching-up process?*, Office for Official Publications of the EU, Luxembourg, 2003.

Europe Action Plan at the spring Council meeting in 2004, as well as the recent Kok Report and the new i2010 initiative launched on June 1, 2005.[4]

Fulfilling such ambitious goals, however, crucially depends on whether national governments and regulators will be able to stimulate investment and competition in their telecommunication (hereafter telecom) infrastructures. Recent data show that both US and EU telecom industries have started to rebound, after the 'boom and bust' phase at the beginning of this decade. The sector's worldwide revenues have climbed from $388 million in 1991 to $952 million in 2003.[5] The European Information Technology Observatory (EITO) has recently estimated growth of the telecoms sector in Europe at 3.7% for 2005 and 3.3% for 2006, whereas the US market is expected to grow by 3.1% in 2005 and 3.2% in 2006. Europe accounts for 30.7% and the US for 21.6% of the €1.126 trillion global telecoms sector.[6] As shown in Table 1, nine of the world's top ten telecommunication firms are based either in the US or in the EU, except the Japanese giant NTT DoCoMo.

The current resurgence of investment and growth in turn calls for action by national governments to adapt their regulatory frameworks to the changing industry landscape and to open up their markets to competition from national and foreign carriers, to the advantage of end-users. Thus scholars and policy-makers are devoting attention to spurring transatlantic dialogue for the creation of an integrated US-EU telecoms services market. Such an integrated market is still hindered by the persistence of diverging regulatory frameworks, incompatible standards and non-tariff barriers to inward foreign direct investment (FDI). Yet, starting with the 1998 EU-US Mutual Recognition Agreement (MRA) on communications equipment, many steps have been taken toward enhanced cooperation by both sides toward further integration. These initiatives have been transposed into positive, constructive endeavors after the 2004 EU-US summit, where officials pledged continued cooperation in the area of telecommunications during the Brussels meeting of the annual Information Society Dialogue (ISD) on September 17, 2004.

---

[4] See the report by V. Kok, *Facing the Challenge* (retrieved from http://europa.eu.int/growthandjobs/pdf/kok_report_en.pdf), November 2004 and the European Commission's Communication, i2010 – A European Information Society for Growth and Employment, COM(2005)229, Brussels, June 1, 2005 (report retrieved from http://europa.eu.int/information_society/eeurope/i2010/index_en.htm).

[5] The source of this data is OECD Key ICT Indicators, 2005. Mobile service revenues only accounted for 7% of overall revenues in 1991 and reached 35.3% in 2003.

[6] See EITO (2005), op. cit. In the IT sector, the opposite occurs: the US accounts for 38.7% and Europe for 33.8% of the global market.

Table 1. Top 10 Telecoms Services Firms ($ millions and number employed)

| Company | Country | Revenue 2000 | Revenue 2002 | Revenue 2003 | Employees 2000 | Employees 2002 | R&D 2000 | R&D 2002 | Net income 2000 | Net income 2002 |
|---|---|---|---|---|---|---|---|---|---|---|
| NTT | Japan | 92,679 | 87,948 | 91,026 | 224,000 | 213,062 | 3,178 | 3,118 | -603 | -6,657 |
| Verizon | US | 64,707 | 67,625 | 67,734 | 260,000 | 245,000 | – | – | 11,797 | 4,079 |
| France Telecom | France | 30,480 | 46,600 | 52,048 | 188,866 | 211,554 | 530 | 680 | 3,313 | -20,500 |
| Deutsche Telekom | Germany | 37,559 | 50,650 | 50,528 | 170,000 | 255,896 | 642 | 849 | 5,437 | -23,195 |
| Vodafone | UK | 11,929 | 33,109 | 47,962 | 29,465 | 67,178 | 109 | 164 | 838 | -23,413 |
| SBC | US | 51,374 | 43,138 | 42,310 | 220,090 | 175,980 | – | – | 7,800 | 5,653 |
| AT&T | US | 46,850 | 37,827 | 36,480 | 84,800 | 71,000 | 313 | 254 | 4,669 | -13,082 |
| Telecom Italia | Italy | 27,516 | 31,200 | 32,983 | 107,171 | 101,713 | 247 | 124 | 3,231 | 781 |
| BT | UK | 28,356 | 30,685 | 30,460 | 132,000 | 108,600 | 552 | 540 | 2,111 | -1,093 |
| Telefonica | Spain | 24,100 | 31,800 | 26,739 | 145,730 | 161,029 | – | – | 725 | 1,800 |
| Total | – | 415,550 | 460,582 | 478,270 | 1,562,122 | 1,611,012 | 5,570 | 5,729 | 39,317 | -75,626 |

Note: Revenues for 2003 are based on the financial year reported in 2003 or the most recent four quarters.

Sources: OECD, IT Outlook (2004) and OECD, Key ICT Indicators (2005).

The future transatlantic dialogue in the communications field will necessarily have to take into account the changes that have occurred in the telecoms industry over the past few years. These changes include the ongoing transition from wireline to wireless telephony, fast-growing competition from all-Internet protocol (IP) networks, fixed-mobile substitution and increased convergence between end-to-end communication technologies and broadcasting services, which promote 'premium' content as one of the main spurs of success for all kinds of network operators. For this reason, the first section of this paper provides a brief overview of major trends in the telecoms industries on both sides of the Atlantic, identifying key drivers and consolidation trends in the fixed-line and mobile sectors. The second section illustrates some of the remaining obstacles that hinder the creation of a transatlantic telecoms market, with specific emphasis on existing non-tariff barriers between the EU and the US. The third section concludes by suggesting possible advantages that might follow from enhanced regulatory convergence and cooperation for global industry operators as well as for consumers.

## Industry Trends: A Global Reshape

The worldwide telecoms industry is changing at a breathtaking pace. Only a few years ago, telecoms markets in most countries were simply the realm of state-owned (EU) or privately owned (US) monopolies. The first wave of liberalization started in the US with the breakup of AT&T in 1984. Later, the US 1996 Telecommunications Act and the European Regulatory Framework on Electronic Communications created important pre-conditions for greater competition in wireline and mobile telephone markets. Today, both of these pieces of legislation appear hardly suited to govern market change effectively and efficiently.

The fixed-line sector is increasingly going wireless and IP-enabled, whereas the mobile sector is rapidly moving to broadband, becoming a viable substitute for fixed voice and data services. The number of mobile subscribers has already overcome that of fixed-line users, and fixed-mobile substitution is one of the main causes for the gradual margin erosion suffered by traditional fixed-line incumbents. Such operators – although still enjoying large market shares in most EU countries – are now struggling to resist the increased competitive pressure from mobile and voice-over-IP (VoIP) service providers, which are credited with better market prospects and higher margins (especially third-generation or 3G players). Finally, the convergence between Internet-based communication technologies, broadband technologies and broadcast services has significantly reshaped the competitive arena, paving the way for future inter-platform competition. The growing importance of valuable premium content as an impetus of consumer demand is leading industry operators to adopt comprehensive market strategies (such as 'triple play'), in which network operators increasingly take the role of platform operators competing in multi-sided markets.

As a result, the competitive strategies adopted by most industry operators have become increasingly 'consumer-centric', as consumer attention is emerging as the scarcest and (thus) most precious resource in an all-IP world. Accordingly, players in the fixed, mobile, broadcast and content industries are now becoming familiar with new challenges, such as 'competition for eyeballs' and inter-platform competition, which call for new revenue-sharing models focused on enhanced cooperation with competitors (so-called 'co-opetition'), content providers and device manufacturers. The new, proactive role of consumers in expressing their preferences also leads to increasingly diversified pricing strategies, which require careful use of versioning and flat pricing schemes. In this changing landscape, consumers are becoming 'pro-sumers' and many industry players are reverting to regional strategies instead of striving to become global.

All these developments certainly exert an impact on the policy options chosen by regulators. It is therefore hardly surprising that telecoms regulators on both sides of the Atlantic are currently in the process of thoroughly reviewing their respective regulatory frameworks. Accordingly, issues such as technological neutrality and hands-off regulation for new emerging markets will be under the spotlight in the coming months.

### *From Wireline to Wireless and Beyond*

The motto for fixed-line telecommunications companies (hereafter telcos) is now 'mobility'. The goal of mobility has spurred a massive migration to wireless access technologies, which include short-range solutions (such as 801.11a, 802.11b (WiFi), RLAN, HiperLAN, HomeRF or Bluetooth) and emerging technologies with extended range – the most important being 802.20 (HiperMAN) and 802.16 (WiMAX). Of these, WiFi and WiMAX, both promoted by Intel, represent the most reliable prospects for fixed-network operators, although they are at a very early stage, especially in Europe. Given the increased convergence and substitution between fixed and mobile services, these platforms are likely to complement 3G (and 4G) cellular technologies in the near future. In particular, WiFi-deployed hotspots are expected to grow ten-fold between 2003 and 2007, reaching more than 404,000 worldwide, of which 93,300 are likely to be in the EU and 103,200 in the US.[7] Revenues are also expected to skyrocket, from \$3.3 billion in

---

[7] Data derived from ON World Inc., *European Hotspots: A rapidly growing ecosystem*, San Diego, CA, 2004.

2003 to \$6.4 billion by 2007.[8] WiMAX revenues are expected to reach \$5.4 billion in 2007. This technology, currently in its infancy, promises to cover 15 to 20 miles at the outstanding speed of 15-20 megabits per second, thus faster than WiFi and 3G.

It is unclear, however, whether current wireline operators will exploit the potential for innovative solutions. First, it is quite hard to imagine where such operators will find the necessary financial resources for a rapid roll-out of next generation networks (NGNs), given the current shortage of revenues in this industry. As a result, equipment manufacturers such as Intel and giant mobile operators such as T-Mobile, Nextel and NTT DoCoMo are taking the lead in WiFi deployment. Second, for incumbent wireline players incentives to invest are further jeopardized by converging all-IP technologies. In fact, Internet service providers (ISPs) are in a privileged position for reaping the benefits of local loop unbundling (LLU) and increased broadband deployment. The emerging VoIP technology is said to promise up to 40% savings in the operating costs of the voice network.[9]

VoIP really has a disruptive potential. Although it is currently being used as Internet telephony with voice traffic routed on a 'best effort' basis over PC-Internet-PC, PC-Internet-PSTN and PSTN-Internet-PSTN networks, the next generation will include voice-over-broadband (VoBB), which allows for high-quality voice transmission over an NGN rather than over the public Internet. Once such a transition is complete, VoIP operators will simply be able to offer high-quality voice and data services at lower price. Hence, the new challenge for incumbent voice operators on both sides of the Atlantic is to move their networks to VoIP. According to a recent study, massive migration to VoIP will take place mostly in the 2009-14 timeframe, but many small businesses and consumers will be moving over between 2005 and 2009.[10]

Industry operators active in the promotion of these new technologies are advocating regulatory relief that would allow them to deploy new infrastructures without having to face heavy-handed regulation. Hands-off regulation for "new and emerging markets" is considered key for innovation in the fixed-line market.[11] In this respect, as explained below, the US and EU seem to be converging on a common path.

---

[8] See "No Wires, No Rules", *Business Week Special Report*, April 26, 2004.

[9] See Analysys Research, *The Role and Impact of WiMAX and Proprietary BWA*, Cambridge, November 2004.

[10] As estimated by InStat, *Carrier NGN Migration Strategies set VoIP Timing,* University of Reading, April 2005.

[11] See for example the KPMG report, *A Tough Road to Recovery*, London, 2005.

## Trends in the US Fixed-Line Sector

Prior to 1984, primarily a single firm, AT&T, supplied both local and long-distance telephone services in the US. In 1984, following a 1982 antitrust settlement with the US Department of Justice, AT&T was broken up into a number of regional firms (so-called 'baby bells' – regional Bell operating companies or RBOCs) providing local services and one long-distance provider that retained the AT&T name. Between that time and the explicit deregulation of US telecommunications with the entry into force of the 1996 Telecommunications Act, the US telecoms industry was characterized by an artificial regulatory segregation of local exchange telephony from long-distance telephony, which arose principally from the consent decree signed by the US Department of Justice and AT&T in 1984.[12] While local services were considered essentially a natural monopoly and as such were subject to rate regulation, the market for long-distance calls was considered potentially competitive and gradually experienced entry by alternative providers.[13] As a result, between 1984 and 2002, per-minute long-distance prices fell by more than 80% after adjusting for inflation,[14] whereas local exchange carriers (RBOCs) were expressly prohibited from manufacturing equipment, offering 'information services' or long-distance services outside their local access and transport areas (LATAs). After failing to obtain relief from the court enforcing the AT&T decree, the RBOCs turned to a legislative solution. In 1996, they finally obtained it, but the price was high: a new asymmetric regulatory regime and the liberalization of entry into local and intrastate markets.

The 1996 Telecommunications Act deregulated long-distance telephone services, local exchange telephone services and local cable television

---

[12] Modification of Final Judgment, reprinted in *United States v. AT&T Co.*, 552 F. Supp. 131, 226-34 (D.D.C. 1982), *aff'd sub nom. Maryland v. United States*, 460 US 1001 (1983).

[13] This trend was heightened by the FCC inadvertently allowing MCI to begin offering long-distance services without explicit FCC permission, then inhibited by the D.C. Circuit Court in the so-called 1978 *Execunet I* case. See *MCI Telecomms. Corp. v. FCC*, 561 F.2d 365 (D.C. Cir. 1977) and the description in G.O. Robinson, *The Titanic Remembered: AT&T and the Changing World of Telecommunications*, 5 Yale J. on Reg., 517 (1988), pp. 523-27. On the slow emergence of a competitive environment in long-distance services, see H.A. Shelanski and J.G. Sidak, *Antitrust Divestiture in Network Industries*, 68 U. Chi. L. Rev. 1, 40 (2001).

[14] As reported in the *2005 Economic Report of the President*, Chairman of the Council of Economic Advisors, transmitted to Congress on February 2005, US Printing Office, Washington D.C., p. 146.

services. As a result, the RBOCs were finally allowed to enter the lucrative long-distance markets under the condition that they provided unbundled access to any entrant that wished to use part of their networks (the so-called 'unbundled network elements' or UNE) at just, reasonable and non-discriminatory conditions, based on the TELRIC pricing.[15]

The 1996 Act, initially welcomed with enthusiasm as a 'Camelot moment', soon proved inadequate to regulate the fast-changing US telecoms industry efficiently.[16] First, the mandatory unbundling obligation has been increasingly considered as an insurmountable hurdle for investments in (DSL) broadband deployment by RBOCs. Second, the so-called 'silos' approach adopted by the Act – in which each type of telecommunication service (broadcasting, telephony, cable television and information services) is subject to its own regulatory structure, seems to have significantly stifled competition in the market and proved hardly consistent with the 'layered' approach required by the new all-IP networks. Under the 1996 scheme, wireline telephone companies were subject to 'common carrier' regulation under Title II of the Communications Act of 1934, and their retail services were subject to the traditional division of regulatory authority between the FCC and the states. On the other hand, use of the airwaves, such as for over-the-air broadcasting or cellular telephone services, was regulated completely or in part under Title III, which, among other things, preempted most forms of state regulation. In addition, cable services were regulated under Title VI, which essentially divided regulatory responsibility between the FCC and local franchising authorities, but generally exempted cable providers from common carriage obligations.

It is no surprise, given such 'regulatory apartheid', that cable operators have taken the lead in broadband deployment.[17] The legacy of the 1996 Telecommunications Act is the main explanation for the cable-intensive nature of broadband connection in the US.[18] Figure 1 shows the enormous

---

[15] TELRIC stands for total element long-run incremental cost.

[16] Senate Commerce Committee Hearing, Voice over Internet Protocol, February 24, 2004.

[17] The definition of regulatory apartheid was given by Peter Huber, quoted in T.W. Hazlett, *Explaining the Telecommunications Act of 1996: Comment on Thomas G. Krattenmaker*, 29 Conn. L. Rev, 217 (1996).

[18] Another explanation is that DSL is constrained by the distance between the subscriber and the central office. DSL over a copper wire only works within 18,000 feet of a central office facility. See *inter alia*, A.A. Gilroy and L.G. Kruger, *Broadband Internet Access: Background and Issues*, Issue Brief for Congress, Congressional Research Service, Washington, D.C., updated April 4, 2005.

increase in high-speed lines that occurred in the US between 1999 and 2004, with cable broadband rising from 1.4 million lines in 1999 to 18.6 million in 2004, with a growth of 15% in the first six months of 2004 alone.[19]

*Figure 1. High-Speed Line Growth in the US, 1999-2004*

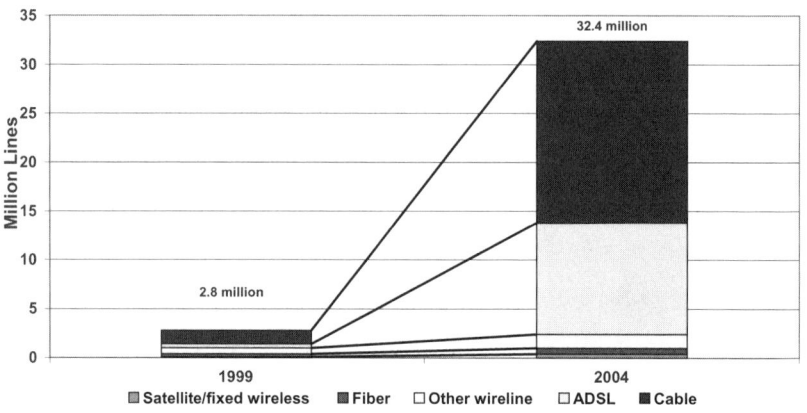

*Source:* FCC's High Speed Services for Internet Access Report, 12/04.

Overall, RBOCs have experienced constantly decreasing margins from traditional voice services. The most (if not only) relevant source of profits today is provided by wireless services and by the adoption of multi-market strategies, such as that offered by triple play.[20] The FCC attempted to remedy the uncertain prospects for DSL with its 2003 Triennial Review Order (TRO), which was challenged in the US Court of Appeals and finally approved in December 2004.[21] Under the TRO, the FCC no longer required local exchange carriers to lease their lines to competitors at wholesale rates,

---

[19] See US FCC, *High-Speed Services for Internet Access Report*, Washington, D.C., December 2004.

[20] RBOCs are currently trying to reach triple play in two main ways: a) through developing fiber-to-the-home connections (FTTH), which promise enormous speed – up to 500 Mps shared over a maximum of 16 subscribers; and b) by signing marketing agreements with satellite providers, such as DirecTv (Qwest) and EchoStar (SBC). See FCC, *High-Speed Services for Internet Access*, Washington, D.C., December 2004.

[21] See Gilroy and Kruger, op. cit.

as was required by the 1996 Telecom Act. This will lead RBOCs to raise their rates by as much as 30% in 2005 on 13 million leased lines, once the contracts expire.[22]

Today, cable companies still hold the lion's share of broadband connections (68%). In 2004, however, telcos outpaced cable operators in subscriber growth for the first time, by focusing on price instead of speed. The price for DSL broadband services is reported to have fallen down substantially from February 2002 to January 2005. In 2002, SBC and Verizon both priced their monthly DSL subscriptions at $49.95, whereas in January 2005 Verizon priced it at $29.95 and SBC at $26.95.[23] New prospects for former baby bells spurred a rapid phase of industry restructuring. As of today, former long-distance giants AT&T and MCI are being acquired by RBOCs such as SBC and Verizon, respectively.

The US fixed-line industry appears increasingly characterized by infrastructurally based competition. The 2004 broadband policy advocated the efficient auctioning of spectrum for the development of new technologies – e.g. the upperbands (>24Ghz), the lowerbands (multipoint distribution services, <3Ghz) and a 'hands-off' approach to technologies such as WiFi and WiMAX, which remain not subject to licensing. WiFi is growing fast in the US, with 24,000 hotspots already in place. Yet industry analysts are still uncertain about the potential for WiFi as a stand-alone service, given the prospects of WiMAX development in the medium-term as well. Presently, SBC and Verizon offer WiFi mostly as an add-on service to their DSL promotions, while T-Mobile and other mobile operators charge a separate subscription fee for it.[24]

The hands-off approach to regulation was also applied to IP-enabled services such as VoIP. The FCC has taken advantage of its silos-approach legacy by classifying VoIP as an 'interstate information service' in November 2004, therefore exempting it from state regulation just as with cable modem services. More recently, the FCC has started its IP-enabled services proceedings in order to assess whether VoIP is to be considered a telecom or an information service.[25] Meanwhile, VoIP has already become a reality in

---

[22] See Deloitte Touche Tohmatsu, *Reconnected to Growth – Global Telecommunications Industry Index 2005*, New York, 2005.

[23] See the "Bucks for Broadband Summit" presentation by FCC Commissioner K.J. Martin at the summit in Frankfort, Kentucky on January 12, 2005.

[24] See Deloitte Touche Tohmatsu, *TMT Trends: Predictions, 2005 – A Focus on the Wireline Sector*, New York, 2005.

[25] An example is the order issued by the FCC on May 19, 2005, requiring VoIP providers to "supply enhanced 911 (E911) emergency calling capabilities to their

the US. According to a recent study by the Yankee Group, almost 1 million US customers will subscribe to VoIP services by the end of 2005 and by 2008 VoIP will serve as many as 17.5 million households. Cable operators such as Cablevision and Time Warner are taking the lead in this sector, which has so far been dominated by Vonage, and will gain 56% market share by the end of 2005. Increased competition is also coming from firms active in the computer industries, including Microsoft and hardware manufacturers such as Cisco, 3Com and Intel.

## Trends in the EU Fixed-Line Sector

Compared with recent developments in the US fixed-line sector, most EU member states lag far behind in terms of technological advancement. This is also owing to the relatively recent and still incomplete liberalization of national markets, which started in the 1990s but was only officially attained on January 1, 1998; it was then further promoted by the adoption of the EC Regulatory Framework for Electronic Communications, which entered into force on January 1, 2003.[26]

Under the new regulatory package, telecoms services are not classified in rigid categories. National regulatory authorities (NRAs), in charge of enforcement, are called to perform detailed market analyses in order to identify (and notify) operators with significant market power (SMP) in a given set of markets. Such analyses are more rooted in economics than in formal pre-defined categories, requiring NRAs to perform the so-called 'SSNIP test'[27] and to rely on a notion of SMP that reflects that of dominance under Community competition law. In addition, Reg. 2887/2000 on local loop unbundling provides that all SMP operators meet all reasonable requests

---

customers as a mandatory feature of the service". On that occasion, the FCC also clarified that "[t]he IP-enabled services marketplace is the latest new frontier of our nation's communications landscape, and the Commission is committed to allowing IP-enabled services to evolve without undue regulation" (WC Docket Nos. 04-36, 05-196, May 19, 2005).

[26] The new regulatory package consists of the Framework Directive (2002/21/EC, OJ L 108, April 4, 2002, p. 33), the Access Directive (2002/19/EC, OJ L 108, April 4, 2002, p. 7), the Authorization Directive (2002/20/EC, OJ L 108, April 4, 2002, p. 21), the Universal Service Directive (2002/22/EC, OJ L 108, April 4, 2002, p. 51), the Radio Spectrum Decision (676/2002/EC, OJ L 108, April 4, 2002, p. 1), the Directive on Privacy and Electronic Communications (2002/58/EC, OJ L 201, July 31, 2002, p. 37) and the Regulation on Unbundling of the Local Loop (2887/2000/EC, OJ L 336, December 30, 2000, p. 4).

[27] SSNIP refers to small, significant, non-transitory increase in price.

for unbundled access to their local loop and related facilities under transparent, fair and non-discriminatory conditions, which entail cost-oriented pricing. Nevertheless, no formal reliance on the long-run incremental cost (LRIC) model by NRAs has been mandated by the EC legislation.

The main changes introduced by the 2002 regulatory package were the adoption of a more comprehensive definition of 'electronic communications', including:

- broadcasting, telecoms and cable TV networks and services (but excluding content);[28]

- emphasis on 'technological neutrality';

- the replacement of licenses with authorizations;

- a mandate for EU member states to decide whether to introduce secondary trading in the radio spectrum; and

- the provision that sector-specific regulation would be rapidly dismantled in case effective competition developed in the relevant markets.

The economic benefits of the new regulatory package for the fixed-line sector today seem promising.[29] As regards fixed-voice services, the last few years have exhibited a significant reduction in prices and a marked increase in the number of operators. Between 2001 and 2003, the average market share of incumbent operators in the EU-15 decreased from 86.9% to 76.8% for local calls, from 72.8% to 66.5% for calls to mobile phones, from 71.3% to 67.4% for long-distance calls and from 64.9% to 59.9% for international calls. Furthermore, the Commission reported encouraging results for LLU activities. In 2004, Europe scored an impressive 110% increase in unbundled local loops (fully unbundled and shared lines) in the EU-15, jumping from

---

[28] The Framework Directive (2002/21/EC, OJ L 108, April4, 2002) applies to all networks and services conveying signals "by wire, by radio, by optical or by other electromagnetic means, including satellite networks, fixed (circuit- and packet-switched, including Internet) and mobile terrestrial networks" (Art. 2a).

[29] The overall electronic communications market has grown by 4.6% from 2003 to 2004, reaching €277 billion. The Commission has estimated that the liberalization of the telecommunications and electricity markets would lead to an increase in GDP and employment levels of 0.4% and 0.6% respectively, four years after the liberalization, and a GDP increase of 0.6% ten years after liberalization. See European Commission, "Structural reforms in labour and product markets and macroeconomic performance in the EU", Chapter 2 in *The EU Economy: 2002 Review*, Office for Official Publications of the EU, Luxembourg, 2002.

1.8 million in July 2003 to more than 3.8 million in July 2004. This result is particularly important as a signal of enhanced market opening to national and foreign investors. In the five years to 2003, non-incumbent fixed-line operators invested as much as €70 billion in the EU-15 for the development of new infrastructures.

A lot still needs to be done, however, as regards broadband deployment, although the last year has shown encouraging results. The European Commission has reported advancement in broadband deployment to reach more than 85% of the EU-15 population, but the average broadband penetration rate in the EU-25 is still at 9%, as opposed to 11.5% in the US. Figure 2 shows the broadband penetration rate for most advanced OECD countries.

*Figure 2. Broadband Subscriptions*

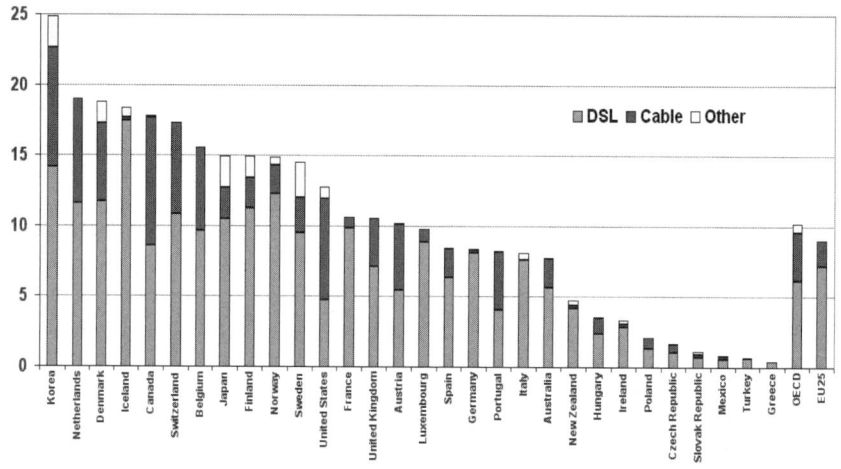

**Broadband Subcribers for 100 Inhabitants, by Technology, December 2004**

Source: OECD Key ICT Indicators (December 2004) and European Commission's i2010 (31 May 2005)

The slow broadband catch-up in most EU member states also depends on the incumbents' major share in most national markets, which still averages 76.8% in local calls (more than 90% in accession states), 67.4% in long distance calls, 66.5% in calls to mobile phones and 59.9% in international calls. The new entrants' market share in the broadband market is now at 46.7%, with significant recent increases in DSL technology – which accounts for 78% of the broadband market. Whereas incumbent telephone companies have traditionally dominated this market, the new entrants' share reached 30.8% in 2004.[30]

Evidence also shows that countries that do not rely solely on DSL for broadband availability are those in which broadband has developed more rapidly. Examples of countries in which cable and DSL have been actively competing include the Netherlands, Denmark and Belgium. Another major problem faced by EU member states is the slow speed attained by its current broadband infrastructure. As the European Commission has recently acknowledged, "the EU is a long way behind its international competitors on network speed". It added that nearly 10% of Japan's 15.4 million broadband subscribers were connected through fiber optic cable with downlink rates of up to 26 Mbps in 2004. In the EU, few of the 40 million subscribers are connected with a bandwidth above 3 Mbps.[31]

The limited speed of EU broadband connections also threatens the development of new services. One example is VoIP, which is still an embryonic market in Europe. Only recently, a number of VoIP offerings have started populating the European market, ranging from pure players like Gossiptel and Sipgate in the UK, Freenet in Germany, to broadband players that offer it as an add-on service such as Free, Neuf Telecom and Tiscali in France and FastWeb in Italy.[32] Even though EU regulators – in particular, OPTA in the Netherlands and OFCOM in the UK – are taking action to exempt VoIP from heavy regulation, the lack of sufficiently fast connections hampers the penetration of IP-enabled services. Moreover, the relatively modest penetration of cable broadband leaves VoIP mostly in the hands of national incumbents, which account for 69.2% of DSL offerings and seem to have scant incentives to promote a service that promises to erode the margins of fixed-voice services further.

Regarding wireless access technologies, Europe hosted roughly 24,000 Wi-Fi hotspots in 2003; it is expected to have 93,300 by 2007.[33] Major

---

[30] See European Commission, *Implementation of the Regulatory Framework in the Member States – 10th Report*, COM(2004) 759 final, Brussels, December 2, 2004a.

[31] Ibid.; see also the Commission's Press Release "i2010 – A European Information Society for growth and employment", MEMO/05/184, Brussels, June 1, 2005.

[32] See the Briefing Paper by the Telecom Infotech Forum, *IP Telephony and Voiceover Broadband*, Hong Kong, December 2004 (retrieved from http://www.trp.hku.hk/tif/home.php).

[33] Data derived from ON World, op. cit.

companies such as British Telecom and France Telecom, however, have already started trial experiments with WiMAX. Wireless access technologies in Europe can operate in many different parts of the spectrum, licensed and unlicensed. The four main suitable bands are the UMTS TDD spectrum (1.9-2.0 GHz), which was included in most UMTS licenses; the band set aside for UMTS extension (2.5-2.6 GHz); the 3.5 GHz spectrum, which in most countries is intended to be used for fixed wireless networks/the wireless local loop; and the 450 MHz spectrum previously used for analogue mobile services. With the exception of the 3.5GHz spectrum, the bands are mostly unused, as licenses have either not been awarded yet (in the UMTS extension band), licenses have been awarded but are not being used (in the UMTS TDD band) or licenses have just expired (as in the analogue 450 MHz spectrum).[34]

Given the initial stage of wireless access in Europe, no market effect can be reported to date. The promising development of new access technologies, however, will certainly help new entrants in overcoming the LLU problem. The future shape of EU telecoms services – just as on the other side of the Atlantic – will be a matter of competition between wireless broadband and mobile broadband services. The European Commission's i2010 initiative identifies the development of broadband as the key enabling factor for convergence among telecommunications, media and electronic devices. For this reason, during 2005 and 2006 major regulatory reforms are expected in this sector, starting with a review of the Directives on Television without Frontiers and Universal Service (end of 2005) and later a more comprehensive assessment of the new Regulatory Framework on electronic communications (June 2006).[35]

Meanwhile, industry trends show that the 'boom and bust' of telcos in Europe is being replaced by a period of slow resurgence. Consolidation in the industry is taking place at high speed, mostly between fixed and mobile operators: France Telecom, for example, took total control of Orange, Wanadoo and EQUANT; Deutsche Telekom recently announced its intent to purchase T-Online, its affiliated Internet service provider, and, Telecom Italia is re-acquiring its mobile subsidiary TIM. Some attempts to stimulate investment in Europe are coming from a gradual lowering of local loop charges by some national regulators. In May 2005, for example, the Regulatory Authority for Telecommunications and Posts (Reg TP), the German regulator, cut charges by 9.75% from €11.80 to €10.65 in an attempt to bolster local competition for broadband services. Nevertheless, local and

---

[34] See Goldman Sachs, *WiMAX and Family: Threats and Opportunities*, New York, September 7, 2004.

[35] See the European Commission (2004a), op. cit.

regional telecoms carriers suspended their plans to invest around €500 million in DSL development in some 700 local areas as charges remained above €10.[36] Similarly, Ireland's regulator cut LLU charges by more than 50% starting on February 1, 2005, in its attempt to boost broadband catch-up.[37]

Overall, the broadband market today appears far more competitive than the traditional fixed-voice market. Table 2 shows that incumbents rely almost exclusively on DSL technology, whereas new entrants also rely on other technologies (for 46.1% of connections). The most relevant obstacle for new entrants is in some cases the high wholesale prices compared with competition-driven low retail prices for residential subscriptions. In some countries (the Czech Republic, Estonia, Cyprus, Latvia, Lithuania and Slovenia), the line rental for full unbundling is higher than the retail subscription fee for residential customers. This form of 'price squeeze' makes it impossible for an LLU-based entrant to make positive profits from (only) selling voice telephony subscriptions to end-users.[38]

## Mobile technologies: Will 3G Break Even?

Just as has occurred in the fixed-line industry with the advent of wireless access technologies, the mobile sector is increasingly exhibiting signs of convergence between the US and EU member states. Such convergence will be boosted by the introduction of 3G platforms, which are reducing (but not eliminating) the problem of incompatible standards on the two sides of the Atlantic. For 3G platforms, the International Telecommunications Union (ITU), following its IMT-2000 initiative, defined and adopted five families of standards – the CDMA-2000, the WCDMA (UMTS), the TD-SCDMA, the UWC-136 and DECT+. Currently, all 3G commercial mobile data services are based on either the CDMA-2000 or the WCDMA, with increased competition from the TD-SCDMA, adopted by the powerful China Academy of Telecommunication Technology.

---

[36] See Reg TP, "Regulatory Authority Lays Down Further Conditions for Local Network Competition", Reg TP press release, Bonn, April 29, 2005.

[37] See the Commission for Communications Regulation (ComReg), "ComReg Announces 50% Cut in Local Loop Unbundling Process Charges", Media Release, Dublin, December 22, 2004 (retrieved from http://www.comreg.ie/_fileupload/publications/PR221204.pdf).

[38] See P. de Bijl and M. Peitz, *Local Loop Unbundling in Europe: Experience, Prospects and Policy Challenges*, Working Paper No. 29/2005, International University in Germany, Bruchsal, February 2005.

*Table 2. Number of Lines along with Wholesale and Retail Prices in Europe (July 2004)*

| | Number of lines | | | | | Wholesale and retail prices (euros) | | | | |
|---|---|---|---|---|---|---|---|---|---|---|
| | Incumbents' broadband lines | % DSL lines | Entrants' broadband lines | % DSL lines | % LLU | Fully unbundled line | Average total cost | Rental of shared line | Average total cost | Residential subscription fee |
| Austria | 249,400 | 100.0 | 456,325 | 23.3 | 100.0 | 10.90 | 15.40 | 5.50 | 14.50 | 15.98 |
| Belgium | 731,825 | 100.0 | 712,848 | 22.1 | 54.4 | 11.60 | 16.30 | 1.70 | 6.50 | 16.80 |
| Cyprus | 14,520 | 99.8% | 0.0% | 0.0% | 0.0% | 11.70 | 17.00 | 7.30 | 14.00 | 9.97 |
| Czech Republic | 30,000 | 100.0% | 46,000 | 13.0% | 0.0% | 15.50 | 42.00 | 8.70 | n.a. | 9.44 |
| Denmark | 539,343 | 79.2% | 299,807 | 45.0% | 100.0% | 8.60 | 12.50 | 4.30 | 7.40 | 16.00 |
| Estonia | 51,876 | 97.9% | 50,895 | 0.2% | 40.5% | 8.90 | 13.70 | n.a. | n.a. | 6.26 |
| Finland | 411,800 | 74.5% | 160,300 | 58.3% | 100.0% | 11.30 | 25.30 | 5.70 | 15.50 | 11.77 |
| France | 2,358,200 | 96.3% | 2,557,287 | 86.8% | 71.4% | 10.50 | 17.10 | 2.90 | 9.40 | 13.00 |
| Germany | 4,704,906 | 99.9% | 710,341 | 82.5% | 100.0% | 11.80 | 15.80 | 2.40 | 7.50 | 15.66 |
| Greece | 10,245 | 100.0% | 15,686 | 80.9% | 100.0% | 10.40 | 13.40 | 5.20 | 9.10 | 12.38 |
| Hungary | 111,228 | 91.0% | 111,751 | 36.7% | 100.0% | 11.80 | 24.40 | 4.30 | 16.90 | 12.86 |

*Table 2. Cont'd.*

| | | | | | | | | | |
|---|---|---|---|---|---|---|---|---|---|
| Ireland | 45,360 | 94.9% | 20,210 | 61.8% | 100.0% | 16.80 | 26.90 | 9.00 | 19.30 | 24.18 |
| Italy | 2,475,881 | 99.2% | 1,043,916 | 73.5% | 99.9% | 8.30 | 11.60 | 2.80 | 7.10 | 14.57 |
| Latvia | 27,427 | 97.8% | 6,477 | 0.0% | 0.0% | 9.00 | 13.40 | 4.50 | 8.90 | 6.34 |
| Lithuania | 31,986 | 99.5% | 56,293 | 4.0% | 100.0% | 12.50 | 20.40 | 6.70 | 16.80 | 6.66 |
| Luxembourg | 18,630 | 97.2% | 6,704 | 60.1% | 59.0% | 15.80 | 31.30 | 7.50 | 23.90 | 18.40 |
| Malta | 4,511 | 100.0% | 9,227 | 74.9% | 0.0% | n.a. | n.a. | n.a. | n.a. | 6.56 |
| Netherlands | 1,053,000 | 100.0% | 1,319,529 | 24.3% | 100.0% | 9.60 | 12.00 | 1.90 | 5.00 | 18.16 |
| Poland | 181,501 | 100.0% | 10,806 | 100.0% | 0.0% | n.a. | n.a. | n.a. | n.a. | 9.71 |
| Portugal | 530,422 | 49.1% | 137,128 | 27.3% | 100.0% | 12.00 | 19.00 | 3.00 | 10.30 | 15.07 |
| Slovakia | 9,900 | 100.0% | 11,785 | 61.1% | 0.0% | n.a. | n.a. | n.a. | n.a. | 7.39 |
| Slovenia | 54,236 | 97.6% | 22,103 | 4.1% | 100.0% | 15.30 | 21.50 | 7.00 | 12.80 | 10.70 |
| Spain | 1,536,148 | 99.9% | 1,231,479 | 44.7% | 100.0% | 11.40 | 13.20 | 3.00 | 5.50 | 15.28 |
| Sweden | 439,000 | 98.9% | 647,167 | 38.9% | 40.5% | 11.40 | 15.30 | 5.40 | 15.40 | 13.75 |
| UK | 1,117,474 | 99.8% | 3,278,087 | 50.0% | 14.6% | 13.30 | 24.40 | 3.40 | 13.90 | 16.84 |
| EU-25 | 16,738,819 | 96.3 | 12,922,151 | 53.9 | 67.1 | 11.75 | 19.18 | 4.87 | 11.99 | 12.95 |

*Source:* P. de Bijl and M. Peitz, op. cit.

With its 379 million subscribers, Europe has taken the lead on mobile services, with a penetration rate in some countries now around 100%. Increased fixed-mobile substitution has led a substantial portion of the population to become 'mobile only' in some European countries.[39] Table 3 presents the number of mobile subscriptions and forecasts up to 2007, showing that US mobile subscribers are expected to grow at an average annual rate of 10.5%, therefore reducing the gap with Europe. Yet both the US and EU markets are faced with a slow migration from 2.5G to 3G. Initial hopes for a rapid transition have now transformed into a more cautious outlook. Consumers still do not find 3G services compelling, mostly because of limited coverage and poor handset performance.[40] As a result, mobile operators in the EU and – to a lesser extent – in the US are still looking for the 'killer application' that will finally drive demand toward 3G.

*Table 3. Mobile Subscriptions, 2003-07*

|  | 2003 | 2004 | 2005 | 2006 | 2007 | CAGR* % |
|---|---|---|---|---|---|---|
| Western Europe** | 361,440 | 383,972 | 402,042 | 418,502 | 433,098 | 4.6 |
| Eastern Europe | 111,885 | 150,417 | 172,384 | 185,432 | 194,010 | 14.8 |
| Total Europe | 473,325 | 534,389 | 574,427 | 603,934 | 627,108 | 7.3 |
| US | 157,625 | 175,713 | 195,718 | 215,561 | 235,204 | 10.5 |
| Japan | 80,027 | 85,729 | 90,834 | 96,919 | 104,090 | 6.8 |
| Rest of the world | 639,224 | 847,008 | 986,547 | 1,115,616 | 1,236,552 | 15.6 |
| World | 1,404,201 | 1,642,840 | 1,847,526 | 2,032,029 | 2,202,954 | 11.9 |

* CAGR refers to compound average growth rate; ** includes Turkey.

*Source*: EITO report (2005), op. cit.

---

[39] Ireland's Commission for Communications Regulation recently estimated that almost a quarter of the country's households are now 'mobile only', with no family member having a fixed-line subscription at all (*ComReg Trends Report Q1 2005*, prepared by Amárach Consulting, ComReg, Dublin, April 2005).

[40] The European Commission reported in its *Implementation of the Regulatory Framework in the Member States – 10th Report* (2004a, op. cit.) that "In most cases 3G networks have limited coverage, mostly concentrated in the largest cities, and population coverage ranges from around 80% in the United Kingdom and Sweden to less than 10% in those countries where services started to be offered at the end of year" (Annex 2, p. 50).

## The EU's Path toward 3G

During the last few years, most EU countries have experienced the successful entry of new players in the mobile industry and in some countries the entry of 3G operators have led to as many as five mobile network operators (MNOs) populating the market.[41] Revenues from mobile services exceed those of fixed-voice services. Continued strong growth of 7% was achieved in 2004, driven in part by mobile data services. The European Commission reported an average penetration rate of mobile technologies as high as 87% in the EU-15 and 83% in the EU-25. This result is certainly remarkable, given that the penetration rate was only 18% in 1998 and 52% in 2000.[42] Further, the average market share of leading mobile operators fell from 46.6% in 2003 to 43.2% in 2004, because of further market opening and the gradual achievement of effective competition. Faced with intense competition, firms operating 2.5G mobile services are striving to achieve new profit streams through increased segmentation strategies, mostly based on a careful use of flat (pre-paid) pricing and micro-payments and group pricing for residential and business customers. Yet future growth in Europe crucially depends on the availability of value-added services and a rapid transition to 3G platforms.

As regards 3G, 75 licenses have been granted in the EU-25, with Germany, Italy, the Netherlands, Austria and the United Kingdom being the only member state to have granted licenses to five operators.[43] The first player to enter the EU market – the Hong Kong-based firm Hutchison – announced in April 2005 that it had signed up more than 3 million customers in the UK, thanks to steadily increasing demand for its next-generation technology. As of March 30, 2005, the operator had 3.02 million UK customers, compared with 1.2 million in September 2004 and 361,000 in March 2004, owing in

---

[41] Such a market structure is said not to be financially viable, given the substantial economies of scale that characterize the mobile sector and increased inter-platform competition by fixed-line operators and ISPs. As a result, a consolidation process is expected in the next few months.

[42] Some commentators, however, have argued that such an impressive result was facilitated by the adoption of the so-called 'calling-party-pays' principle, which leads mobile operators into a situation of substantial monopoly when terminating calls on their networks. The US adopted a 'receiving-party-pays' principle. Anyway, the Commission announced that the average fixed-to-mobile termination rate for SMP operators in the EU-15 fell by 14% between July 2003 and July 2004.

[43] See European Commission (2005), op. cit., Annex 2, p. 51.

the main to its improved network coverage, a wider range of handsets and content, and general improvements in the 3G technology on offer.[44]

The EU adopted a top-down approach to standardization in the deployment of 3G platforms. The UMTS standard was chosen through a number of measures taken at the EU and national levels, starting from the EU UMTS decision of 1998.[45] Nevertheless, the auctioning of spectrum licenses for 3G services faced a number of insurmountable problems. The most important of these were the stark differences in the terms of the licenses granted as well as in the auction design chosen by individual member states, ranging from beauty contests (Finland, France, Norway, Spain and Sweden) to standard auctions (Austria, Belgium, the Netherlands, Switzerland and the UK) to a hybrid design (Greece and Italy). In most cases, these methods resulted in an extremely high level of bids.[46] Consequently, most operators are still on their way to recovering from financial losses incurred during the auction process, which could not be recouped so far given the slow take-up of 3G platforms among European consumers.

Currently, more than €116 billion is reported to have been spent on 3G licenses in Western Europe. The highest prices for 3G licenses were paid in Germany (€8.4 billion) and the UK (€ 7.7 billion). The reaction of stock markets to these huge investments have been negative, with many mobile operators facing a downgrade in their credit ratings and a decline of their market value because of the high debt exposures. This impact further complicates the arduous task of collecting funding to cover rollout costs, estimated at €7.8 billion for Deutsche Telekom and €13.7 billion for British Telecom.[47]

---

[44] See "Hutchison Whampoa Profits Take 3G Hit", *Financial Times*, March 31, 2005.

[45] Decision No. 128/1999/EC of the European Parliament and of the Council of 14 December 1998 on the coordinated introduction of a third-generation mobile and wireless communications system (UMTS) in the Community.

[46] See J.M. Bauer et al., "Transition Paths to Next-Generation Wireless Services", Presentation at the 32nd Research Conference on Communication, Information and Internet Policy, Arlington, VA, October 1-3, 2004. For a critique of the auction design chosen for UMTS licenses, see P. Klemperer, *Auctions: Theory and Practice*, Princeton: Princeton University Press, 2004.

[47] See the estimates by McKinsey & Co. in *Comparative Assessment of the Licensing Regimes for 3G Mobile Communications in the European Union and their Impact on the Mobile Communications Sector*, final report for the European Commission, Brussels, June 25, 2002.

More recently, the EU has sought to remedy the uneasy case for 3G spectrum licenses by thoroughly reconsidering its spectrum policy and allowing for various forms of facilities sharing, such as site sharing, tower sharing, radio access network sharing, and a geographical split of the network or full network sharing. Several NRAs have approved sharing agreements, following the decision issued by the German regulator Reg TP in 2001. A centralization of spectrum policy – so far left in the hands of member states – seems to have been put on the agenda for the review of the regulatory framework that will enter into force in June 2006.

Finally, some degree of uncertainty in the EU market is related to the approach of NRAs to the regulation of mobile termination charges for 3G operators. Given Europe's current calling-party-pays regime, all mobile operators can be said to hold SMP in the market for mobile termination. Additionally, the UK's OFCOM seems to be considering the regulation of charges for calls terminating on Hutchison's 3UK network.[48] Such a move would run counter to the 'hands-off' approach normally reserved to emerging markets such as 3G services.

## The Long Road to 3G in the US

Unlike the EU, and in line with its traditional regulatory approach, the US has adopted a market-driven strategy to the standardization of mobile technologies. This strategy eventually led to the emergence of three incompatible standards: GSM (Cingular, T-Mobile), CDMA (Sprint, Verizon) and iDEN (Nextel). Licenses for 2G were not issued until 1995 – a significant delay compared with the EU, where mobile operators obtained 2G licenses between 1989 and 1992. The 10-year delay in the introduction of 2G services was estimated to have created potential welfare losses of approximately $50 billion per year.[49] Further, the 2G band allocation adopted in the US (in the 1.9 GHz range) currently prevents use of the band chosen in most EU member states.

The 3G band allocation began with a Memorandum signed by President Bill Clinton on October 13, 2000, establishing guiding principles for the FCC and

---

[48] 3UK is currently appealing OFCOM's June 2004 ruling that the company has significant market power because it owns a network and thus has control over the termination rates it charges. So far, 3UK has been exempt from regulation since it operates only a 3G network. See "OFCOM's termination rate regulation update may affect 3G", Dow Jones Newswires, May 19, 2005.

[49] See J. Hausman, "Valuing the Effect of Regulation on New Services in Telecommunications" in *Brookings Papers on Economic Activity 1997*, The Brookings Institution, Washington, D.C., pp. 1-38, 1997.

the National Telecommunications and Information Administration (NTIA) to identify the 3G spectrum. Although the attempt to meet the initial deadline set on November 15, 2000 failed, the FCC eventually issued its final report on the allocation of band frequencies in the 2500-2690 MHz band and in the 1755-1850 MHz band on March 31, 2001.[50] Later on, in September 2001, the FCC added a mobile allocation to the 2500-2690 MHz band. In June 2002, the NTIA published a report containing an assessment of the viability of accommodating 3G services in the 1710-1770 MHz band and in the 2110-2170 MHz band. As the 90 MHz band was already allocated to other services, however, the FCC did not seek to relocate existing licenses. As a result, the actual availability of this band for 3G services is still uncertain. The Chairman of the FCC recently announced that 3G licenses would not be auctioned before summer 2006.[51]

The first launch of (unlicensed) 3G services was made by a regional carrier, Monet Mobile, in October 2002. In October 2003, Verizon Wireless began offering high-speed mobile Internet access services in Washington, D.C. and San Diego, California, using the EV-DO technology, which allows for maximum data transfer speeds of 2 Mbps. In 2004, AT&T Wireless (later acquired by Cingular Wireless) announced the commercial availability of wideband CDMA (WCDMA) or UMTS technology, in Seattle, San Francisco, Phoenix and Detroit.

At present, the US mobile industry is highly competitive and fast changing, dominated by aggressive inter-network competition and increasingly sophisticated market strategies. At the end of 2004, six nationwide operators and more than a hundred regional operators served the US market. Today, the acquisition of AT&T Wireless by Cingular, the proposed Sprint/Nextel merger and recent talks about a possible Verizon/Alltel merger are revolutionizing the competitive landscape, with Cingular Wireless currently the top player and as many as 21 mobile virtual network operators (MVNOs) active in the market.[52] As regards competition policy, the FCC has carefully

---

[50] See the FCC report, *Spectrum Study of 2500-2690 MHz Band: The Potential for Accommodating Third Generation Mobile Systems Seeks Comment on Final Report in Pending Spectrum Allocation Proceeding* (ET Docket No. 00-258), FCC, Washington, D.C., March 30, 2001. See also the NTIA report, *Federal Operations in the 1755-1850 MHz Band: The Potential for Accommodating Third Generation Mobile Systems, Interim Report*, Washington, D.C., November 15, 2000.

[51] See "Powell Says FCC Plans to Auction 3G Spectrum in Summer of 2006", *Tech Law Journal*, December 29, 2004.

[52] See T. Hazlett, *Rivalrous Telecommunications Networks With and Without Mandatory Sharing*, Working Paper 05-07, AEI-Brookings Joint Center,

scrutinized the possible anticompetitive effects of the Cingular/AT&T merger, identifying those markets in which the merged entity would have 70 MHz or more in at least part of the market. The FCC held that "the merger could result in an imbalance in the availability of spectrum that would cause other carriers to be more spectrum-constrained than Cingular at a later point in the deployment of next-generation services" and gave leeway only after Cingular committed to divest spectrum holdings in excess of 80 MHz in all areas.[53] Similar scrutiny is expected for the Sprint/Nextel merger.

Future prospects for the mobile sector in the US crucially depend on the availability of additional spectrum. US mobile operators currently use 170 MHz of spectrum, which is approximately 100 MHz less than players in other developed countries. A recent study shows that allocating additional spectrum to mobile services would produce huge consumer gains: the average price per minute of use would decrease from $11 cents to $8.5 cents if an additional 80 MHz were made available and to $6 cents if 200 MHz were allocated to mobile operators. The resulting consumer surplus would be approximately $32 billion per year in the case of an additional 80 MHz.[54]

## What's Next?

As clearly emerges from the analysis of the telecoms services markets in the US and EU, technology is already leading transatlantic markets to converge. US and EU industries still diverge in many respects, notably in the deployment of wireless access technologies (with the US taking the lead) and in 3G rollout (with the EU running ahead, although not without problems). The future shape of the telecoms industry crucially depends on the convergence of fixed and mobile technologies, as well as on the increasing convergence of the telecoms, multimedia and broadcast industries.

Against this backdrop, enhanced transatlantic dialogue could provide valuable contributions in areas such as:

- **Technological neutrality**. The US in particular still exhibits a mixed landscape, with cable operators and emerging VoIP operators being exempt from state regulation. Most EU regulators still have to take action on VoIP. Both the US and EU will have to consider regulating

---

Washington, D.C., March 2005.

[53] See the FCC's *Cingular-AT&T Wireless Merger Order,* 19 FCC Rcd. 21522 (2004), §9.

[54] See J. Hausman, "From 2G to 3G: Wireless Competition for Internet-related Services", in R.W. Crandall and J.H. Alleman (eds), *Broadband: Should we Regulate High-Speed Internet Access?*, AEI-Brookings Monographs, AEI-Brookings Center, Washington, D.C., December 2002.

content as it is a main driver of consumer demand in an era of convergence. In addition, the need for a light touch in regulating emerging markets needs to be restated, especially for 3G services.

- **Standardization**. 3G was a failed attempt to close the never-ending debate on the incompatibility of standards adopted in the US and EU for mobile communications. The same problem occurs in digital terrestrial television, where the ATSC technology is incompatible with the established DVB-T standard adopted in the EU. Currently, the International Telecommunication Union is still in the process of defining the specific features of the oncoming 4G platforms, expected to be standardized in 2007 and deployed from 2010. The advent of 4G technologies is anticipated to put an end to the fixed-mobile dichotomy, leading to inter-technology integration into an open wireless architecture.[55]

- **Future regulatory frameworks**. Both the US and the EU are in the process of thoroughly reconsidering their existing regulatory frameworks. Both will need to take action by the end of 2006, if they want to preserve some chance of achieving their stated ambitions of the US having universal broadband coverage by 2007 and the EU having the most dynamic and competitive knowledge-based economy by 2010. The creation of a more homogeneous and pro-competitive regulatory environment on the two sides of the Atlantic is crucial for these goals as well as for the future welfare of consumers in the US and the EU.

As regards regulatory cooperation, the creation of an integrated transatlantic market for telecoms services is still hindered by the existence of restrictions to market openness and inward FDI in the US as well as in most EU member states. Accordingly, the next section focuses on pending issues in bilateral EU-US trade negotiations on telecoms.

## Trade and Investment: Prospects for EU-US Dialogue

Trade and investment issues in telecommunications services have been subject to extensive debate over the past few years, especially after the GATS negotiations on basic telecommunication services were concluded on February 15, 1997 in the form of a Fourth Protocol to the GATS, known as the WTO basic telecoms agreement, which entered into force on January 1, 1998. The EU and the US then declared their intention to foster bilateral cooperation on trade and investment with specific respect to information society issues, with the declared aim of achieving full liberalization of the transatlantic market. Table 4 shows data for the import and export of

---

[55] See Bauer et al. (2004), op. cit.

communications services in the US and in a number of EU member states in 1996 and 2002, showing a substantial increase in trade. In 2002, the US was the leading importer and exporter of communications services. Among the leading exporters were also the UK, France, Belgium-Luxembourg, the Netherlands, Germany and Ireland, while the UK, Italy, France and the Netherlands were also among the leading importers of communications services.

On R&D investments in the ICT sector, however, the EU seems to lag far behind the US, as recently confirmed by the European Commission in its i2010 Communication. As shown in Table 5, in 2002 the level of private investment in ICT in the US was more than three times higher than the corresponding figure for the EU-15, whereas public sector investment was 2.5 times higher. Indeed, Japan invested more than the EU-15 in R&D in the ICT sector.

*Table 4. Trade in Communication Services, 1996-2002 ($ million)*

| Country | 1996 | | 2002 | |
|---|---|---|---|---|
| | Import | Export | Import | Export |
| Austria | 338 | 361 | 633 | 431 |
| Belgium-Luxembourg | 1,274 | 448 | 2,238 | 1,311 |
| Czech Republic | 77 | 64 | 172 | 262 |
| Finland | 155 | 194 | 232 | 255 |
| France | 582 | 417 | 2,262 | 1,725 |
| Germany | 2,025 | 2,692 | 1,409 | 3,381 |
| Greece | 71 | 78 | 207 | 264 |
| Ireland | – | – | 1,162 | 468 |
| Italy | 536 | 944 | 983 | 2,569 |
| Netherlands | 648 | 668 | 1,494 | 1,540 |
| Norway | 216 | 172 | 330 | 220 |
| Poland | 315 | 203 | 164 | 188 |
| Portugal | 281 | 172 | 248 | 217 |
| Spain | 642 | 443 | 922 | 1,022 |
| Sweden | 211 | 161 | 623 | 576 |
| UK | 1,649 | 2,091 | 2,912 | 3,035 |
| US | 3,543 | 8,792 | 4,372 | 4,546 |

**Source:** OECD, *Information Technology Outlook 2004*, Paris, 2004.

*Table 5. Investments in ICT Research, 2002*

| CT R&D | EU-15 | US | Japan |
|---|---|---|---|
| Private sector investments | €23 bn | €83 bn | €40 bn |
| Public sector investments | €8 bn | €20 bn | €11 bn |
| Inhabitants | €383 mn | €296 mn | €127 mn |
| Investments/inhabitant | €8 | €350 | €400 |
| ICT R&D as % total R&D | 18 | 34 | 35 |

*Source:* IDATE Foundation, *Investment in ICT Research, Comparative Study,* Montpellier, 2002.

As regards barriers to trade and investment between the EU and US, bilateral negotiations have led to identifying major pending issues, mostly related to existing regulatory obstacles to inward FDI caused by federal and state regulations (US) and by incomplete market liberalization (EU). The next two sections briefly describe these issues.

## Barriers to Inward FDI in the US

Although the *2005 Economic Report of the President* acknowledges that "direct investment into the United States by foreign firms can increase the competitiveness of US domestic firms"[56] through increased competition with welfare-enhancing outcomes for consumers, in a number of cases the US has proven reluctant to allow FDI in the telecommunications sector. The European Commission has repeatedly invited the US government to tackle the following issues in order to allow full access of foreign (EU) companies to the US market:

- **The ECO-test**. In November 1995, in the run-up to the WTO agreement on basic Telecoms the FCC adopted a rule on the entry of foreign-affiliated carriers into the US market, by introducing the so-called 'effective competitive opportunity test' (ECO-test). In the aftermath of the basic telecoms agreement, the FCC replaced the test with a 'refutable presumption' that entry by a foreign-affiliated competitor is pro-competitive, but retained a 'public interest' criterion that can still be invoked to deny a license to a foreign operator in the presence of trade or foreign policy concerns, or a very high risk to competition. These rules

---

[56] See the *2005 Economic Report of the President,* op. cit.

are said to create uncertainty for foreign operators wishing to invest in the US. Yet the system has been extended to satellites licensed by WTO countries.[57]

- **Common carrier radio licenses and broadcast licenses**. Foreign direct investment in US companies holding common carriers radio licenses is limited to 20% by Section 310 of the 1934 Communications Act. This rule – which also applies to the broadcast sector – seems contrary to the commitments undertaken by the US within the WTO basic telecoms agreement, and inevitably limits the freedom of EU firms to invest in US companies. As the EU has expressly stated, "the US broadcasting market today is hardly accessible to foreign media companies".[58]

- **Satellite operators**. After the basic telecoms agreement, the US has kept a market access restriction on satellite-based services – i.e. protecting the monopoly of Comsat although formally abolished by the 2000 ORBIT Act. European satellite operators such as Intelsat, Inmarsat Ventures plc. and New Skies N.V. have experience substantial barriers to entry and suffered from complex and lengthy proceedings in their attempts to enter the US satellite market. In addition, the US has taken an exemption to the most-favored nation principle for one-way satellite transmission of direct-to-home, direct-broadcast-satellite and digital audio services. This exemption was considered by the European Commission as a measure that "may impair European interests".[59]

- **Rigid taxonomy of services**. American commitments within the WTO framework on value-added services strongly depend on the domestic classification of services as communication or information services, which in turn depends on the legacy of the silos approach adopted in the 1934 and 1996 legislation. Such classification arrangements may, according to the European Commission, affect the ability of new players to enter the US market in the near future.

- **Incompatible standards**. Entry of European companies in the US market can be highly dependent on the standards chosen in the US for deployment of given technologies. This influence of course mostly applies where the EU already holds widely adopted standards, as is the case of mobile telephony and digital terrestrial television. Accordingly, the European Commission has highlighted the need to promote further

---

[57] See European Commission, *2004 Report on US Barriers to Trade and Investment*, Brussels, December 23, 2004b.

[58] Ibid.

[59] Ibid.

cooperation on the development of common or interoperable standards for 3G mobile telephony and for digital terrestrial television, where the US ATSC technology is incompatible with the established DVB-T standard adopted in the EU.

## Barriers to Inward FDI in the EU

Similarly, the US trade representative (USTR), in reviewing the operation and effectiveness of US telecommunications trade agreements, pursuant to Section 1377 of the Omnibus Trade and Competitiveness Act of 1988, recently identified remaining barriers to investment in EU member states and at the Community level. The most relevant barriers cited are the following:

- **Slow market liberalization, especially in the fixed-line sector**. The effective ability of US firms to enter the EU market successfully relies on the correct and timely implementation of the new regulatory framework by national governments and NRAs. It also relies on the approach that will be adopted by national competition authorities on anticompetitive conduct by incumbent firms – for example, in cases of margin squeeze, such as by Deutsche Telekom and Telecom Italia. In its 10th implementation report, the Commission highlighted that primary legislation still has to be adopted by five member states (Belgium, the Czech Republic, Estonia, Greece and Luxembourg), while secondary legislation has not been fully transposed into national law by another eight member states (Spain, France, Cyprus, Latvia, Lithuania, Poland, Slovenia and Slovakia).[60] A timely implementation of the new package in laggard member states would certainly contribute to further boosting the telecom sector in the EU and open up the market to US firms. As was explained earlier, the average market share held by incumbents in most EU member states remains quite large, and potential new entrants often envisage difficulties in reaching the critical mass for profitable entry.

- **Use of incompatible standards**. The US has always adopted a market-driven (bottom-up) approach in selecting communications standards, especially in the mobile sector, whereas the EU has always relied on a committee-driven top-down approach. For these reasons, the use of incompatible, non-market-driven standards by some EU countries has been heavily criticized by US officials over the past few months as harming US firms in their attempt to enter the EU market profitably. US Ambassador David Gross clearly condemned such tendencies during the recent Information Society Dialogue, stating, "This must stop".[61]

---

[60] See European Commission (2005), op. cit.

[61] Quoted from the remarks of Ambassador David A. Gross before the Digital

- **Excessively high interconnection prices (especially in Germany)**. The USTR has in several instances remarked that the incumbent operator in Germany, Deutsche Telekom, was refusing to guarantee provisioning times in private lease contracts. The question of whether the German regulator, Reg TP, is sufficiently equipped to contradict Deutsche Telekom's refusals to offer competitors access to private circuits and ISDN lines – seen as a form of raising rivals' costs – has been raised by several US firms as a major obstacle to entry in one of the largest telecoms markets in the EU. On February 28, 2005, Deutsche Telekom announced that it will lower its local and long-distance fixed-line tariffs and will offer, for the first time, a flat rate tariff for high volume callers.[62]

- **Excessive mobile termination charges (mostly in Germany)**. A major issue raised by the USTR is that of mobile termination rates, currently subject to a fierce debate at academic and industry levels. Countries that have adopted a calling-party-pays model, such as most EU member states, normally exhibit higher termination rates than receiving-party-pays countries (such as the US), since each MNO can freely set the price for the termination on its own network and uses its monopoly position to subsidize its retail tariffs and (often) handset manufacturers – the so-called 'waterbed effect'. Nevertheless, the USTR has complained that the German regulator Reg TP is setting mobile termination charges way above those of other calling-party-pays countries such as France and the UK.

Figure 3 shows the level of mobile termination charges as of January 2004. Since then, most EU NRAs have already taken action to reduce termination charges. The French regulator, for example, required annual reductions of 17% and 24% plus a third (yet unspecified) reduction from 2005 to 2007, estimating a savings of €250 million for final consumers in 2005 alone. The Italian regulator also required SMP mobile operators to lower their termination charges to €8.7 cents by 2007, a reduction of more than 40% from the current rate (€12.6 cents). Figure 4 shows the decrease in average mobile termination charges observed in the EU-15 from July 2001 to July 2004.

---

Economy Workshop, Brussels, September 16, 2004.

[62] See "Deutsche Telekom Responds to Competition with Cut-Price Calls", TeleGeography (www.telegeography.com), February 28, 2005.

*Figure 3. Mobile Termination Rates*

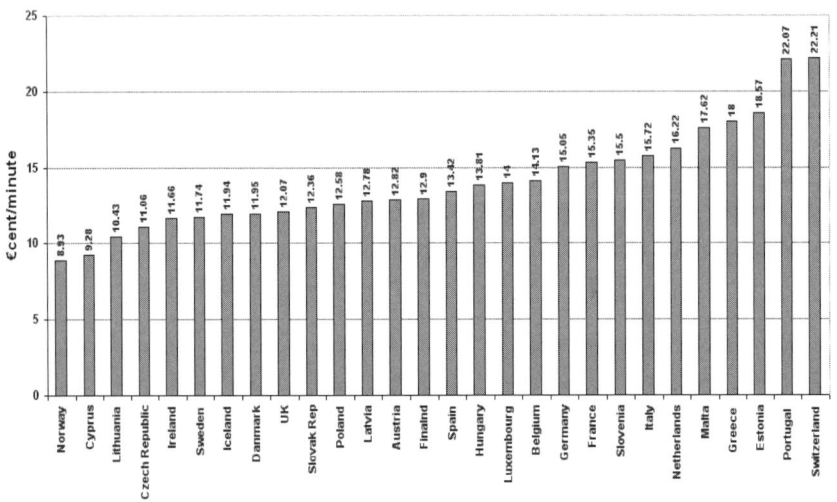

Source: IRG snapshot on mobile termination rates (July 2004)

*Figure 4. Fixed-to-Mobile Interconnection Charges*

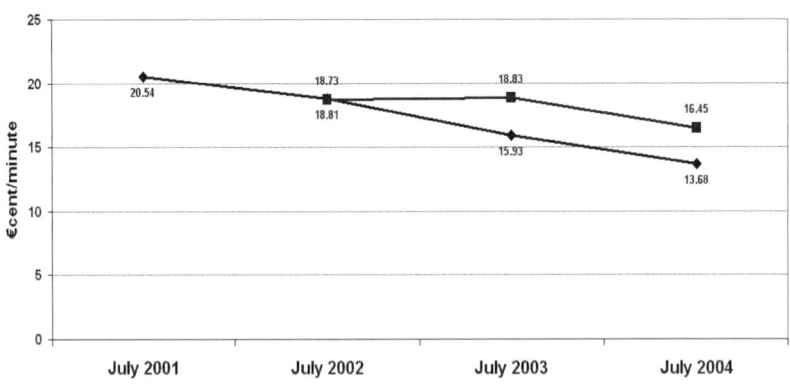

Source: European Commission, 10th Implementation Report (Dec. 2004)

## Conclusion: Can the US and EU learn from each other?

Enhanced cooperation between the US and the EU in the telecoms sector is likely to bring valuable improvements in terms of innovation and long-term consumer welfare. Both *de facto* and *de jure* restrictions to competition and investment still exist on either side of the Atlantic, and national and Community regulators are envisaging important changes in their current regulatory frameworks to account for the changing competitive and technological landscape in the industry. Although hard to quantify with precision, the economic benefits that would follow from the creation of a more integrated transatlantic market for telecoms services would undoubtedly be substantial.

In some respects, the US and the EU can both learn from each other in reconsidering the appropriateness of their regulatory frameworks in the field of electronic communications. In the US, growing criticism of the 1996 Telecommunications Act has even led one commentator to argue in favor of reviewing the US law "with an eye on Europe" – i.e. on the 2002 EU Regulatory Framework, which adopted a more flexible approach to regulation based on a systemic view and on the convergence of sector-specific regulation and competition policy.[63] Many authoritative scholars have expressed similar views over the past few years.[64]

The US also seems in great need of enhanced technological neutrality, although the FCC has been reconsidering the differential treatment of cable and DSL operators in the fiercely debated *Brand X* case, currently under scrutiny by the US Supreme Court.[65] On the other hand, Europe seems to lag behind in market liberalization, the standardization policy and spectrum allocation, especially after the disappointing adventure of UMTS licensing. Most importantly, the EU seems to be falling behind most OECD countries in promoting public and private R&D investments, which lie at the core of technological innovation.

---

[63] J.B. Speta, "Rewriting US Telecommunications Law with an Eye on Europe", preliminary draft (retrieved from http://web.si.umich.edu/tprc/papers/2004/ 322/Speta%20TPRC%202004.pdf, August 31, 2004).

[64] See for example P.W. MacAvoy and J.G. Sidak, *What is Wrong with American Telecommunications?*, John Olin Working Paper Series No. 17, Yale School of Management, New Haven, CT, 2000.

[65] See "Fight over Line Sharing between FCC and Brand X Reaches Supreme Court", NewsTarget (www.newstarget.com), April 6, 2005.

If next-generation regulations converge on a more competition- and investment-oriented regulatory environment, consumers in both the European Union and the United States will reap substantial benefits in the years to come.

The European Commission, in assessing what is now called the 'cost of non-Lisbon' (i.e. the costs of not implementing its ambitious program to bolster European competitiveness and innovation), has estimated that the liberalization of the telecommunications and electricity markets would lead to increases in GDP and employment levels of 0.4% and 0.6% respectively, four years afterwards. Further, a GDP increase of 0.6% could be expected ten years after the liberalization.[66]

Recently, the European Commission has also calculated that increasing the EU's total research and development expenditures from 1.9% to 3% of GDP by 2010 (to reach the targets set out in the EU's Lisbon agenda), compared with the status quo (no increase in R&D spending) would lead to increases in GDP of 1.7% or 0.25% per year by 2010. Furthermore, by 2010, total factor productivity in the EU is estimated to increase by 0.8%, employment by 1.4% and real income by 3%. Additional increases in the European Union's GDP of 4.2%, 7.5% and 12.1% in 2015, 2020 and 2030 respectively are also projected.[67]

In the United States, a recent study on promoting competition through telecoms reform by Hazlett et al., commissioned by the US Chamber of Commerce, analyzed a comprehensive reform package for American telecommunications. Table 6 summarizes the main proposals suggested in the report and the estimated economic impact that would be achieved. The authors further calculated that "each year of delay will cost the US economy about $12 billion of investment spending and about $33 billion of GDP and will deter the creation of more than 212,000 jobs".[68] A number of these reforms, as explained in previous sections, have already been undertaken in the US.

---

[66] See European Commission (2002) op. cit.

[67] See European Commission, *A 3% R&D effort in Europe in 2010: An analysis of the consequences*, study prepared by the Research Directorate-General, European Commission, Brussels, 2004c.

[68] See T.W. Hazlett et al., *Sending the Right Signals: Promoting Competition through Telecommunications Reform*, a report to the US Chamber of Commerce, Washington, D.C., October 2004.

*Table 6. Proposed Reforms to the US Telecommunications Industry*

| Recommended regulatory reforms | Estimates of economic impact |
| --- | --- |
| • Phase out mandatory network sharing rules and, more immediately, regulated wholesale rates set at theoretical costs. | • $58 billion of new capital investment would be generated in five years. |
| • Make 438 MHz of prime radio spectrum available for commercial wireless oper- ators. | • Investment-led GDP would increase by $167 billion over five years.<br><br>• An additional $467 billion would be added to GDP for increased productivity. |
| • Exempt high-speed cable modem and DSL services from common carrier regulation. | • A combined effect of both supply and demand channels totaling $634 billion of additional goods and services, including $113 billion in new tax revenues over five years would be attained. |
| • Exempt Internet services from phone service regulation by states. | • Average employment levels are estimated to increase by more than 212,000 jobs. |
| • Raise funds for universal service directly from general tax revenues rather than from hidden costs that penalize telecom competi-tion and the growth of network services. | • Added consumer value from price competition and innovative new services are envisaged.<br><br>• US competitiveness in the global marketplace would be enhanced. |
| • Distribute universal service funds directly to targeted consumers. | • The rollout of new technologies and advanced networks in knowledge- based industries and applications would accelerate.<br><br>• Social goals such as universal service would be achieved. |

*Source:* Hazlett et al. (2004), op. cit.

# SECTION III

# POLITICS AND MARKETS

# 12. Transatlantic Corporate Governance Reform: Brussels Sprouts or Washington Soup?

## Arman Khachaturyan
## and Joseph A. McCahery

The reduction in barriers to trade and the liberalization of financial markets, transportation and telecommunications have created the basis for the increase in flows of factors of production between jurisdictions. With the prospect of more capital mobility, it becomes conventional wisdom that national governments are prompted to perform their economic policy functions more efficiently. Indeed, the EU and US have developed successful policy strategies over time to encourage more competitive capital, product and labor markets while erecting few barriers that could deter substantial benefits. Nevertheless, many scholars view current efforts with a mixture of skepticism and optimism, arguing that the system of rules and institutions has insufficient incentives and capacity to foster equilibrium levels of efficient investments. At the same time, most serious proponents of liberalization accept that the separate interests within each country may lead to divergences in the optimal outcome with respect to standards. Consequently, much of the debate over finding agreement on the level of optimal standards is thought to turn on whether, all things considered, regulators can press for agreement on the level of standards to set. Underlying this fundamental policy question is the concern that the capacity to come to agreement on higher standards will lead to substantial benefits.

The EU and the US are enjoying increased and unprecedented integration of their economies. Together they account for the largest share of international capital and banking flows, levels of trade, investments and securities transactions. If anything, this transatlantic economic partnership reflects the common will and commitment to strengthen transatlantic relations by upgrading the institutional framework of dialogue, identifying specific challenges, reducing transatlantic trade barriers and promoting bilateral trade. The US-EU summit of 2004 further confirmed the common commitment toward the establishment of a multilateral trading system governed by rules, as well as policies to produce strong and sustained economic growth and to create the cooperative means and best practices to reinforce the underlying basis of the transatlantic economic partnership.

While there are a number of financial and regulatory difficulties that are sufficient to pose a threat to increased transatlantic trade and efficient transatlantic capital markets, the EU and the US launched the Regulatory Cooperation and the Financial Markets Regulatory Dialogue in 2002. The initiative is designed to promote transatlantic trade through establishing better quality regulation and minimize the divergences in the laws and policies of the two jurisdictions. A similar function is also served by the establishment of the Regulatory Dialogue as a forum for discussion of issues of bilateral corporate governance and financial market regulation, which have recently been given increased preference in national regulatory policies.

The high-profile corporate fallouts of recent years have underscored the interconnection and interdependency of transatlantic economies and the need for regulators to work cooperatively to create timely and effective solutions to improve transatlantic auditing and governance policies. Whereas corporate governance failures usually occur at the national level, there is no denying that the recent financial scandals at Enron and Parmalat involved questionable dealings (SPEs, improper swap arrangements and flaws in financial disclosure) that took on a global dimension. These scandals provoked a variety of responses and brought the issue of transatlantic governance and accountability to the attention of law-makers and the public. Responding rapidly to the corporate scandals, the US Congress enacted the Sarbanes-Oxley Act (hereafter referred to as SOXA) in 2002, the most comprehensive legislative package in the history of US corporate regulation since the Securities Acts of 1933 and 1934.

The SOXA introduced sweeping reforms in corporate governance systems of publicly traded companies aimed at increasing the disciplinary systems of managers and gatekeepers. In an attempt to restore public trust and confidence in corporate accounting and reporting, the SOXA was designed to improve the governance and accountability of boards, managers and gatekeepers by inducing increased oversight and monitoring of US-listed companies and reputational intermediaries. In addition to the audit reforms, the SOXA put in place a number of measures specifically designed to counter the governance failures. These include requiring CEOs and CFOs to certify, on pain of criminal penalties, their firms' periodic reports and the effectiveness of internal controls; the imposition of obligations on corporate lawyers to report any evidence of suspected violations of securities law; the prohibition of corporate loans to managers or directors; restrictions on stock sales by executives during 'blackout periods'; and requiring firms to establish an independent audit committee, of which at least one member must be a financial expert. At the same time, the NYSE and NASDAQ quickly proposed new corporate governance guidelines.

The wave of US regulatory reform that followed the collapse of Enron has spilled over into Europe. Most directly, the SOXA applies to non-US firms that are listed on a US exchange and obliges EU audit firms to register with the United States Public Accounting Oversight Board (PCAOB). This extraterritorial application has triggered widespread criticism in Europe. An indirect effect of the events in the US has been to provoke a host of parallel reforms in the EU. Interestingly, EU policy-makers quickly responded to the US scandals by accelerating their own company law modernization and corporate governance reform program that was earlier instituted by the Commission through the High Level Working Group, chaired by Professor Jaap Winter. EU regulators were motivated by a concern to ensure that US collapses are not replicated in Europe, a desire to ensure that domestic and EU legislation reflect best practice and the need to give credibility to claims of regulatory parity for the purposes of negotiations over the extraterritorial impact of US law.

In their second report, the Group recommended strengthening mandatory disclosure obligations for listed companies, granting special investigation rights to minority investors and considering the introduction of a disqualification sanction for directors associated with misleading disclosures. Besides these reforms, the Group suggested the development by EU member states of UK-style codes of best practice, primarily enforced by markets through 'comply or explain' mechanisms, improved investor access to corporate information through the use of electronic dissemination facilities and the strengthening of shareholders' rights to vote via electronic means.

Taking up the recommendations of the High Level Group to establish a new framework for corporate governance, the EU launched its Action Plan in May 2003.[1] The Action Plan is intended to give a fresh and ambitious impetus to EU company law harmonization and is meant to meet three challenges in the area of corporate governance: i) improving the integrity and accountability of board members, ii) restoring the auditors' credibility and iii) promoting fair presentation of the company through sound and reliable accounting and hence, restoring investor confidence and fostering efficiency and competitiveness of businesses in the EU.

This chapter examines the major transatlantic regulatory challenges posed by the latest spate of regulation promulgated on both sides of the Atlantic. While some question whether the reforms are optimally designed to limit future financial frauds or whether they pose excessive burdens for small businesses, EU and US policy-makers, in contrast, contend that it is important to work out cooperative solutions for improving governance performance overall. The development of a 'transatlantic practice' is underway and regulators, lawyers and other parties in the fields of

---

[1] EC Commission Communication, "Modernizing Company Law and Enhancing Corporate Governance in the European Union – A Plan to Move Forward", COM(2003)284 final, May 21, 2003.

accounting, corporate law and securities regulation are influencing its development, leading to the adoption of common standards and convergence in legal techniques to solve similar problems.

Despite these substantive reforms, corporate law remains a domestic matter. Interestingly, securities regulators, who have been developing the recent regulatory innovations, have been a significant influence on the developments that have taken place in EU company law. Similar incursions into the terrain of US corporate law were not significant until legal changes were introduced by the SOXA in 2002. To be sure, impediments remain on both sides of the Atlantic, and questions remain as to whether and how adoption of common standards and convergent measures will influence transatlantic market developments. This policy brief concludes by arguing that regulatory diversity rather than harmonization will be more conducive toward the establishment of a truly transatlantic marketplace. See Table 1 for an overview of the main characteristics of the principal actors on the corporate governance stage of the United States and selected EU member states.

## Transatlantic Regulatory Challenges

In the post-scandal era, the EU and US have continued to face increased transatlantic regulatory challenges. These challenges stem in part from the corporate fallouts and the subsequent regulatory responses, and more comprehensively from the ambition to design an international regulatory and supervisory system of cooperation in accounting and auditing.

Whereas the EU's reform moves remain nascent and have been treated with indifference in the US, the cross-border implications of the SOXA and its 'moral DNA' for US-listed European companies have raised apprehensions and objections in the EU for creating 'unnecessary extraterritorial consequences' and 'unnecessary difficulties'. EU policy-makers and businesses alike have expressed growing discontent that the extension of SOXA requirements to US-listed European companies is costly and might possibly oblige these European companies to de-list from major US markets such as NYSE and NASDAQ. Moreover, the SOXA has been perceived as an attempt to export US corporate governance rules with disregard to the distinct legal and institutional framework in the EU and the very virtue of the EU's approach to regulatory reform. Against this background, a number of pending transatlantic regulatory challenges remain high on the agenda of policy-makers on both sides of the Atlantic. We turn next to the most significant reform measure that has emerged from the governance crises.

Table 1. Main Characteristics of Transatlantic Corporate Governance Players

| Country | United States | UK | Germany | France | Italy |
|---|---|---|---|---|---|
| Employees | *Flexible labor <br> *Low unionization <br> *Employment at will | *Flexible labor market | *Work councils <br> *Co-determination <br> *High skills <br> *Non-flexible labor market | *Work councils <br> *Low unionization <br> *Short-term contracts | *Long-term contracts <br> *Rigid labor market <br> *Medium skills |
| Shareholders | *Institutional investors and individuals <br> *Dispersed | *Institutional investors <br> *Dispersed | *Other non-financial companies <br> *Banks | *Foreign investors <br> *State | *State <br> *Families |
| Government | *Liberal policies <br> *Arms-length <br> *Weak takeover barriers | *Liberal policies <br> *Arms-length <br> *Weak takeover barriers | *Protectionist policies <br> *Medium takeover barriers | *Protectionist policies <br> *Interventionist <br> *Medium takeover barriers | *Protectionist policies <br> *Interventionist <br> *Strong takeover barriers |
| Boards of Directors | *High activism <br> *High % of outsiders due to investor pressure | *High activism <br> *High % of outsiders determined by law | *Moderate activism <br> *Stakeholders as a significant minority <br> *Medium size | *Moderate activism <br> *Minority outsiders <br> *Medium size | *Low activism <br> *Large % of insiders <br> *Medium size |
| Top Management Team | *Professional (finance/MBA) background <br> *Some foreign-born management <br> *Open labor markets | *Semi-professional background <br> *Some foreign-born management <br> *Open labor markets | *Technical background <br> *Few foreign-born managers <br> *Closed labor markets (long-term) | *Common educational backgrounds <br> *State links <br> *Few foreign-born managers <br> *Closed labor markets (long-term) | *Non-professional <br> *No foreign-born management <br> *Closed labor markets (long term) |

Source: "Mastering Corporate Governance", Financial Times, May 27, 2005.

## Internal Controls

The first transatlantic regulatory challenge relates to compliance with SOXA's internal controls standards. According to the SOXA, management of a US-listed company is required to file a report that should state: i) management's responsibilities for establishing and maintaining adequate internal controls and procedures over financial reporting; ii) management's assessment about the effectiveness of the company's internal controls as of the end of the company's most recent fiscal year, including a statement as to whether the controls are effective; iii) any 'material weaknesses' in internal controls that management has identified; iv) the framework used by management to evaluate the effectiveness of the company's internal controls; and v) an outside auditor's attestation to and report on management's evaluation of the company's internal controls and procedures for financial reporting.[2]

Moreover, managers are responsible for creating, maintaining and regularly evaluating the effectiveness of a system of 'disclosure controls and procedures'. As noted above, the CEO and CFO are accountable for reliability and accuracy of both the financial and non-financial information contained in their periodic reports and internal accounting controls. They must personally certify for compliance and take personal responsibility (criminal penalties) for non-compliance.[3]

Whereas the SEC states that such internal controls standards and compliance measures are necessary to enhance US investor confidence and promote deep and liquid capital markets, critics note that the new reporting demands of SOXA Section 404 are perceived in the EU as imposing unjustified costs and time-consuming transitions on all US-listed EU companies. For many types of firms, these regulations impose costs but bring few benefits to investors.

Following intense lobbying efforts from the EU and European businesses and faced with possible delisting of European companies from the US capital markets, the SEC has recently granted a year-long reprieve to non-US listed companies from SOXA's internal controls standards. As a result, European companies have to implement US internal controls standards by July 15, 2006.

---

[2] For more details, see SOXA Section 404: Management Assessment of Internal Controls.

[3] For more details, see SOXA Sections 302 and 906: Corporate Responsibility for Financial Reports.

## Auditing Standards

The second transatlantic regulatory challenge concerns the recent shift in auditing standards. In an effort to create a more independent and accountable audit environment, the SOXA puts significant emphasis on the regulation of not only accounting and auditing practices of a registered public accounting firm but also that of any Certified Public Accountant (CPA) associated therewith, and any CPA working as an auditor of a publicly traded company. The SOXA establishes a direct reporting responsibility between the auditor and the audit committee of the issuer, subjects audit and non-audit services to pre-approval by the audit committee, limits non-audit services to be provided by an auditor to the issuer, clearly defines rules for audit and non-audit service fees, regulates the conflict of interest between the auditor and the issuer, and requires more frequent rotation of lead and review audit partners.

Moreover, following the SOXA's enactment, the SEC ended a long era of self-regulation and established PCAOB as a regulator. Subject to SEC oversight and aimed at protecting public interest in "informative, accurate, and independent audit reports" for publicly traded companies, the function of PCAOB is to: i) register public accounting firms; ii) establish, or adopt, by rule, "auditing, quality control, ethics, independence, and other standards relating to the preparation of audit reports for issuers"; iii) conduct inspections of accounting firms; iv) conduct investigations and disciplinary proceedings, and impose appropriate sanctions; v) perform such other duties or functions as necessary or appropriate; vi) enforce compliance with the Act, the rules of the Board, professional standards, and the securities laws relating to the preparation and issuance of audit reports and the obligations and liabilities of accountants with respect thereto.[4]

As we have already seen, the fact that PCAOB authority extends to any non-US accounting firm that 'prepares and furnishes' audit and accounting services to any US-listed company has further sharpened the focus of transatlantic regulatory dialogue and became one of the major points of contention between the US and the EU.[5] EU policy-makers and industry groups have expressed their discontent that any European accounting firm that provides material services to publicly traded companies in the US should supply its work papers upon the request of the PCAOB or the SEC and be subject to their controls. Moreover, the fact that European accounting companies that do not issue audit reports but are still substantially involved

---

[4] For more details see Section 103 of the SOXA: Auditing, Quality Control, and Independence Standards and Rules.

[5] For more details see Section 106 of the SOXA: Foreign Public Accounting Firms.

in the process of their preparation are treated as a public accounting firms, for SOXA purposes, is likely to cause continued irritation in the EU until convergence or equivalence has been achieved.

Even though EU policy-makers and European businesses have insisted on mutual recognition of equivalent systems of auditing, the SEC remains skeptical of European audit practices, which may impede progress in this area. The SEC takes the view that EU standards, which are largely national and rely on enforcement by national-level regulators, are not adequate in most respects and contrast poorly to the level of regulation in place in the US While the SEC acknowledges that there may be some variation in standards, the US investor is nevertheless entitled to the same level of protection no matter whether the party invests in a domestic or foreign company publicly traded in the US

## *Accounting Standards*

The third challenge in the transatlantic regulatory dialogue relates to the introduction of a single set of global accounting standards. As of January 1, 2005, all listed European companies have to comply with reporting requirements of the International Financial Reporting Standards (IFRS). EU-listed US companies publish their financial statements according to the US Generally Accepted Accounting Principles (GAAP). Whereas EU policy-makers have expressed their willingness to extend the mutual recognition principle to EU-listed US companies reporting in US GAAP, and hence, granting equivalence to US GAAP with the IFRS, the SEC has been so far reluctant to judge the equivalence of IFRS with US GAAP.

The SEC requires that all US-listed companies, including European ones, have to reconcile accounting differences arising from IFRS with US GAAP. This virtually means that US-listed European companies should report according to US GAAP. The position of the SEC reflects the fact that despite the markedly improved quality of transparency and disclosure in the EU since the introduction of more stringent listing rules on national stock exchanges and the enforcement of the IFRS, enforcement of accounting rules in the EU is still national and there is no EU enforcement body. In some new member states there is very weak enforcement of accounting rules. Moreover, even though the Committee of European Securities Regulators (CESR) plays an important role, it does not have 'EU enforcement leverages' or the necessary authority to allow for accounting standards across both sides of the Atlantic offering equivalence.

Nevertheless, the transatlantic regulatory dialogue has already produced positive results with regard to accounting standards. Taking into consideration the transition to IFRS, the SEC has already eased disclosure of historical results by US-listed European companies. Finally, the SEC and EU policy-makers have recently announced a road map that would eliminate the reconciliation requirement for US-listed European companies by 2009.

## De-Listing and Deregistration

As a consequence of sweeping changes in corporate governance, accounting and auditing practices in the US and their across-the-board application to all US-listed companies, the cost of regulatory compliance, possible delisting and deregistration from the US markets by European companies became yet another challenge on the EU and US regulatory agenda. EU policy-makers and business groups alike have warned that they might decide to de-list and deregister because of high regulatory costs and costly transitions that US-listed EU companies will face. Nevertheless, de-listing is not a simple task for European companies with more than 300 shareholders. Indeed, such companies are unable to deregister pursuant to Rule 12(e) and consequently must remain listed on the exchange.

Even though most EU listed companies would not rush to de-list if the barriers were dropped, EU policy-makers have long argued that the SEC should take actions to ease the process of deregistration from the SEC for European companies with more than 300 shareholders. Currently, the SEC is examining ways whether such European companies can be exempted from some corporate governance requirements. It may be an argument to recommend that EU listed companies may opt out of the US measures if the SEC, having assessed all details, is satisfied that the parallel EU measures are sufficient.

## International Regulatory and Supervisory Cooperation

The next challenge in the transatlantic regulatory dialogue refers to the long-running dispute as to greater EU representation and participation in international standards-setting bodies. The EU is keen to have more involvement in the International Accounting Standards Board (IASB) and in the International Auditing and Assurance Standards Board (IAASB) to be able to influence governance thereof as well as the reform process in accounting and auditing initiated by these bodies.

The fact that the PCAOB might 'overrule' the IAASB by extending its system of inspections and investigations to US-listed foreign companies and issue standards independently from those developed by the IAASB as evidenced by the PCAOB Release 2003-023 on "Proposed Auditing Standard on Audit Documentation and Proposed Amendment to Interim

Standards on Auditing",[6] elevated concerns in the EU as to the future of global standards setting in accounting and auditing.

The debate in this area is heating up, but 'the fight' moves into another round with no concrete results so far.

## *A Transatlantic Road Map*

The new US audit and accounting regulatory environment (particularly by limiting the role of the profession) will probably have a major influence on future efforts to establish a convergence model for a global auditing and accounting profession. While the EU's approach offers different regulatory menus, we should expect substantial convergence in the area of governance and disclosure.

Turning our attention to the introduction of new regulatory frameworks, it is important to keep in mind that measures should be left sufficiently flexible in order to accommodate the wide range of firms and corporate law regimes. The more innovative and adaptable a legal system is, the more likely it will be able to supply firms with measures that they require while ensuring an adequate level of investor protection.

In this context, the US legislative reforms introduced in wake of the 2002 governance scandals impose a number of new statutory measures that seek to improve the level of transparency of accounts, ensure auditor independence and limit the abusive actions taken by boards and officers. While such measures have surely taken away some of the shortcomings of the original corporate law regime governing listed firms in the US, they may suffer from several shortcomings as we have seen. In this context, EU listed firms do not have the possibility of opting out of the EU regime. Those who support the introduction of a lower regulatory regime can cite the benefit of allowing investors and firms to enjoy different levels of protection, which is likely to correspond to the diverse needs of investors for information and legal protection. In this respect, the issue of flexibility and reliability of different measures should be examined and assessed.

For the EU, the emphasis on increased use of recommendations by regulators can provide a coherent foundation for reform. Another beneficial aspect might be the use of less intrusive self-regulatory measures which could speed up the process of reform while taking into account the dynamic changes in the market. From this perspective, the role of the EU would be to ensure a certain level of coordination between the member states, and make it possible to provide for certain minimum standards. Either way, focusing solely on

---

[6] For more details see http://www.pcaobus.org/Rules_of_the_Board/Documents/ BriefingPaper2003-023.pdf.

directives and other hard law measures, as opposed to flexibility and national level decision-making, is to ignore arguably the key policy issues for firms for years to come.

Finally, the transatlantic dimension of corporate governance reform represents a unique experiment in corporate law reform. While it is unclear whether EU-US cooperation has make it easier for firms to comply with regulation, made it more attractive for new investment or protected the interests of minority shareholders sufficiently, there may be good reasons to support more extensive cooperation between the EU and US since it may eventually affect capital mobility, and hence, drive product and labor market reforms, leading in turn to lower costs of capital. In this respect, some level of regulatory competition may be necessary to ensure the high rate of flexibility and innovation necessary to create an effective system of corporate law. On the other hand, the increasing trend toward adoption of similar techniques and institutions, accompanied by extensive interest group pressures, may create additional incentives for directors and managers to adopt internal organizational forms that are more efficient. Whether the EU and US will create an effective transatlantic regulatory environment in the various areas of corporate law will depend on how successful the parties are in striking a balance between fostering regulatory competition in some areas to favor heterogeneity of issuers, investors, creditors and to allow them to choose between possible governance structures, while introducing limited harmonization in other areas.

# 13. Climate Change: Could a transatlantic greenhouse gas emissions market work?

## *Christian Egenhofer*

The disagreement between the European Union and the United States over climate change has become one of the most highly publicized and contentious disputes in transatlantic relations. The high-handed manner in which the incoming Bush Administration handled its rejection of the Kyoto Protocol came to symbolize US foreign policy for many Europeans. Despite the best of efforts of the United States to bury the international accord, EU member states agreed to stand up and work together to implement its provisions. Ultimately, the EU succeeded in convincing other countries to ratify the Protocol and to bring it into force without the US. Although this has been touted by many as a major EU diplomatic success, this image is a little misleading in that it tends to obscures the fact that the Kyoto Protocol is actually in rather poor shape. All countries face major challenges in meeting their targets, and there is little likelihood that Kyoto will survive in its current form.[1] With the exception of the EU, only a few countries seem prepared to extend the pure target and timetable approach beyond 2012, when the Kyoto Protocol expires.

Neither the EU nor the US on its own can solve the global climate change challenge. It is only with the is full participation by all major emitters – including the US, the EU, other OECD and fast-growing developing countries – that climate change objectives can be achieved. Moreover, important differences between EU and US carbon constraints – especially if the gap were to widen further – will be a major and increasing source of transatlantic economic and environmental tension. As evidence mounts that climate change represents a significant potential threat to the world and as a scientific consensus continues to support this view, it is evident that the issue will not go away, either in the EU or the US. It is virtually impossible to imagine a further integration of EU and US markets without a resolution of the climate change dispute. On the other hand, an EU-US agreement would almost certainly create a precursor of the future global regime.

This chapter examines practical ways to reach a transatlantic climate change agreement, including prospects for a common greenhouse gas (GHG) emissions market. One bottom-line conclusion is that the deep integration of the transatlantic economy means that both US and European business have

---

[1] See N. Purvis, *Climate Change Policy: Next Steps*, Brookings Briefing, The Brookings Institution, Washington, DC, February 9, 2005.

much to gain by such a market, but also much to lose by failing to achieve it. The possibility for such a market may not be as remote as one thinks. If one believes leading global business associations, there is a growing concern about an increasingly fragmented or even disintegrating regulatory framework. One of the recurring themes in the responses put forward by business is the possible creation of a greenhouse gas emissions market. According to Steve Lennon, Chairman of the Environment and Energy Commission of the International Chamber of Commerce, whose membership includes major US companies, business sees a "global system of emissions trading as inevitable".[2]

## Beyond Kyoto... At Last

Although the real root of transatlantic disagreement is that the EU accepts the need for carbon constraints and the US Administration – as well as parts of the US Congress – as yet does not, the focus of the dispute in the past has been on the Kyoto Protocol. With the entry into force of the Kyoto Protocol, there finally may be an opportunity to move the political agenda beyond Kyoto into the 'post-2012' period and address two fundamental questions. First, how urgent is the problem? And second, what is to be done next?

### *The Changing EU Context*

In the EU, the 'beyond Kyoto' agenda has taken shape with the European Commission's February 2005 Communication on post-2012 climate change.[3] This document explicitly discusses differentiated commitments from a wider circle of participating countries and refrains from proposing targets,[4] partly to avoid renewed international acrimony. According to Henry Derwent, Prime Minister Tony Blair's special representative during the UK's G8 presidency, the door has been opened to more flexibility on the part of the EU on the issue of targets and the nature of commitments.[5]

---

[2] "Business pushes G8 on global warming", by Fiona Harvey, *Financial Times*, June 10, 2005, p. 1.

[3] European Commission, *Winning the Battle against Global Climate Change*, Communication from the Commission to the Council, the European Parliament, the European Economic and Social Committee and the Committee of the Regions, COM(2005) 35 final, February 9, 2005.

[4] Although the Commission has hedged, both the EU Council of Environment Ministers as well as the European Council (which consists of EU heads of governments) have set targets, with conditions.

[5] "We must accept the future may not be like the past and repeat a target and trading approach" (as quoted in the *EU Observer*, April 20, 2005).

To date, the EU has built its domestic strategy on a cap-and-trade program, which is modeled to a good degree upon the successful US emissions trading programs to fight acid rain. The EU emissions trading scheme (ETS), as it is generally referred to in the EU, has become the cornerstone of EU climate change policy. It has also proven to be the most politically acceptable instrument to deal with climate change and to be the instrument of choice at least for the business community. Emissions trading is seen as a means to move beyond traditional 'command and control' environmental policies by establishing a long-term and predictable price signal upon which firms can base investment decisions, while retaining significant flexibility in how they achieve the environmental objective. This approach both reduces costs and increases certainty. The irony, of course, is that the US initially advocated emissions trading against EU resistance, whereas now the EU has pressed ahead with emissions trading while US initiatives are limited to voluntary and state-sponsored schemes.

Yet emissions trading alone cannot explain the relative ease with which climate change policy has been formulated in the EU.[6] Another factor is the relatively modest Kyoto Protocol target. More importantly, however, is the EU's security of supply position with regard to natural gas and its transformation through gas and electricity market liberalization. The strategic positions of the EU and the US in natural gas are profoundly different: according to European Commission data, 80% of global gas reserves are located within an economically transportable distance to the EU, compared with around 10% for the US. These reserves could cover Eurasian demand for 50 years. Hence, switching from coal to gas is a viable, cost-effective short-term policy for the EU, but less so for the US, where the share of coal in power generation is expected to remain stable and continue to account for about half of all fuels.[7] Climate policy will nevertheless put pressure on coal. Any US alternative short of deploying 'carbon capture and storage' would increase concerns about security of supply.

---

[6] M. Wriglesworth and C. Egenhofer, "Security of Energy Supply and Climate Change in the EU: Setting the Stage", background paper for the INTACT Project on Transatlantic Dialogue on Climate Change, March 2005.

[7] According to the International Energy Agency, the share of gas in power generation is projected to more than double in the period from 2002 (15%) to 2030 (35%). The European Commission does not rule out the possibility that 40% of total electricity will be produced from natural gas by that time. See *World Energy Outlook 2004*, International Energy Agency, Paris, 2004. For US figures, see *Annual Energy Outlook – With projections to 2025*, US Energy Information Agency, Washington, DC, 2003.

Against the background of minimal trade-offs – at least in a short-term perspective – between climate change, security of supply and market liberalization, it should not come as a surprise that the energy sector has been broadly supportive of EU climate policy approaches and the EU ETS. A modest carbon constraint, especially when implemented through the EU emissions trading scheme and based on free allocation, has been seen in business circles as enhancing efficiency and even security of supply, as many energy savings measures come at a low or even negative cost.[8] In addition, as long as allowances are given for free ('grandfathering'), the 'competitiveness' effects on industry are minimized.[9] Given that medium-term targets will be more constraining, requiring more radical changes and leading to greater distributional consequences, this relative consensus among stakeholders may come under pressure. This effect can already be observed in during the emerging discussions on the post-2012 EU strategy, as well as on the future of the EU emissions trading scheme.

## The US Political Economy of Climate Change Issues

The EU perception of the US political economy on climate change is that there are various responses on different levels.[10] At the federal, or national, level there is a focus on research and technology programs as well as on voluntary measures. The sub-federal level is characterized by a plethora of state and local government initiatives, including trading schemes. There are advocates for federal regulation, mainly in Congress, as exemplified by the bipartisan McCain-Lieberman cap-and-trade legislation. The business community remains largely divided. Corporations participate in numerous

---

[8] European Commission, *European Climate Change Programme*, Final Report, Brussels, June 2001 (retrieved from http://www.europa.eu.int/comm/environment/climat/eccpreport.htm).

[9] See *The European Union Emissions Trading Scheme: Implications for Industrial Competitiveness*, Carbon Trust, London, June 2004; J. Renaud, *Industrial competitiveness under the European Union emissions trading scheme*, International Energy Agency Information Paper, Washington, DC, December 2004; P. Quirion, and J-Ch. Houcarde, "Does the $CO_2$ emissions trading directive threaten the competitiveness of European industry? Quantification and comparison to exchange rate fluctuations", presented at the EAERE Conference, Budapest, June 2004 (retrieved from http://eaere2004.bkae.hu/download/paper/quirionpaper.pdf); and C. Egenhofer, N. Fujiwara and K. Gialoglou, *Business Consequences of the EU Emissions Trading Scheme*, Report of a CEPS Task Force, Centre for European Policy Studies, Brussels, 2005.

[10] See *Climate Change Activities in the US: 2004 Update*, Pew Center on Global Climate Change, Arlington, VA, 2004; T. Brewer, *The Political Economy of US Responses to Climate Change Issues* (working title; forthcoming 2005).

voluntary initiatives but most oppose mandatory emissions limits.[11] A majority of US public opinion tends to favor stronger climate change policies than those advocated by the Bush Administration,[12] as also do a number of religious organizations and churches.

One result of the impasse over climate change policies at the national government level has been increased activism and cooperation among state and local governments at the sub-national level. It is often noted in this regard that there is a tradition of some states (especially California) taking the lead on environmental issues, with the national government eventually adopting policies that have been developed at the sub-national level. To some extent, this may yet happen with climate change policies.

A growing coalition of Members of Congress – in both the Senate and the House of Representatives – supports a policy of mandatory domestic limits on GHG emissions. Although the coalition is composed predominantly of Democrats, it includes a number of Republicans, and its bipartisan leadership includes Senator John McCain, a prominent Republican. Both the congressional coalition and activist state and local governments tend to hail from the west coast and the northeast. The economic and political significance of fossil fuel industries in many mid-western and southern/south-western states is likely to prevent them from following the trend toward increased mitigation efforts in the far western and north-eastern regions of the country.

As for public opinion, there is a majority in favor of more action than the Bush Administration appears prepared to take. Yet the public is also likely to remain relatively passive about the issue, enabling the US Administration to continue along its basic policy course. Greater public consensus for stronger action may develop as the Kyoto and EU schemes become better known in the US, and as scientific evidence and actual climate events heighten awareness of the implications of climate change. But this is by no means an absolutely certain outcome.

## The Daunting Task of Addressing Global Climate Change

The task to stabilize GHG emissions, as has been laid out in the United Nations Framework Convention on Climate Change (UNFCCC) and ratified by the US, is daunting. Since more than 60% of global GHG emissions relate

---

[11] Some electric power companies have, however, publicly advocated a mandatory cap-and-trade system or a carbon tax.

[12] For a detailed review of public opinion data from 1989-2005, see T. Brewer, "US Public Opinion on Climate Change Issues: Implications for Consensus-Building and Policymaking", *Climate Policy*, Vol. 5, No. 1, 2005, pp. 2-18.

to the burning of fossil fuels, a look at global energy demand projections alone is sobering. In 'business as usual' scenarios, world energy demand is projected to grow by around 60% or even more until 2030,[13] and could even triple by 2050. The principal drivers are economic and population growth, especially in developing countries, which by 2030 will be responsible for two-thirds of the increase in global energy demand. At the same time, the EU and the world at large will continue to rely on fossil fuels as principal fuels.

The World Business Council for Sustainable Development, using scenarios developed by the UN-sponsored Intergovernmental Panel on Climate Change (IPCC), estimates that in order to achieve stabilization of GHG concentrations, there is a need to reduce global $CO_2$ emissions by 22 billion tons of $CO_2$ per year by 2050 – almost as much as today's total global emissions[14] (see Figure 1). This may require a peak of global emissions by around 2020, since GHG emissions stay in the atmosphere for a long time.[15]

*Figure 1. Achieving an Acceptable $CO_2$ Stabilization*

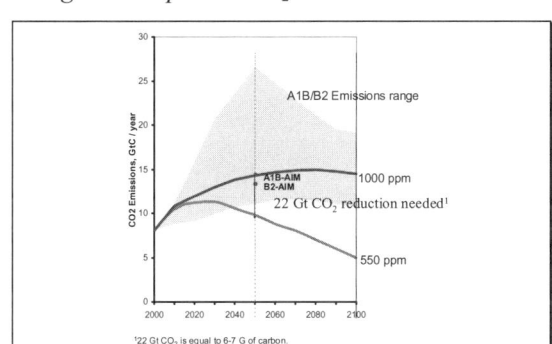

*Source: Facts and Trends to 2050 – Energy and Climate Change*, World Business Council for Sustainable Development, Geneva, 2004 (retrieved from http://www.wbcsd.ch).

To illustrate the scale of the task, a reduction of just 3.3 billion out of 22 billion tons of $CO_2$ (or 1 gigaton out of 6-7 gigatons of carbon) would

---

[13] International Energy Agency, *World Energy Outlook 2004*, op. cit.; European Commission, *World energy, technology and climate policy outlook, WETO 2030*, Luxembourg, 2003; see also *Long Range Economic and Energy Outlook*, ExxonMobil, Irving, TX, 2004 (retrieved from http://www.exxonmobil.com/corporate/Citizenship/Corp_citizenship_energy_outlook.asp).

[14] 22Gt $CO_2$ equals 6-7 Gt of carbon.

[15] $CO_2$, for example, the most important GHG, stays in the atmosphere for 100 years.

necessitate increasing current global wind power capacity 150 times, bringing into operation 1 billion hydrogen cars to replace conventional 30-miles-per-gallon cars, boosting current nuclear capacity five-fold, or using half of the agricultural area of the US for biomass production.[16] Although there are different opinions on whether or not the 2050 goals can be reached with technically proven technology, there is a broad consensus that there is a need for real breakthrough technology (not technically proven) beyond 2050. Pacala and Socolow and the IPPC argue that current technologies could solve the climate problem for the next 50 years, while Hoffert et al. believe that new and revolutionary technologies will be needed.[17]

Thus, it is abundantly clear that the climate change challenge can only be effectively addressed on the condition that all emitters, including all industrialized countries and at least the major emitters among developing countries participate in an emissions-abatement scheme. This requirement has long been acknowledged by the US Administration and Congress, and is also the position of the EU.[18] Participation by the US in any global effort to combat climate change is essential, since the US is the largest emitter of greenhouse gases, accounting for around 20% in 2000.

## No Quick Fix but Progress is Possible

In the aftermath of the Kyoto Protocol negotiations, and especially after the US rejection of Kyoto, numerous alternative proposals to the Protocol have been put forward (see Box 1).[19] When assessing these different approaches

---

[16] See C. Egenhofer and L. van Schaik, *Towards a Global Climate Regime: Priority Areas for a Coherent EU Strategy*, Report of a CEPS Task Force, Centre for European Policy Studies, Brussels, 2005.

[17] S. Pacala and R. Socolow, "Stabilization Wedges: Solving the Climate Problem for the Next 50 Years with Current Technologies", *Science*, Vol. 305, August 13, 2004, pp. 968-972; IPPC, *Third Assessment Report*, summary for policy-makers, Intergovernmental Panel on Climate Change, United Nations, 2001; M.I. Hoffert et al., "Advanced Technology Paths to Global Climate Stability: Energy for a Greenhouse Planet", *Science*, Vol. 298, November 1, 2002, pp. 981-987.

[18] Although there are differences about how developing countries could participate.

[19] For an overview, see A. Torvanger, M. Twena and J. Vevatne, *Climate policy beyond 2012 – A survey of long-term targets and future frameworks*, CICERO Report 2004:02, Center for International Climate and Environmental Research, Oslo (retrieved from http://www.cicero.uio.no); J.E. Aldy, S. Barrett and R.N. Stavins, "Thirteen plus one: A comparison of global climate policy architectures", *Climate Policy*, 3, 2003, pp. 373-397; D. Bodansky, *International*

against environmental, economic or equity criteria, it quickly becomes apparent that there is no magic solution to the climate change challenge. It will take many years to reach a global consensus. This conclusion should not be surprising. An effective response to climate change requires nothing less than aligning the national energy policies of more than 150 countries.[20] Rather than 'reinventing the wheel', however, it seems more promising to build a comprehensive agreement that is based in large part on the Kyoto Protocol structure, while at the same time accommodating a number of additional components, the most important being the *nature of the commitments made* (i.e. the type of targets).

---

*Box 1. Different approaches to the climate change challenge post-2012*

- An international agreement with **absolute – Kyoto style – targets**, but with modifications such as a safety valve, i.e. a maximum price on allowances.
- **Energy** or carbon-**intensity targets** to improve energy efficiency; the ultimate target can be an equal per capita emissions target.
- **Linkages**, i.e. linking participation to R&D cooperation or financial transfers.
- **Environmental conditionality** in which emissions trading is linked to environmental 'progress', e.g. the Green Investment Scheme, or trade-and-back approaches.
- **Sector-specific targets,** i.e. a coordinated approach for domestic policies.
- Coordinated **global carbon taxes.**
- **Technology development** and international cooperation on R&D activities.
- A **combination** of different instruments, such as a combination of the intensity targets, sector-specific domestic measures and technology development in the so-called 'triptych approach'.
- **Orchestration of treaties** focusing on different co-existing commitments under different legal frameworks.

*Source*: Egenhofer and van Schaik, op. cit.

---

*Climate Efforts Beyond 2012: A Survey of Approaches*, Pew Center on Global Climate Change, Arlington, VA, 2004 (retrieved from http://www.pewclimate.org; Y. Kameyama, "The Future Climate Regime: A Regional Comparison of Proposals", *International Environmental Agreements: Politics, Law and Economics*, No. 4, 2004, pp. 307-326; see also Box 1.

[20] J. Ashton and T. Burke, "The Geopolitics of Climate Change", *SWP Comments 5*, Stiftung Wissenschaft und Politik, Berlin, May 2004.

The Kyoto Protocol has set absolute targets for industrialized countries. Despite its merit of relative simplicity as a negotiation tool and its sensitivity to environmental integrity, such an approach is inherently inflexible. It cannot accommodate differences in economic or population growth. The absolute cap approach is generally credited with the successful phasing out of ozone-depleting substances in a multilateral framework under the latter. The latter, however, had special features – such as readily available technologies. Perhaps most importantly, the phasing out of the responsible substances was the *only* solution to avoid ozone depletion. It is also often forgotten that the Montreal Protocol foresaw reviewable exemptions for 'essential uses'.[21] To ensure compliance with the Kyoto Protocol, several approaches have been advanced that reduce the rigidity of absolute targets – including flexible mechanisms, banking provisions, periodic revision of relative short-term targets, transfers and, most importantly, price caps on allowance prices. None of these could ensure a global agreement.

## The Next Priorities

Most scholars and analysts attribute the EU-US climate change disagreement to divergent views on climate science, the role of domestic versus international action, technology, costs, the role of developing countries and the Kyoto Protocol process itself.[22] In order to overcome the climate divide, there is a need for some convergence in all of these areas. This will take time, however. In the meantime, we argue that the EU and the US (governments and stakeholders) should concentrate on three areas likely to be critical for the EU-US climate change agenda: i) a (common) sense of direction, ii) a determination to make the EU climate change policy work and iii) convergence on technology. Progress in these areas is a prerequisite for a more constructive transatlantic dialogue.

---

[21] D.G. Victor, "A Herd Mentality in the Design of International Environmental Agreements?", *Global Environmental Politics*, Vol. 5, No. 1, February 2005, pp. 24-57.

[22] See W.R. Cline, *The Economics of Global Warming*, Institute for International Economics, Washington, DC, 1992; W.D. Nordhaus, *Managing the Global Commons: The Economics of Climate Change*, Cambridge, MA: MIT Press, 1994; W.D. Nordhaus (ed.), *Economics and Policy Issues in Climate Change*, Resources for the Future, Washington, DC, 1998; P.G. Harris (ed.), *Climate Action and American Foreign Policy*, NY: St Martin's, 2000; N. Purvis and F. Mueller, *Renewing Transatlantic Climate Change Cooperation,* The Brookings Institution, Washington, DC, April 19, 2004; D. Michel (ed.), *Climate Policy for the 21st Century: Meeting the Long-Term Challenge of Global Warming*, Center for Transatlantic Relations, Johns Hopkins University, Washington, DC, 2005.

## A (Common) Sense of Direction

The first important step is to forge a common understanding between the US and the EU on the urgency of climate change and to demonstrate together the will to achieve more ambitious reductions and technological innovation. The EU has tried to provide direction after EU heads of governments in March 2005 endorsed a target to limit the global average temperature increase to 2°C and indicated a willingness to explore with other countries the possibility of a reduction target for industrialized countries of 15-30% for GHG emissions by 2020 on a 1990 basis.

The UK intends to use its G8 presidency to develop a package of practical measures to cut emissions, focusing largely on technology as well as building a partnership with rapidly developing economies to find a way to combine economic growth with a low-carbon economy. This is an opportunity to inject fresh political momentum toward a new global consensus. The focus on technology and developing countries as the keys to tackling climate change has been a key US demand for some time. It is important, however, that this new strategy not only responds to the concerns of the current US Administration, but also to those of other stakeholders, notably business, as reflected in the following remark by a representative of Tony Blair's government: "Business and the global economy need to know that this isn't an issue that is going to go away".[23]

## Making EU Climate Change Policy Work

It is now up to the EU to show that climate change policy can be undertaken without ruining the economy. Implementation of the EU ETS has already given strong signals to the US. Successful EU performance can help change the minds of US stakeholders. The EU ETS is increasingly seen globally as the world standard for GHG emissions trading and not just by Kyoto Protocol countries. US scholars are watching the EU ETS intensively. The total value of current EU allowances of permits stands at around €50 billion, as the allowance price has risen to almost €20 recently. This might be too big a market to ignore. It is often forgotten that climate change policy can have important benefits beyond climate policy objectives. Such co-benefits of climate change measures are the reduction of local pollution caused by NOx or SO$_2$, less congestion or noise from transport, innovation and technological

---

[23] H. Derwent, "The G8 and the Post-2012 Agenda", presentation at the 2005 Third Annual Brussels Climate Change Conference, Centre for European Policy Studies, Brussels & EU Conferences Ltd., April 19-20, 2005.

leapfrogging and employment.[24] In fact, most studies assume that the benefits of reducing local air pollution are higher than the costs of reducing greenhouse gas emissions.[25] In short, climate policy is likely to have significant benefits that are not yet explicitly acknowledged. The examples of BP, Entergy, Toyota or Rio Tinto show that reducing GHG emissions can yield net profits.[26] Finally, as the case of the Kyoto Protocol has shown, when the US is absent, other countries will proceed to define the international agenda as they deem most appropriate.

## Convergence on Technology

It is a widely held view that technology will play the decisive role in ultimately achieving stabilization of GHG emissions at politically acceptable levels. Furthermore, international cooperation to promote the development and diffusion of new breakthrough technologies has appeared as the single most important initiative to rebuild transatlantic relations. Unfortunately, the EU and the US have found themselves supporting two polar views: technology push versus market pull.[27]

The technology-push approach argues that the principal emphasis should be on technology development, financed through typical, public R&D programs. Proponents argue that it would be preferable to invest in the short term in R&D and to adopt emissions limitations later, when new technologies will have lowered the costs of limiting GHG emissions.[28] The

---

[24] E. Jochem and R. Madlener, *The Forgotten Benefits of Climate Change Mitigation: Innovation, Technological Leapfrogging, Employment, and Sustainable Development*, OECD, Paris, 2003.

[25] See *Ancillary Costs and Benefits of GHG Mitigation: Policy Conclusions*, ENV/EPOC/GSP(2001)13/FINAL of 17.4.2002, OECD, Paris, 2002.

[26] BP calculated that reducing GHG emissions by 10% below its 1990 level had a net benefit of $650 million. See J. Browne, "Beyond Kyoto", *Foreign Affairs*, Vol. 83, No. 4, August 2004, pp. 20-32.

[27] See M. Galeotti and C. Carraro, "Traditional environmental instruments, Kyoto mechanisms and the role of technical change", in C. Carraro and C. Egenhofer (eds), *Firms, Governments and Climate Policy – Incentive-based Policies for Long-term Climate Change*, Cheltenham, UK: Edward Elgar, 2003; M. Grubb and R. Stewart, "Promoting Climate-Friendly Technologies: International Perspectives and Issues", INTACT Project Paper, March 2004; L. Goulder, *Induced Technological Change and Climate Policy*, Report for the Pew Center on Global Climate Change, Arlington, VA, October 2004.

[28] See K. Humphreys, "The Nation's Energy Future: The Role of Renewable Energy and Energy Efficiency", testimony to the Committee on Science of the US House of Representatives, February 28, 2001; J. Edmonds, "Toward the

market-pull approach argues that technological change is an incremental process emanating primarily from business and industry, induced by government incentives. Profit-seeking firms would respond with technological innovation.[29]

There is a growing consensus that neither 'technology push' nor 'market pull' on its own will be able to meet the climate change challenge. The International Energy Agency, for example, argues that energy efficiency improvements offer the greatest potential to reduce GHG emissions in a 2030 perspective. Such improvements depend critically on government incentives.[30] At the same time, it is increasingly accepted that new and technically unproven (i.e. breakthrough) technologies need to be developed in the long term to meet the stabilization objective of the UNFCCC. In short, incentives for abatement and innovation are inexorably linked.

Since longer-term targets can only be met by the development of new technologies and the massive diffusion of both new and existing technologies, the EU also needs a greater focus on technology. This will become increasingly apparent after 2012, when the modest sacrifices that have had to be made among EU countries until now give way to starker distributional trade-offs and harder political choices. Such trends may prod the EU toward greater convergence in thinking with the US, where the strong emphasis on technology is already apparent.

## The Business Dimension

In the light of the EU's firm position and America's economic and political pluralism, business may well need to take to the lead in overcoming the transatlantic climate change disagreement. If anything, climate change will become more important with regard to such issues as emissions trading, other regulations, carbon liabilities and risks, and investment decisions, as well as questions of 'image'.

US-based firms are already affected by the tangible implications of the Kyoto Protocol and the EU ETS. Large multinational firms have many operations in EU countries and in other nations operating under Kyoto Protocol provisions. Not only are their affiliates directly subject to emissions

---

Development of a Global Energy Technology Strategy to Address Climate Change", paper prepared for a strategic roundtable at the Global Energy Scenarios of the World Gas Conference, June 2, 2003.

[29] M. Grubb, J. Koehler and D. Anderson, "Induced Technical Change: Evidence and Implications for Energy-Environmental Modelling and Policy", *Annual Review of Energy and Environment*, 27, 2002, pp. 271-308.

[30] International Energy Agency, op. cit.

limits, but they are indirectly affected, for instance, by changes in energy prices. Multinational companies will be increasingly exposed to the EU ETS and other national or regional climate change initiatives. Multinational companies could draw upon their experience with the US $SO_2$ and NOx trading programs to their benefit in the allocation process of the EU ETS. More generally, the Kyoto Protocol and the EU ETS will deepen experiences with carbon management. This was among the reasons why US companies have set up a pilot trading program with the Chicago Climate Exchange, where major firms are building a market for trading emissions allowances. To date, however, brokers, market-makers in general, certifiers and other service companies from the US and elsewhere increasingly see the significant emerging market in the EU. Once the market is up and properly running, the annual €50 billion EU carbon market should turn over at least four or five times more than the underlying physical stock of allowances. Carbon emissions dwarf those of the US sulphur scheme. And the EU market is likely to be only the beginning. If Russia, Ukraine, Canada or Japan join, let alone the US, the sums become gigantic. No wonder the Chicago Climate Exchange has set up a fully-owned subsidiary in the EU, in Amsterdam. Nobody would want to miss that market.

Increasingly, investors and analysts will inquire about carbon liabilities and carbon strategies. Tangible evidence that these multilateral and regional regulatory systems can function effectively is likely to have a subtle but potentially profound impact on the thinking of US business leaders, and thus accelerate the process of change in the US.[31] The concept of a 'carbon-constrained' world will no longer be a hypothetical vision of the future; it will be a palpable fact of the present, with important implications for strategic business thinking. A strong European presence in the US and international discussions could reinforce this impression.

Furthermore, these developments are likely to lead to increasing pressures from the financial services sector (including investment banks and brokerage houses, as well as insurance companies) and from religious and other organizations on firms in fossil-fuel industries to report their carbon exposure and to respond more positively to climate change issues.[32] Once it is firmly understood that climate change policy is here to stay, many

---

[31] This is argued by T. Brewer in *Political Economy Models of Strategic Behaviour: Explaining Firms' Responses to Global Warming* (forthcoming 2005).

[32] See *Corporate Governance and Climate Change: Making the Connection*, Coalition for Environmentally Responsible Economics, Boston, 2003; Carbon Disclosure Project, *Carbon Finance and the Global Equity Markets*, Innovest Strategic Value Advisors, New York, 2003.

businesses may – albeit reluctantly – accept regulation. They may ultimately prefer uniform federal rules, and possibly more consistent international regulations, over a patchwork of state, federal, regional and international regimes.[33] Finally, companies cannot forever defer necessary capital investments, for example in the power sector, because of an unsettled climate policy.

## A Transatlantic GHG Emissions Market: Could it work?

At the time of the Kyoto Protocol negotiations in 1997, the US attempted to create a global GHG emissions market as the backbone of a global climate change agreement. Emissions trading would not only reduce abatement costs significantly, it would also ensure a global carbon price, which was thought at least to some extent to accommodate concerns of 'competitiveness'. As this has not worked, analysts and policy-makers are exploring bottom-up approaches, i.e. linking together different emerging national or regional trading schemes.[34] Such a market could easily be worth $100 billion.

The main benefit of bringing together different schemes is cost reduction, which is a key concern in the US debate. Linking effective and transparent national or regional emissions trading schemes or creating global sector-specific (i.e. industry-wide) emissions trading schemes is seen by European business as a means to ensure a global carbon (clearing) price at least for the industrial sector.[35] As previously mentioned, there are important initiatives in the US, notably the McCain-Lieberman draft bill for a US cap-and-trade program and the Chicago Climate Exchange.

Some have suggested that the EU and the US should negotiate a transatlantic climate change agreement that would include a joint emissions trading program.[36] The EU ETS Directive would allow for this, and other countries could join. But could it work? There is no insurmountable obstacle to linking widely differing schemes. Differences in design could be resolved by technical fixes,[37] although at the price of reduced market efficiency. That

---

[33] See Brewer, op. cit.

[34] See *Greenhouse gas market 2003 – Emerging but fragmented*, International Emissions Trading Association, Geneva, 2003.

[35] Egenhofer, Fujiwara and Gialoglou, op. cit.

[36] S. Eizenstat and D. Sandalow, "The Years after Tomorrow", *New York Times*, July 5, 2004.

[37] E. Haites, "Harmonisation between national and international tradable permit schemes: CATEP synthesis paper", paper prepared for the OECD global forum on sustainable development: CATEP country forum, March 17-18, 2003; W. Blyth and M. Bosi, *Linking non-EU domestic emissions trading schemes with the*

price would be worth paying, however, if it meant the engagement of both sides of the Atlantic to work together to tackle climate change.

## *What would be needed?*

First, the EU would need to accept that the EU ETS can be linked with countries that have not joined the Kyoto Protocol. In the longer term, the reference to the Kyoto Protocol becomes obsolete in any event, since it expires in 2012. There are some signs of a new willingness on the part at the EU to trade with non-Kyoto Protocol countries. For example, Alexander de Roo, the former MEP who was responsible for steering the Linking Directive through the European Parliament to amend the EU ETS, has proposed opening the EU ETS to individual US states operating cap-and-trade programs. Exploratory talks have already begun between EU decision-makers and US state representatives on possible linking. The new EU focus on participation is likely to strengthen this approach.

Second, to assuage US fears of 'uncontrollable' costs, the EU should consider permitting a price cap on allowance prices of any joint scheme, which would fix a maximum allowance price (per ton of $CO_2$ for example) as a safeguard against rocketing $CO_2$ prices. This is why it has been called a 'safety valve'. There are promising signs in this regard: the European Commission has been holding exploratory – although very preliminary – talks with Canada about the possibility of linking with a price-capped scheme. There is a drawback, however. Linking the EU ETS to a scheme with a price cap would almost certainly split the market and reduce economic efficiency. It would therefore be better for the EU and the US to agree on a common price cap. If the EU and the US could agree on a price cap of, say, $25 per ton of $CO_2$ – which is slightly less than the current EU price under the emissions trading scheme – there would be no need to negotiate quantitative emissions targets between the US and the EU or at a multilateral level. The price cap would in effect function as a globally harmonized carbon tax as long as the allowance price reached the level of the price cap, as has been advocated by many scholars and practitioners both in the US and the EU in the aftermath of the Kyoto Protocol negotiations.[38]

---

*EU emissions trading scheme*, International Energy Agency, Washington, DC, June 17, 2004 (COM/ENV/EPOC/IEA/SLT(2004)6).

[38] See W.J. McKibbin, and P.J. Wilcoxen, "The role of economics in climate change policy", *Journal of Economics Perspectives*, Vol. 16, No. 2, 2002, pp. 107-129; R. Kopp et al., *A Proposal for Credible Early Action in US Climate Change Policy*, Resources for the Future, Washington, DC, 1999; D.G. Victor, *The Collapse of the Kyoto Protocol*, Princeton, NJ: Princeton University Press, 2001; H.D. Jacoby and A.D. Ellerman, "The safety valve and climate policy",

Third, such an approach would not do away with the need to set an absolute cap in the US, which many oppose. The fact that the cap could be set domestically either at national or state level could, however, reassure those in the US who fear they may find themselves hostage to multilateral agreements.

From the EU side, this would require a change in the EU ETS Directive, which could be achieved following the 2006 EU ETS review.

### Why We Would Gain

Although the case for a common GHG emissions market may be compelling in theory, it is no panacea. Such a market will create winners and losers. Hence, there is a need to ensure that there will be sufficient benefits for business on both sides of the Atlantic.

What would business gain?

1) A uniform regulatory framework across the two major global economies would be established, including one market price for carbon, which would most likely become the global price. If history is any indicator, many businesses may come to prefer a single, uniform regulation – provided it is efficient – over a patchwork of different regulations.

2) The cost of achieving a given target would decrease, since a larger and more liquid market is more efficient. A joint market offers the potential to achieve more reductions at the same price or the same reduction at a lower price.

3) Most importantly, a joint EU-US emissions market with a price cap has the potential of offering a robust, stable and long-term price incentive, which if properly designed could provide the kind of long-term inducement that will be needed to successfully tackle the climate change challenge. The challenge can only be met with major new investment in energy and transport. Such investment is most likely to respond to a stable and long-term price signal.[39] We would expect this to be in the interest of business.

---

MIT Joint Program on the Science and Policy of Global Change, *Report*, 83, 2002; J.C. Hourcade and F. Ghersi, "The economics of a lost deal: Kyoto-The Hague-Marrakech", *The Energy Journal*, Vol. 23, No. 3, 2001; C. Philibert and P. Criqui, "Capping emissions and costs", paper prepared for RFF-IFRI workshop, Paris, March 19, 2003.

[39] Initially the price signal would need to be limited in order to avoid excessive costs because there are no 'killer technologies' that could revolutionize existing carbon mitigation technologies. As technology develops, prices may go up.

One should remain realistic, however. At this stage it is unclear whether such an approach would work. There are many issues to be resolved, including questions regarding the appropriate institutions (i.e. who should run the scheme?), the compliance system, litigation procedures, allocation in a joint scheme and more generally, distributional effects. It is also highly uncertain whether the potential benefits – mainly long-term – could convince those businesses that are opposed to mandatory action to agree to such a scheme. Regardless of the merit or the possibility of a joint emissions market, there remains a need for a serious dialogue within the business community on what can be done about climate change. Failure to achieve an EU-US rapprochement on climate change that includes business will result in continuous friction on climate change with inevitable negative repercussions on transatlantic relations. Industries in some EU member states are understood to be exploring the idea of special import border measures to offset energy price differentials in US goods if the US continues to refuse to move on climate change. While such measures have previously been limited to theoretical discussions,[40] a (non-binding) European Parliament resolution in May 2005 put the issue on the political agenda for the first time.[41] For corporate leaders who lobby hard for a free transatlantic marketplace, this is the clearest sign yet that such efforts are wasted without a solution to the transatlantic climate change dispute. Huge differences in carbon constraints on both sides of the Atlantic would of course make further market integration almost impossible. This fact alone should be incentive enough for business to have a look again at the options to overcome the transatlantic disagreement.

Why not be bold? A breakthrough in one of the most controversial areas of transatlantic dispute would give a major boost to the prospect of a more integrated EU-US market.

---

[40] T. Brewer, "The Trade Regime and the Climate Regime: Institutional Evolution and Adaptation", *Climate Policy*, Vol. 3, No. 4, pp. 329-341, 2003; T. Brewer, "The WTO and the Kyoto Protocol: Interaction Issues", *Climate Policy*, Vol. 4, No. 1, pp. 3-12, 2004; *Climate and Trade Rules: Harmony or Conflict?*, Report by the National Board of Trade, Sweden, January 2004.

[41] European Parliament Resolution on the Seminar of Governmental Experts on Climate Change (B6-0278/2005) of May 12, 2005.

# 14. REACH: Getting the Chemistry Right in Europe

## *Jacques Pelkmans*

O nce REACH, a buzzword in the EU,[1] reached Washington, it almost immediately raised eyebrows. The attention is justified. After the EC 1992 program deepening the internal EU market and following the introduction of the euro, nothing has caused more tremors and lobbying efforts in the European Union than REACH. Some degree of turbulence has spilled over frontiers and across the Atlantic as well. This essay cannot hope to explain and properly analyze REACH with its 1,200 pages of proposals, rules and annexes, not to speak of the numerous suggestions for amendments. Instead, this paper aims to introduce the non-specialist reader to REACH from an economic and regulatory point of view. The perspective assumed in the following is that of 'better regulation', an avowed goal of the EU since the turn of the century and a decisive – though not exclusive – reason why REACH was proposed. The US government has applauded recent EU attempts to subject regulation to 'regulatory impact assessment' (RIA). The Transatlantic Business Dialogue (TABD) has insisted for many years that regulation on both sides of the North Atlantic should be justified by market failures and that their resolution ought to exhibit net benefits to society while minimizing the burden to business. At this general level of policy-making, the EU and the US, as well as their business communities, agree. Let us now see whether a sober, analytical account of REACH fits the well-agreed perspective. In taking a detached view, some suggestions of improvement or correction will be provided.

## REACH: A Primer

REACH is a proposal from the European Commission to EU member states and the European Parliament to overhaul the entire EU chemicals regulation and replace it with a single system with very different rules and incentives, as well as a modest degree of centralization. Since REACH applies to the whole value chain of chemicals and their derivatives, including applications to millions of intermediate and final goods, practically no industry escapes the reach of REACH.

---

[1] REACH stands for Registration, Evaluation and Authorization of Chemicals. For further information on existing rules, see V. Maglia and C. Rapisarda Sassoon, "The chemical industry and regulation", in G. Galli and J. Pelkmans (eds), *Regulatory Reform and Competitiveness in Europe, Volume II* (Cheltenham: E. Elgar, 2000).

Although hazards differ enormously between chemicals, there is nevertheless agreement that the EU needs an overall and detailed chemicals regulation. In other words, in too many instances, the risks are such that a light form of regulation is excluded. But even fairly intrusive and burdensome regulation can be in the public interest if the risks justify it. However, precisely when regulation cannot be light, the danger of having no regard to cost and genuine benefits at all looms large. Current EU chemicals regulation is unduly costly and cumbersome while inadequate for the kind of risks which have to be addressed (i.e. the benefits). The existing stock of EU regulation, comprising more than 40 directives and regulations, has been built up haphazardly over time and is in great need of being overhauled. Mere consolidation and clarification of current regulations would not do, for at least two major reasons. First, incidents, accidents and research in health and environment have increased awareness that the hazards of chemicals need to be better understood in advance of their application or use. There is a huge information gap. The second reason for the overhaul to go beyond mere consolidation and classification is that the competitiveness of the European chemical industry is not well served by the current regulation and probably adversely affected by it. Without watering down the health, safety and environmental objectives driving the legislation, an overhaul of EU regulation could significantly reduce the costs of implementation (*ceteris paribus*) as well as almost certainly improve the incentives for innovation and the supply of new substances. These two critical considerations have dominated the debate about the chemical industry ever since 1996.[2]

In February 2001 the European Commission adopted a White Paper entitled 'Strategy for a Future Chemicals Policy',[3] the starting point of the REACH regulation. Its objective was to 'develop an integrated strategy for a future chemicals policy promoting sustainable development.' It noted that even the seemingly comprehensive EU regulation showed gaps, was extremely complicated, and was excessively costly, given its tendency to lean towards a zero-risk approach with few exemptions. Moreover, the discrimination between so-called 'existing substances'[4] and 'new substances'[5] was found to have no basis in the associated risks, while exercising a deterrent effect on chemical innovation, hence causing a long-run threat to the competitiveness

---

[2] COM(96)187, Communication from the Commission, *An Industrial Competitiveness Policy for the European Chemical Industry: an example*. See also Maglia and Rapisarda Sassoon (op. cit.), and KPMG (1997).

[3] COM(2001)188 of 27 February 2001.

[4] On the market in September 1981 and listed in the EINECS registry; see Regulation 793/93.

[5] Listed in the ELINCS and regulated under Directive 67/548.

of one of Europe's best performing industries. At the same time the heavy-handed regulation never led to a much deeper and wider knowledge of the hazards or risks of thousands of chemicals, let alone to a systematic management of chemical risks for health, safety and environment. It should be noted that these considerations as well as the need for radical reform to address these shortcomings were widely shared by EU member states and by stakeholders.

REACH amounts to a switch to a single, coherent system based on two new principles. First, it shifts the responsibility for risk assessment from the authorities to the industry for all chemicals produced, used and imported, thereby reversing the burden of proof for putting safe chemicals on the internal market. Second, it aims to reduce drastically the lack of knowledge on the risks of the tens of thousands of chemicals traded in the EU internal market. It tries to achieve this by subjecting existing and new chemicals indiscriminately to registration procedures and subsequently, dependent on preliminary risk assessments, to further testing obligations for a proper risk assessment ('evaluation'). As proposed in the 2001 White Paper, registration is always a prerequisite (above the 1 ton threshold), based on elementary data. The idea is: no data, no market. A small subset of chemicals of very high concern would require specific permission by the authorities.[6]

Given the massive exercise of subjecting many thousands of existing chemicals to at least basic testing, a ten year transition period is foreseen to allow the registration to be built up over time, with certain priorities. The highly technical and comprehensive nature of monitoring and supporting this rather involved process was thought to require an autonomous European Chemicals Agency.

REACH has no less than seven objectives:

- protection of health and environment
- competitiveness of the EU chemical industry
- no fragmentation of the internal market
- increased transparency
- integration with international efforts in this sector
- promotion of non-animal testing
- conformity with the EU's obligations under the WTO.

---

[6] The White Paper already identifies subsets such as Persistent Organic Pollutants, and Carcinogenic Mutagenic Reprotoxics. Note that PBTs (persistent, bio-accumulative, toxic) have meanwhile been included in the list for compulsory registration. This may happen to vPvBs (very persistent, very bio-accumulative).

The burden of a negligent past (very little and selective knowledge of the risks of some 30,000 existing substances) can cause extremely high costs for testing and reporting. Even though such costs are only incurred once, they are bound to be disproportionate, if one presumes (quite reasonably) that many preliminary assessments would not show any serious risks. All these substances have been in the market for many years and a large number of them have few if any traces which would point to hazards.

To contain the costs, the White Paper (which is, of course, not yet an official proposal, only a set of suggestions for debate) first sets a threshold for registration (above 1 ton) and estimates that some 80% of the existing 30,000 or so substances would require no more than registration. Note that the 1 ton was also suggested for new substances, which amounts to an immediate relief (given that the existing threshold is as low as 10 kg!).

## Turbulence about High Costs and Unclear Benefits

REACH has been characterized as the most debated piece of environmental legislation in EU history. It has also been one of the most fiercely attacked regulatory reforms.

The run-up to the REACH draft and its RIA offer ample evidence that RIAs are far more than straight-forward technical exercises. The process of moving towards a draft REACH proposal in May 2003 and a formal proposal by the Commission to the European Council and the European Parliament in October 2003, with an accompanying RIA, was turbulent. Stakeholders such as the chemical industry, the business association UNICE, environmental NGOs, EU member states, the US and Japan (and their chemical industries) and, at a technical level, the OECD, all exercised varying degrees of influence from the very outset. In addition, vigorous national debates (notably in Germany) prompted a range of alternative, quasi-RIAs by ministerial advisory councils and private consultants (contracted, respectively, by the German, French and later Italian chemical industry). Without any legislative proposals on the table, alarming cost calculations were already dominating the debate. Three prime ministers (of Germany, France and the UK) wrote a public letter of appeal to the president of the European Commission at the time, Romano Prodi, an unprecedented move in Europe on such a topic.

Rather than a serious attempt to improve the chemicals regulation in Europe, a 'battle of REACH' broke out, causing delay and wasting political and business energies. Such intense debate in the absence of actual (even preliminary) proposals served to harden positions, fed tendencies to exaggerate the potential consequences of REACH, and to inject misleading or biased information simply to be heard above the cacophony. Quasi-RIA proposals by stakeholders generated further confusion by focusing narrowly on the private interests of those stakeholders (e.g. by zooming in on the perceived 'costs' for the chemical industry) without explicit and balanced consideration of the EU public interest. But also NGOs also took very fierce and antagonistic positions that were driven partly by mistrust and partly by a zealous campaign to advance rather extreme applications of the 'precautionary principle,' which inspires REACH. This principle encourages government promotion of research or even action or intervention despite a lack of sufficient scientific knowledge, if there are signs of great but not fully understood damage or of irreversibility. It typically applies to climate change, where great uncertainty does not prevent action. In REACH, too, risk reduction is to be achieved in the absence of sufficient knowledge. But the question is to identify whether and where at least some tentative signs of serious hazards or risks for existing substances can be found, and not to indiscriminately subject all substances to high-cost procedures.

As a result of the early turbulence on REACH many participants in the later legislative process had already positioned themselves. The pre-2000 consensus in terms of objectives and major lines of reform splintered and fragmented when it came to considering how REACH would work in actual practice. The most striking and painful error made during the run-up was the singular emphasis on *costs*. Any regulation, European or otherwise, should first and foremost be justified by its potential *benefits*. European society is better served by the knowledge of why the EU wishes to regulate chemicals in a new way, with the best available range of quantitative estimates of the 'value' of those benefits, than by a sole focus on the costs in the absence of precise proposals. The Commission should have spent resources and political energy on a more informative debate about the (occupational and public) health and environmental benefits of REACH and the choices that – even in the presence of great uncertainty – follow from an exposition of them. It should have attempted to show much more convincingly the links between the overall design of REACH and the benefits pursued.

Emphasizing the benefits of REACH was made intrinsically very difficult by its chosen design. REACH has two stages, but all attention in the run-up to the draft proposal of May 2003 concentrated on the first stage. This stage could well take 10-12 years. Its sole purpose is to *collect information* on hazards and risk. Since most existing chemical substances do not appear to be problematic, the need to collect information via testing and registration burdens the industry with many years of costly preliminary risk assessments that are not likely to offer many additional benefits in terms of health and the environment. Whereas a strong case can be made that the burden of proof for *new* substances should be shifted to industry, which companies can consider as 'sunk costs' to put the product on the market (more or less as with medicines), the case for subjecting many thousands of existing substances already in use, without apparent drawbacks, to extensive information procedures is much weaker.

Emphasizing the benefits of stage 1 of REACH becomes exceedingly hard because most of the direct gains will be limited to hazard (and to some extent risk) information that in most cases is likely to confirm experience. In contrast, the benefits of a new procedure for new substances as well as the benefits of stage 2 [evaluating 'risky' chemicals and authorizing (or prohibiting) very risky chemicals] are much more straightforward and far less controversial, even if costly.

## Main Technical Issues in the REACH Debate

REACH is extremely technical, particularly when it comes to testing and evaluation. These technicalities make it difficult for non-experts to grasp the meaning of the debate and to appreciate the (net) benefits of this giant regulatory reform. This brief section offers a basic primer of the main technical issues. For readers wishing to get a more comprehensive view of REACH, it is good to know that the process of getting to the REACH proposals went through four steps: the early debate to forge a general consensus; the fierce positioning and technical studies following the 2001 White Paper; the preliminary draft proposals of early May 2003;[7] and the final proposal of October 2003[8] and its RIA.[9] The essential differences between the May and October proposals are found in cost cutting measures (see below) and a greater role for the European Chemical Agency. The basic idea behind REACH is described below.

**Registration** concerns chemical substances produced or imported over one ton – approximately 30,000 substances. Information requirements are

---

[7] Proposal concerning REACH, 6 volumes. For consultation up to late June 2003, see the DG Enterprise website, (see http://europa.eu.int/comm/dgs/enterprise/index_en.htm).

[8] COM 2003 644 (03) 'Proposal for a REGULATION OF THE EUROPEAN PARLIAMENT AND OF THE COUNCIL concerning the Registration, Evaluation, Authorisation and Restriction of Chemicals (REACH), establishing a European Chemicals Agency and amending Directive 1999/45/EC and Regulation (EC) {on Persistent Organic Pollutants}' of 29 October 2003.

[9] SEC (20031171/3 of 29th October 2003, Commission Staff Working Paper, "Regulation of the European Parliament and of the Council, concerning the Registration, Evaluation, Authorisation and Restrictions of Chemicals (REACH), establishing a European Chemicals Agency and amending Directive 1999/45/EC and Regulation (EC) {on Persistent Organic Pollutants}", Extended Impact Assessment {COM(2003)644 final}.

proportional to the volumes of the substances. There are different deadlines for each volume threshold (1 ton, 100 and 1,000 tons). The rationale is that different tonnage gives an idea of potential exposure.

**Evaluation** is the second stage, required for substances produced over 100 tons (an estimated 5000 substances) as well as substances produced at lower volumes but about which there are particular concerns. The European Chemical Agency's role at this stage is to help in the prioritization process, using still-to-be-developed risk-based criteria. A resolution procedure is foreseen for cases in which member states do not agree on which substances to evaluate.

**Authorization**, the last stage of REACH, concerns a certain category of substances of very high concern (like the vPvBs as in footnote 6 or endocrine disrupters), representing approximately 5% of substances.[10]

**Restriction** is an additional safety net category providing for EU-wide restrictions. The European Chemical Agency (ECA) and any member state can propose such restrictions.

The October 2003 proposal strengthened the ECA by charging with it with a coordinating role. It manages the registration stage, plays a vital role in the stage of evaluation (by determining criteria for selection of 'evaluation' substances) and gives opinions in the authorization and restriction cases. The original 'one-stop-shopping' idea behind the ECA is thereby compromised.

It is important to understand that REACH affects almost anything made with chemicals or their derivatives. Thus, REACH is *not only and perhaps not even primarily about the chemical industry*. Bulk chemicals and a very wide spectrum of fine chemicals typically move down the value chain to all kinds of intermediate producers in many ways – testimony to the central place chemicals have occupied in manufacturing. Some of those second layer producers are called 'formulators'. They include many small and medium-sized enterprises engaged in extremely product-specific (and often confidential) applications and, in some cases, receiving a limited but rewarding turnover per application. They create complex combinations of substances and/or innovative blends with subtly different properties, often for highly specific use by specialized customers in practically every industry. Those customers form the third layer in the value chain. Some of their products use chemicals only to a very small degree, while others combine many different intermediate products with enormous varieties of combinations (a car, for instance).

---

[10] Note that there is no volume-based exemption for authorization or restriction.

In short, REACH is likely to affect all industries to some extent, if only because of the new burden of information and registration requirements for many inputs they may use. Moreover, various sectors are bound to be hit very differently.

The costs for downstream users quickly became a great concern in business circles. Given extensive intra-firm linkages across continents but especially within US and EU companies, high levels of foreign direct investment and trade (documented in chapter 2 of this book), these concerns swiftly spilled over to manufacturers worldwide. Since the cost of testing in the first layer of the value chain will have to be shared by second- and third-layer companies, it becomes critical to understand whether particular substances would need to be withdrawn or replaced with cheaper or 'safer' substances. If testing and registration costs exceed substitution costs, the market for a particular substance will melt away. If no alternative substance is available, certain products may be withdrawn, with potentially huge impact on the second layer 'formulators' – often small and medium-sized companies – who tend to generate many distinct usages of a substance. This could, in turn, lead to extra costs and complications for final products, including time-to-market problems for fast-moving industries such as computers or technical textiles.

In early studies for the German and French chemical industries,[11] the impact on downstream users was asserted to be extraordinarily costly – several hundred times the basic costs of testing and registration for the first layer. As a consequence, huge turnover losses and job losses were calculated. One analysis, termed the 'hurricane scenario', projected a decline in German GDP by more than 3%! Clearly, these studies were simply not credible for a sectoral reform of a sector already strictly regulated. The analytical basis for alternate, 'quasi RIAs' was weak, biased and, in some cases, not transparent. Nevertheless, they formed the basis for a wholesale attack on the Commission's proposals that politicized the REACH debate and engaged leading European political figures. The Dutch EU Presidency commissioned a sober overview[12] of 36 different impact studies on REACH, which threw cold water on such alarming lobby attempts.

After the initial outraged response by business to REACH, the Commission was forced by the European Council to refine its impact study through a series of case studies, based on close collaboration with well-selected groups of downstream users in the second and third layers. The resulting KPMG

---

[11] See Arthur D. Little, 2003, Economic effects of the EU substances policy, for BDI, Wiesbaden; Mercer, 2003, Study of the impact of the future chemicals policy, Paris.

[12] Ecorys and Opdenkamp Adviesgroep, 2004, *The impact of REACH*, 25 October 2004.

study[13] demonstrated, for four different industries and in great detail, that the withdrawal issue is marginal. This is so for good marketing, transaction cost or sunk cost (of innovation) reasons. The four case studies included a cluster of '(in)organic' sectors ( such as steel, cement, ceramics, paper, glass, etc.), the electronics sector (in particular, the printed circuit board assembly), the automotive sector and that of flexible packaging.

Let us briefly mention a few other technical issues. Many substances never reach the consumer in a pure chemical form. Substances are often included in final articles or are mixed with many other substances. An important issue has been to what extent, and indeed in what cases, substances should be included under the REACH regime. Applying REACH to imported substances might not meet the WTO test of compatibility of technical barriers. The final REACH proposal addresses this concern by specifying that 'the obligation to register or notify a substance contained in an article' only applies when a series of conditions are met (volume threshold, intended release, etc.).

Much attention has focused on whether two further categories of substances should be included in REACH, and to what extent: intermediates and polymers. A cost-effective way of testing polymers has not yet been found. Polymers are usually not hazardous. The final proposal suggests exclusion of polymers from registration.

Another controversial REACH issue concerns the right-to-know and transparency. The 2001 White Paper envisaged the establishment of a central database, but without giving details. The final 2003 proposal tried to strike a balance with a list of safety related data that is never confidential and a shorter list of items (precise tonnage, exact formulas, etc.) that is always considered confidential. Dependent on the case, there is still a lot of concern among innovative second and third layer businesses on the practical safeguards about confidentiality.

## Better Regulation with REACH?

What ultimately matters for European public interest and for world trade and investment is whether REACH can be viewed as 'better regulation'. At the present stage, any evaluation has to be tentative. I shall touch upon the following aspects, which might help the reader to make an informed

---

[13] KPMG Business Advisory Services, 2005, *REACH, further work on impact assessment, a case study approach*, executive summary. For general reference, see KPMG, 1997, *Chemicals, The Single Market Review series, Series I, No. 5*, Luxembourg (Office of Official Publications of the EU, 1997) and London (Kogan Page, 1997), p. 232.

judgment: objectives, proportionality (a core requirement in EU law and sensible from an economic point of view), benefits and costs.

One is struck by the numerous objectives the Commission aims to achieve through the new chemicals legislation. There are far too many objectives and no clear prioritization among them in the RIA. From the general spirit of the document one may deduce that the main objectives to be reached are the protection of human health and environment as well as the competitiveness of the chemicals industry. However, nowhere it is explicitly recognized that there may be trade-offs between these two 'main' objectives. Indeed, the ultimate nature of REACH's design will determine how severe these trade-offs are likely to be.

The Commission has stated that it will not present alternatives to the REACH proposal. This is a remarkable position, to say the least. Indeed, the fact that no policy alternatives are suggested raises a major methodological problem. It is particularly remarkable since the Commission's own methodology paper on RIAs[14] states clearly that proper assessment hinges on thinking in terms of alternative policies.

The Commission asserts firmly that it has been rigorous in its efforts to make the proposal 'proportionate' – the RIA argues that "care ... taken [that REACH]... is not excessive in terms of scope, costs and administrative burden". Furthermore, a range of reduced requirements (compared to the first draft) including e.g. lighter obligations for SMEs (low-volume substances) and exemption periods for innovation all aim to 'lessen' the impact on the industry. CEFIC (the European chemical industry) suggests that the proposal is very administrative and the procedure extremely cumbersome. They fear it would undermine the competitiveness of the chemicals industry. On the other hand, environmental NGOs suggest that the concessions made in the final proposal of the Commission were the result of heavy lobbying from the industry (and, they suggest, captured governments), putting in danger the very health and environmental benefits of the proposal. Thus, one could argue that the Commission was caught in the middle trying to strike a balance. This may be so, but a follow-up document on the implementation details of REACH, with many flowcharts about procedures and processes, does show that the complications and technical requirements in the various

---

[14] COM(2002)276 of 5 June 2002, Impact Assessment; see also the statement of the present author in the REACH hearings in the European Parliament, 19 January 2005.

stages, and the data flows and exchange with the Agency, are extremely intricate and numerous.[15]

When studying *benefits and costs*, one first has to appreciate the vast difference in timing between the two. If the objectives are meant to reflect the benefits, the REACH debate has been misleading because in the first stage of ten or more years there are, inevitably, few and minor benefits. Most of the current debate is about information gathering, culminating in registration – essentially stage 1 of the new regime. Thus, the first objective, health and environment, is not even in sight yet! One may only begin to pursue health and environmental objectives via authorization and restrictions at best late in the first stage, but mainly in the second stage, which may not start before 2016 or even later. For the second objective – competitiveness of the chemical industry – stage 1 of the regulation appears almost entirely as a cost, except for new chemicals, where innovation might be stimulated and evaluation facilitated. As to existing substances, these chemicals are already in use; the very hazardous or persistent ones are largely known. The critical difference between today and the new regime is that nowadays the (national) authorities have to carry the burden of proof before existing chemicals which are reported to possibly entail some hazards or risks, can be taken off the market or subjected to restrictive use. In many thousands of cases this is not likely to be an issue. REACH should eventually enable member states, on the basis of the advice of the Agency, to intervene and regulate with far better knowledge, but the up-front costs are considerable, with the benefits of extra knowledge by definition unknown. However, once stage 2 begins (or, in some cases, already in stage 1) the step of authorization in the framework of REACH still requires a risk management procedure (stage 2 of REACH) with case-by-case RIAs that would add to the bureaucratic burden of the chemical companies and invite more lobbying.

Some attempts have been made to calculate the occupational and public health benefits of REACH, but most analysts believe it is almost impossible to assign monetary values to the environmental effects. Moreover, such benefits would only start being significant 10-20 years after implementation of the new regulation. Since the Commission has not compared alternative approaches, also ranges of benefits cannot be compared. What has been shown are merely back-of-the-envelope calculations of crude benefits based on DALYs:[16] essentially one guesstimate, no range of benefits, and some

---

[15] European Commission, "The REACH proposal, process description", June 2004, Commission website, DG Environment, REACH Implementation Project No. 1.

[16] Disability adjusted value of life methodology, a variant of SVOL, as employed by the World Bank.

illustrative examples. Worse still, the Commission's RIA did not readjust benefits even though the revised proposal of October includes a series of fairly drastic cost cutting measures. If these measures have no effect whatsoever on benefits, one naturally wonders why they were included in the first place.

Admittedly, assessing benefits in this area is tough. The challenge of quantifying the positive impact of the regulation is that we do not know how many of the substances are hazardous and to what extent they are hazardous. This knowledge gap prevents a comprehensive benefit analysis. With regard to long run benefits, anecdotal evidence and fragmented knowledge suggest that chemicals lead to a number of diseases (cancer, skin disorders, etc.); a better understanding of the properties of chemicals could thus help reduce problems of public health. Nevertheless, EU health and safety rules are already strict in the workplace. As far as the environment is concerned, there is a huge knowledge gap, effectively preventing any attempt to calculate such benefits. An illustration by Pearce and Koundouri,[17] based on what they call 'conservative assumptions,' predicts health-only benefits of approximately 50 billion euros over a period of 20-30 years (starting 10 years after the implementation of REACH). In a simpler calculation the Commission came up with the same 'illustrative' figure.

The total direct costs (that is, testing and registration) of the May 2003 draft proposal were estimated to be around €12.6 billion over an 11-year period. The RIA of the final October 2003 proposal, which included a series of cost-cutting measures, estimated a reduction in total direct costs by an astonishing €10.6 billion to less than €3 billion (also incorporating minor changes). In short, the October proposal reduced the May proposal estimates of direct costs by 75%!

No matter what one's views are about REACH, the remaining direct costs would not seem to be so problematic, given that they extend over such a long period and that there is enormous turnover in the chemical industry in Europe. Even so, Table 1 strongly suggests that the original proposal was disproportionate. What about overall economic costs to industry, including the costs of withdrawals and substitution? Here there are at least two tales to tell. One is that the new series of case studies (see footnote 13) confirms that the initial fears of industry were wildly exaggerated. The other tale is based on attempts to come to grips with this issue via economic modeling. Since no econometric model of the EU chemical industry exists, the Commission employed a monopolistic-competition simulation model developed by Canton and Allen. The first version (which was unpublished, but the results

---

[17] D. Pearce and P. Koundouri, 2003, The social costs of chemicals, a report for WWF-UK, London/Brussels.

of which were used publicly by Commissioner Liikanen) came to enormous (present value) estimated costs ranging from 13.6 billion euros to as much as 40 billion euros. The final Canton and Allen study not only slashed this cost range down to between 2.8 to 5.2 billion euros (the latter being only one-eighth of the previous maximum), the modeling device was adapted as well, testifying to the analytical difficulties of grappling with this complex question.[18]

*Table 1. Estimated cost reduction of REACH, October 2003*

| Measure | Saving |
| --- | --- |
| Major reduction in requirements for Chemical Safety Reports | - € 6,450 million |
| Exclude Polymers, pending selection criteria | - € 1,900 million |
| Increased use of QSARs | - € 950 million |
| Reduced requirements for 1 to 10 tonnes | - € 500 million |
| Lighter requirements for transported intermediates | - € 600 million |
| Other factors | - € 200 million |
| **Cost savings** | **€ 10,600 million** |

[18] J. Canton and C. Allen, *A microeconomic model to assess the economic impacts of the EU's new chemicals policy*, European Commission, DG Enterprise, November 2003. This is not the place to discuss the modelling issues. For the economically trained reader, it suffices to say that monopolistic competition is hardly the kind of model suitable for the chemical industry as it assumes free entry and exit (hence, erosion of market power over time). Canton and Allen (2003) simplify (for understandable reasons) by assuming that each firm in their model produces one imperfectly substitutable product; as a consequence, product withdrawal also changes the number of firms, and this has implications for the adjustment process. Their simulation hinges critically on the elasticities of substitution and a substitution parameter derived from the mark-ups over costs. Although it is ingenious as a solution in the absence of empirical models, it is doubtful whether this approach is appropriate.

## REACHing the US?

US business has every interest in following REACH carefully. The chemical industry is of course directly affected. Potentially, the stakes could be high. The chemical industry is the largest exporting sector in the US. Recent annual exports to the EU hover around $20 billion while importing some $40 billion from the EU. Both industries have many, sometimes large affiliates across the North Atlantic and annual US direct investment outflows to the EU add up to some $4 billion. Going beyond the chemicals themselves (the first layer of the value chain), it is estimated that well over $400 billion of 'downstream products', made by US firms with chemicals, are sold in the EU, be they exports from the US or from other affiliates in Europe or in third countries.

The US chemical industry has essentially pursued a similar approach to REACH as the European industry. This is not so surprising, given the strong presence of both industries on both sides of the North Atlantic. What is interesting is that the US administration has intervened very powerfully in the debate, and its strand of arguments and queries seem to reflect industry views and concerns – so much so that the considerable support among US environmental NGOs and in health circles for REACH never seems to get much hearing in Washington, DC. There are many in the US who take the view that the US better consider REACH as a future standard for proper chemicals regulation and information gathering. The Waxman report is a product of the frustration of NGOs and their supporters around Capitol Hill. It unveils in extreme detail, based on official documents, how the US government has mainly echoed the industry position while refusing to give any hearing to the avowed benefits of REACH also for the US.[19] In any event, at the OECD level modest new research and testing programs about chemicals have been initiated. The US fears that the EU might ignore or bypass these cooperative efforts, even though they are least-cost and more risk-based (rather than hazard-based, like REACH).

Concerning the objective or constraint of WTO compatibility, several WTO members led by the US have reacted to the REACH proposal. They expressed concerns that the draft regulation could have discriminatory effects, especially where (chemical) substances in (final) articles are concerned. The line of argument is that it could be hard for importers to know the substances included in the article (confidentiality concerns) or they

---

[19] The Waxman Report – see Committee on Government Reform, minority office, "The Chemical Industry, the Bush Administration, and European Efforts to Regulate Chemicals", http://www.house.gov/reform/min/inves_admin/admin_reach.htm [2004].

may not dispose of the necessary know-how to perform the testing procedures of the regulation.[20]

## Outlook and Conclusions

Writing in late spring of 2005 it seems that the greatest turbulence about REACH is over. The proposals have been adjusted on the cost side and more in-depth studies indicate that initial fears were exaggerated. The original underlying idea of an approach based on the precautionary principle, implying that one should undertake every attempt to improve knowledge in the presence of unacceptably great uncertainty, has been upheld, but its unreserved application has become far more measured. Fears now center more on how the European Chemical Agency can and should operate, including how it can truly offer 'one-stop-shopping'.

The European Parliament has not proposed any official amendments at this moment of writing. Therefore, it is hazardous to predict how REACH will eventually be adopted. Members of the European Parliament have invested considerable effort in trying to understand the merits and needs of this major reform. Several informal proposals by MEPs have been aired but intense consultations continue. MEPs would seem to be aware that the present regulatory system for chemicals is not a good option. Reform is badly necessary; the decisive question is how far, how fast and how intrusive the impositions on business will be, given the broad consensus about the need to know much more about the long term health and environmental consequences of chemicals.

---

[20] For other potential problems REACH might present in a WTO context, see the statement by Professor Marco Bronckers at the European Parliament hearings of January 19, 2005.

# 15. All quiet on the transatlantic front? Deficits, Imbalances and the Transatlantic Economy

## Daniel Gros and Thomas Mayer

The dollar seems to have stabilized in early 2005, at least relative to the euro, after several years of strong decline. While the euro was appreciating against the dollar, the rapid movement in the bilateral rate generated considerable concern in Europe. However, with new-found relative stability, European concerns about the 'excessive' strength of the euro have abated, and exchange rate developments therefore no longer provide a source of transatlantic friction.

The massive swings in the dollar/euro rate seem to have had little impact thus far on the transatlantic trade imbalance. It is usually overlooked that until as recently as 2003, the bilateral US deficit with Europe was as large as that with China. Over the last year this has changed somewhat; the transatlantic imbalance has stabilized whereas the US deficit with China (as that of the EU with China) has continued to increase.

Even today, however, the US deficit with the EU still remains one of its largest bilateral deficits, but until now this has generated little political heat. There are two reasons why the transatlantic trade relationship should be the most robust bilateral trade relationship in the world.

First, the EU and the US produce similar goods, which is not the case in US-China trade. There can thus be no accusations of cheap labor and social dumping across the Atlantic.

A second reason why the transatlantic trade imbalance generates little political heat stems from the huge amount of two-way foreign direct investment (FDI) that has flown across the Atlantic over the last few decades.[1] The accumulated stock is now so large that about one-half of all transatlantic trade is intra-firm trade. This implies that even large shifts in the bilateral exchange rate do not lead to strong protectionist pressures. DaimlerChrysler can just shift production from one side to the other and will not lobby for protection on either side of the Atlantic. Moreover, when a firm produces on both shores of the Atlantic, there is no clear link between the exchange rate and its profits.

---

[1] See chapters 1 and 2 of this volume; also Daniel S. Hamilton and Joseph P. Quinlan, *Partners in Prosperity: The Changing Geography of the Transatlantic Economy* (Washington, DC: Center for Transatlantic Relations, 2004).

There are thus solid reasons why trade issues are not the source of transatlantic friction. Nevertheless, there remains one source of potential conflict: the huge ongoing US current deficit. For US policy-makers, the solution to this problem (if it is regarded as a problem at all) lies in Asia, especially with the exchange rate policy of China. Many Europeans, however, regard insufficient US savings as the root cause. This chapter argues that these two views in isolation are both wrong, but that, in combination, they provide a convincing explanation. They also point to the forces that might bring the US deficit back to more reasonable levels.

In substance, our argument is that the US deficit is the result of the emergence of the desire on the part of the rest of the world, in particular emerging markets, to massively increase their savings. The desire by emerging markets to run large current account surpluses had to be balanced by deficits elsewhere. Why did the US, and not Europe, provide the counterpart to the massive emerging market surpluses? We argue that this is due to a combination of a different policy response to this common shock and a difference in economic structure, particularly in the housing market. A corollary of this view is that a correction of the US deficit does not necessarily require a massive revaluation of the euro against the dollar. The correction could come from a gradual fall in emerging market surpluses accompanied by higher real interest rates and hence slower demand growth in the US.

## Emerging Market Booms and Busts: The Primary Driver for the US Current Account

In order to find the roots of today's US current account deficit, one has to go back almost a decade and to look outside the US. The best time period in which to start is the mid-1990s, when equity markets were booming all over the world on the back of expectations of intensifying globalization and a revolution in 'information and communication technologies'. Emerging markets were then becoming popular destinations for international investors, particularly as their markets were opening up and offering high-growth potential and attractive rates of return. However, the emerging markets' boom came to an abrupt halt in 1997, as a combination of lax fiscal policies, rigid exchange rates, rapid consumption and investment growth led to widening current account deficits financed by large short-term capital inflows. Indeed, outside of Asia and Eastern Europe, foreign direct investment constituted a small share of the financing of the current account deficits. These were the classical ingredients that provoked the crises that occurred in one country after another between 1997 and 2002.

What happened next constitutes the core element of the mechanism leading to the US deficit: shut out of international capital markets and forced to embrace tough IMF medicine and to elect more conservative governments, emerging markets began adopting sound economic policies. Fixed exchange rates were abandoned, current account deficits turned into surpluses, large primary surpluses were generated by the public sector (*pace* George Stiglitz), short-term external debt was eliminated and the depleted stock of international reserves was replenished to record levels.

Figures 1 and 2 show the cumulated current account position of East European, Asian, Middle Eastern and Latin American countries.[2] From a cumulated deficit of $78 billion in 1995, emerging markets turned their current accounts into a sizeable surplus of $81 billion in 1999, as fiscal and monetary policy tightening improved public and private savings-investment balances. Since 1999, competitive currencies and high commodity prices allowed emerging markets to generate even larger current account surpluses, reaching an estimated $328 billion in 2004 (of which about one-half was owed to oil producers – more on this later).

*Figure 1. Emerging Markets Current Account Position*
     *($ billions)*

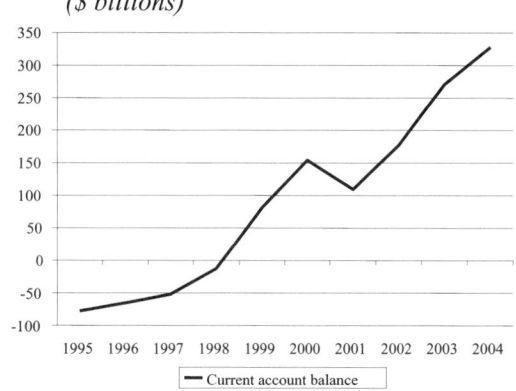

*Source*: IMF, *World Economic Outlook*, September 2004.

---

[2] The group of emerging market economies was built from IMF country groupings. Current account aggregates were computed by adding the current account balances (in US dollars) of these groups. The savings and investment ratios of our group of emerging markets were calculated as the weighted average of the IMF country groups on the basis of purchasing power GDP weights given by the IMF. The source of all data is the IMF's World Economic Outlook Data Base from September 2004.

*Figure 2. Regional Contributions to Current Account Balances in Emerging Markets ($ billions)*

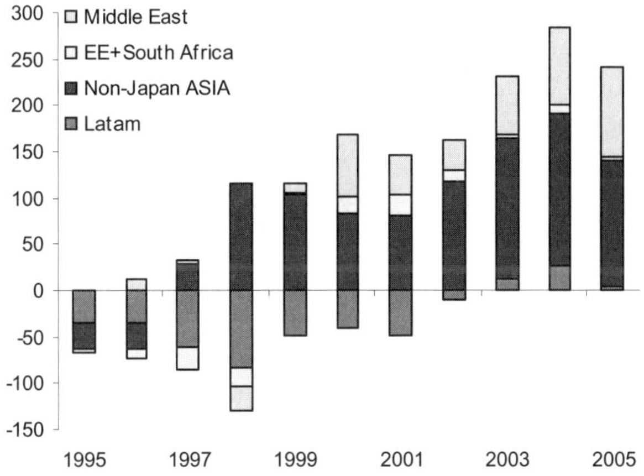

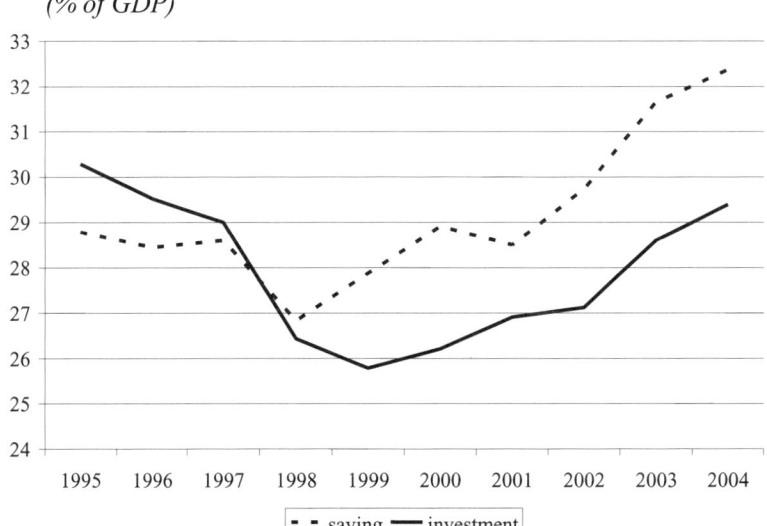

*Source*: Deutsche Bank Global Markets Research.

Figure 3 shows gross national savings and investment relative to GDP for the same group of countries (the difference between the two series indicates the group's external balance and thus its net export of savings).

*Figure 3. National Savings and Investment Positions in Emerging Markets (% of GDP)*

*Source*: IMF, *World Economic Outlook*, September 2004.

As emerging markets' crises unfolded in the second half of the 1990s, emerging markets slashed their investment spending sharply. In 1998, national savings also fell, as a number of countries plunged into severe recession. Thereafter, however, savings recovered thanks to domestic austerity policies, while investment followed only with a lag and at a more moderate pace. As of 1999, in a major change from past behavior and against the conventional wisdom of development economics, emerging markets began exporting large and growing amounts of savings to the rest of the world. In more recent years, exports of savings from emerging markets were boosted further by rising commodity prices.

## G-3: After the Boom, the Investment Bust

While emerging-market countries experienced balance-of-payments crises and stabilization recessions in the second half of the 1990s, industrialized countries enjoyed an economic boom on the back of surging stock markets and euphoria about the benefits of new information and communications technologies. Hence the emerging market bust had little impact on activity in the G3 (although the collapse of the hedge fund Long Term Capital briefly led to fears of a credit crunch). The lower demand for capital from emerging markets was rapidly absorbed by the huge increase in investment in the US. This was the first leg of the contribution of the emerging markets to the US deficits, which then began to increase considerably.

During 2000, however, the boom turned into a bust as the valuation of 'new economy' equities climbed to irrational highs. In the event, the equity markets' decline triggered a sharp drop in investment, as companies struggled to repair their balance sheets by paying off debt, and industrially advanced economies fell into stagnation or recession.

Throughout the second half of the 1990s, industrially advanced countries, and especially the US, had been net importers of international savings, reflecting a rise in investment following the new technology boom that had not been matched by a corresponding rise in domestic savings. After 2000, however, investment in industrialized countries fell, just at the time when emerging market countries stepped up their exports of savings (Figure 4).

At the beginning of the new millennium, global capital markets therefore were suddenly confronted with a rising supply of savings from emerging markets and falling demand for these savings from industrialized countries, which were experiencing an investment recession. There was only one way to equilibrate the global supply and demand for savings: global real interest rates had to fall. This is illustrated in Figure 5, which shows the developments of the ratio of world investment to GDP and real US 10-year government bond yields, which we use here (somewhat loosely) as a proxy for the global real interest rates.[3] The drop in investment (relative to GDP) in the industrialized countries (shown in Figure 4) pushed down the global investment ratio (as the rise in emerging markets' investment was too weak to compensate for the investment weakness elsewhere). As the investment ratio fell, real interest rates fell.

*Figure 4. Emerging Markets' Savings and Industrialized Countries' Investment Positions (% of GDP)*

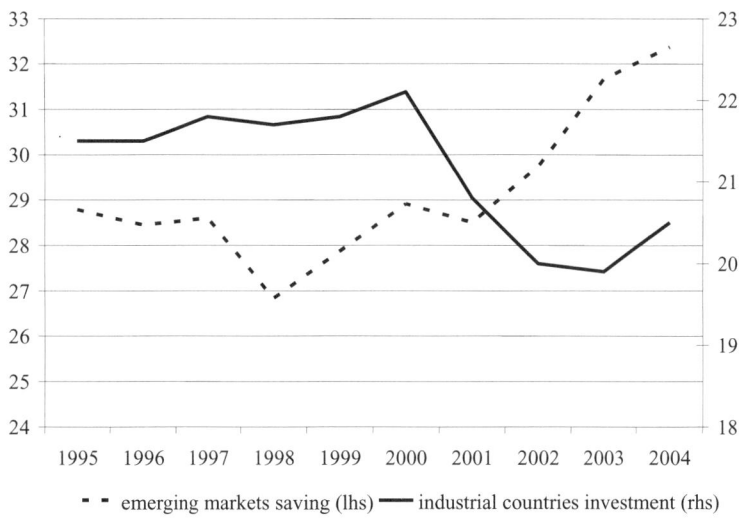

emerging markets saving (lhs) — industrial countries investment (rhs)

*Source*: IMF, *World Economic Outlook*, September 2004.

As we shall argue in more detail below, the decline in real interest rates eventually helped turn around the decline in investment and depressed savings in industrialized countries. At this point we just want to comment briefly on the breakdown of the relationship between lower investment and lower interest rates over the last two years. With investment showing a strong recovery, real interest rates should have risen; but they did not. Why? The next section will illustrate a quite different source of savings that has suddenly appeared on the global scene: the surplus of the oil-producing countries.

---

[3] To calculate real interest rates, we simply deflated nominal US bond yields with the US private consumption deflator.

*Figure 5. Global Investment and Real Interest Rates*

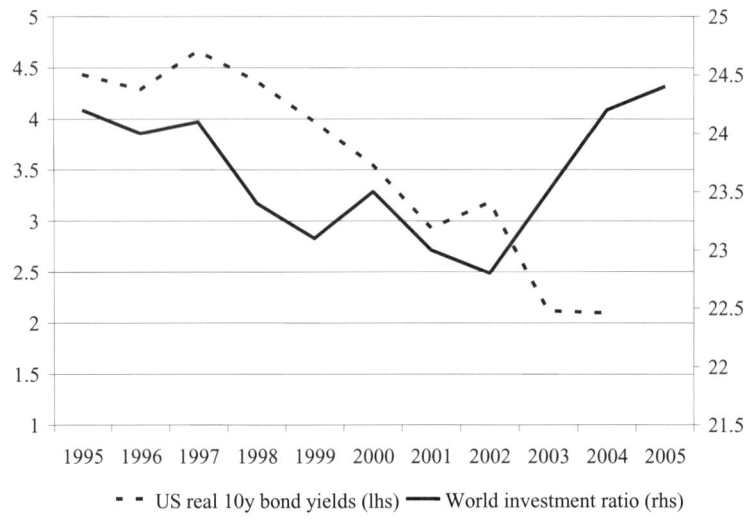

*Source*: IMF, *World Economic Outlook*, September 2004.

## Oil Prices and the Sudden Emergence of Another Source of Excess Savings

More recently, i.e. since 2004, another source of excess savings has appeared and grown very rapidly in the form of the rising surplus of OPEC countries. This surplus is destined to grow even further in the current year as oil prices have stayed above the average 2004 level. The reason for the emergence of this surplus is quite simple: oil-producing countries have a lower propensity to consume beyond their income.

There are several reasons why OPEC and other oil-producing countries are not spending their windfall immediately. First, despite the existence of futures market pricing, there is considerable uncertainty about the future path of oil prices, and thus the marginal propensity to consume is less than one in the short run. Second, the international financial institutions are urging governments of oil-producing countries to build up stabilization funds, advice that has been at least partially taken. This implies that governments are saving a substantial part of the windfall that accrues to them in the form of higher royalties in order to raise national savings.

These two mechanisms are fundamentally very similar: both are based on the uncertainty surrounding future oil prices.

A simple calculation can show that the magnitudes involved are significant. Around 50 billion barrels a day are produced by countries that are not themselves big consumers. An oil price increase of $20 a barrel (e.g. from $30 to $50/barrel) implies a transfer to these producers of about $1 billion per day, or around $370 billion per annum. If about one-half of this amount is initially saved, the increase in the oil price observed over the last year and a half is equivalent to a negative demand shock of about $180-$200 billion for the oil-consuming countries. This alone would be equivalent to a drop of the investment ratio in both the US and the eurozone of around 1% of GDP – not far from the actual increase in global investment shown in Figure 5 above. Under reasonable assumptions, the oil shock could thus have contributed just enough ex ante savings to maintain the global savings/ investment balance at the level it was when savings were depressed in 2001- 03.

## A world out of balance?

A fall in global real interest rates was required to equilibrate the global market for savings and enforce the ex-post identity of real savings and investment. This alone would not explain why the US deficit would increase; in principle one could have expected both the EU and the US to provide the counterpart to higher emerging market savings. However, the fall in real interest rates had a completely different impact on the two sides of the Atlantic. There are two reasons for this asymmetry: policy-makers reacted differently and this interacted with differences in economic and financial structures.

*Differences in policy-makers' reactions.* The investment bust required a new term structure of interest rates at a lower level, which involves the adjustment of both market and policy interest rates. Given their control over the short end of the yield curve, central banks played a key role in bringing real rates lower. Their reaction was promoted by the perceived shortfall of investment and excess supply of savings that were threatening the economic outlook and raising the spectre of deflation.

Here is a first transatlantic difference: the Federal Reserve was able to slash interest rates much more strongly than the ECB for the simple reason that it had hiked rates much more in the run-up to the boom in 1999-2000 (to 6.5% compared to 'only' 4.75% in the eurozone). At the same time, high productivity growth in the US kept inflation in check so that the Fed could lower interest rates to 1%, a fall of 5.5 percentage points. The ECB lowered rates 'only' by one-half of this amount, when it stopped the easing cycle at 2% in 2003. With inflation under control, the fall in nominal long-term rates was fully reflected in real rates, as shown for the US in Figure 6.

*Figure 6. US Nominal and Real Interest Rates and Inflation (%)*

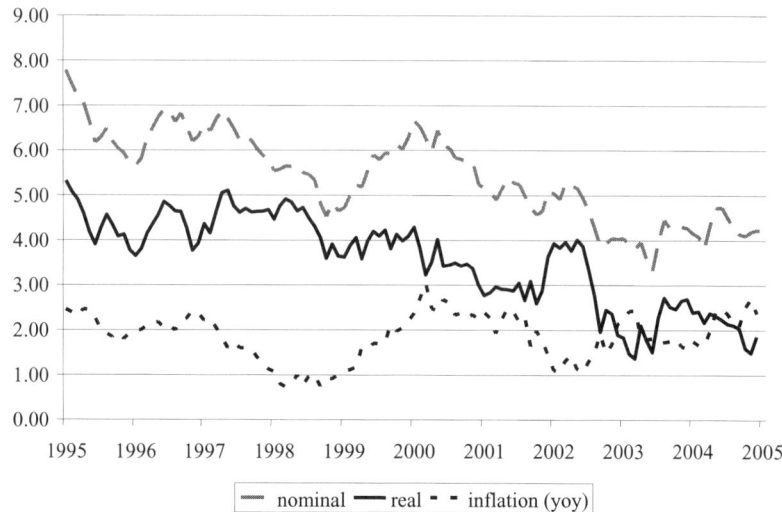

*Source*: IMF, *World Economic Outlook*, September 2004.

As discussed earlier, the decline in real rates was needed to balance the global demand and supply of savings. While the demand for savings by investors responds directly to changes in real interest rates, real and financial assets are the key catalyst for real interest rate changes to affect the supply of savings by private households in the industrialized countries.[4] With the decline in real interest rates raising asset prices, consumers felt wealthier and were inclined to reduce their savings. Real estate markets played the most important role here. Figure 7 shows how real private consumption grew strongly .in countries where housing prices also increased strongly.

Clearly, while the decline in real interest rates was a global phenomenon, demand and supply conditions in specific real estate markets mattered. For instance, housing prices rose only slightly in Japan and Germany, where a supply overhang existed, but they rose at an accelerating pace in the US.[5]

---

[4] To illustrate this point, consider the following standard investment and consumption functions: (1) $I = I(r)$; (2) $C = C(Y,W(r))$. Equation (1) relates investment to the real interest rate and equation (2) relates consumption to income and wealth, which itself is a function of the real interest rate (with a decrease in r raising W).

[5] Of course, there are large regional differences even within countries. The US average value results from a property boom on both coasts, while prices seem to

This constitutes another reason for transatlantic divergence. The impact of differences in the evolution of housing prices is compounded by differences in financial markets: in the US, most mortgages carry an option for the holder to refinance the mortgage should interest rates fall. Moreover, the ratio of the value of the house that can be mortgaged is typically higher in the US than in most of continental Europe. Since the transactions cost of this re-financing is low, it is not surprising that millions of US households took advantage of lower long-term interest rates to 'extract equity' from their homes. Little of this financial engineering is possible in Europe. Accordingly, most continental European countries are positioned below the line in Figure 7 (indicating a lower consumption response to a given increase in housing prices), whereas the US and other Anglo-Saxon countries are above the line.

*Figure 7. Housing Prices (Q303) and Real Private Consumption in 16 OECD Countries, 2003 (% yoy)*

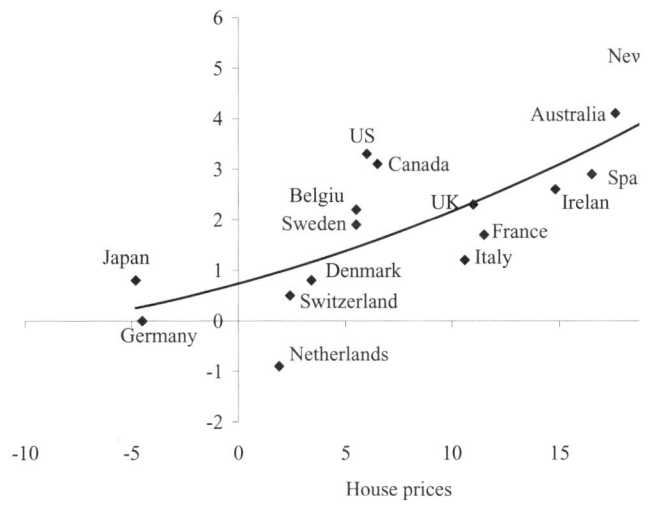

*Source*: OECD and *The Economist*.

Fiscal policy also played an important role in restoring equilibrium in the global savings market. In particular, the US government turned from a net saver to a large dis-saver, absorbing a considerable amount of global savings and helping to stabilize domestic demand in the US. Here is another

have moved relatively little in the center of the country. Even in those European countries (much smaller than the US) where on average housing prices did not increase greatly, there were localized booms.

transatlantic difference: euro area countries had much less room for fiscal policy maneuver because, again, they had not really tightened their policy during the boom. The difference in fiscal policy is even larger than the difference in monetary policy. We use as the best indicator the cyclically adjusted deficit because the direct 'automatic' impact of the cycle on budgets has already been taken out of this measure. At the start of EMU, Euroland governments were already in a weak position with a cyclically adjusted deficit of around 1.5% of GDP, which then was allowed to deteriorate to around 2.5% of GDP in 2002, with very little change over the last four years. By contrast, the US started the period under consideration with a cyclically adjusted *surplus* of over 1% of GDP and was thus in a much better position to use fiscal policy actively for demand management purposes. Due to a combination of spending increases and tax cuts, the US budget balance policy swung rapidly into a deficit of now over 4% of GDP on a cyclically adjusted basis, and the overall swing between 1999 and 2004 was equivalent to over 5% of GDP, five times larger than that for Euroland.

Through these mechanisms, national savings were eventually reduced much more in the US than in Europe, allowing the former to absorb the surplus savings of emerging markets at a time of lower investment activity, without triggering a major world recession. However, this left the world with a considerable international current account imbalance.

In sum, the large decline in real interest rates and the emergence of unprecedented current account imbalances were the corollary to the stabilization of the world economy at a time of huge changes in global savings and investment flows. This common shock had a totally different impact on the two sides of the Atlantic because different starting conditions led to quite different policy responses.

The result of the extraordinary policy stimulus administered in the US is shown in Table 1. US gross national savings as a share of GDP fell sharply from its 1995-97 average to 2004, while investment remained broadly stable (thanks to the rebound in 2004). As a result, the recession of 2001 remained short and shallow, but the national savings-investment deficit increased considerably (see Figure 8). Developments in the UK and Central and Eastern European countries (CEECs) were similar to those in the US. In contrast, the drop in national savings in Japan and the eurozone fell short of, or just compensated for the drop in investment. Since consumption did not compensate for the fall in investment, growth in these regions trailed that of the US.

Table 1. Changes in savings and investment ratios, 2004
relative to 1995-97 (% of GDP)

|  | Savings | Investment | S-I |
|---|---|---|---|
| United States | -2.7 | 0.4 | -3.1 |
| Japan | -3.0 | -4.5 | 1.5 |
| Euro area | -0.7 | -0.7 | 0.0 |
| United Kingdom | -1.4 | -0.1 | -1.3 |
| CEECs | -1.2 | -0.5 | -0.7 |
| Emerging markets | 3.8 | -0.2 | 4.0 |
| CIS | 6.1 | -2.2 | 8.4 |
| Middle East | 4.9 | 0.0 | 4.9 |
| Western Hemisphere | 1.9 | -1.6 | 3.4 |
| Asian NICs | -2.1 | -8.1 | 6.0 |
| Developing Asia | 4.7 | 1.6 | 3.1 |

*Source*: IMF, World Economic Outlook Data Base.

Figure 8. US Savings-Investment Balances
(% of GDP)

*Source*: DB Global Markets Research.

In most emerging markets (with the exception of the Asian newly industrialized countries – NICs), national savings rose significantly between 1995-97 and 2004, while investment rose only a little or fell. In the NICs, however, the savings-investment balance rose significantly because of the large decline in investment. As we argued above, this reflected in large part a change in economic policies aimed at reducing dependence on capital imports by creating a savings-investment surplus. In some regions, notably in the Middle East and the CIS, an improvement in terms of trade resulting from rising commodity prices added to the savings surplus.

In contrast to Japan and Euroland, however, emerging markets managed to grow fast during these years on the back of strong export growth to the US and EU. Many of these countries prevented their exchange rates from appreciating against the US dollar and hence fully benefited from rising US import demand. With private sector capital flows militating against an external savings surplus, countries had to intervene in the foreign exchange markets, occasionally on a large scale, to stabilize their exchange rates. Through this exchange rate policy, they effectively taxed consumption and subsidized exports, and turned their savings surplus into a rise in official foreign exchange reserves.

Table 2 shows changes in current accounts corresponding to changes in savings and investment balances. The current account position of emerging market countries improved by almost $400 billion between 1995-97 and 2004, while the current account position of the other countries/regions listed in the table deteriorated by some $500 billion. Within the latter group, the current account position of Japan rose while that of the euro area remained broadly unchanged. Thus, increases in the current account surpluses of emerging markets and Japan financed to a large degree the increase in the current account deficits of Anglo-Saxon and Central and Eastern European countries.

*Table 2. Changes in Current Account Balances, 2004, 1995-97 ($ billions)*

|  | 2004 | 1995-97 | Change |
|---|---|---|---|
| United States | -631.3 | -119.5 | -511.8 |
| Japan | 159.4 | 91.2 | 68.2 |
| Euro area | 72.2 | 76.0 | -3.8 |
| United Kingdom | -43.3 | -8.9 | -34.4 |
| CEECs | -44.2 | -15.4 | -28.8 |
| Emerging markets | 327.7 | -65.1 | 392.8 |
| CIS | 61.4 | -2.0 | 63.4 |
| Middle East | 103.5 | 6.3 | 97.2 |
| Western Hemisphere | 9.0 | -48.3 | 57.3 |
| NIC Asia | 85.0 | 2.1 | 82.9 |
| Developing Asia | 68.8 | -23.2 | 92.0 |

*Source*: IMF, World Economic Outlook Database.

## Implications for Transatlantic Relations

As anticipated in the introduction, this analysis has one simple implication for transatlantic relations: the main mechanism to rein in the US current account deficit is not the bilateral exchange rate dollar/euro, but an increase in global interest rates, which would compress US excess demand for savings from the rest of the world. It is thus possible that all will remain quiet on the transatlantic front.

# 16. Transatlantic and Global Dimensions of the Lisbon Agenda

## Fredrik Erixon

A t a European Union summit in March 2000, member states agreed to launch a new EU-wide reform program – the Lisbon agenda – aiming to make the EU the most competitive and dynamic economy in the world by 2010. According to the Lisbon European Council, achieving this goal required a transition to a knowledge-based economy and society by better policies for the information society and R&D, as well as by stepping up the process of structural reform for competitiveness and innovation and by completing the internal market.

At the time of the Lisbon summit, the current recession in major EU economies had not yet started. The macroeconomic environment of the EU was rather good; indeed, some claimed that Europe was experiencing the best macroeconomic outlook for a generation. At the peak of the 'dotcom' era, there was a widespread feeling of an ascending Europe. Yet to the discerning observer, there were signs of problems. Unemployment remained persistently high in spite of the economic boom. Ample evidence signaled that the EU economy was once again lagging behind that of the US. The post-World War II catch-up period of the European economy had ended by the early 1970s. European productivity continued to rise faster than US productivity and GDP per capita grew with roughly the same factor over the following decades, but a clear shift of pattern occurred in the 1990s. The convergence of productivity between the US and the EU then ended. US productivity geared up while European productivity growth slowed down. This trend was also manifested in GDP figures: the average annual growth in 1995-2000 was 4.1% in the US and 2.7% in the EU-15.[1]

Of greater concern to many in Europe was the slow pace of the general transformation of the industrial economy into a knowledge-based one. Again, the US seemed to develop faster than Europe. Investment in the information and communications technology (ICT) sectors was higher, and the diffusion of new technology much faster in the US than in Europe. Overall, the organizational structure of the US economy seemed to be more conducive to

---

[1] See B. van Ark and R. McGuckin III, *Performance 2004: Productivity, Employment, and Income in the World's Economies*, Research Report R-1351-04-RR, The Conference Board, New York, 2004.

a 'third industrial revolution' and a step up in the value-added chain.[2] Therefore, to promote structural reform, innovation and growth – and generally increase competitiveness – the EU embarked on a comprehensive economic reform program.

This chapter takes a closer look at the Lisbon agenda and its method of reforms. Of particular interest is the missing link of an 'external dimension' in the agenda, especially a transatlantic dimension, which could enable EU member states to use international cooperation in a wider context to leverage reforms and growth. The chapter argues that the EU has much to gain from widening the perspective of the Lisbon agenda and advancing the multilateral liberalization of the world economy as well as bilateral efforts of the same kind together with the US.

## The Lisbon Agenda

The Lisbon agenda is a comparatively far-reaching reform program that cuts across many policy areas. It has recently been under review. The revised Lisbon agenda, as proposed by the Commission, will be of a different sort than the original agenda in terms of tools and methods for implementing reforms.[3] Having found it difficult to persuade member countries to deliver the reforms and implement the Lisbon strategy, the new Commission has suggested a 'new partnership' for promoting reforms but has not yet specified the details of the process. Nevertheless, the key spheres are still the same: innovation, liberalization, enterprise, employment and sustainable development. Below is a brief description of these areas.[4]

*1) Innovation.* The EU has to increase the role of innovation-based production in order to avoid competing with low-cost countries in future.

---

[2] Studies by the consulting firm McKinsey (*Service Sector Productivity,* McKinsey, Washington, DC, 1992) and W.W. Lewis ("The Power of Productivity", *The McKinsey Quarterly*, No. 4, 2004) suggest that the low level of competition in the European service sectors explains the difference in the ICT effect on productivity growth between Europe and the US. These findings were confirmed by R. Gordon in *Why was Europe Left at the Station when America's Productivity Locomotive Departed?*, NBER Working Paper No. 10661, NBER, Cambridge, MA, 2004.

[3] See European Commission, *Working Together for Growth and Jobs, Next Steps in Implementing the Revised Lisbon Strategy*, Commission Staff Working Paper, SEC(2005) 622/2, Brussels.

[4] The purpose of this description is to present the general thrust of the agenda, not to offer a comprehensive examination or to address every specific goal.

Therefore, spending on research and development has to rise. Although it has risen moderately since 2000, it is still well below the target of 3% of GDP and the US level of R&D spending (2.7% of GDP). The low level of European spending on R&D is assumed to explain the difference in the number of patents between the US and the EU. According to Eurostat's structural indicators, the number of applications to the European Patent Office per million inhabitants was approximately 48 in the US and 32 in the 15 member states that made up the EU prior to enlargement (EU-15). The difference in patent applications to the US Patent and Trademark Office was even larger, more than four times higher in the US than in EU-15. To step up innovation in Europe, member countries should increase Internet access and promote new technologies.

*2) Liberalization.* The EU Single Market is not yet complete. Many sectors, especially service sectors, are still not integrated in an EU-wide economy. The overall market liberalization strategy in the Lisbon agenda is ambiguous; it is unclear to what extent liberalization of the service sectors should be dealt with under the Lisbon heading. Yet some sectors are notably targeted in the strategy: telecom, gas, electricity, transport, postal services and financial services. The agenda calls for deregulation of the telecom sector, liberalization of gas and electricity markets, and increased competition in transport (particularly of rail services). Moreover, the markets for financial services should be opened up for European competition and member states are being generally pushed to promote a single market in services.

*3) Enterprise.* The Lisbon agenda aims at improving the business climate of the EU and at stimulating risk-taking and new companies. Small and medium-sized enterprises are particularly noted as important for the future of the EU's economy and for achieving rising employment. The prospects for an entrepreneurial-based economic future seem to be rather weak, however. According to the Global Entrepreneurship Monitor, a much larger share of the population in the US is involved in entrepreneurial activities than in the EU.[5] Equally disappointing to the EU is the fact that many more Americans prefer to be self-employed.[6] This characteristic is not necessarily an obstacle in raising the number of new companies in the EU, but a more entrepreneurial spirit is explicitly mentioned in the agenda as instrumental to achieving a more dynamic EU economy. According to the agenda, it is also of great importance to expand the volume of venture capital accessible to EU

---

[5] See the *Global Entrepreneurship Monitor 2004 Report,* GEM Consortium, Babson Park, MA, 2005 (retrieved from http://www.gemconsortium.org).

[6] See *Entrepreneurship*, Flash Eurobarometer No. 160, European Commission, Brussels, June 2004 (retrieved from http://europa.eu.int/comm/public_opinion/flash/fl160_en.pdf).

start-ups, simplify the regulatory structure, promote competition and scale-down subsidies to industries, and make procurement rules more accessible.

*3) Employment and social inclusion.* This area is the most politically challenging for reforms in the agenda. It cuts directly into the welfare model of many countries and addresses general concerns of the 'European social model'. Unemployment and the low level of workforce participation are problems in many European countries. In the second half of the 1990s and the first years of the new millennium, unemployment in Europe fell. In recent years, it has started to climb again. The goals of the Lisbon strategy are to raise the general workforce participation ratio to 70% (it is today well below 65%), the participation ratio of women to 60% and of older workers to 50%. The agenda seeks to foster a general upgrade in skills by halving the number of youths lacking secondary education and generally promoting a culture of lifelong learning. In addition, member countries are to consolidate public finances, increase the effective retirement age and reduce the number of persons at risk from poverty and social exclusion.

*4) Sustainable development.* During the Swedish presidency of the EU in 2001, sustainable development was added to the Lisbon agenda. The Kyoto Protocol target of reduced greenhouse gas emissions is now part of the agenda (which aims at an 8% reduction from the 1990 level by 2010), as well as reforms to increase the share of renewable sources in the provision of electricity and to stop the depletion of biological diversity.

## Models of European Reform

The Lisbon agenda is about comprehensive economic reforms in Europe. In this respect, the Lisbon agenda clearly carries the emblem of the EU and European cooperation. Yet, the assignment of reform delivery has not been addressed to the EU institutions. The strategy is largely based on issues where the EU in itself cannot make the decisions owing to its lack of (jurisdictional) competence.

In a limited number of fields, there is a clear assignment of EU policy decisions, but the main mission for EU institutions is to bring a more significant EU dimension to the national policy arenas by monitoring and evaluating member countries. The underlying role of the Commission and the Council is to be a 'midwife of good policies' and smooth reform processes by providing benchmarks and experiences from one member state to another.

The EU institutions can at times also put pressure on member states. It is true that the EU is rather toothless if member countries are not willing or able to deliver the reforms necessary to achieve the Lisbon targets. Yet that does not necessarily translate into an ineffective role for the institutions. An innovative and dedicated Commission can leverage reforms if it is sufficiently sensible and knows when and where to push for them. The history of the EU provides many examples of critical moments when EU institutions have helped to dissolve nationally based coalitions by concerted reform packages in several or all member states.

Until now, however, the 'external dimension' of the Lisbon policy process has ended in Brussels. In spite of the global character of many of the Lisbon issues, there is not an external dimension pointing to – or perhaps more importantly, *using* – international cooperation in a wider circle as a method to achieve structural reforms and to enhance EU competitiveness and growth potential. Given the ambitions of the agenda – not to say the general significance of the global economy and international cooperation today – it is hardly controversial to assert that the EU is missing opportunities to achieve its goals when the policy dimension is wholly focused on the nexus of Brussels and European national capitals.

Furthermore, it is particularly strange that the agenda is largely energized – for some even defined – by a bipolar world of the 'EU versus the US'. True, in the jargon of international competitiveness there is of course a strong element of comparisons with other countries. What is more, comparison can also be invigorating for the EU economy, as well as the other economies, given the greater presence of institutional competition in world affairs. Competition generally promotes better results and raises the general awareness of the upsides and downsides of specific policy options. This precept also applies to competition among nations. Nevertheless, that is a bit beside the point with regard to the Lisbon agenda. The agenda is primarily about increasing growth potential by improving policies. It is a program for structural reforms. Although having many objectives, its shining aspect is finding, developing and instituting methods – and momentum – of reforms. In structural reform processes of this kind, institutional competition has often been an effective strategy for achieving good results.

Viewed in a historical EU perspective, the 'Lisbon idea' of structural reforms can arguably be seen as a policy innovation. Of course, member countries have launched reform programs many times before. In the policy milieu and the institutional setting of the EU, however, the Lisbon meeting was the first time that member states agreed to have a common and extensive agenda in many politically sensitive fields of policy where the EU lacks (jurisdictional) competence and jointly advance a growth policy based on a transformation of the economy and economic policy.

The traditional model of EU (or EC) growth promotion – or put differently, the political economy of European cooperation – has been increased competition by market expansion and economic integration. The basic idea of the European Community (along with many other international institutions) was to tie European countries closer together through increased economic integration. Many other policy areas have been integrated into the European cooperative structure, particularly after the Maastricht Treaty, but a main feature continues to be economic integration – not only for its effects on integration per se, but also for its merits of providing economic growth by increasing competition and pushing for structural reforms. It is therefore warranted to characterize the traditional EU model of growth promotion as a policy based on lower barriers to trade and intensified competition.[7] The Single Market of 1992 is of course the prime example of this model, but the economic integration of the EU in the multilateral trading order has also been pivotal. It is hard to quantify the effects of this policy model on growth, but many studies point to the importance of economic integration to growth in the European post-war period.[8] At times, it has even been the main vehicle.[9]

---

[7] H. Siebert makes a passionate case for this 'Schumpeterian' model of European affairs in his publication *The New Economic Landscape in Europe*, London: Basil Blackwell, 1991.

[8] According to a study by the European Commission (2003), *The Internal Market – Ten Years without Frontiers*, SEC(2002) 1417 of 7.1.2003, the internal market has had a tremendous effect on the European economy. EU GDP in 2002 was 1.8 percentage points or €164.5 billion higher, thanks to the internal market. When adding together the additional annual GDP generated by the internal market since 1992, the European Commission claims that there has been a total GDP effect of €877 billion.

[9] As discussed by P. Krugman and R. Lawrence and others, technological progress is overall a more powerful force of structural change than trade liberalization. Of course, this has also been true for European countries during most of the 20th century. Nevertheless, it does not translate into a lack of effectiveness of the route of trade liberalization to achieving structural change. Nor does technological progress provide a political framework for achieving such change. Looking at structural change from the policy side, increased market integration through trade liberalization is often a more viable strategy for politicians since they do not – at least to the same extent – control the factors by which a country can achieve structural change by technological progress. See P. Krugman and R. Lawrence, *Trade, Jobs, and Wages*, NBER Working Paper No. W4478, NBER, Cambridge, MA, 1993. See also Banks (2003), who shows for example how Australia achieved structural reforms and increased productivity and made Australian business more competitive in the world markets by unilateral trade liberalization.

The Lisbon agenda also contains policy reforms of this ilk, particularly the program to liberalize the energy, financial, telecom and transport sectors. Completing the internal Single Market is also a targeted goal and the original agenda from 2000 went as far as to suggest an internal market for services, although the explicit commitments from member states were, to put it mildly, ambiguous. Furthermore, at the European Council's spring meeting in Brussels 2004, an 'external dimension' of international economic integration was also added to the strategy.

The market expansion element of the Lisbon agenda is, however, limited. The external dimension has not yet been defined or integrated in the general framework, not to mention in targeted goals for member states. The overall *motif* of the agenda, before and after the revision, is to climb the value-added chain through a comprehensive reform program aiming at making many policy areas more conducive to growth. This effort is arguably an essential shift of policy focus for the EU.

First, there is a change of *economic mode*. Instead of addressing the unfinished business of the Single Market and continuing with more market integration in general (internally as well as externally), the Lisbon agenda directs attention to the contributions to growth from research, technology, and innovation.

Second, there is a difference in *policy method*. On balance, the agenda is based on prescriptive policies in these areas, instructing countries what to do, rather than a proscriptive method of policies, prohibiting countries from specific actions. If the monetary union is excluded, the mode of economic cooperation in Europe has historically been of the proscriptive kind.

Third, there is a shift of *governance structure*. The current reform program is largely based on a model of governance where the Commission is not the vehicle of the reform process or in charge of the agenda. In previous programs, the Commission has often played a more significant role in delivering reforms. That was possible because those programs rested upon policy reforms for which the EU actually had exclusive competence.

That is not to say that EU leaders made a bad decision in Lisbon when heading for comprehensive policy reforms. On the contrary, the EU's quest for increased growth needs a systematic overview over many fields of policy. There are, however, several pieces missing in the current agenda. In particular, EU leaders have devalued the possibility of enhancing growth by using closer market integration – internally as well as externally – to leverage policy reforms and structural adjustments. This link is the most apparent one missing in the strategy. The following sections examine the possibility of enhancing prospects for growth by integrating an external dimension in the Lisbon realm, particularly a transatlantic one.

## Themes of the Transatlantic Dimension

In spite of the rapid ascent of Asia and China in international economic affairs, the transatlantic economy is still the vehicle of the world economy. In two other chapters in this volume, Daniel Hamilton and Joseph Quinlan estimate that the transatlantic economy – including two-way trade and foreign affiliate sales – totals approximately $3 trillion. Transatlantic trade accounted for approximately 8% of the $9.1 trillion in world exports of merchandise and commercial services in 2003. These figures may not sound like striking examples of the size of the transatlantic economy, but if intra-EU export is excluded, the transatlantic share of exports rises to more than 20% of the world total. In 2003, the US constituted 22% of the EU's merchandise exports and 15% of its merchandise imports.[10]

Yet the structure of the transatlantic, or the world, economy is no longer dominated by trade flows. Foreign direct investment (FDI) and foreign affiliate sales have in later decades increased rapidly in importance. This increase is owing to what economists call a *proximity-concentration trade-off*; if the cost of exporting products to other countries is higher than maintaining capacity in multiple markets, companies tend to substitute trade by investments in foreign affiliates. Considering the geographical distance between Europe and the US, and the decreasing barriers to investing in the other continent, the transatlantic economy has steered into a foreign affiliate-based relationship. The sales by US or European foreign affiliates are much larger than their respective exports to one another. The total output of US foreign affiliates in Europe was $333 billion in 2000, and inversely, European affiliate sales in the US amounted to $301 billion. The EU has also been the largest recipient of US FDI and vice versa.[11]

By every standard of measurement, the United States and the European Union are the main axis of the world economy. Furthermore, given the size of their economies, even a small annual percentage growth of trade and

---

[10] The data here were derived from the WTO Statistics Database; for a historical perspective of transatlantic trade, see A.G. Kenwood and A.L. Lougheed, *The Growth of the International Economy 1820-2000*, London: Routledge, 1999.

[11] See the chapters by D.S. Hamilton and J.P. Quinlan in this volume; see also D.S. Hamilton and J.P. Quinlan, *Partners in Prosperity: The Changing Geography of the Transatlantic Economy*, Johns Hopkins Center for Transatlantic Relations, Washington, DC, 2004; and also J.P. Quinlan, *Drifting Apart or Growing Together? The Continued Primacy of the Transatlantic Economy,* Johns Hopkins Center for Transatlantic Relations, Washington, DC, 2003.

foreign direct investment in the transatlantic dimension represents the bulk of world growth in the respective indicators when counted in nominal terms.

One could easily believe that the sheer size of the transatlantic economy is a sign of finished business in view of barriers to further economic integration. In addition, judging from basic trade theory, the major benefits of trade stem from trade with countries that have a different set of factors of production. The EU and the US, largely having similar production structures, should accordingly look for improved economic cooperation primarily with other countries and not with each other.

Notwithstanding the importance of improved trade relations with developing countries, this theory is a simplification of trade relations and can be misleading when setting priorities for policy. Put differently, there is a lot to be gained for the EU – as well as the US – by pushing transatlantic economic integration further. This is particularly true with regard to structural reforms.

### Transatlantic Dimensions of the Doha Round and Beyond

The Doha Round of the World Trade Organization (WTO) is at the center of efforts to liberalize trade. Despite several setbacks in the negotiations, the Doha Development Agenda (DDA) remains the core part of developing a world trading system more open to cross-border economic exchange. True, trade liberalization today is often achieved through bilateral agreements or in regional trading blocs. The last decade has witnessed an explosion of the number of so-called 'preferential trade agreements'. Such agreements tend to be important stepping-stones to multilateral agreements, but as a method of bringing larger openness to trade, and increasing the actual volume of trade, they are overrated.

Despite the justified critique of a lack focus on market access in the DDA, the current round will, if completed, deliver many benefits to countries and the world economy. According to a study by the World Bank, the welfare gains from a successful round of multilateral trade liberalization amounts to roughly $250 billion.[12] The benefits will primarily come from liberalization of trade in agriculture and services. In addition, strengthening the rules of anti-dumping and countervailing measures, and clarifying legal uncertainties causing confusion in some trade disputes will undoubtedly add further benefits to WTO countries.

The Doha Round is, however, a development round, explicitly designed to address the concerns of the developing countries. Developed countries of

---

[12] See *Global Economic Prospects 2005: Regionalism and Development*, World Bank, Washington, DC, 2004.

course have a stake in the round, but many of their issues have been put aside, for both good and bad reasons. This context simply means that efforts to increase the economic integration in fields of greater economic importance to the developed world are not sufficiently addressed in the current round.

Furthermore, for a variety of reasons, some analysts hold that the WTO no longer has the tools to address issues of increased market access in areas important to the developed world, notably with regard to trade in services and the so-called 'deep-integration' issues.[13] This perspective may turn out to be an overly pessimistic view of the WTO, but it is probably true that it will take many years before a new round, targeting developed country issues, can be completed. If the Doha Round finishes in 2008 and a new round starts in 2010, it may well be beyond 2015 before a thorough multilateral program of market access issues in the service sectors, following the completion of the new round, are implemented.[14]

This point is not a critique of the WTO. Yet the conclusion is that there are plenty of reasons for countries – not only developed ones – to chart other paths to achieve further economic integration, even as they pursue Doha.

## *Agriculture*

Liberalization in agricultural trade is the centerpiece of the current round. If significant changes are not made in the agricultural negotiations, in border protection as well as in subsidies, there will probably not be any agreement at all. Many developing countries, particularly the large food exporters in the Cairns Group, will veto any accomplishments in other fields of the round unless barriers to trade in agriculture are brought down substantially. Therefore, it is of utmost importance for the EU and the US, the main parties blocking increased market access in agricultural trade, to find ways to deliver agricultural reforms in order to secure success in other areas.

It is not only developing countries that stand to benefit from a liberal regime in agricultural trade. Indeed, consumers in Western countries – particularly in the EU and the US (not to mention those affected by the protectionism in

---

[13] According to this view, too many countries are involved in WTO negotiations today. If the WTO is going to stick to the principle of a single undertaking, it will be difficult to achieve results.

[14] Multilateral negotiations on increased trade in services will probably continue on a sectoral basis between the rounds, as they did between the end of the Uruguay Round and the start of the Doha Round, but real business is often conducted in rounds where several issues and fields are addressed.

Norway and Japan) – will be better off with lower prices on foodstuffs.[15] To the efficient agricultural producers in Western countries, liberalized trade also opens new trading opportunities.

There are many issues of importance to the transatlantic economy in the agricultural negotiations in the Doha Round. Taking stock of non-Doha issues and developments, many other concerns and opportunities in the agricultural sector could easily be added. In view of the Lisbon agenda as well as the WTO, the central concern is again finding a way for the EU and the US to avoid being the mouthpieces of agricultural interests in trade negotiations, which clearly hampers developments in other fields of the economy where trade liberalization is called for. There are two concerns in the nexus of transatlantic trade and agricultural trade affairs that are especially important to address.

First, there is a need to clarify rules on the use of hormones – and other artificial methods – in agricultural production and, if this is not possible, negotiate solutions to conflicts over this type of affair. The example of hormone-treated beef is a case in point.

This case may not be a big issue if measured in welfare gains and losses. The EU ban on imports of animals or meat from animals that have been treated with synthetic hormones equaled, at the time of implementation, a loss of US beef exports of $100 million. The US retaliation in 1999 on imports from the EU amounted to approximately $120 million. Thus, in comparison with losses owing to other trade conflicts, or in view of what can be accomplished by other efforts in trade liberalization, this problem is perhaps not of the magnitude to put it high up the agenda.

On the other hand, $220 million is a substantial loss and there are other concerns involved. According to some analysts, the respective measures of the EU and the US have targeted agricultural production where the competitiveness of the two parties is relatively high – a review, to put it mildly, not equally applicable to other parts of US and EU agricultural production – which thus stirred up feelings among farmers about the benefits of international trade. The French farmer José Bové, a leading activist in the anti-globalization movement that reached headlines after its supporters destroyed a McDonald's restaurant in France, is perhaps the prime example. Not to put too fine a point on it, his antipathy to international trade, globalization and the WTO was based on – or energized by – the use of hormones in meat production and the US retaliation on up-market food

---

[15] J. Francois et al. estimate the annual welfare loss caused by the CAP to the average family to be about $1,200 in *The Cost of EU Trade Protection in Textiles and Clothing,* Swedish Ministry of Foreign Affairs, Stockholm, 2000.

produced by farmers in France. In other words, this trade dispute, bearing small importance to the overall trade patterns of the conflicting parties, helped to produce one of the strongest waves of critique against the world trading order in many decades.

Along with the politics of the use of hormones and other related issues, clarification and further negotiations are needed in a wider perspective. The US Department of Agriculture estimates that the effects of *questionable* restrictions of trade on the ground of public health, which is one of the legal bases for restricting trade in Article 20 of the GATT, equals a loss of \$5 billion of agricultural, forestry and fishery exports from the US.[16] A substantial part of that sum is owing to import restrictions and prohibitions in the EU. The sheer size of the export loss to the US makes it an important issue that undoubtedly will cause trouble in transatlantic relations and the WTO in the future. Tensions are also likely in view of the rapid technological development in the agro-food sector, which will generally increase the stakes in the issue of artificial treatment of animals and crops. Many other parts of the sector (e.g. beverages) will also become involved.[17]

Second, the EU and the US have a common problem of vociferous interest groups blocking reforms of subsidies to agriculture and attempts to liberalize trade in the sector. According to the OECD, the Producer Support Estimate (PSE), a measure indicating the share of farm income coming from subsidies, is 37% in the EU and 18% in the US.[18] These high levels of subsidies have produced an unhealthy political economy rewarding rent-seeking behavior (or in the words of noted trade economist Jagdish Bhagwati, "directly unproductive profit-seeking activities")[19] that clearly distorts trade and efforts toward increased trade openness. Furthermore, not only trade is affected. In the latest EU enlargement, a tremendous manifestation of the fall of the old iron curtain world, the accession process was (and still is) delayed by EU-15 farmers suspecting decreasing subsidies. According to informed observers, the step up in agricultural subsidies in President George W.

---

[16] D. Roberts and K. De Remer, *An Overview of Technical Barriers to US Agricultural Exports*, Staff Paper AGES-9705, Economic Research Service, US Department of Agriculture, Washington, DC, 1997.

[17] In the dispute over hormone-treated beef, it had already been noted that of the six hormones at issue, the one that the EU had identified as most dangerous was found in a more concentrated form in products other than beef – eggs and cabbage, for example.

[18] See *Agricultural Policies in OECD Countries at a Glance, 2004 Edition,* OECD, Paris, 2004.

[19] J. Bhagwati, *Free Trade Today*, Princeton: Princeton University Press, 2001.

Bush's first administration was part of a wider package to win support for other reforms and to secure Republican seats in the mid-term elections to the US Congress.

The question is how the EU and the US can avoid spending a lot of energy to protect farming lobbies and instead focus on issues where they an interest in increased market access. The ideal strategy is to choose liberalization regardless of choices made by other countries. A unilateral strategy is not feasible, however, for either the Europeans or the Americans. In a situation where a small producing sector with huge benefits from the status quo has won over a large consumer interest with small costs, the workings of institutional competition does not seem to function as it should. Other forms of cooperative strategies are therefore called for. A more realistic alternative is to seek concerted efforts by the two parties involving lowered trade barriers to third countries as well as a preferential access to each other's markets. Although this strategy is no doubt sub-optimal, it may not be as difficult and cumbersome as it sounds, for the reasons explained below.

The bounded tariff rates from the Uruguay Round, after converting non-tariff barriers to tariffs, are indeed still high. The bounded rate of border protection for sugar in 2000 was 152% in the EU and 91% in the US. For dairy products, the equivalent figures were 178% and 93% respectively. Border protection for meat and wheat is lower on both sides of the Atlantic.[20] Viewed together with the PSE for the EU and the US, this simply means that there is a long way to go before trade is fully liberalized in the agricultural sector and that there are possible options of preferential-style transatlantic trade agreements without slowing down the process of opening markets for third countries, especially for developing nations. The positive aspect is the separation of producers that are competitive in a transatlantic market (but not necessarily in the world market) from producers that cannot compete in any open trade regime at all.

Admittedly, there are numerous pitfalls in this type of policy, but by offering far-reaching caps on subsidies and zero tariffs in intra-transatlantic agricultural trade the strategy can leverage comprehensive, multilateral trade liberalization in agriculture in later rounds. In such a process, farm lobbies could not defend the status quo by pointing to general differences in the production milieu. The playing field would be largely leveled. Being a stepping-stone to multilateral liberalization, this can represent a push toward increased efficiency for already (and comparatively) competitive farmers in the European Union and the US, and increase the market for high-cost

---

[20] M. Ingco, "Tariffication in the Uruguay Round: How Much Liberalization?", *The World Economy,* July 19, 1996.

producers in niche markets, enabling them to lower the average cost per product.

In other words, as a complement to preferential agreements with developing countries (e.g. the Central America Free Trade Agreement (CAFTA), the Everything-but-Arms agreement and the African Growth and Opportunity Act), incremental steps toward a worldwide liberal trade regime, the EU and the US can undermine the fabric of agricultural protectionism by giving efficient producers a larger stake in trade.

## *Services*

Of greater economic importance to the EU and the US is liberalized trade in services. It is difficult to estimate the welfare gains of future trade liberalization in services but all existing estimations point to huge increases in welfare. A study by the Australian Department of Foreign Affairs and Trade suggests an increase in global welfare by $250 billion if trade distortions in the provision of services are cut by 50%.[21] Almost 30% of these welfare gains would go to the EU and 25% to the US and Canada. Several World Bank studies also estimate substantial gains from the liberalization of trade in services, but not of the same magnitude as the Australian study.[22]

These assessments reflect that the vast share of production in developed countries is within the service sectors, and that many of these sectors have, for a variety of reasons, not been integrated in a world trading system. This lack of integration is partly a result of the slow pace of liberalization in services trade. The General Agreement of Trade in Services (GATS) was born in the Uruguay Round and was the first set of multilateral rules ever established for services trade. Although riddled with exceptions, GATS

---

[21] See the Australian Department of Foreign Affairs and Trade, *Global Trade Reform: Maintaining Momentum,* Canberra, 1999 (retrieved from http://www.dfat.gov.au); see also the conference presentation by G. Banks, "Gaining from Trade Liberalisations: Some Reflections on Australia's Experience", Australian Government Productivity Commission, Canberra, 2003 (retrieved from http://www.pc.gov.au/speeches/cs20030605/cs20030605.pdf).

[22] See *Globalization, Growth and Poverty: Facts, Fears and an Agenda for Action*, World Bank, Washington, DC, 2001; see also the World Bank's publication on *Globalization, Growth, and Poverty: Building an Inclusive World Economy,* Oxford: Oxford University Press, 2002. In 2000, P. Dee and K. Hanslow estimated the welfare gains by services trade liberalization to be $133 billion in *Multilateral Liberalisation of Services Trade*, Staff Research Paper, Australian Government Productivity Commission, Ausinfo, Canberra, 2000.

extends the traditional GATT principles of national treatment and most-favored nation status to trade in services. At least in theory, these aspects should be added. In practice, however, GATS is quite defective and had, from the beginning, limited ambitions. Only a few sectors are being addressed by this agreement; a more defining character of the agreement, in fact, is the absence of many service sectors.

The GATS negotiating agenda in the DDA is ambiguous. Many sectors are involved but countries have not made very far-reaching commitments. The initial offers from the EU as well as the US indicate low aims for increased services trade. Many service sectors addressed in the Lisbon agenda, notably in the financial and telecom sectors, are also part of the GATS agenda. Nevertheless, it is not possible to say what will be accomplished in these fields of policy in the current WTO negotiations. The odds against comprehensive trade liberalization in those sectors are, alas, high. Many WTO countries have yet to come far in the liberalization of certain sectors and the multilateral agenda must take into account the point of departure for those countries.[23] True, other countries can go much further in making commitments to service trade liberalization – and they probably will in some sectors – but the sheer difference in regulatory openness puts a restraint on the ambitions of the negotiations.

In view of the Lisbon agenda and transatlantic economic integration, there are some prospects for increased market access in the Doha Round; but is it not also warranted for the EU and the US to consider other ways to further services integration, particularly across the Atlantic?

### Financial Services

The financial services sector is another area addressed in the Lisbon strategy.[24] Liberalization of trade in this sector could bring substantial welfare gains, particularly to the EU. As with many goods, liberalization of services brings static benefits as well as dynamic benefits. Notwithstanding the importance of static benefits (trade liberalization reduces the effect of trade restrictions on the wedge between domestic and foreign prices), the dynamic benefits are perhaps the most important, particularly in view of structural reform and growth promotion. The generation of new knowledge,

---

[23] A. Mattoo et al. construct an openness index of the financial and telecom sectors, showing substantial differences between countries – see *Measuring Service Trade Liberalization and its Impact on Economic Growth: An Illustration*, Policy Research Working Paper No. 2655, World Bank, Washington, DC, 2001.

[24] For more on this sector, see the chapter by K. Lannoo in this volume.

the upgrade of the quality of intermediary products, the inflow of new technology and the effect of competition – to mention just a few benefits – generally promote growth. Although these factors have large impact on all trade, and exchange within a country too, they particularly affect the financial sector. This sector essentially facilitates economic production and thus has many spillover effects all other sectors of the economy.

According to a rather conservative estimate, liberalization of financial services could bring static welfare gains of nearly $25 billion. Approximately 15% of those gains would be generated in the EU.[25] Yet the prospects for substantial liberalization of trade in financial services in multilateral negotiations are rather thin. As was shown in the Uruguay Round negotiations on financial services liberalization – where a final agreement was reached in December 1997, well beyond the end-date of the Uruguay Round[26] – it is indeed a complex area touching upon regulatory structures and practices, many of them are not usually issues in the negotiating arena of trade.[27]

The commitments made in the 1997 agreement did not go beyond the already accomplished liberalizations among the OECD countries. This result reflects the differences between WTO countries; developing countries, generally having few stakes in financial services liberalization, start from a different position than OECD countries with regard to regulatory openness. Not really being able to find methods for reciprocal negotiations, the agreement started with commitments of domestic financial reforms that were not particularly relevant to most developed countries. The next step of financial services liberalization will probably continue along that path. Additional efforts to liberalize trade in financial services must therefore occur through cooperation.

What can be done to strengthen the transatlantic dimension of financial services exchange? Actually, there are many reforms that could speed up financial services integration – in the banking and insurance sectors – most of which address non-tariff barriers.

---

[25] See G. Verikios and X.-G. Zhang, *Global Gains from Liberalising Trade in Telecommunications and Financial Services*, Staff Research Paper, Australian Government Productivity Commission, Ausinfo, Canberra, 2001.

[26] An interim agreement was reached in 1995, but without US acceptance of the most-favored-nation treatment, because of emerging market reluctance on reciprocal market access.

[27] Some of the concerns, such as capital account liberalization and convertibility, border on the responsibility of the International Monetary Fund (IMF).

The core challenges to the integration of financial services across the Atlantic are differences in regulatory structures and practices. Some of them are non-discriminatory and comply with the principle of national treatment (e.g. prudential measures), but cause high transaction costs. Others are discriminatory to foreign providers or exercised in a manner bordering on it.

To mention one example, European insurance companies have trouble entering the US market owing to general regulatory differences among US states (insurance regulation is largely a non-federal issue) and, in particular, state reinsurance laws that discriminate against foreign reinsurers. This feature of the US market is of significant importance to EU providers as well as many American insurance companies. The high transaction costs for European providers, relating to differences in state regulations, apply equally to many other sectors. Many transatlantic regulatory dialogues, aiming at improving regulatory compatibility, have ended with a note of despair because of the difficulties in discussing and negotiating with the US states instead of federal government authorities.

This problem is not solely an American one. In the EU, there are still differences in parts of the financial services legislation. Moreover, parts of the EU Financial Services Action Plan that have already been agreed, and which seek to improve competition and regulatory structures, have not yet been fully implemented. Thus, US companies entering the European market may have to obtain licenses from several countries for specific operations, and, similarly, comply with different sets of regulations and supervision practices. This problem has particularly affected foreign banks seeking to establish a presence in the EU. It has taken them long time to obtain certain licenses. With regard to prudential regulations, the EU has applied different approaches depending on whether the entering party is a branch or a subsidiary.

Many other examples could be added to this list of regulatory incompatibilities, but it seems there are two tracks in strengthening transatlantic integration in financial services. The first track directs attention to the harmonization of rules and the second to a mutual recognition approach to home-country control. The former implies regulatory convergence and developing common regulations where it is relevant and necessary. The latter points instead to using the home country's rules and supervision mechanisms in exercising prudential regulations.

These two tracks are not mutually exclusive. In fact, it is difficult to organize the home-country approach without some harmonization of basic regulations and vice versa. Both tracks also run the risk of being infeasible given the specific circumstances attached to the regulatory structure of the two parties. If it is not possible to develop a common regulatory structure within a country or within the EU, it is presumably an even more cumbersome project in an international setting. On the other hand, as with the political economy of the EU, international cooperation can also provide a method for dissolving national or state-based opposition to liberal reforms. The US federal government and the EU Commission have tried to reform on numerous occasions but without success. Perhaps the strategy of Jean Monnet, a 'founding father' of post-war European cooperation, is applicable here. When he encountered opposition to European integration, he used a simple strategy: enlarge the context.

### Telecommunications

As with financial services, the telecommunications sector is part of the Lisbon agenda, as well as the current WTO round.[28] The sector has grown rapidly over the last decade and has contributed substantially to productivity growth and thus 'spilling over' to many other parts of the economy. According to one estimate, a full liberalization of telecommunication services could increase the growth rate in a country by 1%.[29] Another study assesses the gains from partial liberalization of the sector to approximately €20 billion, of which the EU-15 would gain about €3 billion.[30]

To continue the comparison with financial services, the process of liberalizing trade in telecommunications has been slow and an agreement could not be reached in the Uruguay Round. Today, the WTO agreement contains an annex on telecommunications and a reference paper on the pro-competitive regulations of telecom services, but the commitments are few and there is a huge difference between OECD countries and developing countries regarding the status of the telecommunications sector and interests in the WTO process. In addition, many of the issues in current negotiations are largely concerned with non-tariff barriers.

There are, however, important differences between the two sectors: the structure of the market and the ownership of the major firms. For a long time telecommunications were viewed as a public good and a 'market failure'. The sector has largely been within the government domain and overseen by state monopolies. In spite of recent deregulations and privatizations, current or former state-owned firms dominate the market. In Europe, they control approximately 70% of the market for long-distance calls (even a larger share

---

[28] For more on this sector, see the chapter by M. Tyler and M. Scott in this volume.

[29] Mattoo et al., op. cit.

[30] Verikios and Zhang, op. cit.

in the local call market) and in many countries, their share of the market seems to move upwards. Not surprisingly, Europeans have to pay much more for their telecommunication services than their American counterparts.

The structure of the telecommunication markets 'level the playing field', to borrow that phrase, in current WTO negotiations; basic structural reforms are not only an issue for developing countries but for the developed countries as well. At least this makes it a bit easier for the reciprocal framework of trade negotiations to operate. On the other hand, American and European companies largely dominate the telecommunication markets. Following the mercantilism approach to trade negotiations (the present trade ideology in most countries), there is thus a risk of the negotiation turning into a game of concessions given by developing countries (particularly emerging markets) to the transatlantic countries. This strategy would imply low pressure on the developed countries to continue with structural reform.

There are also transatlantic concerns in the telecommunications sector. The use of different standards in telecommunications has made it difficult to integrate the two markets. Discriminatory barriers continue to be an obstacle to further economic integration. Regulated markets in the EU and the presence of state-owned firms clearly present hurdles for American companies looking for business opportunities. America also has unfinished business in opening up its markets. The immediate threat from 2000 is hopefully under control, but there still seems to be a strong body of opinion arguing for restrictions on firms partly owned by foreign companies seeking to compete in the US.[31]

### Non-Tariff Barriers and the Movement of People

Differences in rules and regulations also slow down development in other areas of transatlantic services integration (the transport and energy sectors, for example). Accounting standards differ as well as licenses and diplomas for professionals. For legal services, architectural services, medical services, engineering services and many other professional service sectors, there are different educational requirements and different rules and standards for acquiring a 'license to operate'. This barrier clearly prevents greater transatlantic services trade. If lawyers, architects or physicians have to re-educate themselves before crossing the Atlantic for a new job or delivering a service, fewer will be interested in such an adventure. True, this is not only an issue for the transatlantic partners, but they have the largest stake in a

---

[31] In 2000, Senator Ernest Hollings introduced a bill attempting to block the acquisition of Voice Stream by Deutsche Telecom.

more effective process of unifying standards or instituting a mutual recognition process.

To this hurdle should also be added the difficulties in obtaining visas permitting a natural person to work in the US and the EU. This issue – also known in the GATS lingo as the 'mode 4 supply of services'[32] – is on the table in the multilateral services trade negotiations too. One of the barriers to increased trade in services is that often a person must move across a border to be able to provide the service to the customer. On a more general note, one obstacle for many in the process of intensifying trade in services has been the difficulty in dissociating the provision of services from movement of capital and labor. Foreign trade has traditionally been viewed as the export or import of a specific product, not a factor of production. Since service production is often closely linked to a person performing the services, barriers to the movement of people have been barriers to trade. Technological improvements have radically improved the opportunities to trade in services, but the Internet and telecommunications do not substitute for cross-border movements of persons. Most services still require the presence of a natural person in another country.

After the events of September 11, 2001, it has become more difficult for foreigners to obtain visas to the US. For intra-corporate travel and for Europeans, the problems are not as big as they are for small exporters in other parts of the world looking for business in the US. There are still difficulties, however, particularly if the intention is to move to the US. Temporary movements also remain regulated by measures with the purpose of controlling immigration in general.

The EU also has rigorous controls on persons entering the Union in search of long-term work. This not only puts an obstacle to increasing trade in services, it is also a sensitive issue in the Doha negotiations of trade in services. Developing countries have few service exporters in the traditional meaning, but they have many persons interested in moving to a developed country to take a job, often a semi-skilled service job. Developed countries,

---

[32] The GATS is based on a classification of different types of modes in which transactions take place. There are four modalities in the GATS: 1) *cross-border*, where neither the supplier nor the producer moves physically but relies on intermediary services such as telecommunication networks; 2) *consumption abroad*, involving the movement of a consumer to a supplier's country; 3) *commercial presence*, which is the movement of a commercial organization to the consumer's country; and 4) the *presence of natural persons*, the movement of an individual supplier to the consumer's country.

on the other hand, fear the competition from low-paid workers from developing countries but want to have access to their domestic markets.

The transatlantic agenda of mode 4 supply contains several elements. The most important is that the EU and the US have a common interest in avoiding excessive restrictions to the temporary movement of people and reducing the barrier to persons entering in search of employment. This issue is not exclusive to Americans and Europeans, but for people all over the world. Nevertheless, the reluctant parties are primarily the EU and the US. They also have the means to take a leadership role in this domain.

Labor migration is a sensitive issue in the EU. Unemployment among immigrants in many countries is very high and there is fear that new immigrants entering the EU will compete with the unemployed over semi-skilled jobs, particularly in service sectors, which makes any effort to increase the participation ratio of immigrants much harder. In addition, trade unions in service sectors that traditionally have not been integrated in the international economy are fiercely against the idea of persons from developing countries obtaining a job in Europe at a lower salary than the minimum wage. In countries such as Germany and Sweden, which share borders with Eastern European states, this is also an intra-EU concern, as underscored by the recent conflict over the Commission's proposal to create a single internal market for services.

Europeans have to accept the fact, however, that lower salaries are one of the competitive advantages for persons coming from developing countries, and that blocking increased movement of people across borders would create problems for the Lisbon agenda. In many EU countries today, a larger portion of the investment substitutes high costs for low-skilled labor than in the US and other comparable countries. With more flexible labor markets, a larger share of the investment could be released for production higher up in the value-added chain.

Labor market reform is of course controversial. Yet it should be part of the Lisbon strategy (to some extent it already is) and there are opportunities of using international cooperation as a method of achieving reforms.

### Anti-Dumping and Trade Disputes

Over the last decade, there has been a rapid increase in the number of anti-dumping measures filed and taken against foreign producers. Some analysts even talk about an anti-dumping contagion.[33] The US and the EU started the

---

[33] See B. Lindsey and D. Ikenson, *Antidumping Exposed: The Devilish Details of Unfair Trade Law,* Cato Institute, Washington, DC, 2003.

trend of extensive use of anti-dumping measures but now several major developing countries, such as India and South Africa, have followed suit.

The spread of anti-dumping duties is clearly a barrier to trade, especially for developing countries; the majority of anti-dumping actions target exports from developing countries. Clarifying the weak rules of anti-dumping should therefore be an important part of the DDA and there is no alternative to the EU and the US taking the lead role in this process. These two parties are still the most notorious users of anti-dumping duties.

Anti-dumping and, it should be added, countervailing duties are causing problems for transatlantic trade, but it is not a comparatively big concern. True, the increased steel tariffs in the US reached headlines and stirred up feelings in the EU, but the respective parties' use of such measures are largely against developing countries, not against other rich countries.

Of greater concern to transatlantic relations are trade disputes. A number of high-profile cases over the last few years have been worrying. The disputes over hormone-treated beef, the Byrd amendment, the Foreign Sales Corporation, the steel tariffs, and lately, the rising conflict over subsidies to Boeing and Airbus, have all taken a lot of energy and poisoned trade policy affairs. On the one hand, some of these disputes have been settled in the WTO dispute settlement body and thus shown the strength of a legally based trading order. On the other hand, some of the conflicts cannot be settled on the grounds of legal interpretation and have to be negotiated in a diplomatic forum. The dispute over subsidies to Boeing and Airbus is one such conflict, and threatens to block trade policy developments for many years.

This conflict needs to be settled in negotiations between the US and the EU. Returning to concerns in services trade, there is undoubtedly a great scope for liberalization and increasing economic relations in the aviation sector. Few service sectors are still occupied by so many discriminatory regulations as this one. Subsidies to domestic firms are high and there are even rules prohibiting foreign acquisitions of domestic companies. Looking at the civil aircraft transport sector, the picture does not get any better. This sector is not part of the multilateral trading system but based on some 3,000 bilateral agreements, all mainly about rules against free trade.[34] There are small chances of the aviation services sector becoming a part of the GATS. What may be feasible to integrate in the GATS are express delivery services,

---

[34] B. Hindley, *Trade Liberalization in Aviation Services: Can the Doha Round Free Flight?*, Washington, DC: AEI Press, 2004; for more details on the different aspects of the aviation issue, see the chapters by R. Aboulafia and D. Robyn in this volume.

increasing the prospects of better competition in the logistic sector. The main track to increased trade in aviation services is nevertheless successful negotiations of the proposed transcontinental aviation area, which is largely an affair between the EU and the US. Again, a multilateral agreement is better than a bilateral agreement, but given the obstacles, the first step is in all probability a transatlantic agreement opening up this sector incrementally.

## R&D: The Transatlantic Role in Innovation Policy

The purpose of the Lisbon agenda is to steer the EU economies toward innovation-based growth and move up in the value-added chain. As discussed earlier, the focus is explicitly on the contribution to productivity and growth from R&D, technology and innovation. This plan is ambitious, particularly if European leaders are serious about becoming the most competitive economy in the world, perhaps not in 2010 but in a longer-term perspective. There is not only a transatlantic dimension in pushing for and achieving reform in market integration, transatlantic cooperation is instrumental for the EU to achieve higher value-added production.

The EU and the US are, along with Japan and China, the world giants in R&D. A large part of their exports – and sales by their foreign affiliates – is also R&D denominated. This points to the simple fact that trade and international exchange in general is instrumental to innovations and R&D-based growth. Trade flows are not merely the flow of a product; they are also accompanied by knowledge, information, technology and production methods. Therefore, trade is part of the diffusion of knowledge.[35] It should therefore come to no one's surprise that an open trade regime extracts larger benefits from R&D to productivity than the alternative.

Transatlantic cooperation in research and development generally works smoothly, particularly in the business sector. Multinational firms have research centers in several countries and the researchers work together in the same research projects. Overall, it is fairly easy for researchers in the EU and the US to acquire visas to each other's countries. The remaining problems concern other steps in the product cycle, notably making the product of an innovation and taking it to market.

The patent regimes differ. On balance, the US offers stronger patterns in most parts of the process of developing a product and the US generally polices violation of patents more intensely than the EU. This difference is a particular issue for the European countries that miss the opportunity to reap

---

[35] G. Grossman and E. Helpman, *Innovation and Growth in the Global Economy*, Cambridge, MA: MIT Press, 1991.

the full value-added production benefits coming from the later parts of the innovation process.

There are three other concerns where transatlantic cooperation is called for. First, the cost of obtaining patents is higher when applications need to be made to more than one patent authority. Further, within the EU there are the high costs that may be associated with having to acquire patents in several countries. The EU Commission has estimated that an EU-wide patent alone could lower the cost to business by approximately €500 million annually.

Second, there is widespread violation of patents in the world. The OECD has estimated that trade in counterfeit products equals 5-7% of world trade and it is rising rapidly. It is companies from the EU and the US that loses the most from the counterfeit trade and closer cooperation to protect their companies is therefore warranted.

Third, in one of the most innovative sectors, the pharmaceutical industry, there is a difference in rules for parallel trade, causing trouble in transatlantic relations. Depending on developments in this area, the US may in the future bring a case to the WTO where the EU (and possibly others), will be the defending party. This concern should be resolved in negotiations and not be brought to the WTO.

## Conclusion

The Lisbon agenda is a comprehensive reform program for the EU economies. Whether the strategy will be successful largely depends on the methods used for accomplishing reform. This chapter has argued for adding an external dimension – particularly a transatlantic dimension – to the Lisbon process. The benefits of widening perspectives are substantial. Closer transatlantic cooperation will foster increased economic integration across the Atlantic and lead to substantial static and dynamic welfare gains. This market integration approach is especially important in sectors addressed by the Lisbon strategy.

Closer transatlantic ties could also help the EU – and the US – to achieve structural reforms, of both their own economies and the multilateral trading regime in general. This should be of great interest to EU leaders pushing for the Lisbon agenda. The current problem in the Lisbon process is the lack of structural reforms in member states and the inability of the EU institutions to push for them. There are several explanations for this, but one is that EU leaders have devalued the old EC principle of achieving reforms by expanding the market and economic integration. A re-focused agenda, using international cooperation in general, and transatlantic relations in particular, to foster structural reforms would probably be much more successful.

# SECTION IV

# CONCLUSION

# 17. Deep Integration: Opportunities and Challenges for Transatlantic Relations

## *Daniel S. Hamilton and Joseph P. Quinlan*

Given the acrimony between the United States and Europe over the past few years, it is tempting to conclude that the transatlantic partnership has entered its twilight, that the glue that bound both sides of the Atlantic has faded, that each partner has become less relevant to the other. Tempting – but shortsighted.

Some in Europe argue that the EU should be built as a counterweight, rather than as a counterpart, to the United States. They argue for 'emancipation' and seek to define a 'European model' in explicit contrast to an 'American model'. They support the euro and the financial deepening of Europe primarily as ways to put the region on equal footing with the United States and allow Europe to emerge as a legitimate alternative to the US. They define economic relations as a zero-sum battle for global market share and support European initiatives that would enable the EU to 'catch up with America'. Some believe that eastern enlargement can help build such a counterweight.

Such approaches ignore the bottom-line reality that European economies have never been as exposed to the North American market as they are today. Healthy transatlantic commerce has literally become an economic lifeline for some European companies, countries and regions. Dense transatlantic networks of production and innovation are critical for millions of European jobs and for Europe's ability to remain competitive in the global knowledge economy. Many of Europe's largest firms are more at home in the US than in Europe itself. Some US states have stronger economic ties with Europe than do many countries; some European regions invest more in the US than in the EU. As the recent US economic expansion makes clear, what is good for America is also largely good for much of Europe. US affiliate sales are growing fastest in some new EU member states. Efforts to divide Europe from America are only likely to divide Europe itself.

In the United States, there is mounting sentiment that Europe will always lag behind the US economy, that Europe needs America more than America needs Europe, that Europe is less of a partner and more of a prop.

These views ignore the transatlantic underpinnings of continued American prosperity. By a wide but underappreciated margin, Europe is the most important market in the world for corporate America. The region is not only a key source of revenue for leading US companies, it is a key supplier of capital for the debt-stretched United States. European companies are the leading source of 'insourced' jobs in America – millions of Americans owe their livelihoods to European companies based in the United States. European companies are essential sources of taxes for state and local governments. Some regions of Europe have stronger economic ties to the United States than do most countries.

Both partners, of course, face some serious economic challenges. Many European economies remain plagued by slow growth, aging societies, chronic unemployment, rigid labor laws, difficult regulatory environments and weaker productivity. Americans face spiraling budget, trade and current account deficits, daunting social security and Medicare liabilities, stuttering growth and accelerating domestic and foreign debt. But many of these problems could worsen without greater transatlantic cooperation.

The first rule of politics is 'don't forget your base'. The first rule of business is 'don't forget your customer'. Europe and America remain each other's political base and each other's most important customers. Just as Europe was the pivot for American security during the Cold War, Europe today is the geo-economic base for American prosperity in the global knowledge economy. During the Cold War, leaders worked hard to keep transatlantic economic conflicts from spilling over to damage our core political alliance. Today, the growing challenge is to keep transatlantic political disputes from damaging our core economic relationship.

Then there are those who are complacent about the relationship. They understand the openness and significance of the transatlantic economy but don't believe there are many problems to be addressed. "If it ain't broke", they say, "why fix it?"

Given the size and openness of the economic relationship, this is certainly a reasonable view. But it ignores the fact that these very dense connections make the transatlantic economy the laboratory of globalization. It is precisely because the United States and Europe have been at the forefront of a more integrated global economy that the possibilities – and potential limits – of globalization are likely to be defined first and foremost by the successes or failures of the transatlantic relationship. Neither the framework for our relationship nor the ways our governments are currently organized adequately capture these new realities.

Policy-makers need to look more closely at the intersection between deep Atlantic integration and traditional areas of domestic regulation. There is considerable need to work more concertedly to identify 'best practices' for governance that could improve coordination and create safety valves for political and social pressures resulting from deep integration. In democratic societies controversial domestic issues are decided by elections or court rulings. Across the Atlantic such quasi-domestic issues need be managed through new forms of transatlantic regulatory and parliamentary consultation and coordination and more innovative diplomacy that takes account of the growing role of private actors.

If globalization is to proceed and flourish in the future, the US and Europe will have to prove that they can deal with the challenges generated by the deep integration of their economies. If the US and Europe cannot resolve such differences with each other, how will they resolve them with economies much less like their own?

Other voices claim that the transatlantic economic relationship is about the past, and that the future lies in China or India, requiring an attendant shift in transatlantic resources towards 'big emerging markets'.

Certainly China, India and other nations will change our world profoundly, and demand great attention from both Europeans and Americans. Most US and European corporate leaders have recognized that they need to establish a presence in the Chinese, Indian and broader Asian marketplace to remain globally competitive. But most also realize that the bulk of their profits still come from Europe and America. Europe may be struggling to grow, but the size of the market is so huge that 3% growth in Europe would create a new market the size of the entire country of Argentina for companies and investors from the US and other countries. Europe and North America remain each other's most important foreign source of global profits for companies whipsawed by one crisis after another in the emerging markets. Although trade is the benchmark usually used to gauge international economic flows, it is a tremendously misleading guide. International production through foreign direct investment and foreign affiliate sales are far more important mechanisms for international integration – and they flow overwhelmingly across the Atlantic.

Moreover, while many multinationals are engaged in 'asset-exploiting' strategies that take advantage of lower real labor costs, in the case of China primarily in the manufacturing sector and in the case of India primarily in the services sector, a second, seemingly overlooked trend over the past two decades has been the explosive growth of 'asset-augmenting' investments, mainly across the Atlantic, driven by the emergence of intellectual capital as the key wealth-creating asset for most advanced industrialized economies. As asset-augmenting investment has become more important, the locational needs of corporations have shifted from those having to do with access to markets or natural resources to those having to do with access to knowledge-intensive assets and learning experiences – and most knowledge intensive, asset-augmenting activities remain heavily concentrated in micro-regions within the advanced industrialized countries, particularly in Europe and the United States.[1]

Over the next two decades, the prospect of a shift in the global economic balance is very real. But a number of 'big emerging markets' do not necessarily share some of the core legal principles or basic mechanisms that underpin open international commerce. Instead of spending significant political capital on transatlantic trade disputes over bananas or beef, eking out marginal advantage through preferential trade arrangements with tiny markets, engaging in fruitless competition to impose one or another's particular standards in third markets, being tempted into beggar-thy-neighbor approaches to import surges from countries such as China, Europe and the United States could use their current primacy to invest in new forms of transatlantic collaboration that would enable them to be true pathfinders of the global economy.

Some pundits caution that transatlantic economic initiatives could threaten the multilateral system. The reverse seems to be nearer the mark. Given that the transatlantic economy is the axis of the world economy, transatlantic leadership is essential for a strong and effective multilateral trading system. Fredrik Erixon has underscored how the US and the EU must work together and with others through the Doha round of multilateral trade negotiations to extend global prosperity. Further liberalization and reform of the global trading system will give developing countries greater economic growth potential, a greater stake in developing multilateral rules and greater capacity to expand commerce and tackle poverty.

Widening the circle of prosperity through a successful Doha global trade round, however, will not address such pressing 'deep integration' issues affecting the European and American economies as competition policies, standardized corporate governance, more effective regulatory cooperation, tax harmonization and other issues. Nor will it address cutting-edge issues raised by European and American scientists and entrepreneurs, who are pushing the frontiers of human discovery in such fields as genetics or nano-biotechnology where there are neither global rules nor transatlantic mechanisms to sort out the complex legal, ethical and commercial tradeoffs posed by such innovation. There are no patented 'European' or 'American' answers to these challenges. In fact, for most of these issues, neither side has even sorted out the appropriate questions, much less the answers.

---

[1] Vincenzo Spiezia, "Measuring Regional Economies", OECD *Statistics Brief*, No. 6, October 2003; and John H. Dunning (ed.), *Regions, Globalization, and the Knowledge-Based Economy* (Oxford: Oxford University Press, 2002).

Transatlantic leadership is needed, not to challenge or replace multilateral efforts such as Doha with such competitive regional arrangements such as a Transatlantic Free Trade Agreement (TAFTA), but to be true pioneers of the global economy by energizing Doha globally while charting a Doha-plus agenda transatlantically. Erixon explains why the EU and US can advance liberalization together in key sectors included in the Doha Round of multilateral trade negotiations, and simultaneously exploit opportunities for complementary transatlantic market-opening initiatives in such areas as agriculture, services, financial markets, telecommunications, non-tariff barriers and the movement of people, anti-dumping provisions, trade disputes, innovation policies and other areas not yet covered by multilateral agreements.

## A Free Transatlantic Market?

The transatlantic economy is the freest in the world. But it is not free. Our authors have described the many different barriers that continue to hamper the formation of a truly free transatlantic market, the costs that result, the benefits that could come from greater openness and some ways to cope with change.

Services are the sleeping giant of the transatlantic economy. The service economies of the United States and Europe have never been as intertwined as they are today; foreign affiliate sales of services on both sides of the Atlantic have exploded over the past decade. The full potential of the transatlantic service economy, however, remains hampered by internal barriers in the US, but particularly in Europe. Copenhagen Economics estimates that liberalization could result in a total welfare gain of 0.6% of EU GDP, or €37 billion, create up to 600,000 jobs, boost foreign investment by up to 34%. Such an initiative would be the single most important stimulus to the transatlantic services economy. Lack of services reform represents a significant 'opportunity cost' to the US, the EU and the transatlantic economy.

Commercial aerospace is a good example of an open transatlantic market governed by a useful WTO provision. Transatlantic business in this sector is a healthy and mutually beneficial, with both sides importing and exporting $10-15 billion worth of equipment annually, and with deeply intertwined supplier industries. Despite the open nature of transatlantic aerospace trade, however, a joint transatlantic jetliner industry does not now exist, and the sector is marked by bitter divisions between Boeing and Airbus, and between their respective national political backers. Richard Aboulafia wonders whether they will be able to resist the short-term rewards of intervening in commercial jetliner trade, or keep faith in a multilateral framework that has served both sides well.

Even though the EU and US have the largest and among the most deregulated domestic aviation markets in the world, they still limit transatlantic competition and investment. Dorothy Robyn, James Reitzes and Boaz Moselle estimate that a single open transatlantic market for air transport services could boost transatlantic travel by up to 24%, increase consumer welfare by €5.2 billion annually and boost economic output in related industries by at least €8 billion a year, and yet the full potential of this market is hampered by internal barriers on both sides of the Atlantic. As a result, the aviation industry lags in adapting to globalization even as it drives other sectors to globalize.

Garel Rhys explains why the openness of the transatlantic commerce in automotive products provides a benchmark for other sectors. Transatlantic commerce in automotive products, marked by significant flows of investment and trade, is largely free of market distorting arrangements and market failure. Compared with many sectors, the auto industry is an example of best practice in terms of market-opening. Transatlantic automotive commerce, be it in visible trade or capital transfers and invisibles such as R&D, is a major underpinning of the North American and European economies, employing millions of people on both sides of the Atlantic. Although the transatlantic automotive market is largely open, harmonization of regulations across the Atlantic could reduce unit costs by between 5% and 7% and allow the same products – be they components, accessories or sub-assemblies like engines – to be used in both markets. Given the scale of the automotive sector, harmonization of regulations could increase transatlantic commerce significantly.

Françoise Simon explains why the impact of the health care sector on the transatlantic economy is so substantial and expected to grow in the coming decades due to aging populations, consumer demand for innovative medical care and post-genomic advances toward personalized medicine. The biopharmaceutical sector has globalized through the entire value chain, from research to marketing, and offers a high-profile example of transatlantic integration occurring through investment rather than trade. It also offers significant evidence that 'asset-augmenting' strategies are key drivers of integration in the global knowledge economy. Deeper integration is hampered, however, by various barriers on each side of the Atlantic. Although bioscience is emerging as the innovation driver across many sectors ranging from health care to energy, food and bio-defense, and is deeply rooted in transatlantic interconnections, public policies in areas ranging from research funding to pricing and reimbursement lag behind the private sector in spurring transatlantic integration.

In financial markets, Karel Lannoo describes how the exponential growth of transatlantic portfolio investment over the past decade, together with EU financial reforms, has led to a transatlantic financial markets regulatory dialogue tackling concrete issues that could be considered a model for other areas of deeper transatlantic economic cooperation. One result of this dialogue, the April 2005 US-EU agreement on the equivalence of accounting standards, will effectively allow companies to use one single accounting standard in the EU and US. A rolling agenda of specific issues could lead toward a fully integrated transatlantic capital market without replicating at international level the dangers of excessive or opaque national regulatory intervention.

Michael Tyler, Matthew Dixon and Andrea Renda describe why the transatlantic telecommunications sector is a success story of soaring productivity, plummeting prices, rapid innovation and increasingly open transatlantic competition that has had beneficial effects across both continents. The EU and the US are converging in moving towards wireless access and mobile technologies, even though telecom industries still differ in many respects. Further liberalization could result in significant boosts to jobs and GDP, yet barriers remain, notably US federal and state regulatory obstacles to inward FDI and incomplete market liberalization in the EU. This sector is also an example of cutting-edge issues of globalization that are affecting the US and EU first but which neither side has adequately addressed, such as management of common resources e.g. spectrum (perhaps leading to an international marketplace for spectrum rights), and emerging issues of interoperability and intellectual property rights.

The prominent issue of deficits and imbalances underscores the strength and resilience of the transatlantic relationship. Daniel Gros and Thomas Mayer explain that the large and growing US trade deficit with the EU has generated little political heat for two reasons: first, the EU and the US produce similar goods (not the case for China trade), avoiding issues of cheap labor and 'social dumping'; and second, accumulated investments across the Atlantic are so large that more than one-half of all transatlantic trade is intra-firm trade, which means that even large shifts in exchange rates do not generate protectionist pressures. The US current account deficit is also unlikely to generate transatlantic tensions, since it has largely resulted because emerging markets have massively increased their savings. This suggests that the main mechanism to rein in the US current account deficit is not the dollar/euro exchange rate, but an increase in global interest rates, which would compress US excess demand for savings from the rest of the world.

Arman Khachaturyan and Joseph A. McCahery describe how high-profile corporate fallouts of recent years have drawn attention to the interconnection and interdependency of transatlantic economies and the need for regulators and legislators to work cooperatively to improve transatlantic auditing and governance policies. A 'transatlantic practice' in corporate governance is underway – an uneven but palpable process leading to the adoption of some common standards and a certain degree of convergence in legal techniques to solve similar problems. Impediments remain on both sides of the Atlantic, however, and regulatory diversity may actually facilitate the establishment of a truly transatlantic marketplace.

Christian Egenhofer has tackled one of the most controversial transatlantic issues, climate change. Deep transatlantic integration means that US and European business have much to gain by a transatlantic greenhouse gas emissions market, and much to lose by failure to achieve such a market. Once it is up and properly running, the €45 billion EU carbon market should turn over at least four or five times more than the underlying physical stock of allowances. If Russia, Ukraine, Canada or Japan would join, let alone the US, the sums become gigantic. A global greenhouse gas emissions market would easily be worth $100 billion. Huge differences in carbon constraints on both sides of the Atlantic would make further transatlantic market integration almost impossible. On the other hand, a breakthrough in one of the most controversial transatlantic disputes could be a major boost to a more integrated transatlantic market.

Jacques Pelkmans explains how decisions on what may seem to some as a relatively arcane subject can have massive consequences for transatlantic commerce. The European Commission's REACH proposal to overhaul EU chemicals regulation will apply to the whole value chain of chemicals and their derivatives, including applications to millions of intermediate and final goods, including more than $64 billion in transatlantic trade and investments and over $400 billion of 'downstream products' made by US firms with chemicals sold to the EU.

## The Cutting Edge of Globalization

The concept of the Transatlantic Market[2] provides a framework for the broadening and deepening of the market through the removal of remaining barriers to transatlantic trade and investment, similar but not identical to the EU's 1992 Single Market project. It focuses on liberalization of key markets

---

[2]  The Transatlantic Policy Network envisages a target date of 2015 for completing the Transatlantic Market and an accelerated target date of 2010 for four key areas in which regulatory convergence will provide a strategic impetus for the broader transatlantic economy: financial services and capital markets, civil aviation, the digital economy (privacy, security and intellectual property rights) and competition policy (see www.tpnonline.org). Other groups, such as the Transatlantic Business Dialogue, UNICE and the US Chamber of Commerce, have also called for the creation of a 'barrier-free Transatlantic Market'.

in the transatlantic economy and is rooted in the understanding that investment, rather than trade, is a key driver of transatlantic integration.

A key goal of the Transatlantic Market is transatlantic regulatory convergence. As our authors have shown, deep transatlantic integration can mean that domestic non-tariff measures can become transatlantic non-tariff barriers. Most of this is not willful; domestic regulatory agencies are simply not designed to take into account the deeply – but unevenly – integrated nature of the transatlantic marketplace. Regulatory authorities, of course, have the duty to ensure that specific products are suitable for use in their jurisdiction. Given deep integration, however, greater consistency and coordination among EU and US risk assessment and regulatory review procedures can benefit companies, consumers and the broader public.

The US and EU have initiated several useful efforts in this regard, but such cooperation remains nascent and has little political traction with executive or legislative leaders. A high-profile Transatlantic Regulatory Policy Forum, as suggested by various business groups, could break new ground by enabling regular communication and exchange of information on a variety of health, safety, environmental, consumer protection and security standards, examining different approaches to risk assessment. A key premise of such efforts could be recognition of the essential 'equivalence' of testing and regulatory procedures, which are rigorous on both sides of the Atlantic. Rather than seeking to harmonize all standards – an impossible task that is likely to create more bureaucracy, not less – each side could agree to mutual recognition of their respective standards, much as the member states of the European Community agreed to achieve between themselves in the 1980s.[3]

In this regard, it may also be time for a Transatlantic Cecchini Report. In 1988, Paulo Cecchini conducted a comprehensive study analyzing the benefits of a European Single Market. He identified about 300 barriers within the European Community at the time. He estimated the total potential gain for the EC as a whole from removal of these barriers to be around 2000 billion ECU, at 1988 prices, a boost in EC GDP by 5-7% and the creation of 5 million jobs. Cecchini labeled the failure to eliminate these barriers the 'costs of non-Europe'. The Cecchini Report energized political leaders and provided the basis for the EU Single Market process. In the spirit of the Cecchini Report and given the nature of deep transatlantic integration, it would be useful to conduct a comprehensive analysis of the 'costs of non-

---

[3] The US Chamber of Commerce has proposed the interesting notion of a Transatlantic Conformity Mark. Transatlantic products that meet mutually recognized standards could be issued a 'Transatlantic Conformity' (TC) mark, and could be distributed and sold throughout the US and Europe without further testing and certification.

transatlantic'.[4] The recent OECD study cited in chapter 3 is a start, but is limited in that it focuses on a specific package of reforms and does not enumerate the myriad barriers to be addressed. This volume has provided some indication of such opportunity costs, as well as the potential gains to be had from creating a truly free transatlantic market, and has provided some specific sectoral examples and possible 'best practice'. Our cases are illustrative rather than comprehensive, but offer a taste of the challenges and opportunities to come.

---

[4] This proposal has also been made by a number of other groups. See Center for Strategic and International Studies, "Test of Will, Tests of Efficacy", 2005 Report of the Initiative for a Renewed Transatlantic Partnership, Washington, DC, 2005, p. 37 and reports by the Transatlantic Policy Network (www.tpnonline.org).

# About the Authors

**Richard L. Aboulafia** is Vice President, Analysis at Teal Group. He manages consulting projects for clients in the commercial and military aircraft field, and has advised numerous companies, including most prime and many second- and third-tier contractors. He also writes and edits Teal's *World Military and Civil Aircraft Briefing,* a forecasting tool covering over 135 aircraft programs and markets. He writes regularly about the aviation field in such publications as *Aviation Week and Space Technology, Military Technology, Jane's Intelligence Review,* and the *Asian Wall Street Journal.* He has a regular column in AIAA's *Aerospace America.* He offers regular commentary on the aviation industry for US and international media.

**Matthew Dixon** is an associate at Tyler & Company. He has worked as a strategy consultant in the telecommunications and other industries in Europe and the US.

**Christian Egenhofer** is a Senior Fellow at the Center for European Policy Studies (CEPS). As head of the Energy, Climate and Environment Program, he has recently been specializing in EU energy and climate policies, including security of supply, climate policies and emissions trading. He is also Jean Monnet Lecturer at the Center for Energy, Petroleum and Mineral Law and Policy (CEPMLP) at the University of Dundee in Scotland and MBA lecturer at the Solvay Business School of Université Libre de Bruxelles. He is a member of several editorial boards.

**Fredrik Erixon** is Chief Economist of Timbro, the leading free-market think tank in Scandinavia, based in Stockholm, and part of the Swedish Free Enterprise Foundation. He is author of numerous books and papers on international economics and his new book on post-war economic development, *Quid Pro Quo,* will be published in December 2005.

**Daniel Gros** is the Director of the Centre for European Policy Studies, the leading think tank on European affairs. He has served on the staff of the IMF, as an advisor at the European Commission and as Visiting Professor at the Catholic University of Leuven and the University of Frankfurt. He has advised the governments of Russia, Ukraine and other Central and Eastern European countries on trade and exchange rate matters and their relations with the EU. He is currently advisor to the European Parliament and member of the *Conseil Economique de la Nation* (2003-05); from 2001-03 he was a member of the *Conseil d'Analyse Economique* (advisory bodies to French Prime Minister and Finance Minister).

**Daniel S. Hamilton** is the Richard von Weizsäcker Professor and Director of the Center for Transatlantic Relations at the Paul H. Nitze School of Advanced International Studies, Johns Hopkins University. He also serves as

Executive Director of the American Consortium on EU Studies, the EU Center Washington DC. He is the publisher of the bimonthly magazine *Transatlantic: Europe, America & the World*. He served as Deputy Assistant Secretary of State for European Affairs; US Special Coordinator for Southeast European Stabilization, Associate Director of the Policy Planning Staff, Senior Associate at the Carnegie Endowment for International Peace, and Deputy Director of the Aspen Institute Berlin. He has also taught at the University of Innsbruck and the Free University of Berlin. Recent publications include *The New Frontiers of Europe* (2005, ed.); *Partners in Prosperity: The Changing Geography of the Transatlantic Economy* (with Joseph P. Quinlan, 2004); *Transatlantic Transformations: Equipping NATO for the 21$^{st}$ Century* (2004, ed.).

**Arman Khachaturyan** is Restructuring Director of the Armenia Telephone Company and CEPS Research Associate. His areas of expertise include company and securities laws, corporate governance, takeovers, disclosure, comparative corporate law and finance.

**Karel Lannoo** has been Chief Executive of the Centre for European Policy Studies (CEPS) since 2000 and Senior Research Fellow since 1997. He is a member of the European Shadow Financial Regulatory Committee (ESFRC) and has published widely on EU and financial regulation matters.

**Boaz Moselle** is a Principal of The Brattle Group, and heads its Brussels office. Between 2003 and 2005, he was Managing Director of Corporate Strategy at the UK energy regulator OFGEM. Previously he worked in Brattle's London office, where he focused on issues around regulation and competition in a variety of industries including aviation. Before he entered consultancy, he was an Assistant Professor in Managerial Economics at Northwestern University in Chicago. He has a Ph.D. in economics from Harvard University.

**Thomas Mayer** is a Managing Director and Chief European Economist at Deutsche Bank. He and his team provide economic and interest rate forecasts for European countries to Deutsche Bank's clients as well as to the trade and sales desks of the bank. Previously, he worked for Goldman Sachs and Salomon Brothers. Before moving to the private sector, he held positions at the International Monetary Fund in Washington, DC and the Institut für Weltwirtschaft in Kiel. Mr. Mayer has published numerous articles on international and European economic issues in professional journals and commented on these issues in the media. He received a Ph.D. in economics from the University of Kiel and is a CFA charterholder.

**Joseph A. McCahery** is Professor of Corporate Governance and Innovation, University of Amsterdam; Professor of International Business Law at Tilburg University; research fellow at the Tilburg Institute of Law and Economics and the European Corporate Governance Institute (Brussels); and CEPS research associate. His areas of expertise include transatlantic corporate law, corporate finance, the political economy of federalism and securities regulation.

**Jacques Pelkmans** is Jan Tinbergen Chair for European Economics and Professor at the College of Europe in Bruges; Member of the Scientific Council for Government Policy (WRR) in The Hague; and Associate Fellow at the Centre for European Policy Studies (CEPS) in Brussels. Formerly, he was Professor for European Economic Integration at the University of Maastricht; Associate Professor of Economics at the European University Institute in Florence and Professor of Economics at the European Institute of Public Administration in Maastricht. Dr. Pelkmans' current research interests are the EU's trade policy, economic regulation and regulatory reform in the EU, economic regionalism and the economics of technical standards. He is the author of many publications on various aspects of European economic integration and on international trade policy and investment.

**Joseph P. Quinlan** is a Fellow at the Center for Transatlantic Relations at the Paul H. Nitze School of Advanced International Studies, Johns Hopkins University. He specializes in global capital flows, international trade and multinational strategies. He has extensive experience on Wall Street and in the US corporate sector. He lectures at New York University and was appointed as an Eisenhower Fellow in 1998. His publications have appeared in such venues as Foreign Affairs, the Financial Times and the Wall Street Journal. He is the author of the Center's 2003 study, *Drifting Apart or Growing Together? The Primacy of the Transatlantic Economy*; co-author (with Daniel S. Hamilton) of the Center's 2004 study, *Partners in Prosperity: The Changing Geography of the Transatlantic Economy;* and author of three other books, including *Global Engagement: How American Companies Really Compete in the Global Economy* (2000).

**James Reitzes** is a Principal in the Washington, DC office of The Brattle Group, where he provides economic analysis and expert testimony in competition, trade and regulatory matters, particularly in transportation and energy. He has written extensively on international trade and industrial organization, and has consulted with the World Bank on the formation of regional trade agreements. He holds a B.A. in Economics and History from Stanford University and a Ph.D. in Economics from the University of Wisconsin.

**Andrea Renda** is a Senior Research Fellow at the Centre for European Policy Studies, where he manages the regulatory affairs program. He is lecturer in Economic Analysis of Law and Competition Law and Economics at Luiss Guido Carli University in Rome. He is also the Director of New

Media at the Institute for the Economics of Media (IEM) of the Fondazione Rosselli (Rome and Turin). He was formerly a consultant for National Economic Research Associates (2001-03) and a Visiting Professor as the New York Law School (2001). His main fields of research include competition policy, comparative law and economics, the economics of ICT and media industries, regulatory impact assessment and regulation of public utilities. He is currently the Rapporteur of the 2005 CEPS Task Force on Electronic Communications.

**Garel Rhys** OBE is Professor and Director of the Centre for Automotive Industry Research in Cardiff University Business School in the UK. He lectures widely on the economics of the global industry and advises governmental, parliamentary and corporate institutions.

**Dorothy Robyn** is a Principal of The Brattle Group, a Boston-based economic consulting firm. She was a Special Assistant to President Clinton for Economic Policy, with responsibility for transportation, defense and telecommunications. She managed the interagency process on key trade disputes, including the EU's threat to block the Boeing-McDonnell Douglas merger. She has an M.P.P. and a Ph.D. in public policy from the University of California at Berkeley and was an Assistant Professor at Harvard's Kennedy School of Government.

**Françoise Simon** is a professor of business and public health at Columbia University and President of SDC Consulting Group. Previously, she was a Director of Arthur D. Little and a Principal of Ernst & Young, where she developed global strategy practices in health care, high technology and consumer goods. Her corporate experience also includes appointments at Abbott Labs and Novartis. She holds an M.B.A. from Northwestern University and a Ph.D from Yale University. She is co-author of *Building Global Bio-Brands: Taking Biotechnology to Market* with Philip Kotler (Free Press, 2003); *Winning Strategies for the New Latin Markets* with Fernando Robles and Jerry Haar (Prentice-Hall, 2002) and *Europe and Latin America in the World Economy* with Susan Kaufman Purcell (Rienner, 1995). She is a past Vice President and Director of the American Marketing Association and is a member of the Council on Foreign Relations.

**Michael Tyler** has been an internationally recognized consultant, educator and board member in the telecommunications industry since the early 1970s. A former senior executive at British Telecom and faculty member at the Massachussetts Institute of Technology, he is now a Founding Partner and Managing Director of Tyler & Company.